CHRISTIANS AND CHRISTIANITY
IN INDIA TODAY

CHRISTIANS AND CHRISTIANITY IN INDIA TODAY

Historical, Theological, and Missiological Assessments

Edited by

Lalsangkima Pachuau
Allan Varghese Meloottu

FORTRESS PRESS
Minneapolis

CHRISTIANS AND CHRISTIANITY IN INDIA TODAY
Historical, Theological, and Missiological Assessments

29 28 27 26 25 24   1 2 3 4 5 6 7 8 9

Library of Congress Control Number: 2024018120 (print)

Cover design: Kristin Miller
Cover image: Altar in basilica of Our Lady of Good Health in Velankani, Vailankani, Tamil Nadu, India - stock photo from Dinodia Photo/Getty Images

Print ISBN: 978-1-5064-9347-3
eBook ISBN: 978-1-5064-9348-0

CONTENTS

focus has been toward *metatheology* as a contextual theological approach where participation in the divine metanarrative serves as the *telos* of contextual theology. In chapter 7, Lalenkawala deals directly with biblical hermeneutics by critically examining the popular Indian interpretive approaches to argue for an "Indian Biblical Hermeneutics." Lalenkawala argues for a hermeneutical approach upholding the Indian plurality by opening oneself to the text's imaginative, evocative, and even passionate implications heard through the many different voices in public and private settings. In chapter 8, Jose Philip argues for *apologia* as contextual theology for the Indian context. Furthermore, Philip argues for an embodied apologetics method of witnessing as "Truth *enflesh*" (in the flesh). The apologetic of embodied presence guards the gospel from being reduced to a proposition or mere intellectual persuasion. Instead, it nurtures a holistic vision of mission, with an invitational message and a participatory posture, even in the face of persecution and suffering. The theological discussion section concludes with Arpan Christian's historical analysis of the formative process of contextualized Christian hymnody in India. Christianity approaches Indian hymnody through the lens of "missiological interaction" to unfold the multilayered interactions of local Western missionaries, native poets, local congregations, and the various local cultural expressions that gave rise to the hymnody. Such an approach moves away from the common bifurcated perspectives of Indian versus Western hymnody and accounts for the vernacular hymnals, use of English and local languages, musical traditions, and the confluence and divergence of *Bhakti* movements that gave rise to the sung context theologies in Indian Christianity.

Part 3 of the discussion steers toward Indian Christianity's engagement with the sociocultural dimensions. In chapter 10, Manohar James shows the Christian role in Indian political and civic life. Although Indian Christians have been a minority group, James argues that their commitment to nation-building has been remarkable. Through various initiatives, Christians have been at the forefront of promoting human values, advocating for political independence, upholding the dignity of life, and supporting democratic socialism. In chapter 11, we move away from the political aspect to the multireligious cultural identity negotiation of some Christians in India. Vinod John argues that becoming Christian is not straightforward; instead, it involves a constant identity negotiation process for Christians as they practice their Christian beliefs while remaining in their Hindu culture. John especially unpacks the topic considering his ethnographic data gathered from the Hindu devotees of Christ in Varanasi. In chapter 12, Priya Santhakumar Leela discusses the caste realities in Indian Christianity, especially considering the perspective of Dalit Christian women. Leela argues that the marginalization of Dalit Christian women can be understood as "thrice inferior" as they negotiate their identities through being Christian, Dalit, and women. Therefore, as a corrective, Leela calls for the Indian church to uphold and affirm the image of God in the marginalized. Part 3 concludes with a discussion on the most prevalent Indian social reality: multidimensional poverty. In chapter 13, Allan Varghese Meloottu and John Karunakaran, while providing a brief historical analysis of Indian governmental poverty alleviation plans, also show the various historical holistic missiological responses and argue for a more dynamic Christian engagement to work alongside the governmental plans in poverty reduction efforts.

In part 4, the discussion moves toward the contemporary societal health issues dealing with sociomedical and psychological problems that posit missiological challenges to the Indian church. In chapter 14, Hepziba Arputharaj discusses gender inequality in India, highlighting the prevalence of domestic violence. Aruputharaj calls for the Indian church to take on the responsibility to interfere, act, advocate, and educate the society and themselves as part of their missional mandate to be the witnesses of Jesus Christ. In chapter 15, Uma John highlights human trafficking, another social evil often overlooked, especially from the church's missiological encounters. Interacting with human trafficking issues in India, drawing prophetic voices from biblical Prophets, John seeks to empower the church to be the prophetic voice and advocate for uprooting human trafficking, beginning with prosecuting the perpetrators, protecting the victims, and taking actions to prevent further acts of trafficking. In chapter 16, T. S. John engages with the discourse of disability in India, an often-ignored area in mission engagement. John provides an engaging survey of various models of making sense of disability while reflecting missiologically to empower Indian Christians to actively engage with disabled persons. Finally, in chapter 17, the volume ends with a discussion of the mental health crisis in India and how the church could be better prepared missionally to serve those who experience mental distress. Joy Jemina Singh and Allan Varghese Meloottu provide an overview of the mental health crisis in India and propose a missiological model of "walking alongside" (inspired by Luke 24:13–33) as an apt paradigm for an effective mission practice.

Readers may notice from the composition of the authors that we are alumni and current students of Asbury Theological Seminary together with an Indian faculty member. Asbury Theological Seminary has been connected to Indian Christians for a century. Among its alumni are well-known Indian ministers and scholars like Sam Kamaleson, Saphir Athyal, and Siga Arles. For the past few decades, through the combined strength of its faculty with specializations in Indian Christian studies, including Timothy Tennent, Arthur McPhee, and Lalsangkima Pachuau, Asbury Theological Seminary has provided scholarship and produced many scholars in Indian Christian studies. We, the community of Indian scholars of Asbury Theological Seminary, joyfully dedicate this book to Asbury Theological Seminary to mark its centennial, which took place in 2022/23.

INTRODUCTION

Lalsangkima Pachuau and Allan Varghese Meloottu

As he came to the concluding section of his book *The Discovery of India*, Jawaharlal Nehru who later became the first prime minister of India asked himself "What have I discovered?" Part of his response goes, "India is a geographical and economic entity, a cultural unity amidst diversity, a bundle of contradictions held together by strong but invisible threads."[1] The ideal "unity amidst diversity" expressed here, may be credited as the conceptual foundation of India's secularism. Someone recently claimed this concept of unity in diversity to be "India's gift to the World."[2] This claim may be difficult to prove, yet it shows how important it is for the Indian nationality. Even as it faces challenge after challenge to maintain this principle of unity, the fact that it has kept its democracy intact shows India's resilience in unity.

The twentieth century, in retrospect, may be claimed to be the century when the Christian church has been most united if we may apply that same principle of unity, a unity in diversity through mutual recognition among the diverse Christian traditions and practices. In the opening decades of the twentieth century when a quest for unity captured the imaginations of Christian leaders, it was the spirit of mutuality among the diverse churches that led to the ecumenical movement. An early architect of the ecumenical movement, Bishop Charles Brent, used to call for "organic unity," a unity in which each church subjects itself to, and even "subordinates its ideals" to, the whole church which he calls "the perfect Church."[3] More than ever, there appears to be mutual understanding among the different families of churches by the end of the twentieth century, and the family ties of each have been strengthened. Not only has Christianity become a world religion, but Christianity has been increasingly characterized by the multiple forms of practices and cultural values of Christians from everywhere.

---

1. Jawaharlal Nehru, *The Discovery of India* (New York: The John Day Company, 1946), 576.

2. J. Nandkumar, "Independence Diary: 'Unity in Diversity' one of the Most Powerful Thoughts India Gave to the World," *Outlook* (August 15, 2021).

3. Quoted in Eugene C. Bianchi, SJ, "The Ecumenical Thought of Bishop Charles Brent," *Church History* 33, no. 4 (December 1964): 451.

This has now been called "world Christianity," a Christianity in the world characterized by multiple practices, confessions, and traditions.[4]

Indian Christianity has paved the way for the rise of world Christianity in various ways. The variety it represents and the rich history of its experience together with the unique religious diversity of its regions have molded it to be truly at home in the new world of Christianity. Historically speaking, Christianity may have its longest active presence in India. Not only do Christian traditions of the earliest period continue to thrive, but they now mix well with the newest ones. Between one of the oldest churches in the world and the newest Christians today, Indian Christianity has it all. Modern Western missions, from Francis Xavier to Mother Teresa, from Bartholomew Ziegenbalg and William Carey to Amy Carmichael and C. F. Andrews, have produced a variety of rich traditions that have enriched Indian Christianity. In the annals of modern Christian missions, India may have also recorded one of the earliest, if not the earliest, indigenous missionary endeavors in the Global South. The Marthoma Evangelistic Association was founded in 1888 sending cross-cultural missionaries throughout India. Led by nationalist leader V. S. Azariah, indigenous missions thrived with nationalistic fervors in the twentieth century. As John Karunakaran recounts of Indian missionary history, Indian churches have actively engaged in missions for centuries.

Contextual theology as a distinct indigenous theology developed quite early in India, perhaps the earliest in the Global South.[5] It is interesting to note that one of the earliest groups of engaged theologians in India were members of the Brahmo Samaj, a reformed Hindu movement. Well-known early Indian theological thinkers such as Keshub Chander Sen were not Christians technically. Brahmabandhab Upadhyaya was active as a theologian in the opening decade of the twentieth century making use of Indian Brahmanical philosophy as a way of theologizing. The works of an intellectual group, mostly laymen, called the "Rethinking Group" in the first half of the twentieth century, at first, were opposed by Christians but eventually became prominent. The rise of Indian nationalism as a political trend motivated and influenced Indian theology to take its nationality seriously. From the Brahmanical philosophy of nationalist theology in the mid-twentieth century, Indian theology turned "subaltern" by developing new indigenous feminist, Dalit, and tribal theologies in the final decades of the twentieth century. With a rich variety of influences, Indian Christian

---

4. Lalsangkima Pachuau, *World Christianity: A Historical and Theological Introduction* (Nashville: Abingdon Press, 2018), 2.

5. For the development of early Indian theology, see M. M. Thomas, *Acknowledged Christ of the Indian Renaissance* (Madras: C.L.S. Published for the Christian Institute for the Study of Religion and Society Bangalore, 1970).

theology became well established as a field of study by the third quarter of the twentieth century.

Incidentally, much of the missionary cooperation in the nineteenth century that eventually led to the modern ecumenical movement began in India. The exchanges of experiences and ideas during missionaries' summer vacations in hill stations such as in Kodaikanal and Ooty in the South and Mussoorie in the North led to informal fellowships and then to formal conferences. A number of missionary conferences beginning in the nineteenth century prominently in India and elsewhere produced better relationships in the home offices of missions in the West leading to a series of international conferences climaxing in the famous World Missionary Conference in Edinburgh in 1910.[6] As historian Kenneth Scott Latourette stated, Edinburgh 1910 became the "birthplace of the modern ecumenical movement."[7] India seems to be fertile for cooperation amid divergent practices and traditions and such is the case with ecumenical movements within India. The formations of the Church of South India and the Church of North India testify to this in which most of the historical Protestants including Anglicans came together for a united church. What was established as the National Missionary Society in the 1920s became the National Council of Churches in India, a leading conciliar body representing most of the mainline churches in the country. The same kind of spirit may be claimed in the founding of the Evangelical Fellowship of India in the 1970s.

The principle of "unity in diversity" in the spirit of mutuality, thus, is what characterizes Indian Christianity. By the closing decades of the twentieth century, Indian Christianity had come of age. As an active minority community in a culturally and religiously diverse nation, Indian Christianity represents almost every Christian tradition in the world. The life, thoughts, and works of Indian Christians are varied, and yet the common experience of being a minority in a very diverse country held the Christian communities together. This is what this volume tries to capture, and we hope readers will sense the richness of Indian Christianity reflected in the chapters.

This book is divided into four parts dealing with various aspects of Indian Christianity: historical, theological, sociocultural, and missional challenges. There are five chapters in part 1 dealing with historical dimensions. The first three chapters deal with the regional history of Christianity in the South, North, and Northeast. In chapter 1, Allan Varghese Meloottu looks at South

6. See William Richey Hogg, *Ecumenical Foundations: A History of the International Missionary Council and its Nineteenth Century Background* (New York: Harper and Brothers, 1952).

7. Kenneth S. Latourette, "Ecumenical Bearings of the Missionary Movement and the International Missionary Council," in *A History of the Ecumenical Movement, 1517–1948*, ed. R. Rouse and S. C. Neill (Philadelphia: Westminster Press, 1968), 362.

Indian Christianity through various transitionary modes such as assimilation, migration, resistance, accommodation, translation, revival, and indigenization resulting in a polyvalent Christianity where almost all of the major strands of Christian tradition (Orthodox, Catholic, Protestant, and Pentecostal) find their homes in the region. In doing so, this historical narration is a retelling of South Indian Christianity, paying attention to transregional and transcontinental interactions from its beginning to its contemporary form. In chapter 2, Shivraj K. Mahendra deals with Christianity in North India as a first-generation Christian with a Hindu background. While the chapter discusses the history of the roles of mission agencies, persons, and denominations, it also explores the state of Christianity in North India, dealing with its challenges and opportunities. Mahendra demonstrates North Indian Christianity as struggling amid opposition and persecution as well as thriving with optimism. In chapter 3, Lalsangkima Pachuau tells the history of Christianity in Northeast India, focusing on cultural identity struggles and the role Christianity came to play in establishing an indigenous identity for Christians. Although Christianity is a latecomer in Northeast India, Pachuau emphasizes the role of indigenous Christians in the expansion of the faith without dismissing the works of foreign missionaries. Locating Christianity within the geo-ethnic character of the region, Pachuau notes that Christianity is alive in Northeast Indian tribal people, especially with their missionary-minded witness to their faith among their neighbors of other faiths.

After the regional historical analysis, chapters 4 and 5 provide a "grassroots" look into the ecclesial and missional history of Indian Christianity. Matthias Gergan examines the major Christian ecclesial traditions in India, asserting that the seemingly fragmented past and present of Indian churches are not necessarily obstacles but testaments to a diverse unity. In other words, the Indian church offers a way of being a church that is both relevant to the local context and informs the broader church of an essential facet of its identity. In chapter 5, John Karunakaran provides an analysis of the indigenous mission history of India providing an Indian historiographical perspective. It recounts the rich history of Indian Christian missionary engagements from the earliest history of Christianity to the active movement India is seeing today.

Part 2 deals with the theological dimension of Indian Christianity without losing the practical aspects. Thus, it is a combination of theology through theoretical arguments and an analysis of theological practices in India. In chapter 6, Sochanngam Shirik puts forth a theological approach in the form of *metatheology*, prioritizing Scripture's claims and trajectories, allowing it to function as the regulatory epistemological, hermeneutical, and theological principle while at the same time allocating human experiences their due space. While Shirik engages with contextual Indian theologies—tribal, postcolonial, and Dalit—the

Part I

Historical Dimensions

CHAPTER ONE

Tale of Transregional Interactions to a Polyvalent Christianity

A Brief History of Christianity in South India

Allan Varghese Meloottu

Introduction

THE CHRISTIAN COMMUNITY in South India is among the oldest active Christian communities in the world. As Christianity expanded in the region over the centuries, various Christian communities of South India interacted with other Christians around the world, from Syrian Orthodox Christians to Portuguese Catholics, European and American Protestants, and the Pentecostals and Charismatics inside and outside India. Through such interactions, South Indian Christianity has been formed into an "active, kaleidoscopic, complex and intricate" faith.[1] Although attempting to provide a comprehensive account of such a complex, two-thousand-year-old history of Christianity would be a mammoth task, this chapter attempts to map out various key historical moments that shaped South Indian Christianity. I shall pay particular attention to transregional and transcontinental interactions.[2] In doing so, this chapter shows that, over the last two thousand years South Indian Christianity has gone through various transitionary modes such as assimilation, migration, resistance, accommodation, translation, revival, and indigenization resulting in a polyvalent Christianity where almost all of the major strands of Christian tradition (Orthodox, Catholic, Protestant, and Pentecostal) find homes in the region.

To show the evolution of South Indian Christianity meaningfully in its transcontinental and transregional connections, I shall divide the historical

---

1. Daniel Jeyaraj, "South India," in *Christianity in South and Central Asia*, ed. Kenneth R. Ross, Daniel Jeyaraj, and Todd M. Johnson (Edinburgh: Edinburgh University Press, 2019), 143.

2. Klaus Koschorke, "Transcontinental Links, Enlarged Maps, and Polycentric Structures in the History of World Christianity." *Journal of World Christianity* 6, no. 1 (2016): 29.

narrative into four phases using the analogy of sequential springs.[3] The first spring of Christianity highlights the arrival of Christianity in South India and its subsequent assimilation with Syrian Christianity. The second spring is the arrival of Portuguese Catholics in the fifteenth century along with their militaristic agenda and its impact on South Indian Christianity that saw transregional migration and resistance while also experiencing a period of accommodation. The third spring came about with the European Protestant arrival, mainly focusing on the missionary efforts of Bible translation and its impact on vernacularization in South Indian Christianity. The fourth spring represents the transitionary modes of South Indian Christianity in the twentieth century, which went through a renewal in the form of the Charismatic-Pentecostal movement, along with various Protestant and Catholic indigenization efforts. The beauty of South Indian Christianity exists in the coexistence of these varied historical springs and their influence on distinctive Christian traditions as they find belonging in South India.

Brief Geographical and Statistical Note

Before I begin, a word to clarify South India's geography with a brief statistical account of its Christian population. Geographically, South India spreads over five states—Tamil Nadu, Kerala, Karnataka, Telangana, and Andhra Pradesh—and three union territories—Puducherry, Lakshadweep, and the Andaman and Nicobar Islands. However, in speaking of South Indian Christianity, Goa's (the southwestern coastal state) role is undeniable, so it is included in this historical-contemporary analysis of South Indian Christianity. Today, as Pew Research puts it, Christianity in South India accounts for about "half of the Christians in the country," with 2.4 percent of the national population officially adhering to Christianity.[4] Statewise, according to the government of India's 2011 census, Kerala tops the list of South Indian states with 6.2 million Christians constituting 18.38 percent of the state's population. Tamil Nadu follows with 4.4 million (6.12 percent of the population), Karnataka with 1.1 million (1.87 percent), Andhra Pradesh with

---

3. I adopt the typology of four springs from Leonard Fernando and George Gispert-Sauch (*Christianity in India*. [New Delhi: Penguin/Viking, 2004]). However, I adapt them with two divergences. (1) I use them in the South Indian context instead of the Indian context, and (2) I diverge from how Fernando and Gispert-Sauch understands the fourth spring in South Indian Christianity. Given that Dalits have always been integral to the rise and growth of South Indian Christianity from its beginning, I believe the story of Dalits should be integrated throughout the four springs instead of just highlighting it in the fourth spring.

4. Ariana Monique Salaza, "8 key findings about Christians in India," *Pew Research Center* (2021) accessed March 2, 2023, https://www.pewresearch.org/fact-tank/2021/07/12/8-key-findings-about-christians-in-india/

1.1 million (1.34 percent),[5] and Goa with 366 thousand (25.10 percent of the state's population). Among the South Indian territories, Puducherry accounts for 78,550 Christians (6.29 percent of the territory's population) while Andaman and Nicobar Islands have 80,980 Christians (21.28 percent of the population) and only 320 people (0.49 percent of the population) of Lakshadweep Island are Christians. Although Christianity is a minority in all of these South Indian states and union territories, Christianity in South India remains one of the oldest and most diverse Christian communities in the world. Recognition of this diversity prompts us for a fresh historical analysis, specifically focusing on the transcontinental and transregional links and interactions. In rereading and rescripting the story of Christianity in the region, our attention is drawn to the diversity, changes, and variety of transitory modes such as assimilation, resistance, migration, accommodation, vernacularization, and indigenization.

The First Spring
Arrival and Assimilation

Arrival

The first spring of South Indian Christianity begins with the long-held belief that Jesus's disciple Thomas arrived in the region and preached the gospel to the high-caste Brahmins. Although there has been speculation around the historical reliability of Thomas's arrival, the tradition claims that the apostle arrived at the Malabar coast in 52 CE, and, as Susan Bayly writes, "after a period of heroic evangelising and church-building he travelled east to Mylapore, now a suburb of Madras, where he underwent his bloody and spectacular martyrdom."[6] Even though historical evidence is lacking to conclusively claim Thomas's arrival or his martyrdom, in light of the available evidence of maritime trade routes between West Asia and South India, as Robert Eric Frykenberg notes, it is "not implausible" to claim Thomas's arrival.[7] During the first century, South India, with its "paddy-growing areas become the 'core zones' of a rich agricultural and trading

---

5. This statistic includes Christians from the state of Telangana as it was still part of Andhra Pradesh during the census of 2011. It was only on June 2, 2014, that the state of Telangana was officially formed, constituting the northwestern part of Andhra Pradesh with Hyderabad as its capital.

6. Susan Bayly, *Saints, Goddesses and Kings: Muslims and Christians in South Indian Society, 1700–1900.* (Cambridge: Cambridge University Press, 1989), 244.

7. Robert Eric Frykenberg, "Christianity in South India Since 1500: Historical Studies of Transcultural Interactions Within Hindu-Muslim Environments." *Dharma Deepika* 1, no. 2 (1997): 4.

economy with strong links with the maritime entrepots of west Asia and the far east."[8] Therefore, it was common to have merchants visiting coastal South India, and there is a likelihood that Christianity also reached South India during this early stage.[9] Nonetheless, as Kerala historian Sreedhara Menon notes, "the Christians in Kerala continue to attribute to their Church an apostolic origin and call themselves St. Thomas Christians."[10]

Assimilation

Although the Thomas Christians held on to their apostolic succession for the first two hundred years, they soon fell into "a state of disorder," lacking ecclesial leadership.[11] However, in 345 BCE, a merchant named Thomas Cana arrived from the Persian Empire with four hundred Christians and two Syrian bishops, bringing new life to the dying church.[12] Thomas Cana's arrival revived the pre-existing Thomas Christians and provided an association with the Syrian church.[13] Subsequently, the local church "harmonized their church discipline with that of the Syrian Church, without looking at it as something foreign,"[14] marking the beginning of South Indian Christianity's assimilation with Syrian Christianity. Consequently, the South Indian Thomas Christians (who might have been scattered in parts of today's Kerala and Tamil Nadu) embodied Syrian theology, worship forms, and customs. In the following centuries, travelers and other Christians from West Asia mentioned seeing "Nestorian" Christians in South India.[15] Such a Syrian influenced Christianity, assimilated and localized

8. Bayly, *Saints, Goddesses and Kings*, 19.

9. There is also a claim that one of the local kings had invited Thomas to come to South India. Although little is known about the sociopolitical makeup of South India during the first few centuries, there are claims that a Mysore Raja named Gudnaphar had invited Thomas to India.

10. Sreedhara Menon, *Kerala History and its Makers* (Kottayam, Kerala: DC Books, 2008), 44.

11. C. P. Mathew, and M. M. Thomas, *The Indian Churches of Saint Thomas*, rev. ed. (Delhi: ISPCK, 2005), 20.

12. Allan Varghese, "The Reformative and Indigenous Face of the Indian Pentecostal Movement." *International Journal for Indian Studies*, 4, no. 2 (2019): 2

13. Such an alliance might have formed quickly due to both of the churches' common apostolic patrimony in Thomas. "According to the Chaldean or Seleusian tradition, their (Syrian) Church was founded by Mari, a disciple of Addai, whom Mar Thoma sent to Edessa" (Joseph Perumthottam. *A Period of Decline of the Mar Thoma Christians (1712–1752)*. [Kottayam, Kerala: Oriental Institute of Religious Studies, 1994]: 4, footnote 3).

14. Perumthottam, *A Period of Decline of the Mar Thoma Christians*, 4.

15. For details, see http://www.syriacstudies.com/2012/10/05/the-church-of-the-east-mark-dickens/ (accessed on December 1, 2021).

into the South Indian social class/caste structures for centuries. During this long period from the fourth century until the sixteenth century, the church and its doctrines (influenced by the Syriac rites) had been assimilated well to the local contexts and became, in Francis Thonippara's words, "truly an Indian Church rooted in Indian soil."[16] Such an assimilated and localized Christianity remained unchallenged for centuries until the arrival of the Portuguese in the sixteenth century, causing the second spring in South Indian Christianity.

The Second Spring
Conquest, Migration, Resistance, and Accommodation

The second spring of South Indian Christianity is the story of conquest, transregional migration, resistance, and accommodation that spans from 1498 to roughly the 1700s. The pathway for this second spring began when the Portuguese merchant Vasco da Gama arrived on the shores of Kozhikode (Calicut) on May 20, 1498, with the claim that "we come to seek Christians and spices."[17] The initial relations between Vasco da Gama and the local king "were cautious but courteous,"[18] and opened doors for the Portuguese establishment to form "trade agreements with the rulers of Kochi and Kannur."[19] In light of the ongoing attempts to resist the Muslim encroachment into the south, the Hindu empire of Vijayanagara was also happy to establish and further deepen the bonds with the Christian Portuguese traders.[20] However, the Portuguese had long-term plans.

---

16. Francis Thonippara, "From Colonization to Romanization: The Impact of the Synod of Udayamperur on Saint Thomas Christians," in *Heritage of Early Christian Communities in India: Some Landmarks*, ed. G. John Samuel (Chennai, India: Institute of Asian Studies, 2010), 111. Even though the top leadership was still occupied by the Syrians, the local Thomas Christians enjoyed a measure of autonomy in their civil and ecclesiastical proceedings as the archdeacon, who was not a foreigner, was in charge of the local community (Mathas Mundadan, "Indigenization of the Church," in *Indian Christianity*, ed. A. V. Afonso [New Delhi: Center for Studies in Civilization, 2009], 249).

17. Quoted in Robert Eric Frykenberg, *Christianity in India: From Beginnings to the Present* (New York: Oxford University Press, 2010), 121.

18. Frykenberg, *Christianity in India,* 121.

19. Fernando and Gispert-Sauch, *Christianity in India*, 75.

20. It is understood that the Vijayanagara empire came to be established in 1336 CE by the Sangama brothers, Harihara and Bukka, as a resistance against the Invasion of Delhi Sultanates. For a brief history of the Vijayanagara empire, see Akhilesh Pillalamarri, "450 Years Ago, This Battle Changed the Course of Indian History," *The Pulse*, June 20, 2015. https://thediplomat.com/2015/06/450-years-ago-this-battle-changed-the-course-of-indian-history/). According to Pillalamarri, "Within a century, Vijayanagara would grow to be South India's largest empire."

Conquest

Although the Portuguese established themselves by creating parts of South India as the "State of India" (*Estado da India)* in 1505, it was in 1509 with the appointment of Alfonso de Albuquerque as the Portuguese Governor of India, that the new epoch of sociopolitical domination of local Christians by the Portuguese came about. Alfonso de Albuquerque, "a genial colonizer and administrator,"[21] transferred the Portuguese base from Kochi to Goa, as "the conditions in Goa were favourable for a conquest."[22] With five islands located ideally between the Muslim kingdoms of the North and the Hindu Vijayanagar kingdom of the South, Albuquerque entered an alliance with the "Hindu feudal lords of the south and in a military action took the islands of Goa from the control of Adil Shahi, the Muslim sultan of Bijapur."[23] While the Portuguese were critical and intolerant toward the Muslims, they adopted a tolerant outlook toward the Hindus, hoping that they would convert to Catholicism.[24] To make this Catholic conversion of the native Hindus a reality, as Edward Norman notes, "the Catholic religious orders poured in to set up missions and institutions,"[25] propagating the Catholic faith while negotiating tolerance with the local Hindus.

However, such a tolerant attitude soon started to fade. Starting from 1540, perhaps "born of the resurgent Catholic energy of the Counter-Reformation" from the European context,[26] few policies were instituted indicating a switch from religious tolerance to intolerance toward the non-Christians. For example, in 1540, the policy defined as the "rigour of mercy" led to the idea that the "Catholic faith had to be imposed on the population through all sorts of pressures short of physical violence."[27] In 1541, the "confraternity of the holy faith" was instituted specifically for helping "Christians in need and ensured that they get adequate jobs" as opposed to the local Hindus.[28] The subsequent 1557 decree

---

21. Fernando and Gispert-Sauch, *Christianity in India*, 113.

22. Fernando and Gispert-Sauch, *Christianity in India*, 114.

23. Fernando and Gispert-Sauch, *Christianity in India*, 114.

24. Although Catholic Christianity arrived on the shores of South India in the fourteenth century with the arrival of Jordan of Severac in the 1320s, it remained a small Christian presence. For more details see, George Mark Moraes, *A History of Christianity in India, From Early Times to St Francis Xavier: A.D. 52–1542.* (Bombay: Manaktalas, 1964), 98.

25. Edward Norman, "Church of the Bom Jesus, Goa," *History Today* 43, no. 3 (1993): 62.

26. Norman, "Church of the Bom Jesus, Goa," 62.

27. Fernando and Gispert-Sauch, *Christianity in India*, 116.

28. Fernando and Gispert-Sauch, *Christianity in India*, 121.

and the 1560 Inquisition not only made practicing other religions difficult in Goa but also made it impossible to deter anyone (mainly targeting the native new converts) from the Roman Catholic form of Christianity as instituted by the Portuguese. More notably, the demolition of temples and establishment of church buildings in strategic locations indicated the Christianization of Goa under the guise of Portuguese conquest. The churches and convents of Goa, which are today designated as UNESCO world heritage sites, were built during this Portuguese spring of Christianity in South India, and led to Goa being called "the Rome of the East."[29] In summation, the initial religious tolerance of the Portuguese Catholics in Goa was, in fact, as Timothy D. Walker puts it, an "antagonistic tolerance."[30]

Migration

The Portuguese intolerant religious policies in Goa, specifically the Inquisition, prompted the migration of the newly converted native Catholics into other regions of South India. While some converted due to the administrative pressures from the Portuguese colonial rulers, others did so with conviction, mainly by responding to the gospel preached by the Franciscans from 1517 to 1539, starting with Antonio de Loura. However, the Inquisition posited a challenge to these native converts as the policy "sought to purify the native Christians from the influence of their former Hindu traditions and customs."[31] As Carmine D'Costa notes, "As far as the native Christians in Goa were concerned, the Portuguese were unable to separate issues of faith and its cultural expressions. . . . the new Christians could not sever their relationship with their clan, nor could they give up every vestige of their native cultural tradition."[32] Along with this religious cause, economic reasons such as poor living conditions and the excessive land taxation on native Christians by the Portuguese also prompted the native Christians to leave Goa in the 1540s and 1550s.

---

29. Philip Jenkins, "Goa, Rome of the East," *The Christian Century* 134, no. 18 (2017): 44.

30. Timothy D. Walker defines "antagonistic tolerance," as the "anticipate[d] periods of peaceful coexistence between rival groups in a conquered colonial setting, punctuated by periods of violence, and sometimes of extreme violence, including the complete destruction of sites previously shared, and possibly the expulsion of members of defeated rival groups from a contested territory" (Timothy D. Walker, "Contesting Sacred Space in the *Estado da India*: Asserting Cultural Dominance over Religious Sites in Goa," *Ler História*, 78 (2021): 111–134. https://doi.org/10.4000/lerhistoria.8618).

31. Carmine D'Costa, "Migration of Christians from Goa and the Making of the Mangalorean Christian Community in South Kanara (1560–1763)." *Indian Church History Review* 44, no. 1 (2010): 44.

32. D'Costa, "Migration of Christians from Goa," 44.

Later, the attacks on Goa from the Sultan of Bijapur (in 1570) and Shambaji, the Maratha king (in 1683) also prompted further migration of native Christians to Kanara, which by then was ruled by the Nayaks of Keladi. Furthermore, the language policy of 1684 requiring every native Goan Christian to speak in Portuguese was, in fact, an "anti-Konkani legislation" depriving "the native clerics of their advantage of linguistic bond with the parishioners."[33] Subsequently, the indigenously minded native Catholics were prompted to migrate again to neighboring Kanara,[34] joining the Goan diaspora community that was established in the previous century. The product of this migration lives on in the contemporary Christian community in the state of Karnataka, namely in today's Mangalore.[35]

Resistance

While these transregional developments in Goa and Karnataka gave birth to new Christian communities, through force and migration, there was a different story playing out in Kerala, and that is the story of resistance.[36] The initial cordiality between the Portuguese Catholics and local Syrian Christians, which invited them to strike up trade agreements, began to fade as the Portuguese intention to take over the local church became apparent.[37] The Roman Catholic missionaries who came with the Portuguese traders were soon instructed to target Syrian Thomas Christians and propagate the Catholic, or "Latin" way.[38] As part of

---

33. D'Costa, "Migration of Christians from Goa," 47.

34. The Kanara or Canara region, which is also known as Coastal Karnataka, comprises today's three Karnataka coastal districts, namely Dakshina Kannada, Udupi, and Uttara Kannada and Kasaragod Taluk of the state of Kerala.

35. After the Portuguese rule, the Kanara Christians also had to endure the persecutions under Tipu Sultan's reign in the eighteenth century. However, as Fernando and Gispert-Sauch note, "a small community remained faithful to the Catholic religious practice, especially by saying the rosary to Mary and by reciting Thomas Stephen's *Krista Purana* in Konkani." (*Christianity in India*, 129, 130). Despite all these migrations and persecutions, today, "the Majority of Mangalore's Catholics are directly linked with the migrants "from Goa in the sixteenth and seventeenth centuries and brought their language with them: even today they speak Konkani, though they write it in Kannada script" (Fernando and Gispert-Sauch, *Christianity in India*, 128).

36. Parts of this section contain reworking of my previously published work (Varghese, "The Reformative and Indigenous Face of the Indian Pentecostal Movement," 3–4). Although I have described the historical aspects differently in this chapter, it may contain some resemblance to the earlier work.

37. Menon, *Kerala History and its Makers*, 18.

38. Varghese, "The Reformative and Indigenous Face of the Indian Pentecostal Movement," 3.

their Latinizing campaign, they recruited Syrian Christian young men into their seminaries and to the Portuguese military service.[39] However, the Syrian bishops resisted any attempts to lure the Syrian Christians or to replace Syrian ceremonies with Latin, and thus the unrest between the Syrians and the Catholics began. The unrest came to its pinnacle in 1597 with the death of the Syrian bishop Mar Abraham,[40] while newly arrived Catholic Archbishop of Goa, Alexis de Menezes, "saw to it that no new bishop should arrive in Malabar from Mesopotamia" to replace the deceased Bishop Mar Abraham.[41] Using this Syrian leadership vacuum, Menezes set his agenda "to purify all the Churches from heresy and errors."[42] In 1599, by convoking a Synod at Udayamperur (popularly known as the Synod of Diamper), which lasted for seven days, the Archbishop made steps to establish the Roman Doctrine and the Pope's supremacy over the Syrian Christians without compromise. Following the Synod, Syrian books were confiscated for correction or for destruction, and all Syrian clergy were instructed to institute the Latin rituals. In summation, Menezes confirmed the process of Latinization by detaching the Kerala Thomas Christians from their Syrian custom and marked the beginning of "the Westernization of the first Indian Christian community."[43]

However, a good section of the Thomas Christians under the leadership of Archdeacon Thomas resisted the Portuguese Latinization and wrote to the Nestorian, the Coptic, and to the Jacobite Patriarchs in Syria, "asking for a bishop to be sent to Malabar."[44] In 1652 a foreign bishop named Mar Ahatalia, though it is unclear which patriarch sent him, arrived.[45] However, the Portuguese arrested the bishop at the port and imprisoned him, leading to an insurgency by local Syrian Christians that resulted in the Coonen Cross Resolution against the Portuguese and the Roman church on January 3, 1653.[46] The Coonen Cross

---

39. Menon, *Kerala History and its Makers*. 118.

40. Who was the "last Persian Metropolitan of the St. Thomas Christians" (Thonippara, "From Colonization to Romanization," 65).

41. Quoted in Varghese, "The Reformative and Indigenous Face of the Indian Pentecostal Movement," 3.

42. Mathew and Thomas, *The Indian Churches of Saint Thomas*, 32

43. Fernando and Gispert-Sauch, *Christianity in India*, 78.

44. Mathew and Thomas, *The Indian Churches of Saint Thomas*, 40.

45. Fernando and Gispert-Sauch, *Christianity in India*, 78; Mathew and Thomas, *The Indian Churches of Saint Thomas*, 40.

46. The local Syrian Christians gathered outside a church at Mattancherry in Cochin and took the oath on the crooked shaped stone cross. The word "coonen" translates as "crooked."

Resolution resulted in the division of the Syrian Christians, marking "the end of the unity of the Kerala Church."[47] "The ones who remained with the Roman Church came to be known as the 'Pazhayakur' (old party), and the ones who maintained their separation from the Roman Church came to be known as the 'Puthenkur' (new party)."[48] The "new party" of Syrian Christians reintegrated their ecclesial order with the Syrian Jacobite Church, reintroduced oriental customs, and reinstated Syriac as the ecclesiastical language.

Accommodation

While the colonially minded Portuguese administration ventured on conquering Goa with its militarized Christian policies (unscathed by the Jesuit protests against the colonial imposition of Christianity), the Native Goan Christians were migrating to neighboring kingdoms, and the local Kerala Syrian Christians were resisting the Catholic invasion. There were also some missionaries who continued to communicate the gospel. They "ventured into the courts of the *rayas* of Vijayanagar, the places of the Nayakas of Cinji, Madurai, and Thanjavur," attempting to communicate the good news of the gospel as well as contributing to the welfare of the natives.[49] In doing so, "they manifested an entirely different kind of Catholic presence."[50] Most notably, the life and work of Francis Xavier and Roberto de Nobili are noteworthy for their missionary efforts of accommodation which contrasted with the Portuguese militarized Christianity.

Francis Xavier's presence among the Paravas of Tamil Nadu (who were considered as low caste) is one of the early missionary examples of attempting to truly inform the natives of the catholic beliefs and practices beyond mere colonial impositions. The Paravas, as Kaufman notes, "are a body of fishermen, pearl divers, fish dealers, and seaborne traders settled in sixty or more hamlets and villages along the Tamil coast from Kilakarai in Ramnad district to Kanyakumari, and then up the Kerala coast almost as far as Trivandrum."[51] In 1532, the Paravas converted to Christianity at the highpoint of a savage maritime war (1527–1539) between the Portuguese and Muslim naval forces when a delegation of Paravas appealed to "the Portuguese authorities at Cochin for protection against their long-standing rivals, the Lebbai Muslim divers." The Portuguese recognizing "the value of a client community allied to their interests in the struggle to control

---

47. Menon, *Kerala History and its Makers*, 122.

48. Varghese, "The Reformative and Indigenous Face of the Indian Pentecostal Movement," 4.

49. Frykenberg, *Christianity in India,* 137.

50. Frykenberg, *Christianity in India,* 137.

51. S. B. Kaufmann, "A Christian Caste in Hindu Society: Religious Leadership and Social Conflict among the Paravas of Southern Tamilnadu," *Modern Asian Studies* 15, no. 2 (1981): 206.

the Tirunelveli pearl revenues" not only helped to fight off the Muslims but also baptized the Paravas into the Catholic faith.[52] This Paravas conversion was more like, as Kaufmann termed it, a "tactical profession of Christianity" than a genuine embrace of Christianity as a confession of faith.[53] However, Francis Xavier's arrival among the Paravas in 1542, ten years after their supposed conversion, came as a corrective of their mere "tactical" faith. Xavier helped the community to make sense of Catholic Christianity as a confession of faith. Although Xavier was only able to teach them "to make the sign of the cross and to recite garbled Tamil renderings of the Creed and the Ave Maria," the consolidation of a new and distinctive Christian tradition occurred through Xavier.[54] Although Xavier spent only two years in South India, through the force of his personality and the "aura of charismatic authority," as Susan Bayly puts it, "Xavier became a powerful tutelary for the Paravas; in their hierarchy of regional patrons and cult figures he was second only to their most celebrated supernatural patron figure, the miraculous Virgin of Tuticorin."[55]

However, after Xavier, another prominent Catholic missionary who requires a mention is Roberto de Nobili (1577–1656), an Italian Jesuit. De Nobili lived in Madurai for almost forty years (1606–1644) and is known for his lifestyle of missionary witness among the prominent Tamil class. "If Francis Xavier has dealt with the lowest, most polluting segments of Tamil society down the Fisher Coast, Roberto de Nobili dealt exclusively with the highest and most pure."[56] De Nobili immersed himself in the South Indian Brahminic culture and "sought to remove the barriers that lay between the Hindus of caste and faith in Christ by stripping both the Christian message and the Christian messenger of their respective 'cultural encoding'" and embracing the local cultural norms.[57] For de Nobili, this stripping of his cultural encoding meant denouncing his European cultural norms and accepting the South Indian Brahminic *sannyasi* manner of life.

---

52. Kaufmann, "A Christian Caste in Hindu Society," 206.

53. Kaufmann quote is from "A Christian Caste in Hindu Society," 209. For a brief account of the origin and history of the Paravas, see Simon Casie Chitty, "Remarks on the Origin and History of the Parawas," *Journal of the Royal Asiatic Society of Great Britain and Ireland*, 4 (1837). The Paravas, even after conversion to Christianity, remained with a more or less caste-based framework among themselves. "Christianity became in effect a 'caste lifestyle' for the Paravas" (Kaufmann, "A Christian Caste in Hindu Society," 209).

54. Bayly, *Saints, Goddesses and Kings*, 328.

55. Bayly, *Saints, Goddesses and Kings*, 329.

56. Robert Eric Frykenberg, "India," in *A World History of Christianity*, ed. Adrian Hastings (Grand Rapids, MI: Eerdmans, 1999), 169.

57. Cody C. Lorance, "Cultural Relevance and Doctrinal Soundness: The Mission of Roberto de Nobili," *Missiology* 33, no. 4 (2005): 417.

Consequently, de Nobili chose to live in a hermitage rather than in a Catholic mission compound. In addition, de Nobili became well versed in the Tamil language, "developed a Tamil writing style far surpassing the minimal requirements of the colloquial; he learned Sanskrit, Hinduism's classical language, and was probably the first European to be fluent in it."[58] Subsequently, de Nobili was able to communicate the biblical doctrines through the local cultural and linguistic idioms, for example, communicating the thought of incarnation in terms of "divine guru"[59] while also presenting apologetics arguments against the Hindu concepts and theories of the divine.[60] In other words, de Nobili's approach to mission was revolutionary to the extent that it brought a new understanding of gospel accommodation, where his life became a model for numerous other strands of Christianity to envision the faith that is truly India.

In summation, the second spring of South Indian Christianity that came with the Portuguese Catholics presented a multifaceted—conquest, migration, resistance, and accommodation—Christian presence. Through the Portuguese stronghold, on one end, Christianity was seen as a transnational conquering faith (in Goa) because of its military powers that forced a native Christian transregional migration (to Karnataka). On the other side, it also revealed the resisting facet of Christianity (in Kerala), that motivated some to fight to keep the Syrian tradition of Christianity alive in India. Still, some among the Portuguese presented a different kind of Catholicism in envisioning a contextualized faith into the local culture by adopting local religious idioms and lifestyles (in Tamil Nadu).

The Third Spring
Translation and Vernacularization

In addition to the growing Catholic presence in South India, the introduction of Protestant Christianity brought forth a third spring in South Indian Christianity. To mark the beginning of the Protestant presence in South India, King Frederick IV of Denmark commissioned two German Lutherans to join the Danish settlement in India. On July 9, 1706, Bartholomew Ziegenbalg and Henry Pluetschau arrived at Tranquebar, which was followed by numerous Lutheran missionaries joining the mission in Tranqubar (also known as Tarangambadi). From Tranquebar, the Lutheran Christians not only established worshipping congregations in main South Indian cities such as Cuddalore (in 1717), Chennai

---

58. Francis X. Clooney, "Roberto de Nobili, Adaptation and the Reasonable Interpretation of Religion," *Missiology* 18, no. 1 (1990): 26.

59. Lorance, "Cultural Relevance and Doctrinal Soundness," 419.

60. Clooney, "Roberto de Nobili," 26.

(formerly Madras, in 1726), and Tanjore (in 1728),[61] they also established schools, known locally as "*Dharma Pallik-kudams* (public charity schools)."[62]

Translation

For the Protestant missionaries, education and church planting went hand in hand. For the pioneering Ziegenbalg, "the aim of education . . . was not simply the diffusion of knowledge; it was to be part of the equipment of the Christian man, who must be able to read the Word of God for himself and to absorb it into his very being."[63] Therefore, Ziegenbalg and other subsequent missionaries began translating the Bible to the vernacular language which also helped their education mission.[64] Linguistically, although the early Catholic missionaries to South India did not translate the Bible into Tamil, missionaries like Henrique Henrique (1520–1600), Roberto de Nobili, and Constanzo Giuseppe Beshi (1680–1747) "composed original religious texts in Tamil and built up a body of religious terms that proved useful for the early Protestants" like Ziegenbalg.[65] At the same time, with his motivation to provide the Bible (Word of God) for the local Tamils in their language, Ziegenbalg "preferred the colloquial form of Tamil as spoken by the fisherman of Tranquebar to the poetic form of Tamil cultivated by the literati."[66] With his hope to present the gospel to the natives, Ziegenbalg first completed and printed the Tamil New Testament between 1714 and 1715. Although Ziegenbalg's version had to be revised multiple times until it was fit for local reading (and later it was replaced by Johann Fabricius's

---

61. Daniel Jeyaraj, "Embodying Memories: Early Bible Translations in Tranquebar and Serampore," *International Bulletin of Mission Research* 40, no. 1 (2016): 44.

62. Daniel Jeyaraj, "Indian Founders of the Protestant Church in South India," *Indian Church History Review* 35, no. 1 (2001): 78.

63. Stephen C. Neill, *A History of Christianity in India: 1707–1858* (Cambridge: Cambridge University Press, 1985), 31

64. The special interest of the British organization, the Society for Promoting Christian Knowledge (SPCK) in financially supporting the early Tranquebar missionaries encouraged them in the pioneering works of establishing schools and translation efforts (David Packiamuthu, "The Beginnings of Protestant Mission in Madras." *Indian Church History Review* 34, no. 2 (2000): 98).

65. Hephzibah Israel, *Religious Transactions in Colonial South India: Language, Translation and the Making of Protestant Identity*. Palgrave Studies in Cultural and Intellectual History. (New York: Palgrave Macmillan, 2011), 26. For Ziegenbalg, "his reason [to retain the Catholic terms] was that those Christians who were acquainted with such terminology should not be confused with totally new vocabulary." (Daniel Jeyaraj, "Early Tamil Bible Translation in Tranquebar," *Dharma Deepika* 1, no. 1 (1997): 72).

66. Jeyaraj, "Embodying Memories," 47.

[1711–1791] more accurate version in 1772), as Stephen Neil writes, Ziegenbalg's achievement was considerable; for the first time, the entire New Testament had been made available in an Indian language."[67] For the other missionaries who translated the Bible into other South Indian languages, Ziegenbalg's work served as a foundation. Benjamin Schultze, who was a successor to Ziegenbalg, not only took the task of completing the Old Testament translation into Tamil in 1724 (which Ziegenbalg started) but also became the first person to translate "the New Testament into Telugu in 1727 and the Old Testament by 1732."[68]

While Lutheran missionaries took the early step to translate the Bible into Tamil and Telegu, it was the English missionaries (who came after 1880) who translated it into Kannada and Malayalam. One of the reasons for this transition was due to the waning Danish political influence in the region and the ascendancy of the English East India Company, which also coincided with the establishment of the British and Foreign Bible Society (BFBS), along with mission societies.[69] This meant that the task of translating the Bible into South Indian languages passed from German Pietists to British Anglican missionaries, or to those who worked with British mission societies (in some cases Germans working with these mission organizations). Notably, John Hands, from the London Missionary Society (LMS), who was appointed to Bellary, shortly after arriving, committed to the study of the Kannada language (whose script originated from old Brahmi script and closely related to the Telugu script). "By 1811, he was holding services in Kannada and by 1812 had finished translating parts of the New Testament into Kannada, along with a grammar book."[70] In 1825, the whole New Testament was published by John Hands.

However, in Kerala, it was the Church Missionary Societies (CMS) missionaries—Benjamin Bailey, Joseph Fenn, and Henry Baker (who arrived in 1816 and later came to be known as the "Travancore Trio"[71])—who advanced the Bible translation efforts in Malayalam. Unlike any other South Indian

---

67. Neill, *A History of Christianity in India: 1707–1858*, 34.

68. Hephzibah Israel, "Protestant Translations of the Bible in Indian Languages." *Religion Compass* 4, no. 2 (2010): 95. Although the first translations were done by Schultz, Translation Studies expert Hephzibah Israel notes that these translations "were never printed" and so was not accessible to people. Later on, in 1818, it was the Baptists at Serampore who published the first Telegu New Testament (Israel, "Protestant Translations of the Bible in Indian Languages", 95).

69. Of the mission societies, "SPS established in 1825, Church Missionary Society (CMS) in 1814, the London Missionary Society in 1805, and the Wesleyan Methodist Missionary Society in 1816 were Prominent in South India." Israel, *Religious Transactions in Colonial South India*, 30.

70. Chandra Mallampalli, *Race, Religion and Law in Colonial India: Trials of an Interracial Family* (Cambridge: Cambridge University Press, 2011), 28.

71. Garry McKee, "Benjamin Bailey and the Call for the Conversion of an Ancient Christian Church in India," *Studies in World Christianity* 24, no. 2 (2018): 114.

community, until the arrival of the Protestant missionaries, the Malayali Christian community was the only one who had access to the Bible, namely the Old Syriac Bible. However, as Hephzibah Israel rightly points out, "this Christian population in general had no recourse to reading the Bible either in Syriac or Malayalam, [but] unlike other parts of India, the Bible was first translated into Malayalam not for non-Christians but for a largely Christian population."[72] Therefore, the work of "Travancore Trio" was mainly among the Kerala Syrian Christians.[73] The Trio made it clear that their intentions were "not to establish Anglican congregations in Travancore,"[74] but to reform the existing Syrian churches. Particularly, Benjamin Bailey believed that the translation of the Anglican *Book of Common Prayer* to Malayalam would be essential in that reformative task.[75] However, the *Book of Common Prayer* failed to capture the Syrian Christian attention. Instead, it was Bailey's translation of the Bible to Malayalam (completed in 1841) that shifted the trajectory of Christianity into a reformative path.[76]

Vernacularization

Although the initial Bible translations of Bartholomew Ziegenbalg (in Tamil), Benjamin Schultze (in Telegu), John Hands (in Kannada), and Benjamin Bailey (in Malayalam) have gone through numerous revisions by other Western missionaries and native translators, the pioneering nature of the eighteenth and early nineteenth-century European Protestant missionaries are commendable for taking the first step that led the way for others to follow with less difficulty. During the course of the European translation efforts, there were also native "helpers" and disciples who played pivotal roles as evangelists and language consultants.[77] From a broader perspective of Christianity in South India, this wave of translation served as the third spring of South Indian Christianity and shifted the course toward the vernacularization of Christianity.

For example, in Kerala, two reform-minded groups of Syrian Christians emerged as a result of the vernacularization process, breaking away from the Syrian

---

72. Israel, "Protestant Translations of the Bible in Indian Languages," 94.

73. Mathew and Thomas, *The Indian Churches of Saint Thomas*, 56.

74. McKee, "Benjamin Bailey and the Call for the Conversion of an Ancient Christian Church in India," 118.

75. McKee, "Benjamin Bailey and the Call for the Conversion of an Ancient Christian Church in India," 119.

76. Varghese, "The Reformative and Indigenous Face of the Indian Pentecostal Movement," 6.

77. For more on this, see Robert Eric Frykenber's article "The Faith 'Goes Native'" at https://christianhistoryinstitute.org/magazine/article/faith-goes-native.

Jacobite ecclesiastical authority. While the smaller group joined the Anglican Church following the CMS missionaries, the larger group "remained staunchly committed to the ancient Thomas Christian Traditions, [but] still strongly felt the need for internal reforms, both in doctrinal and structural terms."[78] The larger group, led by a local Syrian Jacobite clergy, Abraham Malpan (1796–1845), translated the liturgy from Syriac to Malayalam and began celebrating rites in Malayalam.[79] Another clergy, Kaithayil Geevarghese Malpan, joined in, and together they "abolished prayers for the dead, the invocation of saints, auricular confession, and the unhealthy veneration of sacraments."[80] Such a reformative act to remove all the non-biblical traditional practices and make the biblical message accessible to the people in Malayalam led some to call Abraham Malpan the "Martin Luther of the East."[81] As one would expect, the Syrian (Jacobite) church did not approve of Malpan's reformative efforts, prompting the Metropolitan to excommunicate Abraham Malpan and his congregation.[82] The excommunication led the reform-minded Syrian Christians to establish themselves as the Mar Thoma Church, leading the way for the formation of the Mar Thoma Evangelistic Association in 1888. The following years saw numerous local open-air revival meetings, where people sang songs and preachers expounded from the Bible in Malayalam.

For a Christian community across South India that became accustomed to a more enculturated Syrian and Catholic Christianity, mainly categorized by traditional ceremonies and annual festivals commemorating the saints, the Protestant missionary efforts to make the Bible available in the vernacular language "breathed new life."[83] In this vernacularization process of the Bible, as Daniel Jeyaraj notes, often three cultures met: the Bible culture met the local culture through that of the European missionaries. In this joint venture, the people could hear the Hebrew prophets, Jesus Christ and the apostles speak in their own tongue.[84] For reform-minded, native clergy, this was also a moment of realization

---

78. Robert Eric Frykenberg, *Christianity in India: From Beginnings to the Present* (New York: Oxford University Press, 2008), 248.

79. Fernando and Gispert-Sauch, *Christianity in India*, 176.

80. Stanley J. Valayil C. John, *Transnational Religious Organization and Practice: A Contextual Analysis of Kerala Pentecostal Churches in Kuwait* (Leiden: Brill, 2018), 93.

81. John, *Transnational Religious Organization and Practice*, 93.

82. Mathew and Thomas, *The Indian Churches of Saint Thomas*, 86.

83. A. C. George, "Pentecostal Beginnings in Travancore, South India," *Asian Journal of Pentecostal Studies* 4, no. 2 (2001): 221.

84. This is a paraphrasing of Daniel Jeyaraj's words concerning the significance of the Bible translation into Tamil. Daniel Jeyaraj, "Early Tamil Bible Translation in Tranquebar," *Dharma Deepika* 1, no. 1 (1997): 75.

that, to use Lamin Sannah's words, "no one language had primacy over another and no person might be denied access to God on account of the language he or she spoke."[85] As the Bible became readily available in Tamil, Kannada, Telugu, and Malayalam, the wave of reformations and revivals emerged, leaving a "strong foundation of an indigenous Church in India."[86]

In describing this third spring of South Indian Christianity through Protestant missionary translation efforts, it is also important to highlight how the accessibility of a vernacular Bible and education enabled the Dalits of South India to be empowered. The Dalits were "forbidden to read and hear the sacred scriptures of the Hindus. Thus, they were cut off from all forms of literacy, especially from Hindu sacred texts."[87] Such is the context in which the Dalits were given access by the Protestant missionaries to study at the mission schools and listen to the biblical teachings. Thus, the "accessibility of the Christian sacred Scriptures was an opportunity for empowerment."[88] In other words, for the people with *no-Vedas*, the Bible became their *Veda*, enabling numerous Dalit men and women to be catechists and Bible women working with the Protestant mission organizations pioneering indigenous Christian movements in various parts of South India.[89]

The Fourth Spring
Pentecostal Revival and Indigenization

By the nineteenth century, South Indian Christianity had gone through a series of transitions (assimilation, conquest, migration, resistance, accommodation, translation, and vernacularization), setting the faith on the trajectory toward indigenization. The availability of the Bible in their own language provided a sense of authority and autonomy to the reform-minded South Indian leaders to carry out reforms in their existing churches and to reach out to non-Christians. At the same time, such a native reformative impetus also brought forth a renewal of Christianity, which began in Tamil Nadu (in Tirunelveli) as people started to experience the Holy Spirit in some of their revival gatherings.

---

85. Lamin Sanneh, *Whose Religion is Christianity?* (Grand Rapids, MI: Eerdmans, 2003), 103.

86. Jeyaraj, "Early Tamil Bible Translation in Tranquebar," 75.

87. Sathianathan Clarke, "Viewing the Bible through the Eyes and Ears of Subalterns in India," *Biblical Interpretation* 10, no. 3 (2002): 256.

88. Clarke, "Viewing the Bible through the Eyes and Ears of Subalterns in India," 256.

89. For examples from the states of Andhra Pradesh and Telangana, see Chakali Chandra Sekhar, "Dalit Women and Colonial Christianity: First Telugu Bible Women as Teachers of Wisdom," *Economic & Political Weekly* 56, no. 11 (2021): 57–63.

Pentecostal Revival

One of the earliest revivals that reported Holy Spirit experiences in South India was the Christian Pettah Revival, led by John Christian Aroolappen, a trained Anglican catechist. In his diary entry for August 8, 1860, Aroolappen recorded: "In the month of June some of our people praised the Lord by unknown tongues, with their interpretations. . . . My son and a daughter and three others went to visit their own relations, in three villages, who are under the Church Missionary Society, they also received the Holy Ghost. Some prophesy, some speak by unknown tongues with their interpretations."[90] Aroolappen began to preach beyond the CMS churches to non-Christians following the apostolic pattern of traveling evangelists and embraced an indigenous attitude when it comes to limiting the Western missionary influence on the revival by accepting little or no western funding.

Aroolappen's revival became influential for the revivals in Kerala as Yusthus Joseph (1835–1887), also locally known as Vidhuwan Kutty Achen, attended Aroolappen's meetings and assumed the leadership of the Travancore revival in its early stages which paved the way for the continuation of the renewal in Kerala from Mar Thoma church to Brethren and to the formation of Pentecostal churches in Kerala from 1910 onward.[91] Consequently, in 1926, the first indigenous Pentecostal denomination was formed as the South Indian Pentecostal Church of God (SIPC) under the leadership of K. E. Abraham.[92] The insistence on indigenous leadership of Pentecostal churches prompted them to engage in sending missionaries to various parts of India,[93] eventually removing the "South" from their title and reframing themselves as the Indian Pentecostal Church of God (IPC). Its early indigenous rationale let the leaders to officially register the church in Eluru, Andhra Pradesh, on December 9, 1935.[94] Other Pentecostal

---

90. Aroolappen quoted in, Gary B. McGee, "Pentecostal Phenomena and Revivals in India. Implications for Indigenous Church Leadership," *International Bulletin of Missionary Research* 20 no. 3 (1996): 113.

91. Saju, *Kerala Pentekostu Charithram* [History of Kerala Pentecostals—in Malayalam] (Kottayam, Kerala: Good News Publications, 1994), 49; Michael Bergunder, *The South Indian Pentecostal Movement in the Twentieth Century* (Grand Rapids, MI: Eerdmans, 2008), 26; George, "Pentecostal Beginnings in Travancore, South India," 225.

92. Varghese, "The Reformative and Indigenous Face of the Indian Pentecostal Movement," 11.

93. Roger E. Hedlund, "Indigenous Pentecostalism in India," in *Asian and Pentecostal*, ed. Allan Anderson and Edmond Tang (Oxford: Regnum Books International, 2005), 217.

94. K. E. Abraham, *Yeshuvinte Eliyadasen* [Humble servant of God–in Malayalam]. 4th ed. (Arlington: Vijai & Shirley Chacko, 2015), 281. Stanley M. Burgess, *The New International Dictionary of Pentecostal and Charismatic Movements* (Grand Rapids, MI: Zondervan, 2002), 779.

denominations such as Assemblies of God in India (AG) and Church of God were also established around the same time under the partnership of American Pentecostal missionaries.

IPC's presence in Eluru also marked the beginning of Pentecostalism in the state of Andhra Pradesh.[95] Prior to the arrival of IPC, Christianity in Andhra Pradesh mainly consisted of (a) Catholics, who had remained as a small presence since the sixteenth century and (b) Protestants, beginning with the Lutheran missionaries and then joined by other mission organizations, namely SPG,[96] the American Baptist Mission, Canadian Baptist Mission, Church Mission Society, Zenana Missionary Society, and the South Asia Methodist Mission.[97] However, after the introduction of Pentecostalism, the Pentecostal phenomena[98] began to spread across the state, prompting other indigenously minded pastors to start independent churches, a common trend that emerged in all of the South Indian states. One of the examples is in the formation of the Bible Mission in Andhra Pradesh in 1938, by a Dalit Lutheran Pastor, Mungamuri Devadas, who also served as Sadhu Sundar Singh's "Telugu interpreter during his brief campaigns in the area."[99] Devadas was influenced by the Pentecostal teaching of the Holy Spirit as well as Sundar Singh's visions, dreams, and miracles. Devadas, after being excommunicated from his Lutheran church due to his accusation that "his mother church was not teaching enough about the Holy Spirit,"[100] "claimed that the Lord revealed to him in a vision that he should come out and start a mission and write the name 'Bible Mission' in the air."[101] Today, the Bible Mission of Father Devadas is one of the leading denominations in Andhra Pradesh and Telangana.

---

95. Yabbeju Rapaka, "History of Indian Pentecostal Church of God in Andhra." *Evangelical Review of Theology* 31, no. 1 (2007): 29.

96. The Society for the Propagation of the Gospel in Foreign Parts (SPG).

97. K D. Rajpramukh, *Dalit Christians of Andhra: Under the Impact of Missionaries.* (New Delhi: Serials Publications, 2008), 30–61.

98. Here I use the phrase 'Pentecostal Phenomena' to communicate Pentecostalism as a movement that is beyond a particular denomination. I use the word 'Pentecostal' to mean sharing family resemblance, as Allan Anderson puts it (Allan Anderson, "Varieties, Taxonomies, and Definitions," in *Studying Global Pentecostalism: Theories and Methods,* edited by Allan Anderson, Michael Bergunder, Andre Droogers and Cornelis Van Der Lann. [Berkley: University of California Press, 2010]. 13–29.).

99. P. Solomon Raj, *The New Wine-Skins: The Story of the Indigenous Missions in Coastal Andhra Pradesh,* (Delhi: ISPCK, 2003), 6.

100. Raj, *The New Wine-Skins,* 6.

101. Raj, *The New Wine-Skins,* 8.

It is also important to note that the expansion of indigenous movements such as Bible Mission occurred not only because of its Pentecostal resemblance but also because of its reach among the subaltern Dalit community. As James Ponniah notes, "Devadas was a true subaltern not only because he was born as a Dalit, but because he opted to live a life of simplicity."[102] In other words, the story of Bible Mission testifies to the story of Christian expansion that occurs when "the convergence of the divine and the human [happens] at the site of marginality of the subalterns."[103]

Indigenization

While such an indigenous Pentecostal phenomenon began to spread across South India, there were also inklings of transformation among the already existing Protestant churches to form a unified church in India. Even though the vision for a unified church in South India was forming from the early 1900s,[104] it took until 1947 (immediately after India gained political independence from Britain) for the main protestant denominations—Anglican (Episcopal), Congregational, Presbyterian, and Methodist—to officially inaugurate the new church as the Church of South India (CSI).[105] Even though the Mar Thoma Church of Kerala was not involved in CSI initially, they entered into a "deeper ecumenical relationship as constituent members of the Communion of Churches of India."[106] Although the political independence of India was not a direct reason for such a unified church, the increasing sense of nationalism in the country did influence it,[107] especially in ensuring that CSI would be an "authentically Indian church in matters of finance and personnel."[108] The establishment of CSI was, in fact, a

---

102. James Ponniah, "The Phenomenon of Bible Mission: Exploring the Features of a Local Church on the Margins" in *Mission at and from the Margins: Patterns, Protagonists and Perspectives*, ed. Peniel Rajkumar, Joseph Prabhakar Dayam, and I. P. Asheervadham (Oxford, UK: Regnum Books International, 2014), 69.

103. Ponniah, "The Phenomenon of Bible Mission," 75.

104. Notably in the form of Tranquebar Manifesto in 1919 by various church leaders, including V. S. Azariah, the first Indian Anglican bishop. The manifesto emphasized the importance of congregational, presbyterian, and episcopal elements across the various churches to be united. (George Oommen, "Challenging Identity and Crossing Borders: Unity in the Church of South India," *Word & World* 25, no. 1 (2005): 61).

105. Joshva Raja, "United and Uniting Churches," in *Christianity in South and Central Asia*, ed. Kenneth R. Ross, Daniel Jeyaraj, and Todd M. Johnson (Edinburgh: Edinburgh University Press, 2019), 238.

106. Raja, "United and Uniting Churches," 240.

107. Raja, "United and Uniting Churches," 239.

108. Oommen, "Challenging Identity and Crossing Borders," 62.

reformative move among the Protestant churches as it not only established the Indian leadership over the governance of the Protestant churches, which was started by the Western churches, but in its unified vision, it also presented a prophetic challenge to the rising denominational divisiveness in Western Christianity.

However, reform-minded clergy continued to break away and start new independent fellowships. Such is the story of the Indigenous Churches of India (also known as the assemblies of Brother Bakht Singh). Under the leadership of Bakht Singh, "the first assembly, Jehovah Shammah, was started at Chennai in 1941 as a 'true testimony' for the Lord among people 'dissatisfied with the denominational churches.'"[109] The assemblies prioritized Bible-centered preaching and teaching, aiming for evangelistic outreach (while also instituting Indian-style worship similar to that of Punjabi Sikh Kirtans). Such a priority was an intentional response to the "denominational churches [who] were caught up in the drive for church union, to the neglect of evangelism."[110] The number of assemblies has grown steadily since its beginning making its presence known more prominently in Tamil Nadu, Andhra Pradesh, and Telangana, where it has its headquarters in Hyderabad.

While the fourth spring of South Indian Christianity brought renewal to the existing Protestant denominations in the form of Pentecostalism and indigenization, even in forming new denominations,[111] Catholics were not immune to such transformation. The call for indigenization was also heard loudly among the South Indian Catholic clergy. The most visible effects were seen in the establishment of various Christian Ashrams in South India, notably the Shantivanam in Tamil Nadu (established in 1950) and Kurisumala Ashram in Kerala (established in 1958). The primary aim of these ashrams is to "establish way of contemplative life, based alike on the traditions of Christian monasticism and of Hindu Sannyas."[112] The British Benedictine monk, Fr. Bede Griffiths, was one of the key

---

109. Roger E. Hedlund, "Independents," in *Christianity in South and Central Asia*, ed. Kenneth R. Ross, Daniel Jeyaraj, and Todd M. Johnson. (Edinburgh: Edinburgh University Press, 2019), 266.

110. Hedlund, "Independents," 267.

111. While Pentecostal denominations grew throughout the South Indian states with some large-sized churches, especially affiliated to Assemblies of God, notably the New Life Assembly of God in Chennai (Pastor D. Mohan), Full Gospel Assembly of God Indiranagar in Bangalore (Pastor Paul Thangaiah) and Bethel AG church Hebbal in Bangalore (Pastor Johnson Varghese), independent megachurches such as the Calvary Temple in Andhra Pradesh also were established. See, Jonathan D. James, "Global, 'Glocal' and Local Dynamics in Calvary Temple: India's Fastest Growing Megachurch," in *Handbook of Megachurches*, ed. Stephen Hunt (Leiden: Brill, 2020), 302–322.

112. Antonysamy Sagaraj, "Christianity in India: A Focus on Inculturation," *Research Papers of the Anthropological Institute* 1 (2013), 129, accessed December 1, 2021, https://rci.nanzan-u.ac.jp/jinruiken/publication/item/ronshu1-06%20Sagayaraj.pdf

proponents in establishing these ashrams and was a resident at these ashrams. These ashrams continue to attract people who seek to experience Benedictine Christian Spirituality in a Hindu way. From an educational perspective, the National Biblical Catechetical and Liturgical Center in Bangalore (founded in 1967) was tasked with the objective to "promote the renewal of the Church in an Indian context."[113] Since then, the center has been offering research seminars, courses, and resources for both scholars and catholic clergy to be the church in India, integrating its rich cultural and religious resources in a Christian way.

However, in speaking of the Hindu way of Christianity, it is also important to mention the presence of "Churchless Christianity" as well as "Christ groups" in South India.[114] While Herbert E. Hoefer's study indicates the presence of Christians who are "non-baptized believers in Christ (NBBC)" who remain as Hindus and Muslims while devoted to Christ, Saheb John Borgall's study shines a light on "Christ groups" in the state of Karnataka who consider themselves as a small group of people meeting as "worshiping communities,"[115] akin with local Bhakti movements and Lingayatism, that emphasized experience and devotion to God which went against the Brahminical order of worship.[116]

Both "churchless Christians" and the "Christ groups" are prevalent Christian trends in South India that found their footing during the wave of indigenization of South Indian Christianity along with the Pentecostal renewal wave.

Conclusion

The story of South Indian Christianity has been a testament of a faith that has been transitioning for the last two-thousand years as it encountered multiple Christian traditions, over the course of those years, through various transcontinental links (with Syria, Portugal, Germany, and Britain). While the first spring emerged with the early arrival of Christianity in the first century from Syria, it gave rise to an assimilated nature of South Indian Christianity with the Syrian tradition. The second spring transpired when the Portuguese arrived in the fifteenth century with their Catholic Christianity (along with their political and militaristic agenda). Consequently, South Indian Christianity went through conquest, transregional migration, resistance, and accommodation. Such a momentous era was followed by the arrival of European protestants giving rise

---

113. For more details on the National Biblical Catechetical and Liturgical Center, see: https://www.nbclcindia.org/history.php. Accessed March 6, 2023.

114. Herbert E. Hoefer, *Churchless Christianity* (Pasadena, CA: W. Carey Library, 2001).

115. Saheb John Borgall, *The Emergence of Christ Groups in India: The Case of Karnataka State* (Oxford: Regnum Books International, 2016), 102.

116. Borgall, *The Emergence of Christ Groups in India*, 114–115.

to the third spring in the form of translation and vernacularization. The era of translation opened a non-revocable nature of South Indian Christianity where the vernacular Bible became the authority in the process of indigenizing the faith. However, the final spring was inaugurated in the form of Pentecostalism and its influence in forming independent clusters of Christian communities. This era also witnessed the various indigenization efforts of protestants and Catholics, which continues in different parts of South India.

Collectively, the history of South Indian Christianity is not only the story of how others have imparted their faith tradition to South Indians (through their transcontinental links) but is also about how such traditions were received locally through assimilation, migration, resistance, vernacularization, renewal, and indigenization. Through it all, today, in the context of a Hindu majority India, South Indian Christianity stands as a polyvalent religion, where numerous forms of Christianity assembled under major Christian traditions—Catholic, Orthodox, Protestant, Pentecostal, and independents, claiming to be truly South Indian and Christian.

CHAPTER TWO

Amid Opposition and Optimism

A Brief History of Christianity in North India

Shivraj K. Mahendra

Introduction

WHY SHOULD ANYONE be curious about the story of Christianity in North India? Christianity in North India deserves special attention for at least three reasons: First, North India remains one of the most challenging mission fields in India.[1] Second, it is home to the most persecuted Christians of India.[2] Third, it is a fertile land for some of the most vibrant and growing forms of Christianity in India in our times.[3] Although Christianity is a minority religion in India, it is a *significant* minority, contributing to nation building through pioneering educational, health, and social services. But no single survey, albeit brief, is to be found on North Indian Christianity. There are a few studies dealing with North Indian Christianity, but they are mostly focused on denominations or states.[4] Therefore, this article aims to present an overview of Christianity in North India. In the process, it explores the following questions: What is the status of Christianity in North India? Which mission agencies and denominations have ventured in this part of the nation? What are some of the major institutions? Who are the

---

1. Until recently, Bihar, a north-central Indian state and the third largest state of the nation, was infamously known as "the graveyard of missionaries." See, Alex Philip and Davesh Harish Lal, "Bihar Summit," *Mission Frontiers* (May–June 2015): 30–31. See also, "Life in the Graveyard," *Revival Now!* (April 14, 2019). https://revivalnow.excitingword.org/life-in-the-graveyard/.

2. According to data on attacks on Christians in 2022, the states of Chhattisgarh, Madhya Pradesh, Uttarakhand, and Uttar Pradesh remain increasingly hostile states for Christians in North India.

3. For example, the expansion of Christianity in the North Indian state of Punjab. See, Anilesh S. Mahajan and Sunil Menon, "The Pastors of Punjab: Pentecostal Preachers Find a Fertile Ground among Punjab's Most Oppressed Castes to Spread their Faith and Expand their Flock," *India Today Magazine,* Cover story. New Delhi: November 14, 2022: 43–59.

4. See, for example, Abraham Kunnatholy, *St. Thomas Christians of Madhya Pradesh* (Bangalore: ATC, 2007), and, Shivraj K. Mahendra, *A Christian History of Uttarakhand*, vol. I (Delhi: ISPCK, 2014).

prominent Christians in North India? What are the major themes and issues facing North Indian Christianity today? How are Christians in this part of the world dealing with their challenges and hopes? I explore these questions as a North Indian first-generation Christian with a Hindu background. My attempt is to narrate the story from the perspectives of a historian-missiologist in the making. This is, thus, an insider's overview of the life, history, and witness of Christianity in North India from its beginning to the present. The paper works with historical and missiological frameworks. We shall begin with the location and status of Christianity in North India.

The Location and Status

Geographically speaking, the land above Vindhya mountains in central India is generally considered to be North India. This covers the lands from West Bengal in the east to Gujarat in the west, and it is bordered by Pakistan in the north-west and China and Nepal in the north. North India is home to the river Ganga (aka Ganges) and prominent Hindu pilgrim centers such as Amarnath and Badrinath.

Hindi is North India's dominant language. Other prominent languages include English, Panjabi, Bengali, Rajasthani, Chhattisgarhi, among others. Culturally, North India is a great melting pot of both local culture and cultures of other parts of India. For example, you will find groups of Panjabi people in Uttarakhand and Bihari people in Haryana.

Hinduism is the prominent religion of the land followed by Islam, Sikhism, and Buddhism. The states of Haryana, Himachal, Rajasthan, Uttar Pradesh, and Uttarakhand are the Hindu majority states. Religious demography, like the cultural fabric of North India, remains significantly mixed and from place to place you see high to low population patterns. According to the 2011 census data, 2.3 percent of Indians are Christian.[5] Except in the northeastern states of Nagaland, Mizoram, and Meghalaya, Christians remain a minority in the rest of India, especially in the North.[6] In the 1960s, only about 1 percent of North Indians were Christians. The state-wise official percentage of Christians, according to the 2011 census, is as follows: Bihar (0.12%), Chhattisgarh (1.92%), Delhi (0.87%), Haryana (0.20%), Himachal Pradesh (0.18%), Jammu & Kashmir and Ladakh (0.28%), Jharkhand (4.30%), Madhya Pradesh (0.29%), Odisha (3.0%), Punjab (1.26%), Rajasthan (0.14%), Uttar Pradesh (0.18%), Uttarakhand (0.37%), and West Bengal (0.72%).

---

5. We can only present the 2011 census data as the 2021 Census of India was delayed due to the Covid-19 pandemic and the final results are expected to be published late in 2024.

6. The populations of Christians in the majority Christian states are: Nagaland (88%), Mizoram (87%), and Meghalaya (75%). In the south, Kerala is 18 percent Christian, but that is still only a significant minority.

Note that twelve out of fifteen North Indian states have a population of Christians that is less than 1 percent. Scholars agree that these official figures may not represent the actual numbers. It is estimated that the actual figures would be at least double. There are several reasons for the numeric inaccuracy. First, census officers take the religion of the household based on the religion of the leader. For example, the father may be a Hindu and his wife and children may be following Christ, but they will all be categorized as Hindus. Second, census officers also go by the name of the persons and add their religion by way of assumption. For example, Ram Singh and Rashmi Kumari will be naturally identified as Hindus, whereas Matthew and Mary will be certainly identified as Christians. Third, while the total Christian population is believed to be much higher, the natural rate of Christian population growth is relatively lower than the natural average due to increasing birth control or a lower fertility rate.[7] Fourth, new Christians from special socioeconomic categories do not want to officially identify themselves as Christians. This helps them secure and enjoy employment and other benefits strategically offered by the government. Finally, there is the politics of numbers where the actual Christian population growth may not be officially projected due to influences of the Hindu nationalistic agenda of the Sangh Parivar.[8]

Missiologically speaking, North India may be defined as the "10/40 Window" of India. It is a region characterized by unreached people-groups, hostile Hindutva forces, rampant opposition, and challenging socioeconomic and political conditions. Missions and missionaries from the United States and Europe (mainly up to the Indian independence) as well as from within India (mostly from the South and particularly since the 1940s) have continued to labor for the evangelization, social transformation, and overall development of North India. We shall now turn to their stories.

---

7. Daughrity and Athyal hold that high education rate among Christian women may have an impact on fertility rate. See, Dyron B. Daughrity and Jesudas M. Athyal, *Understanding World Christianity: India* (Minneapolis: Fortress Press, 2016), 169.

8. Sangh Parivar (Lit., Union Family) refers to the Hindu nationalistic group of organizations such as the Vishwa Hindu Parishad (World Hindi Council), Rashtriya Swayamsevak Sangh (National Volunteers Association), Bajrang Dal (Party of Hanuman), the Bhartiya Janata Party (BJP), and the like. While all these groups, except BJP which is a political wing of the Sangh, claim to be cultural and charitable organizations, they are increasingly promoting a religious nationalism achieved through the destruction of the democratic principles and secular spirit and fabric of India.

For a comprehensive study on Hindu nationalism, the Sangh Parivar, and so forth, see, C. V. Mathew, *The Saffron Mission: A Historical Analysis of Hindu Ideologies and Practices* (Delhi: ISPCK, 1999). See also, Lancy Lobo, *Globalization, Hindu Nationalism, and Christians in India* (Jaipur: Rawat Publications, 2002), and Mark Laing, ed., *Nationalism and Hindutva: A Christian Response* (Delhi: ISPCK, 2005).

A Brief History of Christian Missions

The pioneer of Christian faith in North India was apostle Thomas, a disciple of the Lord Jesus Christ. He was the seed sower of the gospel who labored in India in the first century AD. St. Thomas's mission to India had basically two phases: (1) the North Indian phase: This was marked by initial ministry in the northwestern region (present day Pakistan) was chiefly characterized by miracles and charity, and (2) the South Indian phase: The mission in the South was characterized by miracles, baptisms, and planting of churches (in parts of Kerala) and came to an end with his martyrdom in Mylapore, Tamil Nadu.[9]

Some rare archaeological evidence discovered in Udaypur (a small village in Madhya Pradesh) indicates the presence of a Christian church in the eleventh century.[10] However, there is no significant tradition of Christian life and witness in North India until the time of the Jesuit mission at the court of Akbar the Great (1542–1605). Emperor Akbar requested that the Catholic headquarters at Goa (St. Paul's College) send two learned priests with the Holy Bible so that he may study and learn the best of its teachings from them.[11] The leaders at Goa responded with great optimism, sending three Jesuit Fathers, Rudolf Aquaviva (the team leader), Anthony Monserrate (an observant), and Francis Henriques (the Persian convert and translator).[12] They arrived at Fatehpur Sikri (near Agra) on February 28, 1580. This marked the beginning of the Roman Catholic missions in North India. Although Emperor Akbar and his successor Emperor Jahangir (1569–1627) never took baptism, they greatly favored Christianity and

---

9. While the South Indian tradition has ample evidence regarding Thomas's mission, the North Indian tradition relies on significant yet debated sources. For a comprehensive study of apostle Thomas's traditions and evidence, see, George Nedungatt, *Quest for the Historical Thomas Apostle of India: A Re-reading of the Evidence* (Bangalore: Theological Publications in India, 2008).

Sidenote: In December 2022 and January 2023, I visited a few prominent pilgrim centers associated with apostle Thomas in South India. These centers have elegant church buildings and house a relic believed to be of the apostle. Did the church really find the actual bones and has preserved them since then? This calls for another study.

10. See, George Nedungatt, *Quest for the Historical Thomas Apostle of India: A Re-reading of the Evidence* (Bangalore: Theological Publications in India, 2008), 281–304.

11. Edward McLagan, *The Jesuits and the Great Mogul* (London: Burn Oates & Washbourne, 1932), 24. See also, Pierre Du Jarric, *Akbar and the Jesuits: An Account of the Jesuit Missions to the Court of Akbar*, trans. and ed. C. H. Payne (New York & London: Harper & Brothers, 1926), 16.

12. Alice P. J. (Sr. Clerissa), *The Roman Catholic Mission in Agra: From 1781 to 1947,* Published PhD Thesis, (Agra: St. John's College, 1982), 27–31. See also, Henry Hosten, *Jesuit Missionaries in Northern India and Inscriptions on their Tombs, Agra: 1580–1803* (Calcutta: Catholic Orphan Press, 1907).

consequently the Christian mission flourished in Agra and Jesuits reached up to Lahore. However, with the ascension of Shah Jahan (1628) favors were replaced with opposition and persecution.

The eighteenth century saw a new Catholic witness in North India under the patronage of Begum Joanna Zebunisa Samru (1753–1836) of Sardhana (near Meerut). From Muslim dancing girl to the only Catholic ruler in India, Begum Samru's story is fascinating. She was baptized at Agra in 1781 and soon founded the church at Sardhana.[13] Other significant early Catholic missions include Bettiah, Bihar (1703), Raipur, Chhattisgarh (1854), Bhopal, Madhya Pradesh (1871), Jammu & Kashmir (1887), Ajmer, Rajasthan (1890), Shimla, Himachal Pradesh (1910), and Ranchi, Jharkhand (1953). Catholic missionaries built important educational institutions, such as the Convent schools for girls, arts and science colleges, technical and vocational schools for boys, and seminaries, which continue to serve the North Indian society until today.

The arrival of Protestant missions in North India can be traced to the inauguration of the Baptist Mission at Serampore (Sri Rampur) in the 1800s. William Carey and his colleagues Joshua Marshman and William Ward (together known as the Serampore Trio) translated and published the Bible into six languages—Bengali, Hindi, Marathi, Odia, Sanskrit and Assamese—and portions of scripture into over forty other languages.[14] They were dedicated to spreading the gospel through literature evangelism. The Baptist Mission had established stations in Agra (in 1811) and other key places. They worked in Sardhana (Uttar Pradesh), Haridwar and Srinagar (Uttarakhand), and translated the Gospels into several languages of this North Indian Himalayan region.[15] The Serampore missionaries fought against the then prevailing evil practices, such as *Sati* (widow-burning), and worked with a policy "to esteem

---

13. The construction of the Church began in 1809 and was completed in 1822. The Basilica of Our Lady of Graces remains one of the famous Christian pilgrimage centers and tourist attractions today. See, Julia Keay, *Farzana: The Woman Who Saved an Empire: Begum Sumru* (London: I.B. Tauris & Co. Ltd., 2014). See also, James P. Alter, *In the Doab and Rohilkhand: North Indian Christianity, 1815–1915*. Revised and completed by John Alter (Delhi: ISPCK, 1986), 23 and Mahendra, *A Christian History of Uttarakhand*, 33. See also, Raj Bahadur Sharma, *Christian Missions in North India, 1813–1913: A Case Study of Meerut Division and Dehradun District* (Delhi: Mittal Publications, 1988).

14. For a life and legacy of Carey, see, Vishal and Ruth Mangalwadi, *The Legacy of William Carey: A Model for Transformation of a Culture* (Crossway Books: 1999). See also, John C. Marshman, *The Life and Times of Carey, Marshman, and Ward, Embracing the History of the Serampore Mission* (London: Longman, Brown, Green, Longmans, & Roberts, 1859).

15. Languages included Garhwali, Kumaoni, Jaunsari, Paori (Pauri), among others. See, Mahendra, *A Christian History of Uttarakhand*, 36, 63–64. For a history of Bible translation,

and treat Indians always as [their] equals."[16] Thus, they boldly opposed the caste system and every form of discrimination. All evangelical missionaries adopted this policy and it influenced the life and growth of the church throughout North India. This was in sharp contrast to missions in the South where a lenient attitude toward the caste system existed. Carey and team also founded schools for boys and girls and established the Serampore College (1818) for higher learning in arts, science, and theology, which continues to contribute toward nation building.

Other pioneering Protestant missions in the North included the Church Missionary Society (Agra, 1813), American Presbyterians (Allahabad, 1836), the American Methodist Mission (Bareilly, 1856), the London Missionary Society (Almora, 1850), the German Evangelical Missionary Society (Raipur, Chhattisgarh, 1868), the Free Methodist Church and the Pentecost Bands (Raj Nandgaon, 1895), and Christian Church-Disciples of Christ, (Bilaspur, 1930s), among others.[17] Prominent institutions with largely Protestant roots include the Tyndale Biscoe School (Srinagar, J&K, 1880), Isabella Thoburn College (Lucknow, 1870), Christian Medical College (Ludhiana, 1894), Sam Higginbottom University of Agriculture, Technology and Sciences (Allahabad, 1910), Indian Society for Promoting Christian Knowledge (Delhi, 1710), and Presbyterian Theological Seminary (Dehradun, 1969).[18]

Among the Orthodox Churches of India, the St. Thomas Christians (Syro-Malabar tradition) and the Malankara Orthodox Syrian Church, have their presence in Ujjain and Sagar (in Madhya Pradesh) and Delhi and a few other

---

see, J. S. M. Hooper, *Bible Translation in India, Pakistan, and Ceylon*, 2nd ed. rev. by W. J. Culshaw (Bombay: Oxford University Press, 1963).

16. S. Pearce Carey, *William Carey* (London: Carey Press 1923), 248.

17. For histories of Christianity and Christian studies related to pressing issues in some of these places, such as Chhattisgarh, Rajasthan, Punjab, see, Chad Bauman, *Christian Identity and Dalit Religion in Hindu India, 1868–1947* (Grand Rapids: Eerdmans, 2008); John Robson, *The Story of the Rajputana Mission* (Edinburgh: Offices of United Presbyterian Church, 1894); Ashcroft Frank, *Story of Our Rajputana Mission* (Edinburgh: Oilphant, Anderson and Ferrier, 1908); Abraham T. Cherian, *Contribution of Churches and Missions to the Bhils of Rajasthan* (PhD Thesis, AIT, Bangalore, 2005); Alexander T. Daniel, *The Impact of Christian Mission on the Bhil Tribe in Rajasthan* (Delhi: ISPCK, 2012); John C. B. Webster, *A Social History of Christianity: North-West India since 1800* (New Delhi: Oxford University Press, 2007), and John C. B. Webster, *The Christian Community and Change in Nineteenth Century North India* (New Delhi: Macmillan, 1976). See, also, Robert Clark, *The Punjab and Sindh Mission of the Church Missionary Society Giving an Account of their Foundation and Progress for Thirty-Three Years, from 1852–1884* (London: CMS, 1885).

18. A brief history of all these institutions can be accessed from their official websites.

places in North India.[19] The Orthodox mission in the North is also marked
by a seminary, Dharma Jyothi Vidya Peeth: Alexander Mar Thoma Center for
Theological and Developmental Studies (2000), located at Faridabad, Haryana.

The indigenous Independent/Pentecostal and Charismatic Christian
movements comprise some of the largest gatherings of Christians in North
India. Some of them claim a gathering of over one hundred thousand worshippers (Ankur Narula Ministries, Jalandhar); seventy-five thousand worshippers
(Prophet Bajinder Singh Ministries, Kurari), and fifty thousand worshippers
(Yeshu Darbar, Allahabad).[20] The chief characteristics of these ministries are
healing of the sick, deliverance from demonic oppression, extended worship services, manifestations of the Holy Spirit, and preaching of the gospel. People from
various castes, classes, religious affiliations, and nationalities, are increasingly
drawn to them. Their experiences, testimonies, and stories deserve to be studied
for missiological implications and reflections.[21]

Other historic Independent/Pentecostal and Charismatic missions in the
North include the Himalaya Evangelical Mission (formerly, Kashmir Evangelical
Fellowship, Udhampùr, 1971), Indian Evangelical Team (Katra, 1972, Delhi
1986), and Christian Evangelistic Assemblies (Dehradun, 1994). Some of the
prominent Evangelical/Independent institutions in North India include Doon
Bible College (1943), Central India Theological Seminary (Itarsi, 1962), Grace
Bible College (Gurugram, 1972), the New Theological College (Dehradun,
1987), Mission India Theological Seminary (Nagpur, 1993), and Caleb Institute
(Delhi, 2016).[22] These missions and institutions have made, and continue to
make, significant contributions to evangelism, church growth, social work, and
training of spiritual as well as social leaders in post-independence India. From

---

19. See, Abraham Kunnatholy, *St. Thomas Christians in Madhya Pradesh* (Bangalore: ATC,
2007).

20. For Ankur Narula Ministries, visit, www.ankurnarula.org; for Yeshu Darbar, https://shuats.
org/webwapp/yeshu_darbar.asp; Bajinder Singh does not have a website but has over 721,000
followers on Facebook (https://www.facebook.com/prophetji/). All links accessed in January
2023.

21. For a recent study on select indigenous Christian movements, see, Paul Joshua, *Christianity
Remade: The Rise of Indian-Initiated Churches*, ed. Joel Carpenter (Waco, TX: Baylor University
Press, 2022). See also, Shaibu Abraham, *The History of the Pentecostal Movement in North India:
Unfolding its Social and Theological Contexts* (New Delhi: Christian World Imprints, 2017).

22. All the years in parentheses refer to the founding year. Most of these institutions have a
website with a brief history of their origin and development. For a history of New Theological
College, see, Simon Samuel and P. V. Joseph, *Remapping Mission Discourse: A Festschrift in Honor
of the Rev. George Kuruvila Chavanikamannil* (Delhi: ISPCK, 2008).

this brief survey of the institutions and organizations, we shall now turn to some of the notable Christians in North India.

Christians in North India

The lives and contributions of some of the missionaries and local Christians in North India—from widely celebrated or well-known to unsung or lesser-known—will be very briefly introduced in this section. It is impossible to include all the names but here are the most noteworthy.

Among the missionaries, William Carey (1761–1834), the renowned English Baptist, deserves to be noted first. Arriving in West Bengal in 1793, Carey established a mission legacy that continues to inspire generations of Christ followers. From Bible translation and publication to philology, from literacy and higher education to Orientalism, and from relief work and technology to evangelization, Carey and team revolutionized Indian society with outstanding Christian impacts. All these were carried on amid unprecedented challenges related to family, finance, government, mission, and culture. Carey's missiological vision was summed up in his historic saying, "Expect great things from God, expect great things for God."[23] Widely celebrated as the Father of Modern Missions, Carey has also been called "the Father of Modern India."[24]

Oscar T. Lohr (1824–1907) is a lesser-known missionary who performed significant pioneering work in central North India. He was instrumental in founding the German Evangelical Missionary Society (USA, 1867), and became its first Protestant missionary to Chhattisgarh (1868). He established the Christian settlement of Bishrampur (City of Rest) and carried out evangelistic, educational, literary, agricultural, and medical services along with his family and selected local coworkers. Lohr is called the apostle to the Satnami people.[25] Lohr served central North India during one of the most troubled times (due to famine) surrounded with loss and pain.

American Methodist missionary siblings James and Isabella Thoburn have made significant contributions to modernization of the North Indian state of Uttar Pradesh (including Uttarakhand) primarily through education. James

23. For a history and various versions of this 1792 quote, visit, https://www.wmcarey.edu/carey/expect/ (Accessed September 9, 2023).

24. Mission historians have largely honored Carey as the Father of Modern Missions and the Father of Modern Protestant Missions. However, Jeyaraj has argued that that title truly belongs to Ziegenbalg. See, Daniel Jeyaraj, *Bartholomaus Ziegenbalg: The Father of the Modern Protestant Mission* (Delhi: ISPCK, 2007). See also, Vishal and Ruth Mangalwadi, *The Father of Modern India: William Carey* (Sought After Media, 2023).

25. Shivraj K. Mahendra, "Rev. Oscar T. Lohr of Chhattisgarh (1824–1907): The Life, Mission Works, and Legacy of the Apostle to the Satnami People," *Indian Church History Review*, 51, no. 1 (Jan–June 2017): 47–59.

Thoburn (1836–1922) was the first Bishop of the American Episcopal Methodist Church in India and Malaysia. He was a pioneer of Christian education in Garhwal (Uttarakhand). His sister Isabella Thoburn (1840–1901) founded the Lucknow Woman's College (Isabella Thoburn College) and for the first time ever edited a Hindi newspaper *Rafiq i Niswan* (Woman's Friend).[26]

Anglican missionary C. F. Andrews (1871–1940) was an educationist, writer, theologian, social reformer, and churchman. Within North India, Andrews's work extended from Delhi to Kolkata, and outside of India from South Africa to Fiji. He was friends with Mahatma Gandhi, Sadhu Sundar Singh, and Ravindranath Tagore. Andrews was involved in the Indian freedom movement and was instrumental in convincing Gandhi to return to India from South Africa.[27] He was given the title of *Deenbandhu* (Friend of the Poor) by Gandhi, who also renamed him "Christ's Faithful Apostle."

Ernest F. Ward (1853–1937) and his wife Phebe E. Ward (1850–1910) were pioneering Free Methodist missionaries in central India who carried out rural evangelism, church planting, humanitarian services (orphanage, famine relief, etc.), interreligious encounters, and promotion of Christian holiness in Madhya Pradesh, Chhattisgarh, Maharashtra, and Gujarat. The roots of significant institutions such as the Union Biblical Seminary (UBS), Yavatmal College for Leadership Training (YCLT), and Umri Christian Hospital (UCH) can be traced to the groundbreaking ministries of the Wards and their colleagues and mentees. The Wards were instrumental in the conversion of the famous Marathi Christian poet Narayan Vaman Tilak.[28]

Missionary-statesman E. Stanley Jones (1884–1973) was a confidant of US President Franklin Roosevelt, a friend of Mahatma Gandhi, and an inspiration to Martin Luther King Jr., and many other leaders. A graduate of Asbury College,[29] Jones came to North India (Lucknow, in 1907) as a pastor and went

---

26. For more on the life of James Thoburn, see, William F. Oldham, *Thoburn—Called of God* (New York: Methodist Book Concern, 1918). For more on Isabella's life and work, see, James M. Thoburn, *Life of Isabella Thoburn* (Cincinnati, OH: Jennings and Graham, 1903). See also, Linda Joyce Gesling, *Gender, Ministry, and Mission: The Lives of James and Isabella Thoburn, Brother and Sister in Methodist Service.* PhD dissertation. (Evanston, IL: Northwestern University Dissertation Publishing, 1996).

27. See, Eric J. Sharpe, "Andrews, Charles Freer," in *Biographical Dictionary of Christian Missions,* ed. Gerald H. Anderson (New York: Macmillan Reference USA, 1998), 22–23. See also, Benarsidas Chaturvedi and Marjorie Sykes, *Charles Freer Andrews: A Narrative* (London: George Allen & Unwin, 1949) and Hugh Tinker, *The Ordeal of Love: C.F. Andrews and India* (Delhi: Oxford University Press, 1980).

28. For an award-winning study of this lesser-known missionary couple, see, Shivraj K. Mahendra, *Lived Missiology: The Legacy of Ernest and Phebe Ward* (London, KY: Fishers for Christ, 2021, 2023).

29. Now, Asbury University, Wilmore, Kentucky, USA.

on to become one of the most influential interpreters of Christ to the world. He founded the Sat Tal Christian Ashram (Uttarakhand, 1930) and the Nur Manzil Psychiatric Centre (Lucknow 1948). He initiated interreligious encounters called the Round Table Conferences, authored twenty-seven books, published over three hundred articles, and proclaimed "Jesus is Lord" throughout the world. His books have been translated into thirty languages and sold over 3.5 million copies. He promoted global peace and harmony. Jones was twice nominated for the Nobel Peace Prize.[30]

Other notable missionaries in North India include Alexander Duff (1808–1877) the pioneer of English education;[31] William Butler (1818–1899),[32] a Scottish-American missionary who founded the American Methodism in India (Bareilly, 1856); Scottish evangelist sisters Martha Rose and Kay Greenfield and Baptist missionary Dame Edith Mary Brown, founders of Christian Medical College (the North Indian School of Medicine for Christian Women), Ludhiana, Punjab (1894), the first medical school for women in Asia;[33] Donald A. McGavran (1897–1990) of Madhya Pradesh, the missiologist of Church Growth movement and founder of the School of World Mission at Fuller Theological Seminary;[34] Mother Teresa (1910–1997) of the Missionaries of Charity;[35] and Graham Staines (1941–1999), the martyr-saint of Odisha.[36]

---

30. See Anne Mathews-Younes, "E. Stanley Jones: A Granddaughter's Observations and Reflections," accessed December 12, 2002, https://www.estanleyjonesfoundation.com/about-esj/esj-biography/. See also E. Stanley Jones, *The Christ of the Indian Road* (New York: Abingdon, 1925), E. Stanley Jones, *A Song of Ascents: A Spiritual Autobiography* (New York: Abingdon, 1968), and Robert G. Tuttle, Jr., *In Our Time: The Life and Ministry of E. Stanley Jones* (Potomac, MD: The E. Stanley Jones Foundation, 2019).

31. William Paton, *Alexander Duff: Pioneer of Missionary Education* (New York: George H. Doran, 1922?).

32. Clementina Butler, *William Butler: The Founder of Two Missions of the Methodist Episcopal Church* (New York: Eaton & Mains; Cincinnati: Jennings & Pye, 1902).

33. See, Charles Reynolds, *Punjab Pioneer* (Waco, TX: Word Books, 1968).

34. For a very brief study of McGavran, see, Shivraj K. Mahendra, "Exploring the Mission Theology of Donald Anderson McGavran: A Historical and Missiological Exploration," *Indian Church History Review*, 55, no. 1 (January 2021): 59–71. For a complete biography, see, Vern Middleton, *Donald McGavran: His Early Life and Ministry* (Pasadena, CA: William Carey Library, 2012).

35. See, Kathryn Spink, *Mother Teresa: An Authorized Biography* (Grand Rapids: HarperOne, 2016).

36. For more on the life of Staines, see Andrew E. Matthews, *The Least of These: The Graham Staines Story* (Zaccheus Entertainment, 2019), also a motion picture (https://www.theleastofthese.movie/).

Among the indigenous Christians, the names of Sadhu Sundar Singh (1889–1929), the great Indian Christian mystic;[37] Brahmabandhav Upadhyay (1861–107),[38] a pioneer of Indian Christian Theology; Pandita Ramabai Saraswati (1858–1922), the founder of Pandita Ramabai Mukti Mission;[39] and Harry Liddle (1920–1961), the founder of Doon Bible College,[40] deserve to be mentioned. In addition to these missionaries and movement leaders, North India also has both established and emerging theologians and authors. Mittal and Thursby identify the following North Indians as important Hindi-language Christian authors in our times: John H. Anand, Din Dayal, Benjamin Khan, Richard Howell, Shivraj K. Mahendra, Franklin Jonathan, Moti Lall, and others.[41] A study of their lives and contributions, and of numerous English-language Christian scholars in North India, is beyond the scope of this chapter and must be undertaken as separate projects. It also remains to be explored if there are regional language Christian authors in North India besides Hindi. We shall now explore some of the major themes and issues in North Indian Christianity.

Major Themes and Issues

When Christians practice their witnessing faith, they confront contextual issues impacting their life and work as well as that of their neighbors. The following are brief summaries of some of the prominent issues facing North Indian Christianity today.

---

37. T. Dayanandan Francis, ed., *The Christian Witness of Sadhu Sundar Singh: A Collection of His Writings* (Madras, India: The Christian Literature Society, 1989). For a critical biography of Singh, see, Eric J. Sharpe, *The Riddle of Sadhu Sundar Singh* (New Delhi: Intercultural Publications, 2004).

38. For a study of Upadhyay, see, Timothy C. Tennent, *Building Christianity on Indian Foundations: The Legacy of Brahmabandhav Upadhyay* (Delhi: ISPCK, 2000).

39. The most comprehensive and authoritative work on Ramabai comes from Keith J. White, *Let the Earth Hear Her Voice: The Life and Work of Pandita Ramabai* (London, UK: WTL Publications, 2022).

40. For Liddle's brief life and ministry, see V. S. Bhandari, ed., *Doon Bible College Through the Years,* (Dehradun: Doon Bible College, 2018). The publication is based on the research by Barbro Andreasson (1981) and Ruel Singh (2018). See also, Barbro Andreasson, *Doon Bible College, 1944–1981* (Dehradun: DBC, 1981).

41. For a complete list, see Sushil Mittal and Gene Thursby, eds, *Religions in India: An Introduction, Second Edition* (Routledge, 2017). For a brief study of some of these authors' works, see Rakesh Peter-Dass, *Hindi Christian Literature in Contemporary India* (New York: Routledge, 2019). See also, Namrata Chaturvedi, "Masihi Kavya: Reading Christian Devotional Literary Expression in Hindi," *Sambhashan*, 2, no. 1 & 2 (University of Mumbai, 2021): 166–182, accessed December 15, 2022, https://mu.ac.in/wp-content/uploads/2021/08/166-182-Masihi-Kavya-Reading-Christian-Devotional-Literary-Expression-in-Hindi.-Namrata-Chaturvedi.pdf.

Conversion, Persecution, and the Freedom of Religion   Conversion to Jesus
Christ is by far the most debated, misinterpreted, and politicized issue in India
in general and North India in particular. National debates have been conducted
on the theme and several studies, analysis, and reflections have been published
on the nature and motives of conversion.[42] The term generally used for "conversion" in the North is *Dharmantaran,* meaning a "change of religion." Christians themselves prefer to use the term *Man Parivartan,* meaning, a "change
of heart." Due to unwarranted politicized misrepresentation, conversion has
been increasingly misinterpreted as a change of one's allegiance to the nation,
support for the colonial and foreign powers, insult to the religion and culture of
the Hindus, and so forth. As a result, many converts are falsely accused of being
anti-national and have been severely opposed or persecuted in various parts of
India. Persecution includes mental and physical assaults on individuals or groups,
vandalizing of believers' homes, destruction of church properties or places of
worship, expulsion from villages, and arrest by the police. North Indian Christians remain one of the most persecuted people in the world.[43] Among the North
Indian states, Chhattisgarh remains the most difficult place for Christians. Uttar
Pradesh and Uttarakhand are next on the list. While the Indian Constitution
guarantees freedom of religion to all citizens, the state governments have made
specific amendments and passed anti-conversion laws to stop all conversions from
Hinduism to Christianity or Islam, thus taking away the freedom to profess and
propagate the religion of one's choice. Interestingly, there is no law or bill against
conversion from other religions to Hinduism. Existing law is manipulated in
such a way that systematic suppression of Christians is increasing every day.
The *Ghar Wapsi* (Operation Homecoming) movement, characterized by the
forceful reconversion of Christians to Hinduism, is on the rise. Even the police
force, which is supposed to maintain law and order for all, is mostly controlled
by anti-minority elements. Most police officers belong to anti-Christian groups
affiliated with the Sangh family. They just watch while the Christians are beaten,

---

42. See Walter Fernandes, "Attacks on Minorities and a National Debate on Conversions,"
Economic and Political Weekly, 34, no. 3/4 (January 16–29, 1999): 81–84. See also, Sundar Raj,
The Confusion Called Conversion (New Delhi: TRACI, 1986).

43. According to a report published by the United Christian Forum for Human Rights,
New Delhi, nearly six hundred incidents of violence were committed against Christians
between 2022and 2023. See https://www.cwmission.org/united-christian-forum-ucf-issues-
memorandum-on-targeted-violence-against-the-christian-community-in-india/?highlight=ucf
(Accessed September 7, 2023).
    Also, recent violence in Manipur is also a sad case of anti-Christian violence. See the
report by the United States Commission on International Religious Freedom, accessed on
September 7, 2023, https://www.uscirf.gov/news-room/uscirf-spotlight/violence-against-tribal-
christians-manipur-india.

violated, and their properties vandalized. Being a Christian in North India has never been so difficult in history.[44]

Healing, Deliverance, and the Prosperity Gospel Amid increasing opposition, persecution, and uncertainty, however, the stories of miraculous healing and transformation of people appear to be powerful optimisms in North Indian Christianity. Miracles are taking place in terms of healing from various illnesses, deliverance from demonic oppressions, and answered prayers. From Punjab to Chhattisgarh, you can listen to numerous testimonies of transformation of lives through healing and deliverance in the name of Jesus.

I recently met a woman who was bedridden for five long years. Her family resources had been exhausted in her treatment. Her children had to drop out of school to take care of their mother. Her husband had given up hope. He had done everything in his capacity—consulted several witch doctors, offered the required sacrifices, taken his wife to the best hospitals in the region—all for nothing. As a last resort, people advised them to go and "get her prayed." Ceremonial prayer for healing is commonly offered by Christian ministers without charging any fees.[45] Thus, going for prayer or "getting prayed" meant calling to the pastor. The pastor, a friend of mine, visited this family in the middle of the night and prayed for the dying lady. Within two hours of prayer, she got up healthy and full of joy and, today, is a living witness of a miraculous healing. She testifies to the healing touch of Jesus through the prayers offered by the man of God. When nothing worked, prayer to Christ did.[46] This is one of countless stories of healing through prayer.

While people are becoming devotees of Christ through personal experiences of healing, many people are also thronging to the false prophets for the prosperity gospel that is being proclaimed. Prosperity gospel certainly comes as an allurement to conversion, and Christian ministers are accused of converting people through allurement, but such converts are scant and mostly temporary. Crown without the cross is not the way of Christ. Due to lack of a serious personal encounter with Christ, these prosperity seekers easily lose faith. So, the real church growth is not really demonstrated in large gatherings but sustained through individuals and small but faithful groups of Christ seekers.

---

44. For a study on conversion, freedom of religion, and nationalism see, Richard Howell, *Free to Choose: Issues in Conversion, Freedom of Religion, and Social Engagement* (New Delhi: Evangelical Fellowship of India, 2002). See also, Mark T. B. Land, ed., *Nationalism and Hindutva: A Christian Response* (Delhi: ISPCK, 2005).

45. In contrast, village witch doctors require fees for their rituals and performances.

46. This is the story of Purnima Yadav, a Hindu convert to Christ. Interview with Shivraj K. Mahendra, Chhattisgarh, December 29, 2022. Purnima was healed three years before the interview.

Evangelism, Church Growth, and Missionary Training Although evangelistic activities have been officially restricted, the church is growing steadily in
North India. Until recently, we had the freedom to carry out village outreaches,
distribute tracts, and preach in open-air gospel meetings. Now we are not permitted to do so. The doors are no longer open. The opposition is growing stronger
day by day. The opposition is usually from the anti-Christian youth coming
from nearby villages or cities. Every village has an anti-Christian group mainly
composed of a generation of youth that is not willing to listen or talk. Sadly, these
young people have been brainwashed to engage in destructive activities in the
name of the protection of the Hindu religion. Instead of focusing on education,
career, and charity, they have been filled with hatred for others, misguided by
fake religiosity, and blinded by phony nationalism. In many places, they have
been able to stop the entry of itinerant evangelists, but they have not been able
to stop the true seekers. People in need of prayers are not without hope. In most
villages, there is at least one pastor and a small Christian fellowship or house
church. Some of these village pastors, in rare cases, can serve the needy under
the protection of the villagers themselves. Thus, the body of Christ is growing
slowly but steadily.[47] Jesus's seekers are found almost everywhere. In fact, there is
a growing number of anonymous Christians—Christians who are outside of the
organized church but following Jesus enthusiastically. They are making their way
to local churches and increasingly becoming part of the prayer fellowships. God
is also calling young believers from the North as missionaries. They are moving
to seminaries for ministerial and theological training and learning. Interestingly,
a good number of North Indian first-generation Christians are going to South
Indian seminaries for their studies. In a recent visit to the South, I was thrilled
to see several Hindi speaking young Christians in seminaries in Kerala.[48] While
most North Indian seminaries are run by South Indian Christian leaders and are
full of students from the South, most South Indian seminaries are theological
homes to a significant number of North Indian Christians. Although North
Indian Christians are minorities in prominent seminaries, they are promising

---

47. For a study on church growth in the past, see, J. Waskom Pickett, *Christian Mass Movements
in India: A Study with Recommendations* (New York: Abingdon Press, 1933).

48. From December 29, 2022 to January 11, 2023, my wife and I went on a Christian historical
pilgrimage to the South. Beginning with apostle Thomas's place of martyrdom at Mylapore
(Chennai) we traveled all the way to Kodungallur (Kerala), where he landed in the first century
AD. During this trip we visited Gurukul Lutheran Theological College and Research Institute
(Chennai), IPC Theological Seminary (Kottayam), Orthodox Theological Seminary (Kottayam),
and Doulos Theological College (Aluva). Earlier in 2022, we visited the South Asian Institute of
Advanced Christian Studies (Bangalore), the United Theological College (Bangalore), and the
Union Biblical Seminary (Pune). In the North, we have visited the Caleb Institute (Gurgram),
Presbyterian Theological Seminary (Dehradun), and Doon Bible College (Dehradun).

leaders of tomorrow for the church and nation. Their training for ministry is as challenging as their contexts of life and mission. We shall now look at some of the challenges facing North Indian Christians.

Challenges and Prospects

North Indian Christianity faces pressing challenges in almost every aspect of its existence. These challenges range from the opposition of new believers from their families and communities to a lack of identity and leadership in the new community. Other challenges include denominational unity, financial concerns, the church-government relationship, theological education, and so on.

Community Life and Leadership North India's first-generation Christians continue to face discrimination from their families and communities. When the entire family is not following Jesus or sympathetic to Christianity, the individual usually has difficulty living and adjusting with them. Neighbors and community members also mistreat the believers. These challenges create a depressing situation for new Christians who need a supportive atmosphere for their growth. They are constantly faced with challenges to growing spiritually as well as socially. Most new believers are rejected by their families and communities and struggle to find a life partner and livelihood. During the missionary era, such situations were dealt with by relocating new believers to the mission compounds. Nowadays theological seminaries might prove to be temporary places of refuge and growth. However, no matter where they are located, in order to become spirit-filled, productive, and influential Christians, new believers need to live highly disciplined, hardworking, humble, committed, and optimistic lifes. St. Augustine's advice is most beneficial for North Indian Christians today. He said, "Pray as if it all depends on God, work as if it all depends on you."[49] This is exactly what North Indian Christians need to practice with an unwavering dedication. Their testimony of transformation and new life of holiness will determine their positive influence. They must recognize their gifts and use them effectively to serve as emerging leaders in the church, society, and nation. However, they do not have an easy way up to leadership in the new community. Character, qualifications, and experiences are not enough as the structures of organizations and systems of denominations do not necessarily function on these principles alone.

Christian Unity While fully dedicated to serving the nation through various social, charitable, medical, and educational projects, North Indian Christians

---

49. Another version of the quote reads, "Pray as though everything depended on God. Work as though everything depended on you." For a recent study on St. Augustine of Hippo (354–430), see Peter Brown, *Augustine of Hippo* (University of California Press, 2013).

also need to remain deeply united. Christian unity is particularly important in times of opposition and persecution. Historically, North Indian Christianity has actively participated in the twentieth-century ecumenical movement marking its pivotal achievement in the formation of the Church of North India (CNI) in 1970.[50] In addition to CNI, there are regional ecumenical bodies in almost every state of North India, such as the Uttarakhand Christian Council. Within the states, there are district and city level ecumenical groups such as the Clergy Fellowship, the Christian Solidarity Society, and the like. Most of these fellowships have representation of almost all major denominations and independent churches. However, there have been some incidents when in times of persecution of independent house churches, the mainline established churches have tended to withdraw and not to come in solidarity or support. Such situations have raised questions on the unity of Christians. A vibrant and visible interdenominational unity among Christians remains a dream not just in North India, but throughout India.[51] Thus the church in India continues to wait for the fulfillment of the pastoral and ecumenical prayer of the Lord Jesus, "that all of them may be one, Father, just as you are in me and I am in you." (John 17:21). Factors leading to division and disunity among Christians are many. They range from doctrinal-denominational, sociocultural, linguistic-regional, financial, organizational, and personal or individual.

Financial Challenges This is one of the critical concerns in the life of the North Indian church. The dependency created during the missionary era continues to make its presence known through the indigenous and semi-indigenous Christian missions.[52] Semi-indigenous missions are foreign-aided organizations with Indian founders and leaders. While these missions emphasize the need to be self-supporting, they rarely provide any viable alternative to generate income for the church or salary for the pastor. Pastors and evangelists are generally called to work without any promise of financial support. Church women may be provided

---

50. For a complete study of CNI, see D. K. Sahu, *The Church of North India: A Historical and Systematic Theological Inquiry into an Ecumenical Ecclesiology* (Germany: Peter Lang, 1994). For a history of the ecumenical movement in India, see Mathai Zachariah, *Ecumenism in India* (Delhi: ISPCK, 1980). See also V. V. Thomas, *Conciliar Ecumenism: The Beginning of the Former CSI-CNI-MTC Joint Council* (Bangalore: BTESSC, 2008).

51. For an introductory study of the ecumenical movement, see O. L. Snaitang, *A History of the Ecumenical Movement: An Introduction* (Bangalore: BTESSC, 2007). See also, T. V. Philip, *Ecumenism in Asia* (Delhi: ISPCK, 1994).

52. For detailed studies on mission in relation to finances, see Jonathan Bonk, *Missions and Money: Affluence as a Missionary Problem. Revised and Expanded edition* (Maryknoll, NY: Orbis Books, 2007). See also, Paul H. De Neui, ed., *Complexities of Money and Missions in Asia* (Pasadena, CA: William Carey Library, 2012).

with some sewing machines, but that can barely support a family. First generation churches, which are largely independent, unaffiliated, or semi-affiliated, struggle to provide for their pastor, build a place of worship, or send candidates for seminary training. Economically speaking, the condition of the church is very much like the condition of the nation. On the one hand, the North Indian Christian majority is struggling to meet its basic needs, while on the other hand, affluent individuals and organizations are enjoying comfort and glory. Some popular charismatic leaders in North India are demanding ten- to twenty-five thousand rupees (USD 150–300) as fees for special prayers.[53] For a healthy Christian economy in North India, self-supporting pastors and churches must be encouraged and established but at the same time transparency and equality must be maintained in terms of acquisition and distribution of funds and resources by all Christian organizations.

Church-Government Relationship Another crucial challenge facing North Indian Christianity is the relationship between church and government. Following Indian independence, the north-central Indian state of Madhya Pradesh commissioned a study group, the Niyogi Committee, to critically evaluate Christian missionary activities in the region.[54] Based on some preconceived anti-Christian bias and limited data collected from a small number of respondents, the Committee's Report made several recommendations, such as (1) to control the entry and activities of foreign missionaries with intention to convert, (2) to prohibit literature propagating Christian faith, (3) to check the charitable works done by Christian hospitals and educational institutions, (4) to make laws against conversion to Christianity, and (5) to make necessary amendments in the Constitution to regulate conversion to Christianity, and so on. The Constitution of India guarantees every Indian citizen the freedom to profess and propagate any religion (Article 25). However, the article has been amended by several state governments between 2006 and 2022 and anti-conversion laws and religious freedom bills have been passed.[55] Sadly, these laws and bills have been increasingly misused by the anti-Christian elements present in both the government and

---

53. This statement is based on the personal experiences of some of my family members and friends.

54. An online edition of the Committee's report, accessed February 5, 2023, http:// voiceofdharma.org/books/ncr/index.htm. For a recent study of the Report and its implications for Christians in India, see Manohar James, *Religious Conversion in India: The Niyogi Committee Report of Madhya Pradesh in 1956 and Its Continuing Impact on National Unity* (Eugene, OR: Pickwick Publications, 2022).

55. For example, see N. Saiya and Stuti Manchanda, "Anti-conversion Laws and Violent Christian Persecution in the States of India: A Quantitative Analysis." *Ethnicities*, 20, no. 3 (2019): 587–607; Vidhatri Rao, "Anatomy of Anti-conversion Legislation in India: A Comparative Look at

society, resulting in rampant false accusations, human rights violations, hatred, persecution, and illegal arrests and imprisonments. Thankfully, these laws are being challenged and the Supreme Court of India is taking them into consideration.[56] Organizations such as Persecution Relief, the Evangelical Fellowship of India, Chhattisgarh Christian Forum, and others are working toward reporting the incidents and providing legal, moral, and charitable support to the victims of false accusations, violence, and suffering Christians.

Theological Education The primary medium of instruction in most seminaries in the North continues to remain English. But the linguistic context of the ministry is largely Hindi, and related languages such as Punjabi, Marathi, and Chhattisgarhi. Lamentably, there is no higher theological education offered in any of these languages. As of now the highest theological degree offered through Hindi medium is the bachelor of divinity (BD) of the Senate of Serampore College/University,[57] currently offered only at the Allahabad Bible Seminary, Prayagraj (Formerly, Allahabad). At the New Theological College (NTC), a premier seminary in the North affiliated to the Senate, only a one-year certificate in theology is offered in Hindi. Nearly two decades ago, NTC had launched a four-year bachelor of theology program of the Senate in Hindi. My own initial translations of theological books were aimed toward addressing this challenge of lack of theological resources in Hindi.[58] Unfortunately, due to the lack of faculty, resources, and promising students, Hindi theological education is yet to see proper growth. During the Covid-19 pandemic, several online theological schools emerged and are now offering certificate, diploma, and bachelors programs online in Hindi. It remains to be seen how successful these programs will be. There is a general preference to study in English as student see global value in it. In addition to linguistic challenges, there are challenges of curriculum, research administration, and distance and online theological studies.[59] The North Indian church needs to focus on training leaders in the native language of its people.

State Laws," *The Indian Express* (New Delhi: August 16, 2022); and, Stanley Carvalho, "Anti-conversion bill is unconstitutional, unnecessary," *Deccan Herald* (December 7, 2021).

56. For updates, see "SC Issues Notice to Five States on Petitions Challenging Anti-Conversion Laws," *The Wire* (February 3, 2023), accessed February 7, 2023, https://thewire.in/law/sc-issues-notice-to-five-states-on-petitions-challenging-anti-conversion-laws.

57. A BD is the foundational qualification for the evangelistic and pastoral ministry of the church accepted by almost all denominations, especially the mainline churches. It is offered to residents only. Serampore College was founded by Carey, Marshman, and Ward.

58. See, Shivraj K. Mahendra, "Translation as Mission: A Brief History of my Pilgrimage in Hindi Theological Translation," *Indian Church History Review*, 56, no. 1 (January 2022): 63–86.

59. For a general reflection on theological education in Asia, see, Derek Tan, "Theological Education in Asia: Present Issues, Challenges and Future Opportunities," in *Biblical Theology*

Additional notable prospects include being uncompromising Bible-believing Christians witnessing the uniqueness of Christ, prophetically challenging the structures and systems of injustice in the society (and church), honestly and boldly engaging in all possible interreligious dialogues, reaching out to the so-called high castes and elites in the nation, and spiritually empowering the church and her mission in the power of the Holy Spirit.

Conclusion

This chapter has presented a brief outline of the location and status of Christianity in North India, as wells as a history of Christian missions, notable missionaries and Christians, major themes, and challenges of Christianity in the North. Although the seed of the gospel was sown in the first century AD, the notable Christian presence in North India can be dated back to the sixteenth and nineteenth centuries, the eras of early and modern missionary movements. American, British, German, and several other Christian missionaries and mission societies have contributed significantly to the modernization of North India through unprecedented education programs, health care initiatives, and social-vocational services for all Indians. Local Christians have built on existing foundations and also founded new missions and continued to serve the nation, especially her socioeconomically challenged citizens, as true patriots. However, in recent times, their contributions are being forgotten and undermined, and instead of being greeted with appreciation and gratitude, they are being falsely accused of conversion through fraudulent means and of an anti-national outlook. They are also being persecuted for their faith in Christ. Despite all the threats and challenges, churches in North India are growing slowly and steadily. North Indian Christians need strong financial stability, deeper ecumenism, relevant theological training, prophetic encounter with the governments, and transforming witness in the pluralistic context of North India. Many North Indian Christians are right now living like the first century Christians—in fear and uncertainty as well as trust and hope in the Lord Jesus Christ. Christianity in North India is both struggling amid opposition and persecution as well as thriving with optimism along its pilgrimage in mission.

and Missiological Education in Asia: Essays in Honor of Rev. Dr. Brian C. Wintle, ed. Siga Arles, Ashish Chrispal, and Paul Mohan Raj (Bangalore: ATA, TBT, CFCC, 2005), 35–51.

CHAPTER THREE

Identity and Transformation

A Brief History of Christianity in Northeast India

Lalsangkima Pachuau

THIS CHAPTER HIGHLIGHTS some of the unique situations and stories of Christianity in Northeast India. It locates the story of Christianity in the identity struggle of a betwixt and between people (Indian by political-administrative identity yet Sino-Tibetan by ethnicity) and the role Christianity came to play in finding the identity of the people. Christianity is a latecomer to Northeast India, yet Christianity has been joyfully embraced and culturally appropriated by the people of the region producing energetic and thriving Christian communities. Christian history among Protestants somewhat follows the comity agreement, a term developed in the nineteenth-century Protestant missionary movement for "mutual division of territory into spheres of occupation."[1] The narrative will admittedly emphasize the role of indigenous Christians in the expansion of the faith without dismissing the works of foreign missionaries.

The Region and Its Geo-Ethnic Character

Bordered to the north by Bhutan, Tibet, and China, to the south and southwest by Bangladesh, and to the east and southeast by Myanmar, Northeast India is linked to the rest of India by a small strip of land in its northwest corner. Generally, the region is considered to consist of seven states: Arunachal Pradesh, Assam, Manipur, Meghalaya, Mizoram, Nagaland, and Tripura. With Sikkim becoming the twenty-second state of India in 1975, some include Sikkim as part of the region of Northeast India. However, because the state is not directly adjoined to the region and it has quite a distinct history, we will not include Sikkim in this chapter. At the time of India's independence in 1947, all but the princely states of Manipur and Tripura were part of Assam. The states of

---

1. R. Pierce Beaver, "Comity," in *Concise Dictionary of the Christian World Mission*, ed. Stephen Neill, Gerald H. Anderson, and John Goodwin (London: Lutterworth Press, 1970), 123. Also see R. Pierce Beaver, *Ecumenical Beginnings in Protestant World Mission: A History of Comity* (New York: Thomas Nelson and Sons, 1962).

Arunachal Pradesh, Meghalaya, Mizoram, and Nagaland were carved out of Assam as separate states in the 1960s and 1970s.

Two major cultural streams, namely the Indic civilization from the west and the Sino-Tibetan cultures from the north and east, meet here in the region comprising the diverse people of today. From their physical features and languages, the indigenous people share clear common traits with people from the north (China-Tibet) and east (Southeast Asia). Often referred to as "Mongoloids," these groups of people immigrated in waves to their present homes. Scholars identified at least three major linguistic groups: the Monkhmer (Khasis and Syntengs), Tibeto-Burman (Nagas, Kuki-Mizo, and the Bodos), and the Siamese-Chinese (Pkhakials, Khamtis, and Ahoms).[2] Ancient Sanskrit literature referred them as Kirātas.[3] With the mention of the city of Prāgjyotisa (meaning "city of eastern astrology")[4] in the region which is believed to be present-day Guwahati in the two Hindu epics of the Rāmāyana and Mahābhārata in the Purānas (between the third century BC to the eight century AD), Sanskritization of the people in the region has a long history. However, historians opine that the earliest history of Sino-Tibetan migration may have been as early as 2000 BC and concluded that "the prehistoric cultures of Assam have more in common with East Asian and Southeast Asian tradition than with those of the (Indian) subcontinent."[5] Because of the long and sporadic history of the migration from the east and north, the degree of Sanskritization of the people differs vastly. The longer the history of the people's exposure to the Indic religion andculture the deeper they have been Sanskritized or Hinduized. The differences are clear within the Hindu communities of the region. Whereas the Bodo and Assamese Hindu appear quite Sanskritized, the Meitei people who became Hindu more recently (in the eighteenth century) appear relatively less Sanskritic.

The multicultural characters as shaped by the historical experience resulted in what historian Ananda Bhagabati calls, the "geo-ethnic character" of the region.[6] About three-quarters of the region is covered by hilly terrain, and

---

2. B. B. Goswami, "The Tribes of Assam," in *Tribal Situation in India*, ed. K. S. Singh (Simla: Indian Institute of Advanced Study, 1972), 271–272.

3. Rena Laisram, *Religion in Early Assam: An Archaeological History* (Newcastle upon Tyne: Cambridge Scholars Publishing, 2019), 3.

4. Laisram, *Religion in Early Assam*, 2.

5. M. K. Dhavalikar, "Archaeology of Gauhati," *Bulletin of the Deccan College Research Institute* 31/32, no. 1/2 (1970): 137, quoted in Laisram, *Religion in Early Assam*, 3.

6. Annanda C. Bhagabati, "Emergent Tribal Identity in North-East India," in *Tribal Developments in India: Problems and Prospects*, ed. B. Chaudhuri (Delhi: Inter-India Publications, 1982), 218.

one-quarter consists of plains. So-called tribals live mostly in the hill areas, and Sanskritized or Hinduized non-tribals reside in the plains. Here I should mention the artificial and disingenuous creation of "tribal" identity. The difference between tribal and non-tribal in the region is determined by whether the community is Sanskritized or not. Therefore, the people of the region are either Sanskritized religiously or tribalized political by the power outside of them while existing in-between the two great civilizations of Indic India and the Sino-Tibetan East Asia. As I have written elsewhere,[7] the resultant crisis of identity of the indigenous people has led to various political uprisings and movements.

The geo-ethnic character is also reflected in today's ethnoreligious composition of the region. The vast majority of Christians are from tribal communities of the thinly populated hill states while most plains people are either Hindus or Muslims. Assam, the most populous state of the region which has roughly 70 percent of the region's population has a small fraction of Christians.[8] The bulk of Assam's population is Hindu (61.47 %) and Muslim (34.22 %).[9] Similarly, people in the plains and valley regions of Tripura and Manipur are largely Hindus while Christians are from the tribal groups.

Does this distinct geo-ethnic feature also contribute to the ethnopolitical movements that have characterized the region with great intensity since the independence of India? The region has seen identity-based sociopolitical movements with demands for varying degrees of autonomy. Ethnopolitical movements of varying kinds, from [ethno]nationalistic movements and demands for nationhood and sovereignty in Nagaland and Mizoram to the Assamese movement which ranges from anti-foreign immigration to demands for self-rule, and the Tripuri assertion of their indigenous rights and authority, have plagued the region.[10] The alleged involvement of foreign missionaries in these movements (quite popular as political rhetoric in some circles) has largely been debunked, however the role of Christian faith in the formation of their sense of a new sociocultural identity (among the Christians) in Northeast India cannot

7. See Lalsangkima Pachuau, "Nationhood and Ethnonational Identity in Northeast India," in *Indian and Christian* (Delhi: ISPCK, 2019), 180–198.

8. Of the forty-five million people in the entire region according to the 2011 census, 31.2 million, or roughly 70 percent are in Assam. The data is drawn from Census India, "C-01: Population by Religious Community, India—2011," https://censusindia.gov.in/nada/index.php/catalog/11361 (accessed: September 5, 2022).

9. Census India, "C01."

10. For further discussions, see Lalsangkima Pachuau, *Ethnic Identity and Christianity* (Frankfurt: Peter Lang, 2002; Bangalore: Centre for Contemporary Christianity, 2012), and Pachuau, "Nationhood and Ethnonationality in Northeast India," 180–198.

be denied.[11] Deeply ingrained in the people's self-understanding and the cultural ethos of the region's Christians is their Christian identity and practice. To most Mizos, Khasis, Kukis, Nagas, and Garos, there is no cultural identity without their Christianity.

Christians and Christianity in Northeast India

By the time of India's independence in 1947, present-day Nagaland, Meghalaya, and Mizoram had become dominantly Christian. Christianity was also making headway into Manipur although mainly through the minority hill tribals in the north and south while the Imphal valley of central Manipur stayed largely Hindu. According to the 2011 census report, there are roughly 7.8 million Christians in Northeast India which is roughly 28.15 percent of Indian Christians. This percentage is a significant increase from the 1991 census when it was 22.7 percent. Even though only 7.8 million of the 45 million people in the region (17.34 %) are Christians, Christianity is the largest religion in five of the seven states, namely Arunachal Pradesh (30.26 %), Manipur (41.29 %), Meghalaya (74.59 %), Mizoram (87.16 %), and Nagaland (87.93%).[12]

Christians are active and Christianity is vibrant in the region. Sundays are observed as the Lord's Day by most of these societies, and the community values and ethos are largely defined by their understanding and practice of Christian teachings. Their worldviews have been Christianized so much that most of them have closely related Christianity with their sense of ethnic identity. Hindu nationalists popularly allege Christianity to be a foreign religion and Christians are often accused of estranging their native cultures. Such allegations are made because Christians are usually more educated and economically developed than their non-Christian neighbors. Such perception, however, melts when one compares their Christianity with Christianity elsewhere. As Joy Pachuau has demonstrated in her ethnographic study of Mizo Christianity, "the local rootedness" made Christianity a truly Mizo religion in the face of "its alleged 'Western-*ness*'."[13] In my earlier studies, I have also shown how so-called revival

---

11. Pachuau, *Ethnic Identity and Christianity*, 145–175.

12. "Christian Religion Census 2011," *Census of India 2011*. https://www.census2011.co.in/data/religion/3-christianity.html, accessed September 9, 2022. At the time of writing this chapter (Summer-Fall, 2022) the census of India for 2021 had not been completed due to the Covid-19 pandemic. Thus, we rely on the latest census report of 2011.

13. Joy L. K. Pachuau, "Christianity in Mizoram: An Ethnography," in *Christianity in Indian History: Issuers of Culture, Power and Knowledge*, ed. Pius Malekandathil, Joy L. K. Pachuau, and Tanika Sarkar (Delhi: Primus Books, 2016), 47.

movements have connected Christianity with the local cultures and how the indigenous worldviews became Christianized in the new faith.[14]

The three largest Christian groups in the region are Baptists, Roman Catholics, and Presbyterians. According to the calculations of Frederick S. Downs, 89 percent of Christians in the region belonged to churches established by these three denominations in 1971.[15] Most of the Baptists came from the work of American Baptists and are now organized under the Council of Baptist Churches in Northeast India (CBCNEI). They dominate Nagaland, the Garo Hill district of Meghalaya, the larger part of Manipur hills, and pockets of Christian communities in Assam. Until the middle of the twentieth century, the Catholic presence was largely confined to Assam and Meghalaya. Since then, the Catholic Church has been rapidly spreading in other parts of the region. Presbyterians, stemming from the Welsh Presbyterian (formerly Calvinistic Methodist) Church, have organized themselves as the Presbyterian Church of India (PCI) and dominate the Khasi-Jaintia district of Meghalaya, the northern part of Mizoram, the Cachar district of Assam, and part of the Manipur hills. According to Downs, 43 percent of Christians in the region in 1990 belonged to CBCNEI, 26 percent to the Roman Catholic Church, and 23 percent to PCI.[16]

The British Baptist Missionary Society established the Baptist Church of Mizoram in southern Mizoram. Historically and denominationally related to the Mizoram Baptist Church are a few independent churches in the southernmost district of Mizoram. In Tripura the evangelization process began with the Mizo Christian community and was later joined and continued by the New Zealand Baptist Mission under the name Tripura Baptist Christian Union. In the Brahmaputra valley of Assam, other Baptist mission agencies, namely the Australian Baptist Mission and the Baptist General Conference of America, have also been working, and from them, the North-Bank Baptist Association has come into being. Following their immigrant members from southern Bihar (now Jharkhand), the Gossner Evangelical Lutheran Church and the Lutheran Santal Mission also established churches and were involved in evangelistic work among tea garden laborers in Assam. The Anglican presence in Northeast India is meager; indeed, there has been no significant mission effort by any of the Anglican mission agencies.

---

14. Pachuau, *Ethnic Identity and Christianity*, 131–141.

15. Fredrick S. Downs, *Christianity in North East India: Historical Perspectives* (Delhi: ISPCK, 1983), 96.

16. Frederick S. Downs, *History of Christianity in India*, vol. 5, part 5, *North East India in the Nineteenth and Twentieth Century* (Bangalore: The Church History Association of India, 1992), 69n15.

A History of the Christians and their Origins

Other than the princely states of Manipur and Tripura, the entire region was administered under Assam by British colonial rule. After the independence of India, what was Khasia-Jaintia and Garo district became the state of Meghalaya, the Nagaland district became Nagaland state, the Mizo district Mizoram state and the North-East Frontier Agency became the state of Arunachal Pradesh.

Assam and Meghalaya Although Catholics had passed through the region quite a few times, it was Protestants who first established missionary works in the region. The Serampore Mission opened a school first in Guwahati (Assam) in 1829 followed soon by another in Cherrapunji in Khasi hills (now Meghalaya). Both schools closed and the mission was abandoned when Serampore Mission merged with the Baptist Missionary Society in 1837.[17] Meanwhile, the American Baptist Mission arrived in the northeastern part of Assam (now Arunachal Pradesh) in 1836 with the intent of reaching China. When they were unable to move beyond the region, the missionaries gradually turned their attention to Assam itself, adopting it as a field in 1841.[18] That same year, Thomas Jones, the first missionary of the Welsh Calvinistic Methodist Church arrived in Cherrapunji of the Khasi hills adopting the field abandoned by Serampore Mission. Christian growth among the Khasis was slow in the early years and opposition was often violent.[19] The standard of the church membership was high, and the missionaries made no haste in baptizing new converts.[20] There were only twenty Khasi Christians at the end of the first decade (1841–1851).[21]

An early bright spot was the amazing story of Christianity's entry among the Garo people of Meghalaya through two Garo men working in the colonial establishment, Omed Watre Momin and Ramkhe Watre Momin. Through the reading of a Christian religious tract, first found in a garbage bin, the two became Christians. They were baptized in February of 1863. After their futile effort to secure missionaries for Garo Hills from the American Baptist Missionary Society, they decided to resign from their jobs and go back to their home state

17. John Hughes Morris, *The History of the Welsh Calvinistic Methodists' Foreign Mission, to the End of the Year 1904* (Carnarvon: C. M. Book Room, 1910), 72–75; O. L. Snaitang, *Christianity and Social Change in Northeast India* (Shillong: Vendrame Institute, 1993), 67.

18. Milton S. Sangma, *History of American Baptist Mission in North-East India (1836–1950)*, vol. 1 (Delhi: Mittal Publications, 1987), 30–45.

19. Downs, *History of Christianity in India*, 73–74.

20. Morris, *History of the Welsh Calvinistic Methodists' Foreign Mission*, 91.

21. Joseph Puthenpurakal, "Christianity and Mass Movement Among the Khasis: A Catholic Perspective," in Hrangkhuma, *Christianity in India*, 202.

to share their new faith with their fellow Garo people. Thus, "the beginning of the Baptist Mission among the Garos took place in 1864 when the first two Garo converts came to work there."[22]When American Baptist missionary Miles Bronson finally visited Garo Hills in April 1867, he baptized thirty-seven Garo people through whom the first Garo church was formed. He ordained Omed to be the minister of the church.[23]

The zeal to evangelize their own people also began early among the Khasi Christians. By the end of the nineteenth century, the Khasi church had created the Home Mission. By 1940 as many as twenty-four new churches were planted, with more than 2,500 new converts, through the work of the Home Mission.[24] Khasi evangelists contributed greatly to the evangelization of Khasi-Jaintia hills as well as Mizoram later.[25]

Nagaland The names of Edward Winter Clark and his wife, Mary Mead Clark, are usually associated with the pioneering endeavor among the Ao-Nagas of Nagaland. However, the real pioneer among them was Godhula, an Assamese convert who served as Clark's assistant, and who received the "Christian" name Rufus Brown. After learning the basic Ao language, Godhula proceeded to Ao-land without the permission of Clark in October 1871. Suffering threats on his life as well as brief imprisonment, Godhula managed to get across his message of peace and love of God, whom he called the Bread of Love.[26] After a few more trips, the first group of converts, nine in number, were brought to Clark and were baptized in November 1872. Clark moved to Ao-land in 1876 and started evangelization work through preaching, schools, and literature work. He was assisted by fifteen Assamese including Godhula in his early evangelization work of the Ao-Nagas.[27]

With Clark's motivation, other mission stations were opened among the Angami-Nagas, and for a brief period among the Lotha-Nagas. Resistance to Christianity was at first strong, and there were almost no Naga Christians outside

---

22. Krickwin C. Marak, "Christianity among the Garos: An Attempt to Re-read the Peoples' Movement from Missiological Perspective," in Hrangkhuma, *Christianity in India*, 163.

23. Marak, "Christianity among the Garos," 166.

24. J. Fortis Jyrwa, *The Wondrous Works of God: A Study of the Growth and Development of Khasi-Jaintia Presbyterian Church in the Twentieth Century* (Shillong: Mrs. M. B. Jyrwa, 1980), 38.

25. O. L. Snaitang, "Christianity among the Khasis: A Protestant Perspective," in Hrangkhuma, *Christianity in India,* 242.

26. Sangma, "Christianity among the Khasis," 222–223.

27. Joseph Puthenpurakal, *Baptist Missions in Nagaland: A Study in Historical and Ecumenical Perspective* (Shillong: Vendrame Missiological Institute, 1984), 72.

the Ao tribe by the end of the nineteenth century. The drastic reformation in the Ao church in 1894 also considerably reduced the number of Christians. In the first half of the twentieth century, phenomenal growth came about among the Sema-Nagas and the Lotha tribe. Through what Puthenpurakal calls "a chain of reaction," lay native evangelists carried on the work of evangelization, leading to a mass movement among the Semas.[28] The hard resistance by Angamis also began to break down in the 1930s.[29] The major growth of Christianity among these tribes, as well as the initiation and growth among other Naga tribes, began after the independence of India in 1947 and continued after the missionaries left Nagaland in the early 1950s.

The contribution of Naga Christians in the evangelization of Nagaland is enormous. As early as 1898 the missionary report on Ao-Nagas said, "All our churches are now self-supporting."[30] What some called mass evangelization among the Semas came mainly through the work of indigenous evangelists. The number of Christians in Nagaland rose from 98,068 in 1951,[31] to 1,057,940 in 1991,[32] almost double the number in forty years. The percentage of Christians in Nagaland is the highest in the nation (87.93 % in 2011). The fact that the major expansion of Christianity took place in the second half of the twentieth century when most, or all, foreign missionaries had left Nagaland, is a clear witness to the role of Naga Christians themselves in the evangelization of their own land.

Mizoram The pioneer missionaries to Mizoram J. Herbert Lorrain and F. W. Savidge (of a private missionary agency called the Arthington Aborigines Mission, which was founded, funded, and directed by Robert Arthington, Jr.) reached Mizoram in January 1894.[33] The region was earlier visited and planned to be adopted by Welsh missionaries of Meghalaya. When Arthington withdrew the mission, the area was handed over to the Welsh mission. The first Welsh missionary to Mizoram, David Evan Jones, along with Khasi evangelist Rai Bhajur, replaced the Arthington missionaries in 1897. When the southern district of Mizoram was transferred to the Baptist Missionary Society, the two pioneer missionaries returned to Mizoram as the first two Baptist missionaries in 1903.

---

28. Puthenpurakal, *Baptist Missions in Nagaland*, 104.

29. Downs, *History of Christianity in India,* 108.

30. Quoted by Puthenpurakal, "Christianity and Mass Movement Among the Khasis," 116.

31. Downs, *History of Christianity in India,* 108.

32. *Census of India 1991,* Series-1 India, Paper 1 of 1995, *Religion* (New Delhi: M. Vijayanunni, Registrar General & Census Commissioner, India, 1995), xvii.

33. For a biography of Robert Arthington Jr., and a brief account of the Arthington Aborigines Mission, see Lalsangkima Pachuau, "Robert Arthington, Jr., and the Arthington Aborigines Mission," *Indian Church History Review* 28, no. 2 (December 1994), 105–125.

The first baptized Christians received their baptisms in 1899 under D. E. Jones. A third mission society, an independent Lakher Pioneer Mission headed by R. A. Lorrain (the younger brother of J. H. Lorrain), came to work among the Lakher tribe in the southernmost part of Mizoram in 1907. The church planted by this mission came to be called the Independent Church of Maraland.

As in other parts of Northeast India, it was the first converts who made headway in evangelizing their own people. Khuma, one of the first two Mizo converts, is said to have visited almost all villages in Mizoram with a simple message of invitation to everyone he met and each house he visited: "Believe in Jesus Christ."[34] By 1903 the small congregation appointed four evangelists, supporting them with a salary of three rupees each. Starting in 1910, a group of Mizo evangelists, employed by a certain Watkin Roberts under the Thadou-Kuki Pioneer Mission, was sent across the border to Manipur and Tripura, becoming pioneer cross-cultural evangelists.

A series of awakenings referred to as "revivals" in the first four decades of the twentieth century became most instrumental in converting virtually the whole Mizo tribe to Christianity. The awakenings also indigenized Christianity, bringing forth a distinctly Mizo faith.[35] Teams of lay converts affected by the revivals went about sharing their revival experience with their fellow tribe members, spreading Christianity from village to village.[36]

Manipur The two princely states of Northeast India during the British colonial rule—Manipur and Tripura—did not welcome missionaries. William Pettigrew, the pioneer missionary in Manipur, was from the Arthington Aborigines Mission. He entered Manipur in February 1894 and started his work among the Meitei people, the dominant people-group in the Manipur valley. Political conditions later compelled him to move out of the administered valley to the hills where he worked among the Tangkhul-Nagas. Pettigrew changed his denominational affiliation from Anglican to Baptist and joined the American Baptist Mission, which adopted him as its missionary and Manipur as its field.[37]

---

34. Saiaithanga, *Mizo Kohhran Chanchin*, 3rd repr. (Aizawl: Mizo Theological Literature Committee, 1993), 16.

35. For a detailed treatment of the revivals and their contribution to Mizo Christianity, see Lalsangkima Pachuau, *Ethnic Identity and Christianity: A Socio-Historical and Missiological Study of Christianity in Northeast India; with Special Reference to Mizoram* (Frankfurt: Peter Lang, 2002),111–143.

36. Saiaithanga, *Mizo Kohhran Chanchin*, 21.

37. Lal Dena, *Christian Missions and Colonialism: A Study of Missionary Movement in Northeast India, with Particular Reference to Manipur and Lushai Hills, 1894–1947* (Shillong: Vendrame Institute, 1988), 33–35.

Slow and steady was the progress of mission work among the Tangkhuls. The early converts, including some from the Kuki tribes, then took their new faith to their own people. Because of his active involvement in political and other secular activities,[38] Pettigrew was unable to do much mission work. Due to the political restrictions, only a few other missionaries were permitted to enter Manipur, which in turn led the natives to initiate major evangelistic work. The first Kuki to become Christian, Ngulhao, was instrumental in the conversion of at least 334 people. Similarly, it is reported that the efforts of the first Thadou Kuki convert, Nehseh, led to the founding of the first church among his people.[39] The same was true with the Zeliengrong-Nagas and Mao Nagas of the northern and northwestern parts of Manipur.[40] Large-scale growth of Christianity among these tribes took place after the First World War.

The independent Thadou-Kuki Pioneer Mission, founded by Watkin Roberts with the help of Mizo Christians, came to work in South Manipur. This new nondenominational agency was staffed entirely by native workers mainly sent from Mizoram and established itself in the area.[41] When in 1919 this agency extended its work into the neighboring states of Assam and Tripura, it changed its name to North-East India General Mission (NEIGM).[42] Because of conflict and dissension within the mission and clashes with other Protestant missions over allegations of a breach of the comity agreement, NEIGM could not continue its work. In 1922 the mission was suspended from the comity of Protestant Foreign Missions in Bengal and Assam.[43]

Tripura and Arunachal Pradesh   Tripura and Arunachal Pradesh fielded the least number of Christians in the region until the end of the twentieth century. Yet Christian communities in these two states have also been growing in recent years. In fact, Christianity is now the largest religious group in Arunachal Pradesh (30.26 %). Missionaries were not welcomed in the two states for a long time. Tripura did not permit missionaries until 1938.[44] The earliest Christian

---

38. Dena, *Christian Missions and Colonialism*, 37, 39.

39. T. Lamboi Vaiphei, *Advent of Christian Mission and Its Impact on the Hill-Tribes of Manipur* (self-pub., 1997), 63–65.

40. Vaiphei, *Advent of Christian Mission and Its Impact on the Hill-Tribes of Manipur*, 68–82.

41. Dena, *Christian Missions and Colonialism*, 51.

42. For a detailed treatment of the NEIGM, see Vaiphei, *Advent of Christian Mission*.

43. Dena, *Christian Missions and Colonialism*, 53.

44. M. J. Eade, "Golden Jubilee—Tripura Baptist Christian Union," in *Tripura Baptist Christian Union: Golden Jubilee Souvenir, 1938–1988* (Agartala: Tripura Baptist Christian Union, 1988), 10–12.

presence in the state and subsequent mission work began with the Mizo residents in the northeast of the state beginning in the early part of the twentieth century.[45] The Mizo residents received their faith first from Mizoram. A missionary supported by the Tripura Mizo Christians started evangelistic work in 1917 among one of the Tripuri tribes called Darlong. The NEIGM sent a missionary to work with the Mizos in 1918, and among the Darlong tribe in 1919. Other NEIGM missionaries followed, most of them becoming pastors and teachers.[46]

In the meantime, the New Zealand Baptist Mission, which was working across the border in present-day Bangladesh, succeeded in gaining permission to work in Tripura in 1938.[47] Gathering about one hundred Christians, mainly Garos and Kukis residing in the state, the New Zealand Baptist Mission formed the Tripura Baptist Christian Union (TBCU) in December 1938.[48] Until the last missionary left Tripura in the early 1970s, TBCU was led by missionaries of the New Zealand Baptist Mission. The Darlong Church joined TBCU in 1940,[49] as did the Mizo Church, then called Jampui Presbytery, in 1944.[50] Missionary works by Christians from the neighboring states of Mizoram and Manipur increased from the last decades of the twentieth century leading to an amazing growth of Christians among the hill tribes of Tripura from a mere 24,872 in 1981,[51] to 159,882 in 2011.[52]

The present-day Arunachal Pradesh, known until 1972 as North-East Frontier Agency, has a long but insignificant interaction with Christian missions. The first Protestant missionaries of the American Baptist Mission came to the region in their attempt to reach the Shan tribe of northern Burma and southern China. The first American Protestant missionary Miles Bronson landed there in

---

45. Z. Lianthanga, *Tripura a Kohhran lo din tanna leh Chanchintha a darh zel dan* (Vanghmun: Jampui-Sakhan Baptist Association, 1996), 4–6.

46. Lianthanga, *Tripura a Kohhran lo din tanna leh Chanchintha a darh zel dan*, 8–23.

47. Eade, "Golden Jubilee," 12.

48. Hnehliana, "Tripura Baptist Christian Union," in *Tripura Baptist Christian Union: Golden Jubilee Souvenir, 1938–1988* (Agartala: TBCU, 1988), 59.

49. Lianthanga, *Tripura a Kohhran,* 7.

50. Eade, "Golden Jubilee," 2.

51. "Census of India 1981, Series—19, Sikkim, Household Population by Religion of the Head of Household," 18, accessed, March 3, 2023, http://www.lsi.gov.in:8081/jspui/bitstream/123456789/5513/1/50362_1981_HOS.pdf.

52. Population Census, "Christian Population in India 2011," in Christian Religion Census 2011, accessed September 9, 2022, https://www.census2011.co.in/data/religion/3-christianity.html.

1839 but left for Nowgong in Assam after a year.[53] Although the first missionaries of Northeast India may have passed through or landed in the region, there has not been a sustained western missionary presence since then. Between the indigenous religion of the majority tribe called Doni-Polo and the strong influence of Hinduism in the decades after India's independence, Arunachal Pradesh came to be known for its anti-Christian stance. Some people, especially among the dominant Adi tribe, considered Christianity and the modernizing (or Westernizing) tendency associated with it as a threat to their traditional identity.[54]

The Arunachal Pradesh Freedom of Religion Acts of 1978 which followed similar acts in Orissa and Madhya Pradesh, said that "no person shall convert or attempt to convert . . . any person from one religious faith by the use of force or by inducement or by any fraudulent means. . . ."[55] This political development contributed to Christian persecutions, which intensified in the 1970s. Churches reported numerous kidnappings and torture of Christians, dispossession of their belongings, and burning of their houses.[56] The courageous witness of the small Christian community withstood these political pressure and the social ostracization. Meanwhile, Arunachal Pradesh became a major recipient of missionaries from its neighboring states and from other parts of India. The Christian witness in Arunachal Pradesh has resulted in the greatest increase of Christian population in an Indian state during the past four decades. From being a small minority religion in the middle of the twentieth century, Christianity became the largest religion in the second decade of the twenty-first century. In the 1981 census report, there were just 48,274 Christians[57] out of a population of 631,839[58] which is less than 7.7 percent. By 2011, Christianity had become the largest religion with 30.36 percent of the population claiming to be Christian.[59]

---

53. V. K. Nuh, *History of Christianity in Arunachal Pradesh: Focus on Galo Baptist Churches Council* (Council of Naga Baptist Churches, 2006), 11–15.

54. Atul Chandra Talukdar, "Tribal Cultural Revival in Arunachal Pradesh," in *Impact of Christianity on North East India*, ed. J. Puthenpurakal (Shillong: Vendrame Institute, 1996), 486–487.

55. The Arunachal Freedom of Religion Act, 1978, section 3. The Act has been made available online by several organs. This one is quoted from the website of PRS India https://lawsofindia. blinkvisa.com/pdf/arunachal_pradesh/1978/1978AP4.pdf. Last accessed, March 3, 2023.

56. Talukdar, "Tribal Cultural Revival in Arunachal Pradesh," 488.

57. "Census of India 1981, Series—19, Sikkim, Household Population by Religion of the Head of Household," 18, accessed March 3, 2023, http://www.lsi.gov.in:8081/jspui/ bitstream/123456789/5513/1/50362_1981_HOS.pdf.

58. "Census of India 1981, Series—19, Sikkim," 12.

59. "Arunachal Pradesh Religion Population Data," *Census of India, 2011*. https://www. census2011.co.in/data/religion/state/12-arunachal-pradesh.html. Last accessed, March 3, 2023.

The Christian population was 418,732 out of the total 1,383,727 population of the state.[60]

Roman Catholic Church in Northeast India Unlike Protestant missions, the Roman Catholic Church in Northeast India has no particular territory of operation. The first missionary society assigned specifically to the region, the Foreign Missionaries of Milan (PIME), came to the region briefly in 1872, but because of a jurisdiction dispute, no tangible work was done. From 1889 the region was reassigned to the German Society of Catholic Education, popularly known as Salvatorians,[61] which began "Catholic missionary work proper" in the region.[62] During the First World War the German Salvatorians were repatriated, and the work was entrusted temporarily to the Belgian Jesuits (1915–1922), until the charge was handed over to Salesians of Don Bosco in 1922. The Salesian Brothers were joined by Salesian Sisters in 1923.[63]

While numerical growth of Christians was slow under the Salvatorians, the pace of growth picked up with the Jesuits, and then there was major growth from the first decade of the Salesians' work. Until Indian independence, Catholic mission work was confined almost exclusively to present-day Assam and Meghalaya. After independence, however, the Catholic Church experienced spectacular growth in Northeast India. Some new orders joined the effort, strengthening the work together with diocesan clergies. The Catholic community grew tenfold from 70,000 in 1945 to 700,000 in 1990.[64] From the Assam plains and Meghalaya, the Catholic Church soon moved out to Manipur and Nagaland, where it has been enjoying rapid growth.

Conclusion

Christianity is alive in Northeast India, and its transformation of people's lives—social and cultural—has been obvious. Christians are active and missionary minded. The witness of Christians in the region has resulted in the multiplication of their numbers. Such has been their way of being Christian right from the beginning as exemplified by an Assamese role in reaching the Ao-Nagas

---

60. "Census of India, 2011: Religion," accessed September 23, 2016, http://www.censusindia.gov.in/2011census/c-01.html

61. George Kottupallil, "A Historical Survey of the Catholic Church in Northeast India from 1627 to 1969," in *The Catholic Church in Northeast India, 1890–1990* (Shillong: Vendrame Institute; Calcutta: Firms KLM, 1993), 31–35.

62. Downs, *History of Christianity in India*, 92.

63. Kottupallil, "Historical Survey of the Catholic Church," 36–53.

64. Downs, *History of Christianity in India*, 120.

with the gospel, the Khasis with the Mizos, the Mizos pioneering missions in Tripura and southern Manipur, the Nagas, Mizos, and most others in bringing the gospel to Arunachal Pradesh lately.

The term geo-ethnicity may sound awkward, but it helpfully describes the region. The Sanskritization process in the region's history has largely resulted in differentiating between those who are Hinduized and those who continued their primal religions. It has become instrumental in the categorization of the people between tribal and non-tribal in the region. So, the geo-ethnic character of the region has largely been followed by the religious identities of the people. The impact of this distinct feature has been felt in the variety of ethnopolitical movements in the region.

The Protestant story began with Serampore Mission and eventually led to what mission historians called comity arrangements. Ethno-linguistic regions occupied by a mission agency became the church tradition of the region. In some ways, this arrangement aided as well as benefitted the geo-ethnic character of the region. The largest Christian bodies are those with geoethnoreligious crossovers. The Catholic Church is present in every state, the Council of Baptist Churches of Northeast India dominates the region of Nagaland and Garo regions of Meghalaya, Assam, and has a strong presence in Manipur, and the Presbyterian Church of India is present among the Mizos, Khasis, and tribes in the Cachar hills.

CHAPTER FOUR

Ecclesial Traditions in India

A Diverse Unity

Matthias Phurba Sonam Gergan

Introduction

THE DIVERSITY OF India and of ideas of being Indian impact even the writing and imagining of Christian history and its present identity in India. This sentiment is reflected in Robert Frykenberg's statement about Christianity in India, "this is really a history about many separate Christianities, rather than about one."[1] Thus, any attempt to write about the church in India must account for the diversity and plurality of histories, traditions, cultures, peoples, and locations. However, descriptors for the church like "the people of God" (Rom 9:25–26; 2 Cor 6:16) and "the body of Christ" (1 Cor 12:12–17; Eph 3:6; Col 1:14), would indicate that churches despite their plurality ought to contain within them a unity. This chapter examines major Christian traditions in India to make the assertion that the seemingly fragmented past and present of Indian churches are not necessarily obstacles to be overcome. Instead, through its diverse unity, the Indian church offers a way of being a church which is both, relevant to the local context and informs the broader church of an essential facet of its identity.

This chapter presents and contemplates mission efforts that led to the establishment of different ecclesial traditions in the Indian context. Stephen Bevans and Roger Schroeder's assertion that mission is *"prior* to the church and constitutive to its existence,"[2] is foundational to this approach. Taken alongside Michael Goheen's statement—"Ecclesiology is about understanding our identity"[3]—the chapter is also an inquiry into the Christian identity. Straddling the disciplines

1. Robert Eric Frykenberg, *Christianity in India: From Beginnings to the Present*, Oxford History of the Christian Church (New York: Oxford University Press, 2010), vii.

2. Stephen Bevans and Roger Schroeder, *Constants in Context: A Theology of Mission for Today*, American Society of Missiology Series, no. 30 (Maryknoll, NY: Orbis Books, 2004), 13.

3. Michael W Goheen, *A Light to the Nations: The Missional Church and the Biblical Story* (Grand Rapids, MI: Baker Academic, 2011), 5.

of mission and church history, this chapter seeks to present the Indian church as a diverse unity in a manner that holds together the church's mission and its identity in close dialogue with its history. While this approach will lack the depth of inquiry that specialized studies in these individual disciplines could provide, it seeks to display the need and utility of interdisciplinary inquiries in the field of ecclesiological studies.

Due to limitations in its scope, the chapter examines specific events and sections of history to draw a broad-strokes picture of the church in India (limiting the conversation to established formal churches with longer local histories) instead of presenting a comprehensive historical account. The chapter will proceed by looking at early (precolonial) churches in India. Following this, churches formed during the colonial period under Roman Catholic missions and Protestant missions will be examined. Finally, the chapter will turn its focus to later indigenous churches followed by a reflection on how this seemingly disjointed picture of ecclesiologies in India can be understood as a diverse unity beyond mere sociocultural categories and what this can mean for the global church. It must be clarified that the categories utilized for the historical account of churches in India contain immense diversity within themselves. While they are utilized in this chapter as a means to organize and narrate a complex history, they are not meant to homogenize any of the ecclesial traditions they represent.

Early Churches in India

India has had a long and storied Christian presence, with some present-day churches in southern India tracing their origins to Saint Thomas the Apostle from the first century. Woba James lists three views regarding the beginnings of Christianity in India. The most widely held view believes that "Apostle Thomas landed in India in the year A.D. 52 and suffered martyrdom in the year A.D. 72)."[4] A second, less popular view believes that "Apostle Thomas and Bartholomew (the disciples of Christ Himself), brought Christianity to India."[5] The third view credits "a group of Christians migrating from East Syria or Persian Churches"[6] for bringing Christianity to India. Writing about the veracity of the history of Christian origins in India, Frykenberg notes, "it is impossible to establish this antiquity with any more scientific validity than many events of ancient

---

4. Woba James, *Major Issues in the History of Christianity in India: A Post-Colonial Reading* (Jorhat: TDCC Publications, 2013), 31.

5. James, *Major Issues in the History of Christianity in India*, 31.

6. James, *Major Issues in the History of Christianity in India*, 31.

history that are accepted without much question."[7] Thus, much of the evidence presented for early churches in India remains open to scrutiny and doubt, like much of ancient history.

Nathanael J. Andrade details such objections regarding the veracity of the early origins of Christianity in India. A key argument by Andrade relates to what the term "India" referred to in narratives cited as evidence of the early roots of Christianity in India. He argues that "all late antique narratives regarding the evangelization of 'Indians' were almost certainly referring to peoples of east Africa and south Arabia."[8] Andrade posits that "Christianity first arrived and became established in south India due to the fifth-century CE activity of Sasanian merchants."[9] However, A. Jayakumar writes, "no other country in the world other than India claims to have the tomb of St. Thomas. And no other country other than India claims that Christianity was established by St. Thomas."[10] The exclusivity of India's claims to its Christian origins through Saint Thomas and the presence of living churches with traditional narratives passed down through generations make the early Thomas origins of Christianity in India not only possible but highly plausible. Even if one were to agree with Andrade's position, it can be safely said that Christianity and churches existed in India long before the advent of European missionaries.

A. M. Mundadan notes that the early Thomas communities shared several aspects of day-to-day life with the higher castes.[11] He later adds, "the social organization of St Thomas Christians was more or less based on the ecclesiastical organization and religious life."[12] Thus, while they were highly integrated within their context, the churches served as the primary locus for the day-to-day lives of Thomas Christians. In addition, Mundadan notes that the early Thomas Christians, due to their enmeshment with the caste system in the context, "were averse to proselytising."[13] Thus, early Indian churches were deeply enculturated

---

7. Frykenberg, *Christianity in India*, 91.

8. Nathanael J. Andrade, *The Journey of Christianity to India in Late Antiquity: Networks and the Movement of Culture* (Cambridge: Cambridge University Press, 2021), 72–73.

9. Andrade, *The Journey of Christianity to India in Late Antiquity*, 212.

10. A. Jayakumar, *History of Christianity in India: Major Themes* (Kolkata: SCEPTRE, 2013), 11.

11. A. Mathias Mundadan, *History of Christianity in India: From the Beginning Up to the Middle of the Sixteenth Century (up to 1542)*, vol. 1 (Bangalore: Church History Association of India, 1984), 158.

12. Mundadan, *History of Christianity in India*, 1:174.

13. Mundadan, *History of Christianity in India*, 1:191.

into their context which led them to becoming integral members of society. However, this enculturation also compromised the churches' willingness to reach across preexisting communal divides.

Roger Hedlund writes that migrating Syrian Christians came in contact with Indian Thomas Christians in the fourth century with "whom they interacted and amalgamated thus reinvigorating the Indian Christian community."[14] This encounter and the resultant revival show that these churches were open to interaction with other ecclesial communities and the possibility of being changed in the process. However, Hedlund adds, "Gradually everything ecclesiastical in India became essentially East-Syrian."[15] Thus, their dialogue and resultant amalgamation with the Syrian church, beginning with revitalization, later resulted in abstraction from the context. However, this Syrianization of the church has also arguably played a role in preserving its distinct character and traditions across generations and through numerous upheavals.[16] Frykenberg's characterization of these communities is apt: "Hindu in culture, Christian in faith, and Persian or Syrian (Orthodox) in doctrine, ecclesiology, and ritual."[17] The early Indian churches thus show the interplay of continuity and discontinuity with the surrounding context in the formation and preservation of an ecclesial tradition.

The early churches in India provide a glimpse into living churches with their foundations in the earliest forms of Christianity with deep roots in Indian soil. Their survival and continued life represent vital aspects of being church. First, the importance of shared memory passed down through generations bears witness to the church's faith, origins, and struggles. Second, the churches exhibit and live out the need for deep, sometimes treacherous, engagement with the local context and the global church. Third, these communities exhibit the interplay of continuity and discontinuity with the context and other Christian traditions in being church. Finally, these communities offer the possibility of the church being the central interpretative lens for the lived realities of communities, even when Christians are a minority.

Churches of Roman Catholic Missions in India

Concentrated European missionary efforts began in India with the arrival of Vasco da Gama in 1498.[18] Stephen Neill points to the growing power of Portugal

---

14. Roger E. Hedlund, *Christianity Made in India: From Apostle Thomas to Mother Teresa* (Kindle Edition, 2017), 14.

15. Hedlund, *Christianity Made in India*, 15.

16. Hedlund, *Christianity Made in India*, 14.

17. Frykenberg, *Christianity in India*, 112.

18. Robert Eric Frykenberg, "Christians in India: An Historical Overview of Their Complex Origins," in *Christians and Missionaries in India: Cross-Cultural Communication since 1500*, ed Robert Eric Frykenberg and Alaine Low (Grand Rapids, MI: Eerdmans, 2003), 40.

and Spain, which led to Rome handing over primary responsibility for missions to the two states.[19] This arrangement led to a relationship between the two European empires and Rome that brought Christianity to India with an intensity it had not seen before. P. Thomas describes the Portuguese as "Zealous Catholics, they thought they had a mission to convert the people of the East by preaching, if they could, and by the sword if they had to."[20] This form of Christianity mixed with imperialism sharply contrasted with that of the Thomas communities which had grown more organically.

Early forays into India brought clergy who primarily served as chaplains to the Portuguese. The Franciscans were the first missionaries to India in this era—other religious orders followed them. Neill notes that Henry de Coimbra led the first group of Franciscans to India in 1500.[21] The Franciscans encountered resistance from the secular clergy (those who accompanied Portuguese imperial parties) due to their interests often conflicting. This conflict is understandable given the primarily commercial and imperial interests of most of the Portuguese who came to India.

Such tensions encouraged missionaries from various religious orders to venture into regions that were not under Portuguese control. Frykenberg mentions that such missionary forays reached Vijayanagara, Cinji, Madurai, Thanjavur, and even the Mughals in Agra and Delhi.[22] These efforts by the missionaries to move away from areas of Portuguese control "manifested an entirely different kind of Catholic presence."[23] Unlike the close coupling of imperial and missionary efforts evidenced in areas controlled by the Portuguese, these missionary ventures aimed at accommodation, indigenization, close interaction with local cultures, and service as "missionary physicians, scientists, and technicians."[24] The work of Roberto de Nobili—a Jesuit who distanced himself from the "crude, beef-eating, alcohol-drinking barbarians from Europe" and called himself a "Roman Brahman"—famously exemplifies efforts at accommodation and indigenization in Madurai.[25] Distance from centers of Portuguese power made the missionaries take more dialogical approaches, which led to communities that bore the imprints of such accommodation.

---

19. Stephen Neill, *A History of Christianity in India: The Beginnings to AD 1707* (Cambridge: Cambridge University Press, 1984), 111, https://doi.org/10.1017/CBO9780511520556.

20. P. Thomas, *Churches in India* (New Delhi: Ministry of Information & Broadcasting, 1990), 4.

21. Neill, *A History of Christianity in India*, 120.

22. Frykenberg, "Christians in India," 43.

23. Frykenberg, "Christians in India," 43.

24. Frykenberg, "Christians in India," 43.

25. Frykenberg, "Christians in India," 45.

Joseph Thekkedath points to the enormous influence of Francis Xavier (arrived May 1542) on the development of the Indian church. He credits Xavier with systematizing missionary work in India, creating enthusiasm in Europe for missions in India (which led to an increased inflow of missionaries from Europe), and creating a more helpful attitude among Portuguese officials toward the spread of Christianity.[26] Frykenberg describes Xavier's work among the Paravas. Despite not knowing Tamil, he worked with assistants "drilling people in rote recitations of the Lord's Prayer, Ave, the Creeds, and the Commandments."[27] Ines Zupanova mentions Xavier's advice to fellow Jesuit Gaspar Barzeus "to study people around him. It is from them, he wrote, that we can learn more in order to usefully 'fructify the souls, your own and that of your neighbor.'"[28] Thus, despite limitations like the lack of expertise in indigenous languages, Xavier showed a remarkable instinct for learning from the local populace while growing them in the Christian faith in a systematized manner.

Roman Catholic missions in India naturally encountered Thomas Christians. Hedlund notes that despite early cordiality in their relationship, matters quickly worsened.[29] A significant factor that led to the souring of relations was the Roman Catholic Church's attempts at assimilating the Thomas Christians within their fold accompanied by Latinization—characterized by attempts at correcting errors in Thomas Christianity. Matters escalated with the council of Diamper (1599 CE), where "Roman Catholic authorities destroyed many manuscripts and texts of the Thomas Christians that they understood to have contained erroneous works."[30] From the Thomas Christian side, these events culminated at "the Koonen Cross Revolt on January 3, 1653 . . . marking the restoration of Indian autonomy of the St. Thomas Christians of Kerala."[31] These developments have a tinge of irony given the move from local languages to a Syriac liturgy in earlier Thomas Christian history.

This brief account of some events from the early stages of Roman Catholic Christianity in India gives a glimpse into the nature of the churches that came to

---

26. Joseph Thekkedath, *History of Christianity in India: From the Middle of the Sixteenth Century to the End of the Seventeenth Century*, vol. 2 (Bangalore: Church History Association of India, 1988), 1.

27. Frykenberg, "Christians in India," 44.

28. Ines G. Zupanova, "Sinner and Confessors: Missionary Dialogues in India, Sixteenth Century," in *Christianity in Indian History: Issues of Culture, Power and Knowledge*, ed. Pius Malekandathil, Joy L. Pachuau, and Tanika Sarkar (Delhi: Primus Books, 2016), 119.

29. Hedlund, *Christianity Made in India*, 24.

30. Andrade, *The Journey of Christianity to India in Late Antiquity*, 209.

31. Hedlund, *Christianity Made in India*, 24.

be as a result. First, there was a concentration of power and authority in European imperial centers. This issue continued to plague Roman Catholic missions and churches. A 1915 document, *Survey of Roman Catholic Mission,* notes: "A great hindrance to the revival of Roman Catholic missions in India in the nineteenth century was the insistence by Portugal on the patronate accorded to it by the popes in the sixteenth century."[32] This situation led to an impasse wherein the Portuguese could neither appoint new bishops to vacant sees due to their waning power nor were they willing to allow the Roman Catholic church to do the same. The impasse "led to a schism with the church of Goa and to violent conflicts which were not finally settled until 1886."[33] Thus, churches born through Roman Catholic missionary efforts struggled to negotiate imperial and missional goals. Further, this led to an association of the Indian church with foreign imperial power, which continues to plague contemporary Indian churches today.

Second, related to the coupling of imperial efforts with missions, was the conflict of interests between secular clergy and missionaries, like the Franciscans.[34] Further, Thekkedath notes that even religious orders sent primarily as missionaries were not above conflict with each other, often due to their concern "for the honour and reputation of their own religious families."[35] Thus, the churches formed as a result of these missionary efforts also developed along fractured lines with often intense rivalry and mistrust between Christian groups.

The third issue was the Roman Catholic response to the Indian caste system. Missionaries like de Nobili and Xavier worked within the caste categories already present in society, working with higher and lower castes respectively, seeing it as a "social convenience."[36] Being church while working with local social structures remains an issue for the church (beyond Roman Catholicism), centuries after de Nobili and Xavier, as evidenced in the Lausanne Occasional Paper 1 on Donald McGavaran's Homogeneous Unit Principle. The paper while discussing McGavaran's HUP and its impact on the unity of the church argues, "in many situations a homogenous unit church can be a legitimate and authentic church. Yet we are also agreed that it can never be complete in itself."[37] This

---

32. "A Survey of Roman Catholic Missions II British India and Ceylon," *International Review of Mission* 4, no. 4 (October 1915): 638.

33. "A Survey of Roman Catholic Missions II British India and Ceylon," 638.

34. Neill, *A History of Christianity in India*, 126.

35. Thekkedath, *History of Christianity in India*, 2: 9.

36. Thomas, *Churches in India*, 5.

37. Lausanne Committee for World Evangelization, "Lausanne Occasional Paper: The Pasadena Consultation: Homogeneous Unit Principle" (Lausanne Committee for World Evangelization, June 2, 1977), https://tinyurl.com/25wmwc4a.

statement when applied to the idea of caste-based local missions and churches to accommodate the local culture such that, "to be truly indigenous, [it] should be rooted in the soil of its local culture" continues to raise questions of accommodation to indigenous cultures and the prescriptive role of the church in culture.[38]

The churches that arose from Roman Catholic missions, while formed with power differentials between the European imperialists and local indigenous communities, were not formed without local agency. Zupanova points to a text, *Confessionairo*, which was "a libretto for dialogue between a Jesuit confessor and a Parava penitent."[39] While this may appear to be another instrument to impose European Christianity and culture on the locals, Zupanova notes that its translation required "Tamil concepts expressing devotion, guilt, fear, sorrow, desire and hope."[40] This document became crucial in constructing "the Parava's communal self and caste structure" even beyond their time under the Jesuits.[41] Thus, Indian churches, despite power differentials, were still formed through dialogue wherein indigenous communities found ways to adapt and influence European structures.

Protestant Churches in India

Frykenberg argues for using the term "evangelical" for "all Christians who, in their doctrines and ecclesiology, were and are neither Orthodox nor Catholic."[42] He reasons that the term "Protestant" is a more Anglican term. "Evangelical," on the other hand, has its roots in India's Christian history. This term was appropriated from northern Germany—the source of the first evangelical missions in India.[43] However, I use the word "Protestant" for these categories of churches because of its more widespread usage and acceptance in India, in a manner similar to what Frykenberg intends for "evangelical" (acknowledging the utility of the category itself). Further, this usage also differentiates these churches from contemporary evangelical churches from the West which are growing in influence—particularly in urban India.

E. R. Hambye marks 1706 as the beginning of organized Protestant missions in India with the arrival of two Lutheran pastors, B. Ziegenbalg and

---

38. "Lausanne Occasional Paper."

39. Malekandathil, Pachuau, and Sarkar, *Christianity in Indian History*, 120.

40. Malekandathil, Pachuau, and Sarkar, *Christianity in Indian History*, 120.

41. Malekandathil, Pachuau, and Sarkar, *Christianity in Indian History*, 121.

42. Frykenberg, *Christianity in India*, xi.

43. Frykenberg, *Christianity in India*, xi.

H. Plutschau at Tranquebar (Tamil Nadu).[44] This period was one of political transitions, with the decline of Mughal power culminating in the British coming to control most of India.[45] Frykenberg notes that 1706 was also when Constanzo Guiseppe Beschi, a Jesuit missionary among the Tamil, "was about to have such a profound impact upon Tamil learning at its highest levels."[46] Beschi's work was characterized by a high degree of accommodation and acculturation, not dissimilar from de Nobili's. Thus, Protestant missionary work began in India when Roman Catholic missionaries were experimenting with greater levels of accommodation and acculturation and the wider political situation in India was also in a transitory period.

Frykenberg describes the sending context of Ziegenbalg and Plutschau as "a mingling of Enlightenment thought and Evangelical Pietism."[47] The first Protestant missionaries to India came with "a new kind of ecumenical voluntarism and the forming of an altogether new kind of missionary collaboration"— with the evangelical awakening in Britain and America, Moravian sheltering with Count Zinzendorf at Herrenhut, and August Hermann Francke's educational efforts at Halle University in the background.[48] This new approach to missions brought with it a higher emphasis on education with evangelistic zeal for indigenous peoples, combined with less direct ties with European imperial governments or a central ecclesial authority like Rome.

Due to their lack of strong imperial connections, evangelical missionaries often encountered opposition from local European authorities. Ziegenbalg and Plutschau were initially persecuted and harassed by the Danish due to fears that they may endanger their commercial interests.[49] The British also took a largely antagonistic position toward missions due to their commercial interests. However, they softened their official stance after the Charter Renewal Act of 1813, which allowed British missionaries to work in India with a permit.[50]

The debates surrounding missionary efforts and colonial interests became especially significant in the nineteenth century as the British became increasingly dominant. David Mark Rathel's account of the conflict between Anglican

---

44. E. R. Hambye, *History of Christianity in India: Eighteenth Century*, vol. 3 (Banglaore: Church History Association of India, 1997), 1.

45. Hambye, *History of Christianity in India*, 3:1–2.

46. Frykenberg, "Christians in India," 47.

47. Frykenberg, "Christians in India," 47.

48. Frykenberg, "Christians in India," 47–48.

49. Frykenberg, "Christians in India," 49.

50. Frykenberg, "Christians in India," 55–56.

missionaries and the Baptist Missionary Society helps clarify the two approaches. Charles Grant, who served in the British Parliament, was chairman of the East India Company, and was actively involved with the Clapham Sect, is cited by Rathel as an example of the approach to missions from an established church—the Anglicans. Grant based his arguments for Christian missions on Britain's responsibility to "maximize the happiness of her Indian subjects."[51] This envisioning of mission coupled closely with the colonial enterprise was based on the understanding that "Christian witness" would occur primarily "through the efforts of British authorities."[52] Grant's envisioning of Christian missions contained an assumption that British rule in India had a providential purpose within which the church and state would need to work closely together for the ultimate good of its Indian subjects.

Andrew Fuller, who led the Baptist missionary efforts in India, is cited by Rathel as representative of the nonconformist position that "rejected the establishment of a national church."[53] This position was based on the understanding that the kingdom of God was "not of this world."[54] The nonconformist approach led to a closer collaboration with "allies in India" in religious and social matters like the banning of *sati* (widow burning).[55] However, this also led to suspicions of Baptist missions from the ruling British.

Like the Roman Catholics, Protestant missionaries also encountered Thomas Christians in India. Hedlund mentions that their early encounters were positive, with the Church Missionary Society beginning Malayalam translations of the Bible. However, this enterprise led to a schism between reformers and traditionalists in Thomas churches over translating the Bible and the Anglican prayer book into Malayalam. Their contact with Protestants led the reformers to place greater emphasis on "the Bible, sermons and hymns" with proposals for "vernacularization of liturgy and prayer" and the consequent rejection of the "mediatory power of the saints and Mary."[56] Thomas churches saw internal changes and related debates when they encountered Protestant missions just as they had with Syrian and Roman Catholic encounters in the past.

---

51. David Mark Rathel, "Evangelicals, Ecclesiology, and Empire: How Ecclesial Commitments Shaped Early Evangelical Reactions to British Rule in India," *American Baptist Quarterly* 38, no. 2 (2019): 128.

52. Rathel, "Evangelicals, Ecclesiology, and Empire," 131.

53. Rathel, "Evangelicals, Ecclesiology, and Empire," 133.

54. Rathel, "Evangelicals, Ecclesiology, and Empire," 133.

55. Rathel, "Evangelicals, Ecclesiology, and Empire," 138.

56. Hedlund, *Christianity Made in India*, 24–25.

Protestant missions, with beginnings in the Enlightenment and Pietism, emphasized the equality of all humans and education as a means of mission. This orientation led to greater reach with disadvantaged members of society among lower castes. However, the churches formed through these missions were not entirely removed from issues faced and negotiated by previous missions and the churches born of them. They continued to struggle with the relationship between church, state, and missions. Further, many of their efforts were viewed with suspicion and they were often at odds with colonial governance and commercial interests. The role of foreign missionaries and their relationship with indigenous peoples was another area that churches of Protestant missions continued to negotiate. Finally, they continued to engage in a dialectic between their Western origins (the home context of most missionaries) and the context encountered in India. These tensions continued to manifest in their dealings with the caste system and practices like *sati*. Further, even the Western context was not a homogenous reality—exemplified in the conflict between Grant and Fuller. Finally, it must be emphasized that Protestant missions and churches (like all others who came before them) did not begin their existence in a vacuum. The churches born out of these missions were formed in dialogue and negotiation with preexisting churches and the missional efforts that had led to them.

Later Indigenous Churches in India

Paul Joshua defines Indian Initiated Churches (IICs) as "churches initiated by Indian Christians as their own spiritual home, constructed according to local needs, by local people expressing local hopes and dreams and sharing local concerns and struggles."[57] This section will briefly highlight some later indigenous missions and the churches that emerged from them. Joshua locates the IICs after what he calls the "third wave of Christianity . . . with the arrival of the German Lutherans of the Danish-Halle Mission in South India (1706)"[58]— corresponding with the section on Protestant churches in this chapter.

Kirsteen and Sebastian Kim point to some early initiatives by Indian leaders to rethink Christianity from an Indian perspective. Brahmabandab Upadhyay (1861–1907) was a "Bengali Brahmin who became a Roman Catholic, re-laid the foundations of Indian Christian theology on Vedantic Hinduism rather than Greek philosophy."[59] Kim and Kim note other pioneers of Indian Christian

57. Paul Joshua, *Christianity Remade: The Rise of Indian-Initiated Churches*, series ed. Joel A. Carpenter, Studies in World Christianity (Waco, TX: Baylor University Press, 2022), Introduction, sec. "Indian-Initiated Churches," 4.

58. Joshua, *Christianity Remade,* ch. 1, sec. "Christianity in India, " 21.

59. Sebastian C. H Kim and Kirsteen Kim, *Christianity as a World Religion: An Introduction*, ch. 2, sec. "Religions and Caste in South Asia" (Kindle Edition, 2016), 1000.

theology like A. J. Appasamy, an Anglican bishop who used Hindu Bhakti mysticism, and Sadhu Sundar Singh, who lived the life of a *sadhu* (a religious ascetic).[60] They also note "a caste group called Shanars or Nadars in the Tirunelveli district of South India who in 1857 founded the Hindu-Christian Church of the Lord Jesus."[61] These initiatives at rethinking and forming an "Indian Christianity" were distinct from previous efforts at indigenization and acculturation because of their Indian initiators. IICs emerged after centuries of Christian presence in India as Indian leaders began to grapple with their identity as Indians and Christians.

Writing about IICs, Roger Hedlund identifies three broad types. First, those that focus on healing. Second are "brethren or 'Baptistic' groups," including the movement around brother Bakht Singh. Finally, "Holiness" movements like the Laymen's Evangelical fellowship and numerous "South Indian Pentecostal fellowships, denominations, and organizations."[62] Bakht Singh (1903–2000) was born into a Hindu family in Punjab and was brought up as a Sikh as per tradition for the first-born son. During his time in England, he declared himself an atheist and a free thinker.[63] However, on a trip to Canada, he attended a Christian service on a ship where he had a divine encounter. Returning to Canada in 1929 for an Agricultural Engineering degree Bakht Singh borrowed a New Testament Bible from a friend. Reading John 3, he had a personal encounter with Jesus, at which point he said he truly became a Christian. Bakht Singh stayed in Canada from 1930 to 1933 and was mentored by John and Edith Hayward of the Christian and Missionary Alliance Church.[64] During this time, he had an encounter with God in 1932 which led to him surrendering to ministry and returning to India in 1933, where his family disowned him.[65]

Starting as a street evangelist in Mumbai, he developed into an itinerant preacher across denominations in North India.[66] Over time Bakht Singh grew critical of denominational churches and concluded that "the lack of dependence upon the Word was one of the causes for strife and spiritual barrenness among

60. Kim and Kim, *Christianity as a World Religion*, 1009.

61. Kim and Kim, *Christianity as a World Religion*, 1009–1014.

62. Roger E. Hedlund, *Quest for Identity: India's Churches of Indigenous Origin, The "Little Tradition" in Indian Christianity* (ISPCK, 2000), 1.

63. B. E. Bharathi Nuthalapati, *Brother Bakht Singh: Theologian and Father of the Indian Independent Christian Church Movement* (Carlisle, UK: Langham Monographs, 2017), 16–20.

64. Nuthalapati, *Brother Bakht Singh*, 21.

65. Nuthalapati, *Brother Bakht Singh*, 21–22.

66. Nuthalapati, *Brother Bakht Singh*, 22–23.

Christians."[67] These convictions laid the theological foundations for much of Singh's ministry and the churches that grew out of it. The churches that grew out of Singh's work had a strong reliance on the biblical text interpreted through the Holy Spirit, with loosely connected churches catering to the specific needs of their context, with the lines between clergy and laity being blurred.[68] As the movement grew, there was a need to designate and train "full-time workers who had the ability to care for new congregations."[69] Hence, even though Bakht Singh's movement began as a response to the rigidity and lack of adaptability of the organized churches he encountered, it adopted and created its own structures as it grew.

Another earlier example of indigenous churches in India is the communities formed by the work of John Christian Arulappan. Born into a Christian family in 1810 in Tirunelveli, Tamil Nadu, Arulappan was sent by his family to study at the Anglican Christian Mission Society seminary when he was fifteen.[70] Arulappan's encounter with Anthony Norris Groves, "a British leader of the Brethren movement . . . began a seminal stage in his spiritual and ministerial formation."[71] Like Singh's movement, Arulappan's also emphasized scripture over tradition and an accompanying stress on the freedom of the Spirit and the priesthood of believers. He started Christianpettha in 1840 "as a model self-supporting agricultural village."[72] However, unlike other contemporaneous Christian settlements, Christianpettah had Christians and non-Christians living together. Joshua describes Christianpettah as "an example of a home-grown Christian community in a predominantly Hindu context."[73] Singh's and Arulappan's communities can be understood as the next steps in Indian ecclesiological development—indigenous churches responding to indigenous needs under indigenous leadership.

While earlier missionaries like Beschi and de Nobili did work in ways that also sought to address contextual realities, later indigenous churches were different due to their Indian leadership. The churches they formed were a form of ecclesiology from below. However, even this ecclesiology from below was not done in abstraction. On the contrary, these leaders interacted and engaged with Western

---

67. Nuthalapati, *Brother Bakht Singh*, 23.

68. Nuthalapati, *Brother Bakht Singh*, 64–70.

69. Nuthalapati, *Brother Bakht Singh*, 97.

70. Joshua, *Christianity Remade*, ch. 1, sec. J. C. Arulappan and Christianpettah Village, 26.

71. Joshua, *Christianity Remade*, ch. 1, sec. J. C. Arulappan and Christianpettah Village, 27.

72. Joshua, *Christianity Remade*, ch. 1, sec. J. C. Arulappan and Christianpettah Village, 31.

73. Joshua, *Christianity Remade*, ch. 1, sec. J. C. Arulappan and Christianpettah Village, 31.

Christianity and its ideas through mentors and fellow Christians from the West. Thus, while ecclesiastically, the later IICs may appear distinct from churches formed in previous stages of history, a closer examination reveals them to be created through continued dialogue in the church catholic across space and time, in the Indian soil.

A Diverse Unity

A cursory reading of the previous sections may lead to a seemingly disjointed picture of ecclesiologies that happened to inhabit the Indian subcontinent through various accidents of history, leading to the establishment of churches that had little in common other than their shared geographical location. However, a missional-historical reading of the same can show, borrowing from Bevans and Schroeder, that these missionary efforts reveal the church's true nature "as the community engages with particular contexts, under the direction of the Spirit."[74] From this perspective, ecclesiologies in India are united despite their diversity on two fronts. First, through the unity of the *missiones ecclesiae,* various foreign and local missionaries worked in India, joining with the *missio Dei* under the direction of the same Spirit of God across space and time. Second, they are united by the churchs' encounters in mission with the Indian subcontinent through different stages of history and accompanying contextual developments, while maintaining continuity through a shared history (which may be strained at times).

Lamin Sanneh comments, "World Christianity is not one thing, but a variety of indigenous responses through more or less effective local idioms, but in any case without necessarily the European Enlightenment frame."[75] While one may disagree with his choice to contrast World Christianity with Global Christianity as semantic minutiae, one can see that the Indian church does indeed stand as a witness to diverse indigenous responses. However, one may argue, contrary to Sanneh, (in the Indian church) European Enlightenment is also included in the conversation and not necessarily as a distinct foreign voice. Over time, even European Enlightenment (as seen in the Protestant missions) became part of the Indian milieu acquiring a distinctly Indian flavor while still retaining some of its European characteristics.

This brief look at Christian traditions in India offers helpful insights into the very being of the church. First, the church (and missions) is a coming together of the divine and human in one reality. This is seen in the various interplays of

---

74. Bevans and Schroeder, *Constants in Context*, 13.

75. Lamin Sanneh, *Whose Religion Is Christianity? The Gospel beyond the West* (Grand Rapids, MI: Eerdmans, 2003), 219–220.

political histories and geographical particularities, with missionary efforts that led to the formation of the Indian church. Second, the church exists in continuity and discontinuity both within itself and with the Indian context. This is seen in missionary efforts to evangelize India with a diversity of approaches and convictions (sometimes with violent disagreements). It is also seen in the unity in identity as Indians and Christians, among the members of the churches formed, with the diversity in expressions of the same. Third, the church exists with a dynamic yet anchored identity. This was seen in the diversity of approaches to local cultures and critiques of the church from within the church (seen most recently in the IICs), while maintaining unity as a people anchored by a desire to reach others with the gospel of Christ (even this was with its own diversity of approaches and interpretations). Finally, while power differentials do exist (they always have) within the church and in relation to the surrounding context, the less powerful are not simply subsumed by the more powerful. They have agency and implicit power to influence the conversation.

Conclusion

The process of being and becoming church continues even today in India, as is seen in globally connected urban Indian congregations and local forms of "churchless Christianities" like the various *Krist Bhakta* movements. These communities are perhaps the next phase in Indian Christianity, reflecting the increasingly globalized and connected world they inhabit and different understandings of being church. In all this, the Indian church stands in continuity and discontinuity with the global church and within itself, in a manner wherein neither simplistic homogenizing models of unity nor simply affirming diversity will suffice. Instead, by embracing its diverse unity as exemplified by the Indian church, the church can truly live out its identity and be effective in mission, being incarnate in cultures while still critiquing the same from within and being open to the God of mission revealing and taking it in new directions while being anchored on the person and gospel of Christ.

CHAPTER FIVE

The Indigenous Mission Movement in India

From the First Century Onward

John Amalraj Karunakaran

Introduction

THE ACTIVE PARTICIPATION of an indigenous Christian community in God's mission characterizes the spread of the missions movement in India. The involvement of both the Eastern and Western churches contributed to its growth. The history of the missionary movement in India documented by Western and Indian historians typically follows chronological and geographical perspectives and largely relies on documentary evidence portraying the foreign influence on Christian growth without adequately focusing on the indigenous people who were also primary actors. One of the main reasons for this trend is the approach taken to narrate historical events based on the interests of Western readers.

John Webster lists three categories of audiences that determined the purpose of writing history: (1) the academic Christian readership in the Indian context, (2) academic historians in India and abroad, and (3) academics engaged in historical mission studies.[1] Webster points out that most mission histories were written for Western readers to influence their support for mission work in India and therefore only "assign very minor and passive roles to Indian Christians."[2] Lalsangkima Pachuau points out the contention among Christian historians in India between hagiographic accounts of missionary historians and other nationalist historians while differentiating nationalism from indigenous historiography.[3] He explains that indigenous historiography focuses on native perspectives. Pachuau takes the middle ground by giving due appreciation to Western missions while recognizing the indigenous

---

1. John C. B. Webster, *Historiography of Christianity in India* (New Delhi: Oxford University Press, 2013), 2–3.

2. Webster, *Historiography of Christianity in India*, 82.

3. Lalsangkima Pachuau, *Indian and Christian: Historical Accounts of Christianity, and Theological Reflections in India* (Delhi: ISPCK, 2019), 158–159.

contributions and proposes rescripting the Indian history illustrating this with how a few Western missionaries initiated the movement while the native converts spread far and wide.[4] Historian V. V. Thomas divides the contemporary historiographical/theoretical perspectives into subaltern, postcolonial, and contemporary feminism and discusses how the earlier historiographical schools of thought are inadequate while calling for the rereading of history.[5] This essay focuses on the global audience presenting the larger picture of the Christian missionary movement in India while zooming in on the indigenous efforts from the first century to today.

Among many Indian and Western scholars who contributed to the narration of the history of the missionary movement in India, the most outstanding contribution is that of the Church History Association of India's six-volume series on the history of Christianity in India which brings together the ecumenical efforts of Catholic, Protestant, and Orthodox scholars who approach history with the perspective of viewing Christianity in India as an integral part of the sociocultural history of the Indian people. Webster comments that this effort was a "new perspective" that rejected the more institutional approach in favor of a sociocultural history that has become a watershed in Christian historical writing.[6] Chandra Mallampalli refers to the recent publications by historians adopting a bottom-up approach emphasizing the "Indianness of Christianity" and its indigenous agency.[7] Similarly, Roger Hedlund also offers a scholarship that counters the biases that focus on the colonial character of Christianity and argues for the Indianness of Christianity in India.[8] Building on his prior work of rescripting Indian history, Pachuau provides a fresh perspective on the history of the global missionary movement (with an emphasis on Pentecostal and Charismatic movements) as a missiological eye opener using a cross-cultural lens in his writings while focusing on native initiatives.[9]

---

4. Pachuau, *Indian and Christian*, 175.

5. V. V. Thomas, *Understanding Subaltern History: Theoretical Tools* (Bangalore: BTESSC/SATHRI, 2006), x–xiii.

6. Webster, *Historiography of Christianity in India*, 7–8.

7. Chandra Mallampalli, "Historiography and Bibliography: South Asian Christianity," in *The Oxford Encyclopedia of South Asian Christianity*, ed. Roger E. Hedlund, et al. (New Delhi: Oxford University Press, 2012), 311–315.

8. Roger E. Hedlund, *Christianity Made in India: From Apostle Thomas to Mother Teresa* (Minneapolis: Fortress Press, 2017), 1–2.

9. Lalsangkima Pachuau, *World Christianity: A Historical and Theological Introduction* (Nashville: Abingdon Press, 2018).

A glance through these and other outstanding historical accounts of the missionary movement in India shows that there is much value in focusing on the indigenous nature of the movement that has been witness through the centuries to the spread of the Christian faith in India.[10]

The purpose of this chapter is to focus on the indigenous nature of the missionary movement in India within the sociocultural context of India using both Indian and Western historians as my source. I argue that the Christian missionary movement in India was primarily driven by anonymous indigenous believers and gospel workers faithfully sharing the love of Christ with other Indians leading to its growth. They are often recorded in historical documents as native mission agents, local assistants, and cultural informants for foreign missionaries.

First, we will briefly trace the origins of the indigenous missions movement before Western colonization and the key mission events that involved indigenous efforts during the colonial period. Next, we will explore the continuity and discontinuity of the missionary movement during the last few decades of the transition from the colonial era to the postindependence era. Third, we will briefly describe the present status of the indigenous mission movement during the twenty-first century and, finally, conclude with a discussion on the contemporary challenges faced by the Indian missions movement.

The Indigenous Missions Movement
Before the Colonial Era

Recently scholars have affirmed that the missions movement within India by Indians has been present right from the first century. Roger Hedlund comments that "Indigenous Christianity is as old as Christianity itself" and the Indian Christian movement for all its foreign influence continued through the centuries to preserve its indigenous tradition.[11] Robert Frykenberg in his overview of the complex origins of Christians in India traces it to the eastward movement from Antioch by Arabs, Persians, and Zoroastrians to the peoples of India and China in the first few centuries while giving credence to the traditional apostolic origin and their missionary zeal among Indians.[12] Focusing on the historical self-understandings of the Christian communities that trace their origin to the

---

10. Dana Lee Robert, ed., *Converting Colonialism: Visions and Realities in Mission History, 1706–1914*, Studies in the History of Christian Missions (Grand Rapids, MI: Eerdmans, 2008), 17.

11. Hedlund, *Christianity Made in India*, 1, 5–6.

12. Robert Eric Frykenberg and Alaine M. Low, eds., *Christians and Missionaries in India: Cross-Cultural Communication since 1500, with Special Reference to Caste, Conversion, and Colonialism*, Studies in the History of Christian Missions (Grand Rapids, MI: Eerdmans, 2003), 33.

first century, Frykenberg uses the evidence of oral traditions, lyrical epics, artifacts, and genealogies which suggest that the community was self-propagating and self-sustaining. In this regard, historian T. V. Philip addresses two major questions regarding the missionary activities of the Indian Christian community in the early centuries.[13] The first question is about the interaction of the Christian community with the existing Indian society and its identification within the existing social stratification by becoming one of the castes. The second question is whether the Thomas Christians were aware of their missionary responsibility. This leads us to the core issue of how the gospel spread in India in the early centuries given the apostolic tradition origin.

Referring to the St. Thomas Christians and their missionary activities, Philip remarks that there is nothing spectacular to note except that during the medieval period there is significant evidence of the East Syrian missionaries being involved in evangelistic work including the Nestorian merchants, artisans, clergy, and monks from Persia assuming that there were some of Indian origin.[14]

Hedlund testifies that the survival of Thomas Christianity through the centuries in the context of the rise of Islam supports the hypothesis of apostolic origin resulting in a Christian life that was vigorous and not necessarily self-contained.[15] In other words, Hedlund is suggesting that the Thomas Christians have been involved in Christian witness. Philip argues against the popular assumption that the Indian Christian community had no missionary zeal until the European missionary era. In doing so, he critiques the sweeping generalizations of scholars like Stephen Neil, L. W. Brown, and George Moraes and gives evidence of missionary spirit among the early Indian Christian community.[16] He points to efforts made to preach the gospel to Hindu philosophers and scholars in the second century by the Thomas Christians. Philip adds that later during the tenth and the eleventh centuries Indian monks attempted to spread the gospel to the Far East, all the way to China, Central Asia, and the Maldives Islands in the Indian Ocean.[17]

The second piece of evidence is the social integration of Christians with Indian society through their everyday life with caste Hindus. Both Philip and Mundadan use respected theologian Anthony Mookenthottam's comment that

---

13. T. V. Philip, *East of the Euphrates: Early Christianity in Asia* (Delhi: Jointly Published by Indian Society for Promoting Christian Knowledge and Christian Sahitya Samithy, Tiruvalla, 1998), 126–127.

14. Philip, *East of the Euphrates*, 127–128.

15. Hedlund, *Christianity Made in India*, 12.

16. Philip, *East of the Euphrates*, 127.

17. Philip, *East of the Euphrates*, 127–128.

the early Indian Christian community was indigenous with social and cultural roots within the Indian tradition that implied a lived incarnational theology.[18] Phillip agrees with the arguments advanced by Mundadan and comments that this was a different perspective from scholars like Robin Boyd who dismisses this perspective for lack of documentary evidence. He further opines that even though there is not much documentary evidence we can make an inference from other sources and circumstantial evidence.[19]

This takes our discussion back to the questions of whether the first-century Indian Christian community became a caste within the Indian social stratification and how that played out in the spreading of the gospel in India. The academic discussion in this respect has been diverse with some concluding that the Indian Christian community accepted their position in society as one of the castes resulting in a lack of any attempt to bring their non-Christian neighbors into the church. Philip refutes this argument stating that the Aryans and the Sanskritization process was slower and came later, probably around the thirteenth century.[20] K. P. Kesava Menon writes that Indian Christians accepted the Hindu ritualistic observances into their expression of faith making the context "Hindu in culture, Christian in religion, and oriental in worship!"[21] Philip adds that there was much social mobility between the caste systems and those who followed other faiths and this inculturation into the existing society does not mean a lack of Christian witness but a way of exerting Christian influence on the caste system itself.[22] Historian John England points out that during the second century, an invitation by the Indians was sent to Alexandria for missionaries to preach to Hindu philosophers and scholars.[23] Further, in the fourth century, their relationship with the Nestorian church known for its missionary zeal resulted in monks from India being sent overseas to the Far East including

---

18. Mathias A Mundadan, *History of Christianity in India*, vol. 1 (Bangalore, India: The Church History Association of India, 1989), 492.

19. Philip, *East of the Euphrates,* 142. Mundadan, *History of Christianity in India*, 1: 492–493.

20. Philip, *East of the Euphrates*, 127–128.

21. K. P. Kesava Menon, "Foreword," in *Christianity in India: A History in Ecumenical Perspective*, ed. Hormice C. Perumalil and E. R. Hambye (Alleppey: Prakasam Publications, 1973), 6–7. According to John C. B. Webster, in his work *Historiography of Christianity in India* (Oxford: Oxford University Press, 2012), 83, these words are that of Placid J. Podipara quoted by Mundadan in *Indian Christian Search for Identity and Struggle for Autonomy* (Bangalore: Dharmaram Publications, 2003), 22.

22. Philip, *East of the Euphrates*, 128.

23. John C. England, *The Hidden History of Christianity in Asia: The Churches of the East before the Year 1500* (Delhi: ISPCK & CCA, 1996), 66.

Burma where Christian groups trace their origin to this endeavor.[24] There was communal harmony and a spirit of tolerance between the religious communities as the Indian Christians became rooted in local culture and shared a social life with their Hindu neighbors.[25]

The third piece of evidence is the similarities to Christianity found in the Hindu *bhakti* tradition in the literature of the later centuries.[26] Although there is no evidence of the direct influence of the Christian faith in the development of the *bhakti* movement in Hinduism—it is possible that the social interaction between Thomas Christians and their Hindu neighbors had an impact on Hinduism. The similarities and close resemblance to the Christian understanding of God in the *bhakti* movement of the *Dravidian bhaktas* in the South and later in the writings of Ramanuja (eleventh century) and Madhva (thirteenth century) suggest more. Although there are scholars who contend such an influence, Philip argues that Christian witness cannot be measured in conversion numbers but in how society was being impacted across generations. Later there seems to be a decline in missionary efforts as the caste stratification became rigid even as the Mughal rulers dominated the political landscape restricting the freedom of religious practices which had an effect even in places that were not directly under their rule. Although this discussion primarily focused on the Thomas Christians in the South, the presence of Christian communities through the Nestorian church's missionary efforts in the Northern geographical areas cannot be ignored. Evidence of stones marked with a cross has been found in several places across the western coast extending to Gujarat and Sind, the interior southern slopes of Nilgiris, and all the way north to Tankse in Kashmir and Leh.[27] The emergence of the *bhakti* tradition in different parts of India makes it a logical assumption that the small presence of Christians in the Northern Territory also had a significant influence on society except for the increased rigidity in the caste system and the long history of the Mughal empire. Many scholars attribute the caste consciousness of the Thomas Christians to preventing their advancement in mission, but a few disagree.[28]

The Thomas Christians from Kerala were not a closed community as for centuries they expanded because of their zeal through their cultural integration. They practiced the East-Syrian, Chaldean rites in their worship while holding

24. England, *The Hidden History of Christianity in Asia*, 66.

25. Philip, *East of the Euphrates*, 146.

26. Philip, *East of the Euphrates*, 128–129.

27. Perumalil and Hambye, *Christianity in India*, 32.

28. England, *The Hidden History of Christianity in Asia*, 66.

on to the apostolic legacy.[29] Religious processions and pilgrimages were popular and their devotion to church buildings were all opportunities for public witness. They had local priests called *Kathanar* who received basic training by *malpan* or teacher (and in some form of Christian monasticism) who were influenced by the East-Syrian churches. While some families in the Thomas Christian community took it upon themselves to add new members including those from the Nair community and nurture them, others traveled to the Far East and Central Asia.[30] All these glimpses suggest that there was some evidence of missionary activities by the early Thomas Christians even though it may not fit into our present-day understanding of missions.[31] We must consider the indigenous participation in God's mission to refute the narrative that attributes missionary activities only to the colonial era Western missionaries.[32]

The Indigenous Mission Movement during the Colonial Era

During the medieval period, the Thomas Christians had established a good reciprocal relationship with the Eastern Syrian Church. However, the first formal missionary effort of the West was the Latin church expansion project of Pope Innocent IV who followed Pope Gregory IX's idea in 1241 of sending the Cistercians, Dominicans, and Franciscans to preach against the invading Mongols threatening Christian Europe.[33] Soon the project spread to Persia and Asia where India became part of a strategic route to extend to China. It did not seem that India was the destination but rather the midpoint for the many papal emissaries who were traveling using the sea route to China as the land routes through the mountains were challenging.[34] It was in the thirteenth and fourteenth centuries that the Latin mission made its presence known in India. In the beginning, there was mutual respect between the Portuguese and the Thomas Christians as they fostered solidarity. However, the Thomas Christians' self-identification, communal consciousness, and desire for autonomy in ecclesiastical matters created tensions in their relationships.

Around the same timeline, the Western colonial expedition started with the visit of Vasco da Gama who landed in Calicut in 1498 primarily for trade but later leading to the sovereign rule of Goa on the West coast and other nearby

---

29. Perumalil and Hambye, *Christianity in India*, 36–37.

30. Perumalil and Hambye, *Christianity in India*, 37.

31. England, *The Hidden History of Christianity in Asia*, 66–67.

32. Robert, *Converting Colonialism*, 17.

33. Perumalil and Hambye, *Christianity in India*, 38–45.

34. Perumalil and Hambye, *Christianity in India*, 38–39.

islands. As the Portuguese established their colonial rule on the southwestern coast of India with Goa as their capital, it paved the way for a more formal Western colonial influence on the Christian missionary movement.[35] The *Padroado* that legitimized the Western mission efforts was the "means" through which the Christian faith was spread in India by the Portuguese. The first Jesuit who came to India was Francis Xavier who was instrumental in one of the earliest mass movements as he traveled to the fishery communities on the coast and baptized thousands of people.[36]

Before the visit of Xavier, these fishing communities had on their initiative taken baptisms to seek protection from colonial powers that were affecting their fishing livelihood.[37] This was followed by at least two or three instances of mass movements of baptisms among this community with the same motivation of seeking protection. Later after the arrival of the charismatic Francis Xavier, it was observed that there was a lack of adequate Christian teaching. Xavier set up a system of teaching the basic rudiments of the faith through Indian assistants who accompanied him on his travels which resulted in thousands of baptisms.[38] When Xavier left on his further travel, he appointed Indian catechists who became the leaders of the new believers continuing to grow to the extent that these fishing community maintained their Christian identity through several centuries even though they were from the lower rung of society. As much as Xavier needs to be credited for these mass movements, the fact that he did not speak the local language and relied on Indian assistants and catechists shows that the movement grew more indigenously than otherwise perceived. An interesting fact during this period is the internal migration of the new Indian believers especially from the coastal regions into the interior where new centers of Christians emerged and eventually came under Catholic care.[39] As history shows, migrants carry their faith seeking economic livelihood wherever they go influencing through their day-to-day witness.

As the Portuguese established their colonial rule on the western coast of India, the ecclesiastical relationship between the Thomas Christians and Portuguese Christians began to change. The Latinization of the ecclesiastical tradition undermined the Eastern Syrian tradition and loyalty to the Vatican was being actively sought. During this time, Muslim invaders began to colonize

---

35. Mundadan, *History of Christianity in India*, 1: 216.

36. R. E. Frykenberg, "India," in *A World History of Christianity, ed.* Adrian Hastings (Grand Rapids, MI: Eerdmans, 2000), 167–169.

37. Frykenberg, "India," 167.

38. Frykenberg, "India," 168.

39. Perumalil and Hambye, *Christianity in India*, 79.

the remaining parts of Northern and Central India. These colonial powers adversely affected religious freedom as the Muslim rule dominated Northern India and the Portuguese rule attempted to appropriate the Thomas Christians into the Vatican fold. The relationship between the Portuguese and the Thomas Christians became a tug-of-war.[40] The Portuguese thought that the Indian Christians were heretics and needed to be brought into the Catholic church and conform to the Latin way of worship, while the Thomas Christians thought that they were seeking the protection of powerful European brothers out of Christian solidarity and desired coexistence with autonomy in their Christian life and worship.[41]

It is important as we glimpse through the history of the church in India during the medieval times and the colonial period to look at how the Christian faith sustained itself and continued to spread. Firstly, the Thomas Christians strived hard to maintain their autonomy and their unique apostolic identity in a very hostile environment. Mundadan in a summary of nearly twenty centuries of Indian Christians divides the period into four epochs:[42]

1. The first fifteen centuries were the period of the growth of identity and autonomy.
2. The sixteenth to the seventeenth century was the period of interaction with the Portuguese Christians.
3. The seventeenth to nineteenth century was a period of struggle for identity, autonomy, and unity.
4. In the nineteenth to twentieth century, autonomy was restored but unity and identity was challenged.

This shows how the indigenous Indian Christian community weathered the changing political context to continue their existence while some of the churches in the East were almost wiped out by the Islamic invasion. Penelope Carson argues that the early Christian community chose to remain part of the existing social, cultural, and moral order of society as they integrated their faith which resulted in the fact that those who converted to Christianity were not alienated.[43] The challenges of colonial rule of the Muslims and the Portuguese led to sharper boundaries being created within the society based on religious affiliation

---

40. Perumalil and Hambye, *Christianity in India*, 85–87.

41. Perumalil and Hambye, *Christianity in India*, 87.

42. Mundadan, *History of Christianity in India*, 1: 491.

43. Penelope Carson, "Christianity, Colonialism, and Hinduism in Kerala," in Frykenberg and Low, *Christians and Missionaries in India*, 153.

and the demand for loyalty from the rulers. Most scholars focus on the ecclesiastical conflicts especially focusing on the Thomas Christians, who over several centuries challenged the patronage of the Portuguese and papal interference to remain autonomous, but the reality is that through these struggles, they continued to keep the indigenous flame of the gospel alive from generation to generation.

Continuity, Discontinuity, and the Indigenous Mission Movement

After the initial foray of Western colonization began with the *Padroado*, there was a consistent flow of missionaries with the explicit purpose of converting the native Indians. This period was fruitful from the perspective of the Western missionaries as they discovered the Thomas Christians and attempted to adopt them into their fold. Furthermore, the Thomas Christians in the South and other smaller migrant Christian communities scattered in other parts of India also confessed their solidarity with the Western Christians as they sought protection from hostile rulers.[44]

The continuity of mission during colonial rule shows that under the might of Western political and ecclesiastical domination, the indigenous mission had its unique way of being expressed. It was in the context of the *Padroado* that Robert de Nobili arrived in India and took a different focus to win the *Brahmans* for Christ by becoming a *Brahman* himself.[45] He was not alone in his mission as two Indians from the Thomas Christian community were his close colleagues and an Indian *guru* became his master to teach him the social way of life.[46] His interaction with master-teachers in the Hindu temple and interaction with other *Brahmans*, helped him to baptize several Indians amid opposition. In his five decades of work in the Madura mission, he laid the foundation for higher learning in the languages of India and those who followed him created volumes of epic poems, philosophical treatises, commentaries, dictionaries, grammar texts, translations, and apologetic tracts that speak out for the incarnational social life in the Indian cultural setting.[47] Even though most historians do not mention the role of the indigenous Christian community working alongside Robert de Nobili and other Jesuit missionaries, it can be inferred that this volume of literary work and the spread of the gospel in the region could not have been

---

44. Perumalil and Hambye, *Christianity in India*, 79.

45. Frykenberg, "India," 169.

46. Frykenberg, "India," 169.

47. Frykenberg, "India," 169–170.

accomplished without the critical support of the translators, teachers, cultural interlocutors, and above all, the believing disciples.

On the other side of this missionary endeavor in the southern and western regions, the Jesuits were also invited to the famous *durbar* during the reign of Akbar in the northern region where Sunnis, Shias, Buddhists, Brahmans, Jains, and Christians along with many others engaged in religious debates.[48] Although not much evidence is available as to how these debates impacted the common people's perception of the Christian faith, we can infer that these efforts indirectly kept the fragile indigenous Christian communities witnessing presence from being erased by an all-powerful Mughal empire in the northern parts of India.

As the Portuguese colonization waned, there were other colonial powers like the Danish and the French who occupied some territories until the British arrived. Until this time, the Jesuits and the Franciscan missionary movement had the greatest influence as they extended their ecclesiastical patronage to influence the indigenous Christian community to win their loyalty to the Western church while motivating them to reach out to other communities.

When the pietists came on the scene, with the arrival of Ziegenbalg and his friends, they followed a similar path as the Jesuits in learning the local languages and making contributions to the literary advancement but went further in focusing on translating the Bible as their main endeavor along with developing model schools to help with literacy with the support of the local royalty.[49] The missionaries believed that every indigenous Christian should be able to read the Scripture in their tongue. Soon Tamil speaking disciples were trained as catechists, pastors, and teachers and became the primary agents of the expanding mission movement.[50]

During the eighteenth century, the British Empire emerged to occupy almost the whole of the Indian subcontinent which opened the floodgates of mission work across the length and breadth of the country. The protestant mission created more conflicts and tensions with the colonial rulers and between the Catholics, Evangelicals, and indigenous Christians over conversions and contextualization.[51] During this period, a major influence in the South was that of Frederick Schwartz (1750–1798) who gained prominence as the preacher, schoolmaster, diplomat, negotiator, and statesman ending up as protector-regent of a Tamil King.[52] Schwartz's Indian disciples traveled

---

48. Frykenberg, "India," 172–173.

49. Frykenberg, "India," 172–173.

50. Frykenberg, "India," 174.

51. Frykenberg, "India," 182.

52. Frykenberg, "India," 176.

across the Tamil-speaking kingdoms of South India spreading the gospel. The fruit of these disciple-making efforts led to several prominent Tamil-speaking Christians leading the indigenous mission resulting in a mass movement where the now famous Tirunelveli Christians transformed villages, cultures, and society through the nineteenth century.[53] Daniel Jeyaraj narrating the participation of Indians in promoting the Christian mission in India mentions the pioneers Savarimuthu, Rayanayakkan, and Aaron who partnered with the Tranquebar mission in evangelizing, discipling, and pastoring the new believers.[54] They also played an important role in receiving royal patronage for the mission work. Jeyaraj summarizes that "the missionaries needed the Tamil Christians, and the Tamil Christians, in turn, needed the missionaries. . . . Together they accomplished many useful things."[55]

Heike Liebau discusses in detail the role of the group of South Indian Christians under the pioneering Tranquebar mission who were intermediaries between the foreign missionaries and the locals.[56] There were around five hundred Indians among whom were nine country priests and two hundred catechists, schoolteachers, and assistants. They were the social middlemen in the context of the Tranquebar mission who played a significant role in the growing mass movement of converts coming to faith. Liebau categorically states that European missionaries depended entirely on their local assistants who led the religious activities. Stephen Neil points out the first successful ordination of Indian catechists advocated by Welsh missionary John Thomas in South India during the nineteenth century that resulted "in a large number of missions of every conceivable ecclesiastical complexion the number of ordained nationals far exceeded the number of ordained foreigners."[57] These nameless "assistants" were key to the expansion of the mission movement.

Furthermore, the challenges of the British Raj during the nineteenth and twentieth centuries were characterized by social reforms, national

---

53. Frykenberg, "India," 177.

54. Daniel Jeyaraj, "Indian Participation in Enabling, Sustaining, and Promoting Christian Mission in India" in *India and the Indianness of Christianity: Essays on Understanding, Historical, Theological, and Bibliographical, in Honor of Robert Eric Frykenberg*, ed. Robert Eric Frykenberg and Richard Fox Young, Studies in the History of Christian Missions (Grand Rapids, MI: Eerdmans, 2009), 30–39.

55. Jeyaraj, "Indian Participation in Promoting Christian Mission in India," 40.

56. Heike Liebau, "Country Priests, Catechists, and Schoolmasters as Cultural, Religious, and Social Middlemen in the Context of the Tranquebar Mission" in Frykenberg and Low, *Christians and Missionaries in India*, 70–71.

57. Stephen Neill, *A History of Christian Missions*, 2nd ed., The Penguin History of the Church, ed. Owen Chadwick (London: Penguin Books, 1990), 219.

self-determination, and radical revolutionary changes.[58] It was also the time when the gospel was spreading across the country with increasing activities of the missionary and transformed peoples from the lower strata of society, and the emerging literate middle class. As the opposition to conversions of Indians dominated public opinion, the policy of the British government to missionary activity became unfriendly. Frykenberg writes that the East India Company Raj took the support of the Hindu elites to create imperial control by using them as bureaucrats and soldiers shaping modern Hinduism that was hostile to both Indian Christians and foreign missionaries making it unofficially a "Hindu Raj."[59] It was in this sociopolitical context, that the arrival of William Carey and his friends to Serampore (close to Calcutta the then capital of British India) made an important mark in the history of Indian missions. This multi-faceted mission that included bible translations, educational institutions, and social reform became the foundation on which indigenous Christianity was given cultural affirmation and identity. During this "great century of missions" the vernacular Bible translations into hundreds of languages came into reality and involved the participation of indigenous workers.[60] The pioneering work of William Carey who had initiated projects in Bengali, Sanskrit, Hindi, Oriya, and Marathi among fifteen other languages stands out as he was assisted by many natives. These and other missionary projects were launched primarily because Carey innovated "the means" of voluntary societies to achieve specific goals.[61] It is important to note that all these evangelical projects required translators, teachers, and assistants from the existing Indian Christian community and even from non-Christian communities which made it largely an indigenous movement.

One of the major milestones during the nineteenth century is the emergence of the role of women in missions. The formal schools that were established in the early part of the eighteenth century by Alexander Duff and others focused on the education of boys while the social bias against girls' education seemed insurmountable. Missionaries innovated that women can also be sent as missionaries resulting in women teachers sent from England to start schools for girls in Calcutta.[62] The expectation that Indian girls would come to schools failed and

58. Frykenberg, "India," 179–180.

59. Frykenberg, "India," 180.

60. Timothy C. Tennent, *Invitation to World Missions: A Trinitarian Missiology for the Twenty-First Century* (Grand Rapids, MI: Kregel Publications, 2010), 266–267.

61. Tennent, *Invitation to World Missions*, 260–263.

62. Binᵃya Bhūshanᵃ Rāya and Pranati Ray, *Zenana Mission: The Role of Christian Missionaries for the Education of Women in 19th Century Bengal* (Delhi: Indian Society for Promoting Christian Knowledge, 1998), 1–3.

the missionaries changed their strategy to take education into homes where the girls were living.[63] This came to be known as the *Zenana* education movement which became a necessity of the times. Single women missionaries began visiting the secluded apartments of Indian women households among the high-caste Hindu and Muslim families. Since foreign missionaries faced language barriers, teacher training institutions were founded to train Indian women as Zenana teachers who became known as "Bible Women." Roberts estimates that "indigenous Christians working as evangelists, catechists and 'Bible women' typically outnumbered the foreign missionaries and were essential to the spread of the Christian message."[64] For example, in 1900, the *Bible Medical and Missionary Fellowship* reported 154 European missionaries, 197 Indian teachers, and 92 Bible women on their roll.[65]

Another milestone in the indigenous mission movement during the colonial period relates to the northeast region. The hill tribes of Northeast India had a unique experience as Frykenberg suggested that they were neither *Sanskritized* nor *Islamicized* which is only partially correct as history shows that the Assamese, parts of Tripura, and Manipur had been *sankritized*.[66] The others like the Khasis, Garos, Nagas, Kukis, and the Mizos whose animistic "worldviews have been Christianized to such an extent that most of them have closely related Christianity with their sense of ethnic identity."[67] Recounting the history of the gospel movement into the northeast, we must note that the initial efforts by the Serampore mission and other Baptist missionaries in the region of Assam were not hugely successful. It was two young Garo cousin brothers who ventured out of their tribal life for their education and while working encountered the gospel through a tract leading to their baptism in 1863.[68] They eventually became pioneer missionaries in their tribal village and found success in founding the first Garo church. Then the gospel spread to the Khasis who were also very mission minded and soon a Khasi convert went to Mizoram just as an Assamese convert went to the Ao Naga tribe and lived among them and created a chain reaction as the Ao Christians went to other tribes.[69] A similar chain reaction can be traced

---

63. Dana Lee Robert, *Christian Mission: How Christianity Became a World Religion* (Malden, MA: Wiley Blackwell, 2010), 127.

64. Robert, *Christian Mission*, 49.

65. *International Service Fellowship*, Archival Collections, London.

66. Hastings, *A World History of Christianity*, 182.

67. Pachuau, *Indian and Christian*, 159–160.

68. Pachuau, *Indian and Christian*, 164–165.

69. Pachuau, *Indian and Christian*, 166–167.

with all the tribes in the region who have now become Christians. Pachuau summarizes this movement by saying that while the Western missionaries introduced the gospel to a few individuals through education, it was the native converts who often pioneered into new territories as "native assistants" in spreading the success of the missionary movement.[70]

The mass movement of Indians from the lower social strata of society now called "Dalits" was a quest in seeking a new identity. These mass movements from the Dalit communities began during the nineteenth century which gave them a new dignity and status against the power of dominant castes, political majorities, the elite, and the rulers of the day.[71] The seminal work of Waskom Pickett on the mass movements in India shows how the indigenous agency of the Indians advanced the mission movement with case studies from five different regions of India that included Telugu, Tamil, Hindi, Urdu, and Punjabi-speaking people.[72] This sociological research project inspired Donald McGavran to propose the homogenous unit principle to argue that church growth was primarily among units, or groups of people who shared racial, cultural, and linguistic similarities linking homogeneity to context.[73] Both these works led to diverse opinions on the process and motives of conversions within the missional community. During the same time, Gandhi led the nationalists who opposed conversions attributing them to misplaced motives. Webster, building on Pickett's work, comments that this mass movement among the lower strata of society gave the Indian Christian community a new identity as "Dalit" Christians since they now form the majority in the existing Christian population.[74]

The indigenous mission movement gained a significant innovation in contextualization that reflected the Indian spirituality of indigenous Christians in the form of the *Ashram* movement.[75] While the Marathi Poet Narayan Vaman Tilak founded an *Ashram* in Satara, in the western part of India, the Marthoma church coming out of a revival movement ventured into founding *Ashrams* "as a means" to spread the gospel. *Christukula Ashram* founded by two doctors, an Indian and

---

70. Pachuau, *Indian and Christian*, 175.

71. Webster, *Historiography of Christianity in India*, 88–89.

72. J. Waskom Pickett, *Christian Mass Movements in India: A Study with Recommendations*, 2nd Indian ed. (Hazratganj, Lucknow, India: Lucknow Publishing House, 1933), 13.

73. Donald A. McGavran, *Understanding Church Growth*, 3rd ed., ed. C. Peter Wagner (Grand Rapids, MI: Eerdmans, 1990), 223.

74. Webster, *Historiography of Christianity in India*, 91.

75. G. P. V. Somaratna, "Ashram Movement" in *A Dictionary of Asian Christianity*, ed. Scott Sunquist, John Hiang Chea Chew, and David Chusing Wu (Grand Rapids, MI: Eerdmans, 2001), 43–44.

a Scot, at Tirappattur and the *Vidivelli Ashram* founded by two women who were former college professors in South India was inspired by the life and ministry of Sadhu Sundar Singh.[76] Others suggest that this was a response to the Western expression of Christianity and followed similar *Ashrams* founded by the Hindu reformist K. C. Sen, poet Tagore, and Gandhi.[77] Stanley Jones's *ashram* in the Himalayas in North India founded along with two others, an Indian and a Brit, focused on Christian spiritual reflection, worship, and inter-religious dialogue is well known globally.[78] Jones later founded the International Christian Ashram Movement to bring together all those who were involved in similar movements. The Ashram movement reflected the ongoing efforts in indigenizing influenced by the nationalist movement, but it also shows the longing for indigenous participation in the expansion of the Christian mission movement.[79]

The first indigenous mission society in India was the Marthoma Evangelistic Association founded in 1888 establishing Christian ashrams and sending out workers across cultures showcasing the determination of Indian mission leaders.[80] Soon thereafter in the first decade of the twentieth century, the Indian Missionary Society and an inter-denominational mission agency National Missionary Society were established under the leadership of V. S. Azariah in 1903 and 1905. The vision was to share the gospel with other Indians with the principles of "Indian men, Indian money, and Indian management and an area of work where no other missionary society was working."[81] Pandita Ramabai's pioneering work in Mumbai where she founded a destitute home for women which later evolved into the founding of Mukti Mission Society near Pune in the year 1889 must find its place in the mission history narrative that bears witness to the holistic mission role of women in the indigenous movement preceding the initiatives of the Marthomites and Azariah.[82]

---

76. Neill, *A History of Christian Missions*, 441–442.

77. Sunquist, Chew, and Wu, *A Dictionary of Asian Christianity*, 43–44.

78. Anne Mathews-Younes, ed., *A History of the Sat Tal Christian Ashram*, 1st Indian ed. (Lucknow, India: Lucknow Publishing House, 2018), 75–76.

79. Pachuau, *Indian and Christian*, 71.

80. K. Rajendran, *Which Way Forward Indian Missions? A Critique of Twenty-Five Years, 1972–1997* (Bangalore, India: SAIACS Press, 1998), 55.

81. Peter S. C. Pothan, "Indian Missionary Society of Tirunelveli" in *The Oxford Encyclopedia of South Asian Christianity,* ed. Roger E. Hedlund et al. (New Delhi: Oxford University Press, 2012), 333.

82. Robert Eric Frykenberg, "Pandita Ramabai Saraswati: A Biographical Introduction," in *Pandita Ramabai's America: Conditions of Life in the United States* (Grand Rapids, MI: Eerdmans, 2003), 31–32. Pandita Ramabai raised funds from England and the United States

The Indian missions movement cannot be confined only to the founding of institutions but also involves theological reflections by indigenous thinkers. Pachuau asserts that "India has one of the longest continuing histories of theological engagement" and discusses how the indigenization of Christianity identified with the evolving national independence movement.[83] He points out that during the early years of theological reflections reformed Hindus engaged in Christological reflections followed by Christian nationalist thinkers like Brahmabandhab Upadhaya.[84] Later A. J. Appasamy attempted to use the mystical dimension of Hinduism to make the Christian message meaningful to Hindus and this path was followed by a group of theologians calling themselves the "Rethinking Group". The mainstream protestant and catholic theologians followed in further reflections to express the core Christian doctrines in Indian cultural and religious terms often creating more controversies than consensus. Since the independence of India, the theological themes that emerged chronicled among others "Christian encounters with Other Faiths" and "Christian Participation in Nation Building" led by Paul Devanandan and M. M. Thomas which had a global influence through the WCC.[85]

The ecumenical movement in India was an indigenous effort led by V. S. Azariah whose missionary zeal was evident not just in leading the mass movements of converts coming from lower strata of society in Dornakal (and shepherding them) but also in giving voice to the unity efforts to create an ecclesiastical structure that can be truly identified Indian.[86] Azariah's famous cry "Give us Friends" at the Edinburgh conference in 1910, echoed the sentiments of the indigenous mission workers serving alongside the Western missionary enterprise.[87] Azariah's several decades of consultations resulted in the formation of the Church of South India consisting of Anglicans, Methodists, Presbyterians, Congregationalists, and Baptists as an organic union in 1947. Later, similar consultations led to the formation of the Church of North India in 1970. Although some of the existing churches continued to maintain their relationships with

---

to support her destitute work which may be one of the reasons for some scholars not crediting her mission as part of indigenous mission.

83. Pachuau, *Indian and Christian*, 67–69.

84. Pachuau, *Indian and Christian*, 68.

85. Pachuau, *Indian and Christian*, 74–75.

86. John Amalraj, "Learnings from the Missional Church in India" in *A Learning Missonal Church: Reflections from Young Missiologists*, ed. Beate Fagerli, Regnum Edinburgh Centenary Series (Oxford: Regnum, 2012), 69–70.

87. J. Z. Hodge, *Bishop Azariah of Dornakal* (Madras: The Christian Literature Society of India, 1946), 4–6.

their parent denominations, the leadership became indigenous. This ecumenical union became a missional expression of witnessing to the newly independent India.

In the postindependence era, Indians assumed the leadership of institutions established by Western missionaries while others pioneered new mission agencies and institutions both within the existing denominational churches and independent of those denominational structures. It was in the late twentieth century during the seventies and eighties that there was an explosion of indigenous missions resulting in many voluntary mission societies being established that brought the world's attention to the growth of indigenous missions in India.

Indigenous Mission Movement— Contemporary Scenario and Challenges

The Indian missionary movement made a transition from being dominated by denominational societies during the colonial era to indigenous inter-denominational and independent mission societies and churches during the late twentieth century. These movements initially focused on birthing new congregations across the nation through traditional and creative mission strategies characterized by mass movements of Dalits and tribal conversions that spurred the freedom of religion debates intensely during the postcolonial era. This indigenous movement pioneered institutions in primary and higher education and health sectors, caregiving ministries in the form of orphanages and rehabilitation institutions, relief and development agencies, and sociocultural development efforts through literacy and translation projects contributing to nation-building.

The charismatic influence of Sadhu Sundar Singh who lived during the early twentieth century as a mystic declining to identify himself with the foreign missionary denominations is often underestimated. He did not leave behind disciples or build institutions but he did preach and witness to the masses. This has led to continuing debates about the thousands of followers of Christ who chose to remain "unbaptized," a movement scholars have labeled "churchless Christianity". Herbert Hoefer, the author of the book *Churchless Christianity*, has researched this phenomenon to determine if most Indians will join the existing Western-structured church and concludes that this is incompatible with the national culture.[88] Finally, Vinod John, based on empirical data gathered from interviewing Christbhaktas in the holy city of Varanasi, portrays an indigenous movement of followers of Christ which seems to offer an alternative

---

88. Herbert Hoefer, "Follow-up Reflections on Churchless Christianity," *Mission Frontiers*, March-April 1999, accessed April 26, 2024, https://www.missionfrontiers.org/issue/article/follow-up-reflections-on-churchless-christianity.

framework for understanding ecclesiology in a hostile environment.[89] He argues that negotiating the identities of believers from Hindu backgrounds without the extraction and assimilation model and engaging them in their cultural context will blunt the polarizing political discourse in India.

The present church and mission scenario is complex and diverse with traditional and denominational structures in the Western models while newer indigenous models are emerging as independent and networked within the Pentecostal and charismatic streams. There is a huge difference between the growing churches in urban centers partly due to internal migration and growing churches in rural and tribal areas due to indigenous missions.[90] These are all the fruit of cross-cultural indigenous missionary movements in the early centuries before the colonial era, during the colonial times, and postindependence Indian history. Ken Gnanakan points out that it is only when the Church's being and becoming are held together that the totality of the Church is manifested as the people in worship reflecting the nature of the people of God and being involved in the mission as its outflow.[91] The indigenous innovation in church planting was influenced by a spirit of nationalism where it was believed that the Indian mission movement was primarily the responsibility of Indian Christians. However, over the years, the influence of the Western church and in more recent times from countries like South Korea and Nigeria for example cannot be overlooked.

Many spiritual renewal movements starting from the late nineteenth century in South India and in the early twentieth century in North-East India continue to motivate the indigenous mission movement.[92] The Northeast region has witnessed during the nineteenth and twentieth centuries the greatest transformation of the contemporary sociocultural environment among the Mizos, Nagas, Garo, and others leading to a vibrant indigenous mission movement.[93] In the northern region, the visible growth of the church has been comparatively hidden due to the hostile environment and religious discrimination but there have been revivals

---

89. Vinod John, *Believing without Belonging? Religious Beliefs and Social Belonging of Hindu Devotees of Christ*, (Eugene, OR: Pickwick Publications, 2020).

90. Daniel Jeyaraj, "South India," in *Christianity in South and Central Asia*, ed. Kenneth R. Ross, Daniel Jeyaraj, and Todd M. Johnson. *Edinburgh Companion to Global Christianity* (Edinburgh: Edinburgh University Press, 2019), 145–146.

91. Ken Gnanakan, "The Church: Its Mission and Theological Education," *TBT Journal*, 1, no. 1 (1999): 20.

92. Pachuau, *World Christianity*, 161.

93. Kaholi Zhimomi, "Northeast India" in Ross, Jeyaraj, and Johnson, *Christianity in South and Central Asia*, 164–167.

and mass movements among the tribals and the Dalits.[94] A cover story in one of
the leading news magazines describes the indigenous charismatic influence of the
contemporary church in Punjab and illustrates the impact of missions.[95] In the
western region, the sustained mission work over many centuries has borne fruit
amid the apathy and antagonism against tribal and Dalit converts, such that the
indigenous expression of Christian spirituality is noteworthy.[96]

The growth of the Pentecostal and charismatic churches in the late twentieth century continuing into the twenty-first century is another fruit of the
cross-cultural indigenous mission movement which has given birth to new church
denominations and thousands of house churches in rural and urban centers. In the
Indian context, the religiosity of the masses, poverty-stricken living conditions,
and existential tensions between tradition and change acted as a framework for
the emergence of charismatic and Pentecostal Christianity and their involvement
in mission work.[97] The *Yesu Darbar* movement in Allahabad in a Christian university campus that spontaneously attracted thousands of rural people from the
surrounding villages for healing ministry resulted in major outreach in the region.[98]

Rajendran, an Indian missiologist and the then leader of the India Missions
Association claimed that "India is the foremost among Two-Thirds World
missionary-sending countries."[99] This indigenous mission movement is represented
by the India Missions Association with a membership of more than 290 mission
societies, denominational mission bodies, missionary training institutions, and
development agencies that networks hundreds of thousands of cross-cultural mission workers, pastors, and social workers. Rajendran in his doctoral work critiqued
the Indian mission movement in the last three decades of the twentieth century
(1972–1997). He pointed out the challenges of the nation in transition, the Indian
missions' neglect of urbanization, and a few leadership issues, and ended by calling
for a comprehensive vision for the indigenous movement.[100] Pachuau points out

---

94. Leonard Fernando, "North India" in Ross, Jeyaraj, and Johnson, *Christianity in South and Central Asia*, 129–130.

95. Anilesh S. Mahajan and Sunil Menon, "The Pastors of Punjab," *India Today*, November 14, 2022.

96. Atul Y Aghamkar, "West India" in Ross, Jeyaraj, and Johnson, *Christianity in South and Central Asia*, 136–142.

97. Pachuau, *World Christianity*, 111.

98. Leonard Fernando, "North India" in Ross, Jeyaraj, and Johnson, *Christianity in South and Central Asia*, 124–125.

99. Rajendran K., "The Emergence and Expansion of Indian Mission Movement from 1947–2009: A Study into the Successes and Failures," in *Mission History of Asian Churches*, ed. Timothy Kiho Park (Pasadena, CA: William Carey Library, 2011), 45.

100. Rajendran, *Which Way Forward Indian Missions?*

that expanding mission movement in the last decades of the twentieth century was also the period when the Indian Dalit ("subaltern") theology emerged from the margins.[101]

Ebenezer Sunderraj in his analysis of the strengths and weaknesses of Churches and missions, says that the strength and contribution of Indian missions is in planting churches in new areas, among new cultures, languages, and people groups.[102] However, neighborhood evangelism is predominately accomplished by evangelical charismatic churches and denominations. A major characteristic of the indigenous mission movement is its adaptation to the holistic expression of mission in all its dimensions. This is a legacy from the Western missionary movement that built educational, health care, and community developmental institutions across the country even before the missiologists came out with the concept of holistic mission. This has been imitated by the indigenous movements and has helped them to continue to contribute to nation-building.

Answering the question, "What does it mean to be Indian and Christian?" Paul Joshua points to how Christianity was being remade in India through the Indian-initiated churches where the popular piety and the gospel interact among the subaltern perspective and vision from the margins.[103] Joshua provides a case study of six movements spanning India's rural and urban contexts during the twentieth century: Christian Pettah Village, The Indian Pentecostal Church of God, Bakht Singh Assemblies, India Bible Mission, Yesu Darbar, and New Life Fellowship. He suggests that the polycentric nature of missions and the changing center of gravity from historical denominational churches to contemporary forms finds its roots in the indigenous movement.[104]

The indigenous movement in the contemporary scenario is not just confined to India or the traditional missional structures. The marketplace mission and the diaspora mission have led the indigenous mission to grow beyond the borders of India and become global. Hundreds of Indians have moved cross-culturally into neighboring countries like Nepal, Bhutan, Bangladesh, Sri Lanka, Myanmar, and other Southeast Asia nations. The diaspora Indians using the migration route and the opportunities of globalization have gone beyond the Gulf regions, Central Asia, South America, some African countries, and China.[105]

---

101. Pachuau, *World Christianity*, 100–101.

102. Ebenezer Sunder Raj, "Evangelism in India Today," *Second National Consultation*, 8.

103. Paul Joshua, *Christianity Remade: The Rise of Indian-Initiated Churches*, ed. Joel A. Carpenter. Studies in World Christianity (Waco, TX: Baylor University Press, 2022), 17, 189,

104. Joshua, *Christianity Remade*, 189–200.

105. Sam George, ed., *Desi Diaspora: Ministry among Scattered Global Indian Christians* (Bengaluru: SAIACS Press, 2019), 202.

The main challenge of the contemporary scenario is the sociopolitical Hindu nationalism that has created a hostile environment attempting to put an end to conversions and restrict the freedom of religion. This has led the Indian government to increase surveillance on all Christian mission societies, social development agencies, and churches and create mandatory legal compliances that have challenged the society's institutional model of mission. Increased harassment of new converts and persecution of tribal and Dalit Christians have made the church in India find creative ways of continuing its ministry as the doors for the spread of the gospel seem to be closing.

Conclusion

The indigenous mission movement in India from the first century to the contemporary era cannot be attributed only to the human agency whether it is the foreign missionaries or indigenous Christians but to the Triune God who is both the source and owner of the mission. It is God's mission, and we are all called to be partners with Him. As Lesslie Newbigin insists, "any preaching of the Gospel must presuppose an understanding of the triune nature of God" which implies that mission is bigger than the visible church institution, it cannot be confined to the life of the church community, and it cannot be reduced to statistics on conversions and church membership.[106]

This chapter has attempted to explore the indigenous mission efforts of the first-century Thomas Christians. In the following centuries as the colonial powers became influential, we discovered how the indigenous communities continued to play a vital role in the mission movement. Finally, in the postindependence and contemporary era, we briefly glanced through how the indigenous Pentecostal and charismatic movement grew and expanded.[107]

To summarize, the indigenous Christian community from the first century survived by contextualizing their newfound faith within the existing communities to create an identity for themselves often facing a hostile environment. The Eastern churches in their mission work in India shared their theology and liturgy while the Western church focused on Bible translation, literacy and health care, and social reforms that became the launching pad for the indigenous mission movement to become a global movement.

---

106. Lesslie Newbigin, *The Open Secret: An Introduction to the Theology of Mission*, rev. ed. (Grand Rapids, MI: Eerdmans, 1995), 12.

107. Pachuau, *World Christianity*, 161–162.

All these overlapping human networks that include Indians and the global church are here to stay amid political challenges to continue their missions of spreading the message of Jesus Christ as part of the mission of the triune God.[108] In today's global movement of people and ideas, it is the local church community that encourages every believer to share their faith with others using human connections and create a multi-cultural community that worships Jesus as Lord.

---

108. Robert, *Christian Mission*, 176–77.

Part II

Theological Dimensions

CHAPTER SIX

Contextual Theology as Metatheology

A Methodological Inquiry of Selected Indian Contextual Theologies

Sochanngam Shirik

Introduction

I PROPOSE THAT considering contextual theology as metatheology provides a helpful pathway toward reconciling the canonical and catholic principles inherent in theology. Metatheology, as I understand it, is not an attempt to formulate a universal theology for all contexts but a way of thinking about theology that could benefit all contexts. It is a process of theologizing that upholds Scripture as the epistemological foundation, adopts synergistic-developmental hermeneutics, and pursues participation in the divine metanarrative as the theological telos. This theological approach gives space to Scripture's claims and trajectories, allowing it to function as the regulatory epistemological, hermeneutical, and theological principle while at the same time allocating human experiences their due space. To demonstrate the validity of metatheology, as I propose here, I first briefly discuss the nature of contextual theology. Then, I identify three fundamental features underlying contextual theology: epistemological, hermeneutical, and theological triggers.[1] Investigating these three areas opens a window into contextual theology's foundation, method, and telos. While a full-fledged development of metatheology is not possible in this chapter, I briefly show how these three elements are essential drivers of theology and should be taken together to develop contextual theologies.

To better appreciate contextual theology and illustrate these three triggers as the underlying factors, the present study investigates three major Indian contextual theologies as representatives of the broader world of contextual theologies and their foundation, method, and telos. The study focuses specifically on the epistemology of Indian tribal theology, the biblical hermeneutics of Indian

---

1. The relationship of these three elements as they relate to contextualizing the gospel has been cursorily explored in Douglas W. Kennard, ed. *The Relationship between Epistemology, Hermeneutics, Biblical Theology and Contextualization: Understanding Truth* (Lewiston: Edwin Mellen, 1999). The book, which is a collection of articles on each of the title's components, however, does not pursue, except for Kennard's chapter, the symbiotic relationships of the subfields.

postcolonialism, and the decentering of the center of Dalit theology. Lastly, using the previous three categories as anchoring points, I briefly highlight my proposal of metatheology suggesting that this approach does not argue for Scripture to occupy sequential priority but an authoritative foundation; it does not advocate methodological categorial exclusivity but logical subordination to the scriptural category; and it does not pursue exclusively or even primarily otherworldly concerns but the participation in the divine metanarrative by upholding the New Creation ethos as the telos of theology.

What Is Contextual Theology?

The rise of world Christianity coincided with a theological paradigm shift wherein all theologies are consciously recognized as contextual theologies.[2] In this era of world Christianity, the focus has shifted from the contextualization of Christian theology to theologizing in context. While the former emphasizes the meaningful communication of the gospel, the latter accentuates the construction of theology from the local perspective by paying careful attention to the sociopolitical conditions.[3] In this practice of theologizing in context, people's existential experiences become essential interpretive data.[4] However, as the Nigerian theologian Victor Ifeanyi Ezigbo rightly observes, for many it is not clear what contextual theology is exactly: Is it a new field of study and, if so, is it a sustainable theological field?[5] How is contextual theology different from other forms of theologizing? The title of an article precisely captures this dilemma: "What's 'Contextual' and What's 'Theological' about Contextual Theology"?[6]

Used in a prescriptive manner, there is a certain universality (or trans-contextuality) about contextual theology that transcends specific local contexts. While the present context is the immediate and indispensable

---

2. Po Ho Huang, "Revisiting the Methodology of Contextual Theology in the Era of Globalization," in *Wrestling with God in Context*, ed. M. P. Joseph, Po Ho Huang, and Victor Hsu (Minneapolis: Fortress Press, 2018), 24.

3. Lalsangkima Pachuau, *World Christianity: A Historical and Theological Introduction* (Nashville: Abingdon Press, 2018), 94.

4. Justin Ukpong, "Inculturation Hermeneutics: An African Approach to Biblical Interpretation," in *The Bible in World Context: An Experiment in Contextual Hermeneutics*, ed. Walter Dietrich & Ulrich Luz (Grand Rapids, MI: Eerdmans, 2002), 18–22.

5. Victor Ifeanyi Ezigbo, "Contextual Theology: God in Human Context," in *Evangelical Theological Method: Five Views*, ed. Stanley E. Porter and Steven M. Studebaker (Downers Groves, IL: IVP Academic, 2018), 94.

6. Geoff Thompson, "What's 'Contextual' and What's 'Theological' about Contextual Theology? A Question from an Australian Theologian," *CTC Bulletin*, 23 (2007): 94.

theological interlocutor, the proposal to do theology in a particular manner is in itself a universal call, as Geoff Thompson observed.[7] In other words, it is as theological as it is contextual. Marc Cortez differentiates between "intra-contextual" and "trans-contextual theology," with the former focusing on the concerns and ideas of a specific context and the latter "on relating the theological perspectives of its context to those originating from other contexts."[8] Both Thompson and Cortez emphasize that the particular and universal aspects must be simultaneously considered in developing any models and theories of contextual theology. The Indian missiologist and theologian Lalsangkima Pachuau maintains that although "theology can be done in a very particular context as well as in a more general context," the former is not necessarily authenticated by eliminating the latter, and vice versa, for "context is always multilayered."[9] Drawing from Daniel Hardy and agreeing with Pachuau's view on the interweaving nature of context,[10] the Australian theologian Christian Mostert argues for the possibility and necessity of doing general and universal theology without neglecting context-specific theology.[11]

Whereas theologians and missiologists together affirm the contextual nature of all theologies and simultaneously recognize the need for a trans-contextual connection, developing a methodological framework that upholds the universal and particular elements inherent in theology is still needed. Some have proposed that the present experience has a certain priority over the past (Scripture and tradition) in the sense that it is what ultimately validates the experience of the past.[12] Others disagree.[13] Ezigbo's elucidation is helpful but raises more questions.

---

7. Thompson, "What's 'Contextual' and What's 'Theological' about Contextual Theology?" 96.

8. Marc Cortez, "Creation and Context: A Theological Framework for Contextual Theology," *Westminster Theological Journal* 67, no. 2 (2005): 360.

9. Lalsangkima Pachuau, *God at Work in the World: Theology and Mission in the Global Church* (Grand Rapids: Baker Academic, 2022), 15.

10. Daniel W. Hardy, "The Spirit of God in Creation and Reconciliation," in *Christ and Context: The Confrontation between Gospel and Culture*, ed. Hilary D. Regan and Alan J. Torrance (London: Bloomsbury Academic, 1993), 237–238.

11. Christian Mostert, "Is a Non-Contextual Theology Viable?" in *Mapping the Landscape: Festschrift in Honor of Professor Ian Breward. Essays in Australian and New Zealand Christianity* (New York: Peter Lang, 2000), 118–122.

12. Stephen B. Bevans, *Essays in Contextual Theology, Theology and Mission in World Christianity* (Boston: Brill, 2018), 1–2.

13. For instance, the Nigerian theologian Byang H. Kato argued, "Evangelical Christians know of only one theology—Biblical theology as opposed to many contextual theologies—though it may be expressed in the context of each cultural milieu." Kato, *Biblical Christianity in Africa* (Achimota, Ghana: African Christian Pr, 1985), 12.

He contends that no hierarchy is to be attributed to the sources of theology such as Scripture, tradition, reason, and human context.[14] Instead, the relationship between these sources is to be seen in terms of how each occupies specific functions, rather than in the order of hierarchical importance.[15] As promising (and provocative) as Ezigbo's proposal is,[16] and as influential as contextual theology has become, a focused methodological examination of the subject that upholds the authoritative foundation of Scripture while giving context ("context" here includes one's experience, social, historical, and geographical location) its due place is still needed. This chapter investigates a way of theologizing that pays attention to the universalizing and particularizing elements inherent in the fabric of Christian theology. It is a proposal to consider in a particular way the foundation, method, and telos of theology.

Contextual Theology in India
Epistemological, Hermeneutical, and Theological Triggers of Contextual Theology

Tribal theology (henceforth TT) draws deeply from tribal epistemology of life, whereas Indian postcolonial hermeneutics accentuates the hermeneutics of suspicion by positing an alternative reading, and Dalit theology pursues a more inclusive approach by decentering the theological inclination of the dominant theology. While all these three show similar orientations in drawing from the lived reality, resisting the universalistic impulse in the dominant hermeneutical approach, and postulating more inclusive theological directions, each brings out one overlooked aspect more noticeably. Investigating these topics will yield a clearer understanding of the foundation, methods, and telos of contextual theology.

Tribal Theology's Epistemology
The Epistemological Foundation of Contextual Theology

"Tribal theology" can be defined as an indigenous theology that draws its primary resources from the tribal worldview, Christian tradition, and Scripture. The word "tribal" is here used descriptively without any pejorative judgment. While India's TT is not confined to the northeast region of India, in this chapter, the primary engagement is with selective proponents from that region. By "tribal

---

14. Ezigbo, "Contextual Theology," 99.

15. Victor I. Ezigbo, *The Art of Contextual Theology: Doing Theology in the Era of World Christianity* (Eugene, OR: Cascade Books, 2021), 23.

16. One can notice echoes of David Kelsey's view—whom Ezigbo also agreeably cites—that Scripture possesses functional authority as opposed to intrinsic authority.

worldview," I mean the fundamental *commitment* and *orientation* of the tribal people through which they interpret reality. This simplified definition agrees with James H. Olthuis's perceptive observation that "faith" and "historical conditioning" are two important components of a worldview.[17] As Olthuis argues one's search for meaning and purpose in life, organization of values, and relationship to God or pseudo-god "elude our intellectual grasp and strict logical proof" demanding faith rather than a mere rational inquiry. Yet, these faith commitments are shaped by experiences that take place within a particular historical and cultural context.[18] Tribal worldview as a commitment to certain beliefs and practices within a particular historical and cultural context in combination with the Scripture provides the raw data for TT.

While there are diverse voices within TT,[19] one overarching theme is the emphasis on the centrality of the tribal worldview in constructing Christian theology. Whereas theologians differ on what is central to the tribal worldview, they agree that the tribal worldview occupies an essential interpretive and constructive component of tribal Christian theology. Whether it is the emphasis on land or creation as the controlling force of theology as has repeatedly accentuated;[20] or the tribal experience of alienation and community life as the driving factor of hermeneutics as noted by some;[21] or the amalgamation of the various indigenous beliefs and practices as a fundamental interpretive lens, as has been recently argued;[22] the underlying presupposition is that speaking of an unqualified Christian worldview as such but only a context-specific

---

17. James H. Olthuis, "On Worldview," in *Stained Glass: Worldviews and Social Science,* ed. Paul A. Marshall, Sander Griffioen, and Richard J. Mouw (Lanham, MD: University Press of America, 1989), 30–35.

18. Olthuis, "On Worldview," 31–32.

19. For an analysis on some of these issues, see Sochanngam Shirik, "Evangelical Contextual Theology in Northeast India and the Origin and Development of Tribal Theology: A Conversation," *Asia Journal of Theology,* 32, no. 2, (2018): 50–74.

20. To start with, see Wati Longchar, "Tribal Theology: Issues, Method and Perspective," in *In Search of Identity and Tribal Theology: A Tribute to Dr. Renthy Keitzar,* Tribal Study Series: 9, ed. A. Wati Longchar (Jorhat: Tribal Study Centre, 2001), 48–54. Due to Longchar's unrelenting emphasis on the significance of land as the essential hermeneutical key, his theological methodology has been described as a "theology of creation." Bendangjungshi, *Confessing Christ in the Naga Context: Towards a Liberating Ecclesiology,* ContactZone: Explorations in Intercultural Theology: 8 (London: Global Distributor, 2011), 177.

21. K. Thanzauva, *Theology of Community: Tribal Theology in the Making* (Aizawl: Research & Development of AIC, 2004),115–169.

22. Yangkahao Vashum, *Christology in Context: A Tribal-Indigenous Appraisal of North East India.* Christian Heritage Rediscovered–49 (New Delhi: Christian World Imprints, 2017), 111–130.

Christian worldview. The implication is that an authentic contextual theology will emerge only in consideration and incorporation of tribal memory, resources, and experiences.

There are at least two interrelated emphases of TT's epistemology: the dissolution of the sharp transcendence-immanence distinction of God and the conflation of the epistemology of God as Creator and the epistemology of God as Redeemer. Tribal theologians maintain the interconnectivity of the creation and Creator and reject the sharp Creator-creation separation.[23] Proponents are not necessarily eradicating all Creator-creation distinctions but challenging the polarization that they see in some Western epistemic approaches. On the one hand, they are pushing back on a highly anthropocentric theology that sees the God-creation relationship in terms of hierarchy with creation at the bottom. On the other hand, they are also resisting the strict demarcation of God's transcendence and immanence. For them, God is not known through mere reflection but is encountered in the daily affairs of life within one's created space. Since the Creator can be known and encountered only through the medium of creation, the two cannot be sharply separated.

The second characteristic of TT epistemology is an extension of the first: the conflation of the epistemology of God as Creator and God as Redeemer. Given the belief that the relationships between God, humans, and creation are closely connected, tribal theologians consider the whole tribal community as an integral part of the Creator-creation community.[24] This means, among other things, that all tribal people are believed to have a unique relationship with their Creator. Such an intimate relationship is possible, according to Longchar, because God is "organically related to the whole of creation"[25] and because "God reveals and mediates through different cultures."[26] This tribal way of perceiving affirms God's wider revelatory presence that occurs outside the Christian community and without direct reference to Jesus. Although not all tribal theologians will precisely agree with the presented views, the tendency to conflate the epistemology of God as Creator and epistemology of God as Redeemer in Christ

---

23. Longchar, "Inter-Faith Dialogue: A Question from a Tribal Perspective," in *Good News for the North East India: A Theological Reader*, ed. Renthy Keitzar (Assam: Christian Literature Centre, 1995), 100.

24. Because of the perceived interconnectedness of God, humans, and creation in tribal worldview, Thanzauva believes that the most appropriate model of the Creator-creation relationship could be termed the "community model of relationship." Thanzauva, *Theology of Community*, 195.

25. Longchar, "Tribal Theology," 63.

26. Wati Longchar, "The Need of Doing Tribal Theology," in *Tribal Theology: A Reader* (Jorhat: Tribal Study Centre, Eastern Theological College, 2003), 8.

Jesus is still evident in their views, contesting the traditionally held distinction between natural and special revelation.[27] Exemplifying other wider contextual theologies' epistemologies, TT contests the sharp distinction of the traditional Creator-creation relationship and sometimes overlooks such demarcation in the process of theologizing.

TT epistemology, understood within its context, offers some constructive insights into the foundation of contextual theology. At the same time, it reminds us about the need for properly restructuring God's various revelations in the world. We shall now turn to Indian postcolonial biblical hermeneutics to investigate the methodological principle of contextual theology.

Indian Postcolonial Biblical Hermeneutics
Contextual Theology as Contrapuntal and Grassroots Reading of the Text

Defining the term "postcolonial" or "postcolonialism" as it relates to Indian biblical hermeneutics is difficult since the voices within this field are expanding. To begin with, postcolonial studies is a broad field. Different authors attach different values to the term.[28] Additionally, tribal hermeneutics, Dalit hermeneutics, feminist hermeneutics, and even subaltern hermeneutics, are subsets of postcolonial hermeneutics, drawing from postcolonial visions.[29] Therefore, rather than giving a precise definition of the term "postcolonial" in relation to biblical hermeneutics, it is helpful to look at the shared overarching markers.

I discuss two characteristics of postcolonial hermeneutics. The first I call "readings as contentions: from armchair theology to theological arm-wrestling." What is common in all forms of Indian postcolonial hermeneutics is to interpret the text in question, whether Scripture or any other text, through the lens of the interpreter's history, experiences, struggles, and geographical location. This endeavor is typically coupled with criticism of dominant Western hermeneutics—usually the historical-critical method—which some proponents consider to be irrelevant to their context, if not authoritarian. The two terms,

---

27. For example, Vashum, *Faith Seeking Transformation: Rethinking Faith, Theology and Mission in North East India* (Delhi: Christian World Imprints, 2020), 18–19.

28. For instance, Simon Samuel presents four different models of postcolonial biblical readings, each represented by Indian scholars. Samuel, *A Postcolonial Reading of Mark's Story of Jesus* (London: T & T Clark, 2007), 14–32.

29. C. I. David Joy, *Mark and Its Subalterns: A Hermeneutical Paradigm for a Postcolonial Context* (London: Routledge, 2008), 33–60.

"contrapuntal" and "subaltern," highlight important features of Indian postcolonial biblical hermeneutics that are relevant to our case. Although these two
terms do not capture the full force of Indian postcolonial biblical hermeneutics,
they highlight their important facets.

By "contrapuntal" reading, Edward Said means a reading of the text that
takes into consideration the perspective and experiences of both the exploiter
and exploited to unmask the intentional and unintentional interpretation and
the normalization of the process that privileges some at the expense of others.[30]
When applied to the biblical text, it fulfills its goal by incorporating both the
experiences of the exploited and the exploiter to "highlight gaps, absences and
imbalances" in the reading of the text, so that the "reified binary characterization
of Eastern and Western writings" and readings are overcome.[31] This is done by
being "aware simultaneously of the mainstream scholarship and of other scholarship which the dominant discourse tries to domesticate and speaks and acts
against."[32] The ultimate goal is not to read the text univocally, for the temptation
to impose the dominant ideology lurks behind every pretense of uniformity, they
maintain, but to reshape the dominant (or domineering) meaning by upholding
polyphonic voices.

The "post" in "postcolonial" is not necessarily identified as "after" colonial,
as in post-colonial, or as anti-colonial, but as "beyond" colonial.[33] For Samuel,
the "'Post' in postcolonialism as a marker of the 'beyond' may be understood
in terms of consensual-conflictual hybridity or in terms of an ambivalent
affiliative-antagonistic cultural engagement in between the colonist and colonized culture."[34] For Sugirtharajah, postcolonialism not only challenges the
oppressive nature of colonialism but also "recognizes the potentiality of contact
between colonizer and colonized" and attempts to "integrate and forge a new
perspective by critically and profitably syncretizing ingredients from both vernacular and metropolitan centres."[35] The underlying assumption is that our context
always influences and controls our reading to the degree that what we think to be
biblical in one location will not be so in another. For proponents, their respective

---

30. Edward W. Said, *Culture and Imperialism* (New York: Knopf, 1993), 66–67.

31. R. S. Sugirtharajah, *Postcolonial Reconfigurations: An Alternative Way of Reading the Bible and Doing Theology* (St. Louis, MO: Chalice Press, 2003), 16.

32. Sugirtharajah, *The Bible and the Third World: Precolonial, Colonial, and Postcolonial Encounters* (New York: Cambridge University Press, 2004), 281.

33. Samuel, *A Postcolonial Reading of Mark's Story of Jesus*, 3.

34. Samuel, *A Postcolonial Reading of Mark's Story of Jesus*, 3.

35. Sugirtharajah, *Postcolonial Reconfigurations*, 15–16.

experiences of *perceived*[36] colonialism and contexts of dislocation and hybridity[37] provide critical lenses for the *post*colonial hermeneutics they propose.

I label the second characteristic of Indian postcolonial hermeneutics as "interpretations as grassroots endeavors: reading from and with the margins." Another word that captures the spirit of Indian postcolonial hermeneutics is the term "subaltern." As an adjective, my use of the word "subaltern" goes beyond a specific "subaltern hermeneutics." It refers to the deliberate exercise of incorporating the voice of the voiceless. Thus, subaltern hermeneutics is a "hermeneutics from below," which attempts to incorporate the grassroots experience of marginalization, concern for creation care, and orality.[38]

In accentuating the incorporation of the voices of the marginalized, postcolonial hermeneutics raises three important and neglected concerns. First is the need for proper inclusion and representation of subalternity. Gayatri Chakravorty Spivak rightly reminds us that the voices of the subalterns are often silenced. Even in representing their views, the dominant interpreters tend to project their own opinions.[39] Second, and connected to the first concern, is the enterprise of deconstructing modern metanarratives and modern mission historiography that sideline the voices of the margins. Y. T. Vinayaraj conceives of subaltern hermeneutics as an attempt to deconstruct the way subalterns are treated in those narratives.[40] A third concern, which ties together the first two, is the contestation of the uncritical assumption of "context" as a totalizing factor.[41] Patta observes that viewing context as a "totalizing factor" consequently leads to "essentialized

---

36. I use the adjective "perceived" not because I deny the reality of colonialism but because the term and concept are charged with diverse experiences and interpretations. The nature and extent of colonialism I identify may not be what others see.

37. For Sugirtharajah, it is the (voluntary) dislocation beyond his country and hybridized context. For Samuel, it is his liminal location of "in-betweenness" informed by his experience of cultural and geographical dislodgment within his own country.

38. Joy, *Mark and Its Subalterns*, 52–54.

39. Gayatri Chakravorty Spivak, "Can the Subaltern Speak," in *Marxism and the Interpretation of Culture*, ed. Cary Nelson and Lawrence Grossberg (London: Macmillan Education, 1988), 271–313.

40. Y. T. Vinayaraj, "Envisioning a Postmodern Method of Doing Dalit Theology," in *Dalit Theology in the Twenty-First Century: Discordant Voices, Discerning Pathways*, ed. Sathianathan Clarke, Deenabandhu Manchala, and Philip Vinod Peacock (Oxford: Oxford University Press, 2010), 98–99; Vinayaraj, *Re-Visiting the Other: Discourses in Postmodern Theology* (Tiruvalla, Kerala: Christava Sahitya Samithi, 2010), 60–61.

41. Rajbharat Patta, "Towards a Subaltern Public Theology for India" (PhD. diss., The University of Manchester, 2018), 128.

identity," which then destabilizes any contestation of difference and alterity.[42] Comparable to Samuel's and Sugirtharajah's emphasis on the "third space," so to speak, subalternity defies both unanimity and the opposite binary. This refusal to be categorized in one camp is itself a defiance of the Indian caste system that would have them belong to the category devised by those in the so-called upper echelon of Indian society.

The contrapuntal and subaltern readings encompass both "reading from above" and "reading from below." Although such readings are done from the "colonized" space, as a highly academic and theoretical exercise it could be considered "reading from above." Postcolonial ideologies, as Samuel points out, encompass both mini- and metanarrative. By these terms, he means that postcolonial criticism as a mininarrative should be grounded in a particular context and thus necessarily manifest diverse theoretical and practical applications and manifestations. Simultaneously, as a metanarrative discourse, it is a "process to achieve what may be called a universal liberation hermeneutics," and necessarily implies some homogeneity and universality.[43] I suggest that within the broader postcolonial hermeneutical paradigm, contrapuntal and subaltern methods of interpretations as "reading from above" and "reading from below" respectively have the potential for methodological construction of contextual theologies. The combination of grassroots readings and "elite" readings is best exemplified in Dalit theology to which we now turn.

Dalit Theology's Theological Premise and Goal
Contextual Theology as Decentering the Center

One's theological presuppositions and goals are closely connected. Presuppositions influence method and although methods do not always determine the conclusions, they could affect them because method sets the ground rules for how theology is developed, what sources are used, and what questions are asked.[44] Alternately, one's goal will affect the kind of presupposition made and methods chosen. In discussing Dalit theology's assumption and goal, I want to highlight how it represents the wider contextual theology's attempt to decenter the center of theologizing. Negatively, Dalit theology's enterprise illustrates the general dissatisfaction with constructing a center around the dominant interpretation. Positively, it exemplifies the desire for local constructive theologizing that upholds and promotes the integrity of the *Imago Dei*.

---

42. Patta, "Towards a Subaltern Public Theology for India," 128.

43. Samuel, *A Postcolonial Reading of Mark's Story of Jesus*, 4.

44. Mary M. Veeneman, *Introducing Theological Method: A Survey of Contemporary Theologians and Approach* (Grand Rapids, MI: Baker Academic, 2017), 2.

I identify two characteristics of Dalit theology. The first is theology as decentering the center: deconstructing the false god. Dalits (and tribals) are the "outcasts," those unworthy to be considered even within the lowest strata of Indian society by the self-declared gatekeepers of the Indian caste system. Historians note that Dalits continued to face marginalization and discrimination from both the Hindu and Christian "upper" class societies even after they became Christians.[45] This "downgraded" group, who even after becoming Christians continued to face the same denigration and injustice as their fellow non-Christian Dalits, find their comfort and hope not among the fellow Christians who often were insensitive to, if not the instigators of their situation, but in the rejected and marginalized Jesus, whom they considered a fellow Dalit. Their theological stance begins not with some generic good news of the gospel, but by drawing deep into the wells of Dalit experiences and God's special unwavering love and care for them and their condition. Arvind P. Nirmal, arguably the pioneer of academic Dalit theology, claimed that "the primacy of the term 'dalit' will have to be conceded as against the primacy of the term 'Christian'." He went further, "What is 'Christian' for this theology is exclusively the 'dalit'. What this exclusivism implies is the affirmation that the Triune God—the Father, the Son and Holy Spirit—is on the side of the Dalits and not of the non-dalits who are the oppressors."[46] While Dalit theologians today are not so keen on a polarizing approach, Nirmal's point set the tone for the initial phase of Dalit theology.

The rejection and subjugation that Dalit theologians speak of exceed theological and economic marginalization; they include ideologies that manifest in different shapes and forms.[47] While the socioeconomic divide and injustices are emphasized just as in the Latin liberation theology approach, the Dalit struggles add the problem of the caste that is embedded in the very social structure of the Indian context.[48] One's socioeconomic condition could be improved, but caste, like gender, cannot be altered, at least in the Indian context. As M. Gnanavaram aptly points out, "It is much easier and safer for educated non-Dalit, middle-class [Indian] Christians to support liberation theology than to accept their part in

---

45. Poornam Damel, "Dalit Christian Experiences," in *Emerging Dalit Theology*, ed. Xavier Irudayaraj (Madras: Jesuit Theological Secretariate, 1990): 18–34; Joseph D'Souza, *Dalit Freedom Now and Forever: The Epic Struggle for Dalit Emancipation* (Centennial, CO: Dalit Freedom Network, 2004), 29–46.

46. Arvind P. Nirmal, "Towards a Christian Dalit Theology," in *Frontiers in Asian Christian Theology: Emerging Trends*, ed. R. S. Sugirtharajah (Maryknoll, NY: Orbis, 1994), 32.

47. For example, see the insightful article by Philip Vinod Peacock, "'Now We Will Have the Dalit Perspective': Dissecting the Politics of Identity," *The Ecumenical Review* 72, no. 1 (2000): 116–127.

48. Nirmal, "Towards a Christian Dalit Theology," 30.

the cultural oppression of the Dalits."[49] In such a situation, the Dalits find that the only option is to engage in a deconstruction of the theological and ideological systems that in the first place create the problem.

The Dalit pathos, that is, their common experience and suffering, came to occupy a space of temporal priority in their theologizing. This approach challenges "the epistemological foundations of the casteist discourses"[50] upon which some dominant Indian theologies are constructed, directly undermining the Dalit concerns. Therefore, Dalit theology contests not only the dominant Western theologies but also the Indian theologies built on the Brahmanic tradition and any other tradition that excludes marginalized groups.[51] While the act of deconstructing the oppressive narrative is in itself a constructive proposal,[52] Dalit theologians do not only push back the oppressive ideologies and structure, but they also strive for inclusion. The goal is not to create another caste identity but to form an anti-caste collective movement.[53] The Dalit pathos, which invokes empathy and sympathy provides them with both the corrective and constructive theological lens.

The second characteristic of Dalit theology is this: "theology as constructive inclusivism: reconstructing through the Dalit pathos." Although to make their case clear the initial theorizers like Nirmal and others tended to emphasize their Dalitness at the exclusion of other Christians, there is now an attempt to overcome this exclusive approach.[54] In the initial stage, a certain amount of theological exclusivity was called for because Dalit theology was reacting to the dominant Indian theology that attempted to co-opt all other theologizing.[55] The emphasis on Dalit identity and pathos as the paradigmatic locus of theologizing evident in the initial phase of Dalit theology is now being reframed for a more theologically inclusive approach by incorporating the experiences of those who

---

49. M. Gnanavaram, "'Dalit Theology' and the Parable of the Good Samaritan," *Journal for the Study of the New Testament* 50 (1993): 67.

50. Vinayaraj, "Envisioning a Postmodern Method of Doing Dalit Theology," 93.

51. Sathianathan Clarke, "Dalit Theology: An Introductory and Interpretive Theological Exposition," in Clarke, Manchala, and Peacock, *Dalit Theology in the Twenty-First Century*, 23–27

52. Peacock, "'Now We Will Have the Dalit Perspective,'" 121.

53. Sathianathan Clarke, Deenabandhu Manchala, and Philip Vinod Peacock, "Introduction," in *Dalit Theology in the Twenty-First Century*, 6.

54. Clarke, Manchala, and Peacock, "Introduction," 11–14.

55. Clarke, *Dalits and Christianity: Subaltern Religion and Liberation Theology in India* (Oxford: Oxford University Press, 1998), 35–43.

are being oppressed and dehumanized in any form.[56] The paradigm is shifting from victimhood to an active assertion of Dalit identity. The introduction of the Bangkok Declaration and Call of 2009 proclaims "Today, regardless of where we come from, which church we represent, we all become Dalits. Not only for today and during this conference, but also for our life until Dalits are liberated, we all become Dalits."[57] According to Philip Vinod Peacock, reframing the Dalithood from one of fixity to fluidity not only frees Dalits from the constructed binaries imposed on them but also makes provision for others who are marginalized, who do not belong, and who occupy an alternate space to be part of the Dalit struggle.[58]

How, then, does Dalit theology maintain its Dalitness? Peniel Rajkumar believes dialectically upholding the liberative social vision and identity affirmation of the Dalits, coupled with an inclusive approach will yield a constructive theological vision for Dalit theology.[59] This dialectical relationship of methodological exclusiveness and theological inclusion in Dalit theology, according to Clarke, is needed to counter the imposing tendency of the dominant theology and construct an alternative vision for the common good of all communities.[60] However, even in this integrative and inclusive approach, the Dalit struggles and experiences should be allowed to frame the central theological vision, proponents maintain. In this inclusive approach, the core of Dalit theology should arise, Clarke argues, from the pain-pathos of Dalits, without which there is no Dalit theology.[61] While not all can share the Dalit experience, all can identify with the Dalit commitment.[62] The non-Dalit experience *about* and the Dalit experience *of* the Dalithood[63] should be combined for a fruitful Dalit theology.

56. Clarke, Manchala, and Peacock, "Introduction," 13.

57. "The Bangkok Declaration and Call." *Oukoumene WCC*, March 21–24, 2009 https://www.oikoumene.org/resources/documents/the-bangkok-declaration-and-call (accessed August, 8 2023).

58. Peacock, "'Now We Will Have the Dalit Perspective,'" 123–124.

59. Peniel Rajkumar, *Dalit Theology and Dalit Liberation: Problems, Paradigms and Possibilities* (Farnham, England: Ashgate: 2010), 41.

60. Clarke, "Dalit Theology: An Introductory and Interpretive Theological Exposition," in *Dalit Theology in the Twenty-First Century* (Oxford: Oxford University Press, 2010), 21.

61. Clarke, "Dalit Theology," 21.

62. Godson Jacob, "Methodological Issues in Black Theology and Dalit Theology: A Critical Dialogue," *Canadian-American Theological Review*, 7 (2018): 110.

63. James Massey, *Dalit Theology: History, Context, Text, and Whole Salvation* (New Delhi: Manohar), 222.

Using Indian contextual theologies as a departing point, I have briefly discussed the epistemological foundation, hermeneutical methods, and theological telos operational in contextual theologies. Contextual theologies, some in greater intensity, accentuate the worldview of the native as an epistemological lens, emphasize the contrapuntal reading of the text by giving space to the interpretations from the margins, and attempt to decenter any theological center by adopting a constructive-exclusivist posture. Next, I will briefly outline a form of theologizing in context that takes the epistemological, hermeneutical, and theological triggers. A more detailed analysis of each contextual theology presented here, and a detailed discussion of the methods, await future publication.

Contextual Theology from a Canonical Perspective
Contextual Theology as Metatheology

The term "metatheology" is used here not in the sense of discovering one theology *above* all theologies but in the sense of developing theology *about* theologizing. Only in a static understanding of theology can a unified theological construction be possible. I define theology as involving three primary components simultaneously: (1) the contextual *reflection* of God's revelation primarily through Scripture (2) the *(re)imagination* of this reflection in and to concrete time and space, and (3) the *reproduction* of our reflection and reimagination in our personal and corporeal body of Christ. Seeing theology in this manner creates space for the elements of universality and particularity intrinsic to the discussions of contextual theology. The understanding of theology taken here allocates to Scripture the foundational roles both in the product and process of theologizing. Here, the foundation, method, and telos of theology are all considered. The inspired Scripture is the ultimate foundation of theology, the way we (re)imagine the scriptural truth in concrete space and time is our method, and the reliving of our reflection and (re)imagination of the scriptural truth is the telos of theology.

To restate, metatheology is a process of theologizing that upholds Scripture as the epistemological foundation, adopts synergistic-developmental hermeneutics, and pursues the New Creation ethos to the glory of the triune God as the theological telos. This approach does not argue for Scripture to occupy sequential priority but an authoritative foundation; it does neither advocate categorial exclusivity in its methodology but logical subordination to the scriptural category; and it does not pursue exclusively or even primarily otherworldly concerns, but ultimately participates in the divine metanarrative.

Scripture as the Epistemological Foundation

The central point of contextual theology's epistemology as illustrated through the TT epistemology amounts to the nexus of general and special revelation. In encouraging worldwide Christians to seriously consider God's wider work in the world by questioning the strict dualism of general and special revelation, TT epistemology on this particular aspect echoes the rationale of many other Reformed theologians.[64] While the specifics of TT's epistemology or that of Reformed theology could be contested on different levels, what they have shown us is that some traditional theological categories do not always neatly capture the existential experiences of people and contexts. The discussion calls for more nuanced articulations. The false binary of Christians and their views as always aligned with Jesus and the views of others with spiritual darkness needs to be challenged. Thus, TT's affirmation of God's revelation through all creation is not far removed even from the traditional conception.[65] After all, tribal theologians could and do claim that truth looks different from their perspective.

Nonetheless, while the strict separation of general and special revelation may be unwarranted since special revelation builds on natural revelation (grace builds on nature), coalescing the two forms of revelation diminishes the helpful framework of God's work in the world. For one, if we conjoin them, how do we distinguish God's work in the believers' lives and the Church from his work in the world? Additionally, is there not a difference between God's revelation in and through Scripture and his revelation through the Hindu *Vedas* or creation? Yet, the deeper question beneath the veneer of the distinction between the general and special revelation that touches on TT's epistemological claim, and, by extension, many contextual theologies' claims, is the question of whether the saving knowledge of God is mediated to people apart from the written Word

---

64. J. V. Fesko argues that although many early modern reformed theologians—perhaps with the clear exception of Karl Barth—employed natural theology to a varying degree, they were sympathetic to the idea that God's revelation, in some degree, was available to all humanity and that unbelievers could know God as Creator through his general revelation. While they were convinced that natural theology should not draw supernatural revelation under its domain, they also held that God was at work in the world, revealing about his existence and character through his creation. Thus, natural theology was not the result of a human's capacity to reason his way toward God; rather, it is the result of God's revelation through his creation. Fesko, "Introduction," in *Natural Theology: Gerhardus Vos*, trans. Albert Gootjes (Grand Rapids, MI: Reformation Heritage Books, 2022), xvii–lxx.

65. The Asian American Old Testament Scholar Jerry Hwang convincingly argued that "all of Yahweh's created order pulses with a vibrancy that cuts across the physical and spiritual realms while nonetheless diverging from the Eastern pantheism." Jerry Hwang, *Contextualization and the Old Testament: Between Asian and Western Perspectives* (Carlisle, UK: Langham Global Library, 2022), 167.

and encounter with the living Word, Jesus Christ.[66] Although we may entertain an exception to the general rule, the exception does not invalidate the rule. Any claim of special knowledge of God, the dissolution of the transcendence and immanence of God, and the coalescing of the epistemology of God as Creator and epistemology of God as Redeemer must be properly qualified.

While the epistemology of God as Creator and epistemology of God as Redeemer cannot be strictly separated, completely amalgamating them confuses the purpose and goal of each.[67] Those who acknowledge God as the Creator do not necessarily recognize him as the Redeemer.[68] Regardless of the precise nature of distinctions between general and special revelation, Christians have emphasized that human personal knowledge of and relationship with God is made possible because God acted in history and made himself known definitively in and through Jesus Christ (Heb 1: 1–3), the most reliable and authoritative record of which is now preserved in the written word of God. Clarifying this in the theologizing process will yield better clarity to our theologies.

Adopting a Synergistic-Developmental Hermeneutics

Recognizing the authority of Scripture is one thing, interpreting it is another. Synergistic-developmental hermeneutics does not demand that our interpretation "begin" and "end" with the Bible;[69] rather, it gives room for context to occupy temporal priority without compromising the authoritative priority of Scripture. The theological idea of synergism gives room to both God's and human's actions by maintaining that the efficient cause (God) can work through the instrumental cause (human), without undermining the agency of both parties. The Bible is the "foundational but not the final" theological resource because contextual theology starts from the Bible and develops in new directions.[70] The question is not *whether* we move beyond the Bible but *how* we move beyond the Bible.

---

66. Bruce A. Demarest observed that the controversy during his time regarding the relationship between general and special revelation boils down to this question. Demarest, *General Revelation: Historical Views and Contemporary Issues* (Grand Rapids, MI: Zondervan, 1982), 14.

67. Tedla Gebreyesus Woldeyohannes, "Volition, Doxastic Voluntarism, and Knowledge of God" (PhD dissertation, Saint Louis University, 2016), 34.

68. Jack Cottrell, *What the Bible Says about God the Redeemer* (Eugene, OR: Wipf and Stock, 2000), 10.

69. The term "synergistic-developmental" is adapted from Richard N. Longenecker. Longenecker, *New Wine into Fresh Wineskins: Contextualizing the Early Christian Confessions* (Peabody, MA: Hendrickson Publishers, 1999), 147.

70. Timoteo D. Gener, "Divine Revelation and the Practice of Asian Theology," in *Asian Christian Theology: Evangelical Perspectives*, ed. Timoteo D. Gener and Stephen T. Pardue (Carlisle, UK: Langham Global Library, 2019), 16, 25.

Sequential or temporal priority should not be confused with authoritative priority. As Jackson Wu (a pseudonym) noted, confusing the two hinges on an "order fallacy," which assumes that whatever comes first has authoritative priority.[71] So long as the foundation and telos of theology are properly recognized, we will not be hesitant to affirm and adopt methods that emancipate human suffering. The context or experience could be allotted a temporal priority even as the authoritative place of Scripture is upheld. While the discussion of the nature of the telos of "developmental" in the synergistic-developmental model requires much more space, I will conclude that any developmental trajectory must be consistent with the very development within the Scriptures, especially illustrated in how the newer revelation (New Testament) reconceptualized the older revelation (Old Testament). Our development of hermeneutics also must recognize the unique place of biblical writers and their writings in the theologizing process.

The postcolonial deconstruction of the essentializing context that modern metanarrative upholds has important implications for interpretations and contextual theologies. If "context" is not something with clear parameters, as the postcolonial theologians contend, or if it is not absolutely determinable, since it is a socially constructed notion, as Jacques Derrida argues,[72] and if "meaning" is the affair of context, then the inevitable conclusion is that meaning—including the meaning of the biblical text—is indeterminate. If so, the project of deconstructing mission historiography and theologies as many Indian subaltern and Western postmodern theologians are engaging is not only justifiable but also necessary In Derrida's fashion, deconstruction is not *a* method of reading, rather, deconstruction is *the* method of any reading. According to him, this is the case because the text itself demands such reading.[73] However, pursued to the extreme and applied to the biblical text,[74] the distinction of meaning and significance, if such a distinction is legitimate, breaks down. In this scenario, different contexts no longer *draw out* different meanings from the text but *determine* them,[75] blurring the line between our interpretation and the intended goal of the author

---

71. Jackson Wu, *Saving God's Face: A Chinese Contextualization of Salvation Through Honor and Shame*. Evangelical Missiological Society Dissertation Series (Pasadena, CA: William Carey International University Press, 2012), 60.

72. Jacques Derrida, "Signature Event Context," in *Limited Inc*, trans. Samuel Weber (Evanston, IL: Northwestern University Press, 1988), 2–3.

73. Christopher Watkin, *Jacques Derrida: Great Thinkers* (Philipsburg, NJ: P&R Publishing, 2017), 21–23.

74. For example, K. Jesurathnam, "Dalit and Subaltern Hermeneutics in Conversation with Reader Response Method: 1 Kings 22, A Case in Point," *Bangalore Theological Forum*, 48, no.1 (2016): 55.

75. For example, Vinayaraj, "Envisioning a Postmodern Method of Doing Dalit Theology," 99.

and text. The question is whether and in what sense such an argument stands under scrutiny.

The ultimate goal of hermeneutics is neither reproduction nor the repudiation of the dominant reading of the Bible but the proliferation of the mission of God by upholding the integrity of the text in promoting its vision of building and nurturing lives in a specific context. Rather than imposing the grassroots experiences and struggles on the text, hermeneutics is about reading the texts *with* and *through* the lens of the grassroots experiences. This form of reading does not negate the importance of grammatical-historical hermeneutics either;[76] rather, it builds on it. Synergistic-developmental hermeneutics eschews both the binary distinction between the West and the Rest and the tendency of forceful homogenization, looking for commonality while preserving the differences. This intercultural negotiation under the authority of the Scriptures prevents the imposition of any exterior theological motives on a local context that does not take into consideration its existential needs and challenges.

The Participation in the Divine Metanarrative as the Telos of Contextual Theology

Scripture, which is our foundation, also defines the telos of our theology, as our hermeneutical methods help us navigate toward it. Therefore, all our theologizing must take into consideration the Bible's grand narrative. Nicholas Tom Wright reasons, "anyone who professes to regard the Bible as in some way the ultimate source, or even *an* ultimate source, for theological knowledge and understanding, cannot ignore the fact that the Bible . . . presents an overarching narrative which is more than simply a loose frame in which abstract theological teaching happens to be embedded."[77] It is within this story that Christians make sense of their particular stories. Lesslie Newbigin similarly states that it is *through* this biblical story that we make sense of our stories,[78] as much as we make sense of the former with the latter. Likewise, Kevin J. Vanhoozer reminds us that the church's appropriate response to the theo-drama of the gospel is to "participate [in it] more deeply, passionately, and truthfully."[79] Christopher H.

---

76. By "historical-grammatical" hermeneutics, I am broadly referring to the way of interpreting a text through rigorous historical and grammatical analysis.

77. Nicholas Tom Wright, *Interpreting Scripture: Essays on the Bible and Hermeneutics* (Grand Rapids, MI: Zondervan, 2020), 340–341.

78. Newbigin, *The Gospel in a Pluralist Society* (Grand Rapids, MI: Eerdmans, 1989), 38.

79. Vanhoozer, *The Drama of Doctrine: A Canonical Linguistic Approach to Christian Theology* (Louisville, KY: WJK, 2005), 107.

Wright agrees.[80] Therefore, as Richard Bauckham insists, the church's calling is to find herself inside the story of the missionary movement of the gospel.[81] The church's responsibility, then, is to allow this biblical metanarrative to serve as a sort of "biblical social theory"[82] that makes room for unity and diversity. By "social theory," I mean a guiding narrative that informs our thoughts, actions, and goals. As a social theory, the biblical metanarrative has at least three interrelated characteristics: it pursues the New Creation ethos, it makes room for particular stories, and it ultimately seeks the glory of God.

Bible scholars of various fields affirm the establishment of the New Creation as the grand finale of the Bible's storyline, although they differ on how such a telos informs the church's ethos. A. Sue Russell helpfully explains a way for the new community to live out the New Creation ethos. According to her, people enter this new creation community not by detaching from their previous relationships or structures but by participating or indwelling in the Holy Spirit such that this new community no longer operates based on social status defined by worldly structures. Instead, they are now bound by a new relationship marked by mutual respect and sacrifice.[83] In this liminal state, they live anti-structurally. The primary goal of this anti-structural living, I suggest, is not the kind of lifestyle calling for active decentering of the center, be it political, social, or financial, as important as they are, but a subversive living marked by humility, self-sacrifice, and love.

Nonetheless, participation in this grand narrative can take place only through the particularities of our context. This is the second characteristic. After all, the biblical metanarrative is the sum of all the biblical witnesses; the details are as important as the sum. Just as the sum is reliable only if the details are so, the universality makes sense only when the particularities of the contexts are considered.[84] Thus, biblical metanarrative entertains diverse narratives. Drawing from Gérard Genette's distinction of story and narrative,[85] Bauckham suggests that within the single biblical story, there are many different narratives "conveying

---

80. Christopher H. Wright, *The Mission of God: Unlocking the Bible's Grand Narratives* (Downers Grove, IL: IVP Academic, 2006), 22–23.

81. Richard Bauckham, *Bible and Mission: Christian Witness in a Postmodern World* (Grand Rapids, MI: Baker, 2003), 11.

82. This is the central argument of Christopher Watkin's *Biblical Critical Theory*. Watkin, *Biblical Critical Theory: How the Bible's Unfolding Story Makes Sense of Modern Life and Culture* (Grand Rapids, MI: Zondervan, 2022), 30–31.

83. A. Sue Russell, In *the World but Not of the World: The Liminal Life of Pre-Constantine Christian Communities* (Eugene, OR: Pickwick, 2019), 30–54.

84. Bauckham, *Bible and Mission*, 47.

85. Gérard Genette, *Narrative Discourse*, trans. J. E. Lewin (Oxford, Blackwell, 1980).

different information, highlighting different aspects of significance."[86] In this sense, the biblical metanarrative is to be distinguished from the totalizing metanarrative characteristic of modernity.

This grand scheme of seeking the divine metanarrative is translated into a concrete context by considering the local existential challenges and promises. Considering that our pursuit of participation in God's larger story must address the pressing concerns of the context, our method could be tested against the helpful framework of what Ian T. Ramsey calls an "empirical fit."[87] According to Ramsey, theological models unlike scientific models cannot always be verified or falsified by verifiable deductions. Instead, the theological model works more like "the fitting of the boots or a shoe" to the degree that its success or failure is judged by "its ability to match a wide range of phenomena, by its overall success in meeting a variety of needs."[88] Thus, the success of theological models is judged both by their faithfulness to the scriptural metanarrative and their ability to neatly harmonize people's experiential and existential realities consistently.

The third feature of the biblical metanarrative is the pursuit of *Soli Deo Gloria*. In Ephesians 1:6, 12, 14, Paul attributes salvation to the work of the Father, Son, and the Holy Spirit respectively, and exhorts us to give him the glory he deserves. While the word "glory" is also used in reference to humans, the Scripture reserves its primary use for God.[89] We are to render to God what is due him because of who he is and what he has done. Timothy Tennent rightly attributes *missio dei* to the very nature of God: God the Father as the initiator, God the Son as the embodiment, and God the Holy Spirit as the empowering presence of *missio dei*.[90] This perspective, Tennent reasons, affirms and "validates the significance of human history in God's plan," providing "the basis for a robust theology of human culture."[91] The movement toward the New Creation should be elucidated by intentionally and visibly uplifting the triune God, whose character is most visibly manifested in the incarnate Son Jesus Christ our Lord, the author and perfecter of our salvation.

---

86. Bauckham, "Reading Scripture as a Coherent Story," in *The Art of Reading Scripture*, ed. Ellen F. Davis and Richard B. Hays (Grand Rapids, MI: Eerdmans, 2003): 43.

87. Ian Ramsey, *Models and Mystery* (Oxford: Oxford University Press, 1964), 16–18, 38.

88. Ramsey, *Models and Mystery*, 16–17.

89. Harold W. Hoehner, *Ephesians: An Exegetical Commentary* (Grand Rapids, MI: Baker Academic, 2002), 200.

90. Timothy Tennent, *Invitation to World Missions: A Trinitarian Missiology for the Twenty-first Century* (Grand Rapids, MI: Kregel, 2010), 74–101.

91. Tennent, *Invitation to World Missions*, 77–78.

The limitation of the Indian Christian theology drawn from the Vedantic philosophy or theology, as Dalit theologians identify, is that it superimposes ideologies that ultimately disservice the subaltern communities. What could have been a liberating theology for one community became suppressive for another. Therefore, the theology of "decentering" becomes an important prerequisite for centering on the true center. This decentering creates space for the voices of the neglected. Peacock's imaginative and inclusive vision of Dalit theology is instructive. For him, God is not just the God of the Dalits, he is "the God who does not belong."[92] By the phrase, he means God is bigger than any single vision of him, whether that of Dalits or others. He is a "God who slips between the gaps to elude all claims, even universal ones."[93] In other words, "God does not belong, but God is to be found in between."[94] If so, God's personhood is comprehended more fully in and through our relationships. The "other" as opposed to "us" comes to occupy a central category in Peacock's inclusive vision.[95] Such a vision has important epistemological and hermeneutical implications as well: they could be properly appropriated only when we show true solidarity with the "other," those who are suffering and hurting. We cannot be distant observers or noncommitted interpreters.[96] Additionally, a deconstructive inclusivism, as Peacock and subaltern theologians articulate, has a prophetic voice for theologies. It provokes us to ask, as the continental deconstructionist philosopher John D. Caputo asks, "What would Jesus deconstruct" today in our society?[97] We need constant scrutiny of whether our construction of God needs to be decentered to make way for the God of the Bible to occupy the center.

Understandably, owing to their historical marginalization, the vision of Dalit theology is constructed around affirming, restoring, and reclaiming human dignity to give way to a transformative and constructive theological imagination. What Dalit theology teaches us is that reclamation and affirmation of the *imago Dei* cannot be achieved without taking into consideration the specific historical and structural precedents in which such degradation transpired. The aim of contextual theology, then, is to deconstruct any oppressive metanarratives,

---

92. Peacock, "'Now We Will Have the Dalit Perspective,'" 124.

93. Peacock, "'Now We Will Have the Dalit Perspective,'" 124.

94. Peacock, "'Now We Will Have the Dalit Perspective,'" 125.

95. Peacock, "'Now We Will Have the Dalit Perspective,'" 125.

96. Gnanavaram exhorts that we need to continually reform our "non-committal, neutral, or impartial" interpretation. Gnanavaram, "'Dalit Theology' and the Parable of the Good Samaritan," 62–63.

97. John D. Caputo, *What Would Jesus Deconstruct? The Good News of Postmodernity for the Church* (Grand Rapids, MI: Baker, 2007).

recognize and affirm the existing prevailing grace of God within a context, and theologize by drawing insights from the variegated existential challenges and experiences of the people rooted in their history with the end-goal of recentering our ambitions, desires, and life around the true center.[98] I suggest that the biblical metanarrative—which upholds the New Creation ethos, provides space for flourishing individual stories, and seeks the ultimate glory of God—should serve as a Christian social theory under which the tribal, Dalit, or postcolonial concerns are to be pursued.

Conclusion

Theology must seek to be faithful both to the content of the Bible and the context of the people. Navigating the gaps between the content of the Bible and the contemporary context requires more than replicating or revolting against the dominant voice. Using three Indian contextual theological approaches—tribal theology epistemology, postcolonial biblical hermeneutics, and Dalit theology's emphasis on pathos—as windows into the larger contextual theology's foundation, method, and goals respectively, I have argued how these three essential components should be taken together in consideration of any contextual theology. I have proposed that considering contextual theology as metatheology is able to address these concerns. Metatheology takes Scripture as the epistemological lens of theologizing, adopts synergistic-developmental hermeneutics, and pursues participation in the divine metanarrative as the telos of theology. This approach does not argue for Scripture to always occupy sequential priority but an authoritative foundation; it does not advocate categorial exclusivity in its methodology but logical subordination to the scriptural category; and it does not pursue exclusively or even primarily otherworldly concerns, but ultimately seeks to participate in the divine metanarrative. The proposed approach provides space for both the universality of the gospel and the particularity of the given situation.

---

98. Peacock has discussed the problem of essentializing Dalit identity. He shows how such assumption can also be invoked to "reinforce the hegemony of the dominant community." Peacock, "'Now We Will Have the Dalit Perspective.'" 117–120.

CHAPTER SEVEN

Indian Biblical Hermeneutics

Lalenkawla

Introduction

THE TREND OF biblical scholarship is changing and the number of methods for interpreting the Bible have increased in recent years. As a result, there is a significant shift from the dominant traditional interpretation to a context-based interpretation of the Bible. The failure to respond to the context's demands has inspired new contextually-conscious interpretation methods, including an authentic Indian interpretation of the Bible. Sam P. Matthew rightly asserts, "The inability of dominant contemporary biblical exposition to meet the pressing needs of the common people is the basic problem in Indian biblical interpretation. This situation calls for a re-examination of the methods employed for the interpretation of the Bible by Indian biblical scholars/theologians and demands new principles and directions determined by the Indian context."[1] This chapter explores the traditional biblical approaches and viewpoints as well as the problems that these approaches face when applied to Indian biblical hermeneutics. It then offers some suggestions for appropriate Indian biblical hermeneutics. Within the Indian context, I will put a special emphasis on Northeast India.

Calling for an Indian Biblical Hermeneutics

The word "hermeneutics" is from the Greek word ἑρμηνεύω, which means "to interpret," "to explain." It denotes the science or art of interpretation.[2] Indian tribal biblical scholar Renthy Keitzar defines it as, "The science and methodology of interpretation of written [or oral] texts, especially scriptural texts and their meaningfulness to different situations and cultures."[3] In recent times the term has

---

1. Sam P. Matthew, "Indian Biblical Hermeneutics: Methods and Principles," *Neotestamentica: Journal for the Study of the New Testament in South Africa* 38, no. 1 (2004): 100.

2. Milton S. Terry, *Biblical Hermeneutics: A Treatise on the Interpretation of the Old and New Testaments* (New York: Phillips & Hunt, 1885), 17.

3. Renthy Keitzar, "Tribal Perspective in Biblical Hermeneutics Today," *Journal of Tribal Studies* 18, no. 1 (2013): 1.

been used not just to mean the mechanics of interpretation but also as a reference to a more inclusive phenomenon of understanding a text or tradition. In this sense, hermeneutics is not only the mechanics of text-interpretation but also a process of understanding which is part of the total human experience of the world. To put it differently, hermeneutics is the science and art of interpretation that continues to adapt itself to meet the needs of the readers and hearers by drawing meaning for a particular context.[4] It should challenge biblical scholars in different ages depending on varied issues and contexts. As all the writers of the Bible interact with their contextual realities, finding appropriate hermeneutical concerns that can engage and interact with comparable interests is a challenge for Indian interpretation.

It is important to highlight why Indian hermeneutical tools are necessary to interpret biblical texts. Jones Muthunayagom rightly describes the present interpretive context of the Bible and its purpose in India:

> A biblical interpreter from India is affected by certain contemporary problems such as the suffering of the subaltern communities such as the Dalits, Adivasis, the women, the fisherfolk and the poor, the socio-economic disparity being caused by the globalisation, the ecological crises created by the industrialisation and deforestation and the issues related to multi-religious and multi-cultural factors. The purpose of the reading of the bible is to make a proper sense to their respective life situation. The ultimate purpose is to restore life or to bring about liberation or dignity to the affected people.[5]

The husband-and-wife duo of theologians, Mizoram K. Thanzauva and R. L. Hnuni, assert that "biblical hermeneutics no longer remains the monopoly of Western scholars; it has local dimensions as well."[6] Similarly, Razouselie Lasetso has argued that "[h]ermeneutical principles need to be developed to enter the scriptures to find ourselves in the various pages of the Bible as we take the Bible as the Word of God and not simply a book to be read."[7] With reference to the context of Northeast India, Supongmayang Longkumer adds:

---

4. Supongmayang Longkumer, *The Apocalypse of John and Its Subalterns: Implications for a Postcolonial Tribal Context* (Delhi: ISPCK, 2019), 131.

5. D. J. Muthunayagom, "Biblical Hermeneutics in the Context of the Life Experiences of Dalits and Burakumin Communities," *Bangalore Theological Forum* 37, no. 1 (2005): 2.

6. Mizoram K. Thanzauva and R. L. Hnuni, "Ethnicity, Identity and Hermeneutics: An Indian Tribal Perspective," in *Ethnicity and the Bible*, ed. Mark G. Brett (Boston: Brill Academic Publishers, 2002), 343.

7. Razouselie Lasetso, "Tribal Theology and the Bible: A Contextual Reading of the Bible," *Tribal Theology: A Search for Quality Theological Education and Relevant Ministry*, Tribal Studies Series 17, ed. Yangkahao Vashum (Jorhat: Tribal Study Centre, 2009), 34.

The biblical scholars from the North East Indian region attempt to interpret the texts grounded on the existential realities of the tribal people, land, society, culture, belief system, polity, economy, psyche, and so on. As such, some of the major concerns can be the spring-board towards developing hermeneutical tools and is worth noting. The nature of tribal communities in NEI is indeed complex, yet, have commonality as well. No doubt, recognising the uniqueness of each community ought to be treasured without exclusivism and judgmental outlook. At the same time, the ecumenical approaches to the texts will still provide spaces to recognise and embrace the others (tribal and non-tribal) be it community, denominational or faith traditions.[8]

The above observations show the need for appropriate hermeneutical tools for the study of the Bible in the Indian context. The development of the hermeneutical tools must center on the complete human existence and experiences as an Indian in accordance with biblical worldviews.

Traditional Biblical Interpretation

For a long century, the divine inspiration paradigm was the dominant tradition in the history of biblical interpretation. In the seventeenth and eighteenth centuries, a paradigm known as the historical critical method came into being. This diachronic (historical) method dominated Old Testament and New Testament studies for a long time. The historical-critical approach attempts to locate the historical reality and interpret the meaning of the texts from its original author's and a current reader's perspectives. Historical multi-environment inquiries are unveiled through the historical-critical tools which are important to apply to biblical studies. Though the approaches and implications would seem incomplete as the world from where the texts are read is completely different, whereby, critical contextual reading of the texts becomes inevitable.[9] J. F. A. Sawyer therefore strongly argues against the historical criticism by saying that one has to liberate Old Testament study from the grip of archaeologists and philologists, for it is the meaning of the text that is important, not whether it is historically true.[10]

---

8. Supongmayang Longkumer, "Tribal Biblical Hermeneutics: Exploring Theories and Principles," (paper presented at the North East India Society for Biblical Studies webinar, November 26, 2021), 2.

9. Longkumer, "Tribal Biblical Hermeneutics," 1.

10. Hrangthan Chhungi, "Rhetorical Reading of Proverbs 31:10–31," *Mizoram Theological Journal* 7, no. 2 (July–December, 2007): 29.

From the middle of the twentieth century, there was a shift of focus from the study of Diachronic (history) to the Synchronic (literary analytic) approach known as the modern literary criticism or the new literary critical approach. The new literary criticism is not a historical discipline, but a strictly literary one, foregrounding the textuality of the literature. The primary concern of this approach is that it looks at the text as an object, a product, not as a window upon historical actuality.[11] It does not worry about stages of development of the text, rather its focus of interest is mainly upon the literary world created by the text. Its goal is to interpret the current text in its finished form. It emphasizes the unity of the text as a whole.[12] It is in this world that the reader finds meaning and is repeatedly challenged to discover what lies in the deep sea of the text. However, this synchronic approach has no concern for the reader of the text. It merely looks into the artistic character of the text.[13] The limitations of the above two approaches to biblical criticism has been well summarized by Ched Meyers: "If historical criticism betrays the narrative integrity of the text, literary criticism betrays its historical integrity."[14] K. Jesurathnam observes:

> It is no longer the domination of author-centered or text-centered method that dominates the reading and interpreting of the biblical text. A combination of all the methods is also employed for an effective understanding of the meaning of the text. In the author-centered method the "impossible" Sitz-im-Leben behind the text was sought in order to know the "original" community behind the text. This diachronic method has no significance for the present readers of the text. All that this method wanted to do is to trace out the background of the text however speculative it may be. In this method no direct relationship is established between the text and the reader.[15]

---

11. David J. A. Clines & J. Cheryl Exum, *The New Literary Criticism and the Hebrew Bible* (Sheffield, UK: JSOT Press, 1993), 11.

12. Mark Allan Powell, *What is Narrative Criticism? A New Approach to the Bible* (London: SPCK, 1993), 7.

13. Kondasingu Jesurathnam, *Exploring Dalit Liberative Hermeneutics in India & The World: Based on an Ancient Hebrew Prophet, Jeremiah of Anathoth* (New Delhi: Christian World Imprints, 2015), 26.

14. Ched Meyers, *Binding the Strong Man: A Political Reading of Mark's Story of Jesus* (Maryknoll, NY: Orbis Books, 1990), 25.

15. Jesurathnam, *Exploring Dalit Liberative Hermeneutics*, 26.

Contextual Biblical Interpretations

The inadequacy and dissatisfaction with the historical-critical approach led to the development of new methods. Contextual interpretations arose as a critique to traditional interpretations, supplementing it with such as liberation hermeneutics, feminist hermeneutics, Dalit hermeneutics, tribal hermeneutics, and so on.

Liberation Hermeneutics

The rise of liberation theology in Latin America from the late 1960s opened a new avenue of interpretation followed by various other forms of liberation hermeneutics. This mode of interpretation seeks to represent the Christian faith from the perspective of the poor and the oppressed.[16] The movement is rooted in the Christian faith and Scriptures and seeks its ideological superstructure based on the religious reflection in close association with Church organization. The Latin American lead was followed in other oppressive situations especially in other Global South countries.[17] Liberation hermeneutics introduced two important critical tools: hermeneutical circle and hermeneutics of suspicion. The hermeneutical circle begins with the experience of the interpreter and moves to ideological or theological suspicion, to exegetical suspicion, to new interpretation, and then, feeds back to the interpreter's experience of reality, modifying it and starting the process anew. Liberation hermeneutics has influenced some Indian scholars to attempt social reading of the Bible, giving due importance to the socioeconomic concerns of the people.[18]

Feminist Hermeneutics

Feminist scholars began using more than the traditional historical-critical methods of interpretation, adding the newer hermeneutical tools of literary criticism and liberation theology. Phyllis Trible's *God and the Rhetoric of Sexuality* and *Texts of Terror: Literary-feminist reading of Biblical narratives* indicate that a new wave of women's biblical interpretation was on the way.[19] From that point

---

16. H. M. Conn, "Liberation Theology" *New Dictionary of Theology*, ed. Sinclair B. Ferguson, David F. Wright, and J. I. Packer (Nottingham, UK: Inter-Varsity Press, 1988), 389.

17. Marian Hiller, *Liberation Theology: Religious Response to Social Problem. A survey* (Houston: American Humanist Association, 1993), 1.

18. Matthew, "Indian Biblical Hermeneutics," 104.

19. Phyllis Trible, *God and the Rhetoric of Sexuality* (Philadelphia: Fortress, 1978); Phyllis Trible, *Texts of Terror: Literary-Feminist Reading of Biblical Narratives* (Philadelphia: Fortress, 1984).

on, traditional ways of reading biblical narratives, like the Genesis account, that use them to justify exclusion or oppression of women were no longer tolerated. Elisabeth Schussler Fiorenza, in her work *The Power of the Word—Scripture and the Rhetoric of Empire* applies the postcolonial approach to the Bible, from a feminist perspective.[20] Fiorenza speaks about certain emancipative techniques or conscientizing strategies that can meaningfully be incorporated in Indian biblical hermeneutics. They are: (1) a hermeneutics of experience, (2) a hermeneutics of domination, (3) a hermeneutics of suspicion, (4) a hermeneutics of evaluation, (5) a hermeneutics of imagination, (6) a hermeneutics of remembrance, and (7) a hermeneutics of transformation.[21]

Dalit Hermeneutics

Dalit Christians started to read the Bible to unlock its message of liberation in the last two or three decades. The Bible is seen as a fundamental religious resource from which the solid roots of Dalit theological discourse was constructed. Dalit Christians assert their identity and dignity based on the message that in Jesus Christ they find a sense of self-dignity and self-worth that is denied to them by their high caste oppressors. Dalit Christians are thus seeking their liberation from caste-based oppression and affirm their human identity by using the Bible as a potential source of their religious faith.[22] K. Jesurathnam, in his interpretation of Psalm 22, uses strategies and interplay with mechanisms of power in order to subvert such powerful and exploitative power dynamics.[23] Laments "speak in the language of protest in response to acute suffering . . . appeal to God for his (sic) intervention."[24] Dalits identify themselves with this genre of lamentation by identifying themselves with the cry contained in the laments: "The lament cry addressed to God seeks to enter into an intense dialogue with God in order to evoke God's response to the cry of the lamenter." Dalit Christians cry out to their God "in anticipation with and in the light of liberative potential that may ultimately come from God."[25] Jesurathnam suggests the following as a basis for

---

20. Elisabeth Schussler Fiorenza, *The Power of the Word—Scripture and the Rhetoric of Empire* (Minneapolis: Fortress Press, 2007).

21. Fiorenza, *The Power of the Word*, 163–164.

22. K. Jesurathnam, *Dalit Liberative Hermeneutics: Indian Christian Interpretation of Psalm 22* (Delhi: ISPCK, 2010), 5–6.

23. Jesurathnam, *Dalit Liberative Hermeneutics*, xvii.

24. Jesurathnam, *Dalit Liberative Hermeneutics*, 232–233

25. Jesurathnam, *Dalit Liberative Hermeneutics*, 233.

Dalit hermeneutics: (1) hermeneutics of liberative transformation, (2) hermeneutics of protest and action, (3) hermeneutics of suspicion, (4) hermeneutics of identity, and (5) hermeneutics of empowerment.[26]

Tribal Hermeneutics

Tribal theology, by definition, is a contextual theology that arises out of the life experiences of the tribal people in India. It reflects on the indigenous-tribal people's faith experiences and aims to liberate them from oppression, inferiority complex, and alienation. Tribal scholars have contributed to the development of hermeneutical methods. However, they need more substantial and systematic methodological contributions to its epistemology in its entirety. K. Thanzauva understands tribal theology as a contextual theology that synthesizes the gospel and culture of the people. For him, the enterprise of tribal hermeneutics is an authentic interpretation that involves reading of the texts with sensitivity to the reader's own context, to the horizons of the text, and that of the reader's fused. He asserts, "The concern of tribal hermeneutics is not merely understanding the ancient text objectively, but how I know myself in the process of knowing God through the text, and how will I, as an individual person and my society, be transformed by that knowledge?" In search for authentic and meaningful interpretation of the text, Thanzauva lends support for critically taking into account the tribal social and cultural situation. Then he proposes "alienation" as the hermeneutial paradigm, as tribal people have been alienated people throughout their history.[27] Tribal scholars like Maisuangdibou Marianmai propose community hermeneutics as the starting point.[28] For Supongmayang Longkumer, tribal biblical hermeneutics is a tribal reoralizing and remythology hermeneutics. According to him, a tribal reoralizing hermeneutic must, (1) have the goal of bringing about social justice, and (2) value both tribal oral lore and the biblical texts equally.[29] According to K. Lallawmzuala, a tribal hermeneutics/reading is a new approach to the Bible. This approach can be taken as one among many new ways of contextually reading the biblical text in the present day. It is a combination of contextual, liberation, and cultural-anthropological approaches of interpretation.

---

26. Jesurathnam, *Dalit Liberative Hermeneutics*, 233–7.

27. K. Thanzauva, *Theology of Community: Tribal Theology in the Making* (Bangalore: ATC, 2004), 121–122.

28. Maisuangdibou Marianmai, "Reenvisioning Tribal Theologial Hermeneutics," *SATHRI Journal* 24, no. 1 (April, 2021): 66–100.

29. Longkumer, "Tribal Biblical Hermeneutics," 1.

It raises questions and concerns from the Mizo tribal sociocultural, political, and economic contexts. A tribal reading should also be regarded as part of the liberation approach in so far as it is profoundly based on the common principle of the liberation hermeneutics that the interpretation of the Bible should contribute toward liberation of the poor and oppressed. However, the main concern of this hermeneutics is not only to reveal the liberative elements of the biblical texts for socioeconomic liberation (unlike the Latin American liberation), but also for liberation from racial discrimination, sociocultural assimilation, and various forms of alienation. Therefore, a tribal reading will uphold the significance of the tribal communitarian ways of life, cultural values and ethos, and their socioethical principles.[30]

Toward Indian Biblical Hermeneutics

No one theological and biblical hermeneutics can represent the pluralistic India. In further developing Indian hermeneutic, we should seriously consider the social realities of the country. With its wide range of languages, cultures, and faiths as well as striking contrasts, the Indian environment is incredibly complicated. Three obvious elements of Indian social reality are: a caste system that is harsh and pervasive, widespread pluriform religion, and extreme poverty. There is a strong connection between caste, religion, and poverty. In India, poverty has a religious factor as well as an economic one. Poverty is sustained by some systems. Caste, even in its most humiliating form of untouchability, is justified by Hindu scriptures and universally accepted by others, including Christian churches. Other significant aspects of the Indian setting include the fight for survival and freedom from exploitation, violence, and discrimination among Dalits, tribals and Adivasis, as well as the fight of Indian women against patriarchy.[31]

To discuss the Bible and its relationship to the Indian context, the socioeconomic context in India must be taken seriously. Liberation theology had a significant influence on the populace in Latin America due to its reading of the Bible. India has a wide range of religious and cultural variety, in contrast to Latin America and South Africa, which affects socioeconomic elements of daily life.[32]

The contribution of historical criticism in finding out the social location of the authors and editors of the texts is quite significant. In our effort to develop Indian biblical hermeneutics, we do not discount the significance of the

---

30. K. Lallawmzuala, "Hermeneutical Issues in the Old Testament," *Mizo Journal of Theology* 2 no. 1 (Jan–June, 2011): 119–120.

31. Matthew, "Indian Biblical Hermeneutics," 111.

32. K. Jesurathnam, *Old Testament Theology* (Bangalore: Theological Book Trust, 2015), 347.

historical-critical method, instead we supplement it and employ it together with the sociological approach, the anthropological approach, or any other approaches. These approaches can supplement in highlighting the significance and meaning of the historical contexts of the text. They ought to be used as analytical tools to determine the meaning of the ancient texts. Our goal should be to rediscover the text's meaning through its interaction with the current situation and realities, not just to try to interpret the ancient text in an objective manner.[33]

The Indian interpretation of the Bible, in contrast to a historical critical approach, is centered on the interaction between the text and the reader, allowing for the formation of new interpretations. Thus, interpreting the Bible in light of Indian socioeconomic and religious issues has shown tremendous fruit in recent years. For instance, a variety of Dalit and tribal interpretations together with Indian feminist interpretations and older Indian interpretations using Brahminic philosophy make up the Indian hermeneutics. They should co-exist and mutually learn from each other through their interactions. The advent of these readings, some from the margins and others from the dominant society, together make the Indian hermeneutics. The foundation for such a meaning, which was drawn from the text will continue to exist on its own and keep conveying fresh meanings to new readers.[34]

In India, the Bible is usually interpreted by a theologically trained elite. In the context of postmodern biblical interpretation, Walter Brueggemann correctly notes a profound shift in the interpretative groups. He writes:

> The great new fact of interpretation is that we live in a pluralistic con-
> text, in which many different interpreters in many different specific
> contexts representing many different interests are at work on textual
> (theological) interpretation. The old consensus about limits and pos-
> sibilities of interpretation no longer holds. Thus, interpretation is no
> longer done by a small, tenured elite, but interpretive voices and their
> very different readings of the texts come from many cultures in all parts
> of the globe, and from many subcultures even in Western culture.[35]

Thus, the text's imaginative, evocative, and even passionate implications would come from reading along with the many different voices in both public and

---

33. Lallawmzuala Khiangte, "Values and Ethos of the Eighth-Century Prophets: A Mizo Perspective" (PhD diss., School of Theology and Religious Studies University of Wales, Bangor, 2009), 37–38.

34. Jesurathnam, *Old Testament Theology*, 352–353.

35. Walter Brueggemann, *Theology of the Old Testament: Testimony, Dispute, Advocacy* (Minneapolis: Augsburg Fortress, 1997), 61–62.

private settings. For the liberation and emancipation of the communities inside and around us, our viewpoints are continually changing. Indian hermeneutics' role is to support such organizations and biblical interpretations whenever it is feasible. Whichever side takes the initiative, they must be prepared to utilize it for a creative reading of the Bible.[36]

Conclusion

It is crucial to stress that there is no one universal context, culture, or set of experiences when discussing the Indian context. The situation in India illustrates plurality, variety, differences, and a vast range of cultures, worldviews, experiences, and challenges. Several identity-specific readings, such as Dalit reading and tribal reading, have been produced as a result of contextual diversity and differences. On the one hand, it might not be feasible to develop a standard hermeneutic that applies to everyone. On the other hand, the development of Indian biblical hermeneutics benefits from such identity-specific readings. Without ignoring the traditional interpretation of the Bible, Indian biblical hermeneutics is primarily concerned with constructing viewpoints appropriate to Indians and efficiently utilizing materials accessible from the Indian context. It aims to liberate the individual and reform society, resulting in a sense of peace among all people. This goal can be achieved only through an openness to the dynamic activity of the Spirit.

---

36. Jesurathnam, *Old Testament Theology*, 355–356.

CHAPTER EIGHT

Truth *Enflesh*

An Apologia *for Embodied Presence*

Jose Philip

Introduction

I WOULD LIKE to begin with a personal story. In 2017 during an open forum, after almost a decade of working as apologist and evangelist in the Asia-Pacific region, a university student asked if she had to "become an atheist before she became a Christian?" The obvious answer to her question was no. However, to miss the gravity of her question would be almost unforgivable. I had just finished a presentation on the exclusivity of Jesus Christ to a group of students from diverse socioeconomic, cultural, ethnic, and religious backgrounds at a secular university, in a pluralistic society. Though the presentation was well received, the incisiveness of my questioner's query exposed many underlying (and flawed) assumptions I had made of God, the gospel, and the work of apologetics. My apologetic was inadequate, perhaps even a misrepresentation of the gospel invitation, and in a country like India where Christianity is a (persecuted) minority one could ill afford to misrepresent Jesus.

Apologetics, for the most part, is understood as rationally establishing the veracity of the Christian faith. While my personal approach to apologetics is eclectic and conversational, it still privileges reason and rational inference; *agreement* has been the goal of my apologetic engagements. My experiences in the field, however, have not only helped me acknowledge my naivete and inadequacies, but have also encouraged me to find ways to represent Jesus appropriately. And, as I continue my work as an apologist and evangelist, my quest for appropriate models of how to relate to people of other faiths in the manner of Jesus, especially in situations where the Christian community is minority has only intensified. This chapter is one more attempt in that quest.

A slightly modified version of this chapter which includes a summary of the contemporary approaches to Christian Apologetics was published in the *International Journal of Religious Freedom*. See Jose Philip and Godfrey Harold, "Truth enfleshed: An apologia for embodied presence in the midst of persecution in India," *International Journal for Religious Freedom* 17, no. 1 (April 2024): 61–77, https://doi.org/10.59484/BKAE3482

The fundamental changes in cultural and intellectual attitudes over recent years, influenced by confidence in the Enlightenment's dictum of "universal human rationality" behind us has many questioning the purpose of Christian apologetics. This is particularly so in the Indian context, where diversity runs deep and "many gods, many ways" is a prized mantra. From its pantheon to its philosophy, almost anything can be understood differently and appropriated at will. However, with growing nationalistic sentiments and the persecution of adherents to minority faiths—especially Muslims and Christians—on the rise, I believe the question is not whether there a place for Christian apologetics in India, but what apologetics is meant to be and how it could be meaningfully practiced. In other words, the time is ripe for a renewed vision and a revitalized practice of Christian apologetics in India.

In this chapter, I argue that apologetics that is biblically informed offers more than a case for Christ. It offers "Truth *enflesh*" (in the flesh). As a community that embodies and represents Christ faithfully, the task of apologetics is to commend Christ with gentleness and respect, inviting and nurturing participation. The apologetic of embodied presence guards the gospel from being reduced to a proposition, apologetics from being reduced to persuasion, and evangelism from being polarized between proclamation and social action. On the contrary, it nurtures a vision of mission that is holistic, a message that is invitational, and a posture that is participatory, even in the face of persecution and suffering.

In developing an apologetic for embodied presence, I will outline the history of Christianity in India, underlining key developments and highlighting the contextual and contemporary challenges for apologetics in India in the wake of the rise of Hindutva. Next, I will explore the work of apologetics in the New Testament. Finally, I will present an *apologia* for embodied presence—truth in the flesh—as an approach to apologetics that is both biblical its content and viable in the Indian context. But, first, a discussion on the methodology.

Apologia as Doing Contextual Theology for India Today

Christian apologetics is commonly understood as mounting a defense; persuading people to believe in Jesus. This invariably (sometimes unintentionally) reduces the gospel to general propositions and universal truth claims, and the goal of apologetics is to secure agreement. However, for the gospel to be meaningfully understood and faithfully lived out, it has to be contextualized. How else, as Lalsangkima Pachuau asks, will a people make faith practices distinctly their own while allowing others to do the same?[1] Moreover, contextualization

---

1. Lalsangkima Pachuau, *World Christianity: A Historical and Theological Introduction* (Nashville: Abingdon Press, 2018), 91.

is essential for the gospel revealed in Scripture, to take root and bear fruit in cultural soils different from its own, thereby emphasizing the receptor's context. Therefore, critical reflection on the receptor's culture; attending to the contextual realities, is vital to the work of theology. It helps us to both appreciate that God is at work in the world and enables us to participate in God's continuing work.[2] Seen in this light, apologetics is contextual theology.[3] It calls for serious reflection on what the gospel is; how the gospel can be meaningfully articulated and accepted; what it means to become a Christian, and so forth. And, doing so fully cognizant of Christianity's long history in the country, the changing landscape of Indian politics, the upsurge of Hindu nationalism, the implementation of anti-conversion laws, and the rise of religious persecution, to mention a few.

Doing apologetics in India today (as with doing theology) isn't a simple nor a straightforward task. To begin with, as Stephen Bevans rightly points out, taking the contextual realities of human experience into account is not just adding an element; it is "changing the whole equation."[4] I recollect an incident when, after my talk at a university in Australia, a student from an Islamic country asked if he could speak to me in private. His question to me was very simple, "Can I believe in Jesus without making my faith public or be baptized?" My answer to him, while textually appropriate, did not take his context into account and was hardly helpful. He was looking for a concrete way to live out his faith, he was looking for a community; my answer did not deal with his existential struggle, practically. Unfortunately, his predicament is not uncommon. This also provides the first two building blocks of developing an appropriate apologetic for India: the canonical text and the recipient's context.

Given the contextual nature of the Christian message, and the implications of context on the respondent, Bevans highlights the need to pay close attention to the complexities inherent in contexts at two levels. First, at one level, one needs to attend to external factors such as historical events, cultural shifts, and so forth. Second, at another level, one needs to attend to internal factors such as the incarnational nature of Christianity, the sacramental nature of reality, the nature of divine revelation, the catholicity of the church, the nature of God, and the like. Bevans uses six models to categorize the different approaches to contextual theology and plots them along an "experiences of the past and experiences of present" continuum. He warns against adopting any model exclusively as it runs the risk of distorting the theological enterprise. Moreover, Bevans posits

---

2. Pachuau, *World Christianity*, 94–99. Shoki Coe, "In Search of Renewal in Theological Education," *Theological Education* 9, no. 4 (1973): 238–241.

3. The goal of apologetics, in my view, is to serve the purposes of evangelism.

4. Stephen B. Bevans, *Models of Contextual Theology* (Maryknoll, NY: Orbis Books, 2006), 15–16.

that the criteria for judging a model's efficacy is its ability to nurture positive change.[5] This means Christian apologetics demands more than the defense of a proposition; it calls for an explanation that makes sense to the receptor. In other words, apologetics is contextual theology that is "constructive."[6]

Laurie Green, likewise, argues that we steer clear of the deeply misguided "supra-cultural" expectations of our methods; a problem that plagues most apologetic methods, which most apologists seem oblivious to.[7] For any theological task to be transformative, for Green it must be theoretically thorough and practically pertinent. By implication, Christian apologetics must seek to deal with real issues of the people being engaged incarnationally, rooted in context, making divine presence manifest in its heart for the marginalized; all of which demands meaningful presence and participation in context.[8] This provides us with a third building block: the community of believers and unbelievers.[9] There is one final piece to complete this puzzle: the content. What should make up the content of Christian apologetics in India?

Given the contextual-personal nature of the God–human interactions in Christianity, that is, the incarnation, it is important that the content of Christian apologetics be framed around the person and work of Jesus Christ, taking great care to not reduce the person to the proposition. This calls for a multidimensional understanding of Christology. K. K. Yeo is right about the *Christocentricity* of all things; humans growing into the fullness of Christ, not just a monolithic (Western) Christology, but a multidimensional, global view—"while Jesus is singular, Christology is plural."[10] This then ought to be at the heart of our apologetic endeavor, as Peter exhorts, to exalt "Christ as Lord" (1 Pet 3:15).

---

5. Bevans, *Models of Contextual Theology.*

6. Victor I. Ezigbo, *The Art of Contextual Theology: Doing Theology in the Era of World Christianity.* (Eugene, OR: Cascade Books, 2021), 8–9.

7. Using the experience, exploration, reflection, and response quadrilateral to do theology in the community, Green seeks to liberate theology from the clutches of a privileged few and put it into the hands of every Christian, transforming it into "an open system of discovery and transformation" (Laurie Green, *Let's Do Theology: Resources for Contextual Theology* [New York: Continuum International, 2009]: 18).

8. Green, *Let's Do Theology,* 17–37.

9. Doing apologetics that is contextually sensitive, as Ezigbo argues, necessitates "attend[ing] properly to the actual context of the community," which is sufficiently addressed only through the rubric of "love" (Ezigbo, *The Art of Contextual Theology,* 76).

10. Gene L. Green, Stephen T. Pardue, and K. K. Yeo, *Majority World Theology: Doctrine in Global Context* (Downers Grove, IL: IVP Academic, 2020), 241, 216–232. Complementing Yeo's reflections from a Chinese perspective, Andrew Mbuvi's Christology from an African

These four aspects—context, canon, community, and Christ—form the building blocks of doing apologetics in India today. With a distinct commitment to the Lordship of Jesus Christ, and a firm grasp of the canonical text, it is the privilege and responsibility of the community of believers to engage in contextually appropriate ways, so that the yet to believe will know and experience the love of God for them in Jesus Christ, and come to place their faith in him. With this in mind we will consider the fabric of Christianity in India.

From When We Came and Whither Are We Headed
Christianity in India

History of Christianity in India

Christianity in India lacks a clear, distinct, single starting point.[11] Robert Frykenberg observed that Christianity in India can be traced to multiple waves beginning with the "ancient" wave. While the ancient wave of the first four centuries included the apostle Thomas, Hastings notes influences from Babylonian, the Chaldeans, and the Syrian Orthodox Church as well. This was followed (centuries later) by a medieval wave of the Roman Catholic Church in the fifteenth century, and finally the modern, Protestant, wave from the eighteenth century.

While a case can be made that Christianity did take root very early in Indian soil, it had remained relatively subdued and silent for the first fifteen centuries.[12] Christianity's diminutive, noninvasive, and fragile nature in the first fifteen centuries compelled Stephen Neill to label its continued presence "a miracle of church history," and reasoned that it was her distinct language and liturgy that preserved her from being amalgamated into Hinduism.[13]

Much of this changed with the second and third waves of Christianity, when (unfortunately) merchants, mercenaries, and missionary influences rechristened Christianity as a foreign, oppressive faith. Frykenberg observes that Christianity in India after the fifteenth century teetered between systematic exploitation, marginalizing, and murdering Indians on the one hand, and missionaries working

perspective (p. 201–213) and Amos Yong's (p. 237–250) and Rene Padilla's (p. 334–352) pneumatologies from Asian and Latin American perspectives emphasize the same pursuit of multidimensionality.

11. Adrian Hastings, ed., *A World History of Christianity* (Grand Rapids, MI: Eerdmans, 1999), 147.

12. Robert Eric Frykenberg, ed., *Christians and Missionaries in India: Cross Cultural Communications since 1500* (Grand Rapids, MI: Eerdmans, 2003), 36–37.

13. Stephen Neill, *A History of Christian Missions*, 2nd ed. (London: Penguin Books, 1990), 112.

tirelessly to bring them the good news of Jesus Christ on the other. However, after twenty centuries India is still less than 3 percent Christian.[14] The problem today is not colonial imperialism, but a plethora of factors including, of significant importance to the task of Christian apologetics, the Hindutva—Hindu (fundamental) nationalism.

The Birth of a Nation

Several ideologies were at play as India began to find her feet as a sovereign nation. As S. M. Michael argues, India's national consciousness "found its earliest expressions not in the realm of politics but in social and religious reform movements, with the search for an appropriate cultural foundation for Indian society."[15] Michael further notes that three visions of how India ought to be reconstructed in response to her quest for her identity vied for supremacy: (1) Western ideals cradled in the Enlightenment, (2) ancient Hindu traditions, and (3) aspirations of the oppressed and marginalized. The coalescing of these three visions, through multiple iterations, resulted in framing the Indian constitution, granting, guaranteeing, and guarding India's cultural, religious, and ethnic plurality.[16]

Christophe Jaffrelot argues that the framing of the Indian subcontinent as a secular nation with multiple identities—linguistic, caste, and religious identities as part of its national fabric—was largely due to the influence of the Indian National Congress (INC). "For the founders of Congress," Jaffrelot argued, "the Indian nation was to be defined according to the territorial criterion, not on the basis of cultural features: it encompassed all those who happened to live within the borders of British India."[17] While the INC had many credible leaders, none were as charismatic as Mahatma Gandhi and his spiritual son and political heir, Jawaharlal Nehru.

The INC's vision for nationhood was significantly influenced by both Gandhi's universalist definition of Indian nation and Nehru's secular, individualistic, view. Gandhi "looked at the Indian nation as, ideally, a harmonious collection of religious communities all placed on an equal footing. He

---

14. The Pew Research Center finds that "Christians have made up between 2% and 3% of India's population in every census since 1951." Stephanie Kramer, "Religious Composition of India" https://www.pewresearch.org/religion/2021/09/21/religious-composition-of-india/ Published on September 21, 2021, accessed on December 8, 2022.

15. S. M Michael, "Culture and Nationalism: Politics of Identity in India," *Sedos Bulletin* (2003), 3.

16. Michael, "Culture and Nationalism," 3–4. The cradle that nurtured Indian identity, unlike Pakistan which chose nationhood based on a singular religious (Muslim) identity was territorial.

17. Christophe Jaffrelot. *Hindu Nationalism: A Reader* (Princeton: Princeton University Press, 2007), 4.

promoted a syncretic and spiritual brand of the Hindu religion in which all creeds were bound to merge, or converge," and Nehru believed that "the construction of the Indian nation could only be rooted in secular, individual identities."[18] This vision, Gyanendra Pandey argues, Hindu nationalists squarely rejected.[19] And, after seven decades of being the largest democracy and a secular state, it appears as though the country is leaning increasingly toward Hindu nationalism.

India @70 and Beyond
The Ascent of Hindu Nationalism and Hindutva

The clearest articulation of what Hindu nationalism entailed can be found in Vinayak Savarkar's *Essentials of Hindutva* (1923). In this booklet, Savarkar argues why India must be rid of everything foreign and return to 'pure' Hinduism. It was the duty of every true Indian, he insisted, to engage in this quest to purify India and make her a Hindu nation. While originally Hindutva was used (as early as the 1890s) by social reformers such as Chandranath Basu and Bal Gangadhar Tilak to articulate a cultural vision of Hinduism, Savarkar reframed it to delineate a political ideology in his famous work *Hindutva: Who is a Hindu?* (1923). Savarkar's proposal was to envision India as built on the threefold assertion of: (1) a common nation (*rashtra*), (2) common race (*jati*), and (3) common civilization or culture (*sanskriti*).[20]

Savarkar not only disagreed with the INC's vision for a secular India, he disagreed with Gandhi's approach to freedom. Gandhi adopted nonviolence as his political strategy, Savarkar espoused overt and deadly violence. While Savarkar's role in the struggle for India's independence is no match to Gandhi's, his influence must not be underestimated. Notably his influence on Keshav Baliram Hedgewar, the founder of the Rashtriya Swayamsevak Sangh (RSS),[21] and the

---

18. Jaffrelot, *Hindu Nationalism*, 4–5.

19. Gyanendra Pandey, *The Construction of Communalism in Colonial North India* (Delhi: Oxford University Press, 1990).

20. C. V. Mathew, *The Saffron Mission: A Historical Analysis of Modern Hindu Missionary Ideologies and Practices* (Delhi: ISPCK, 1999), 163–192.

21. According to Hedgewar, "The Hindu culture is the life-breath of Hindustan. It is therefore clear that if Hindustan is to be protected, we should first nourish the Hindu culture. If the Hindu culture perishes in Hindustan itself, and if the Hindu society ceases to exist." Moreover, in 2021 the RSS had over a million members, and it argues that there can be only one explanation for this exponential growth in secular India: The emotive response of the millions to the vision of Bharat's national glory, based on the noblest values constituting the cultural and spiritual

Bharatiya Janata Party (BJP), the ruling party of India in 2024, which is not only the largest political party in India, but the largest political party in the world.[22]

While Hindutva is not explicitly a religious party and does not include the ritual or religious tenets in its manifesto, its commitment to secular India is highly contentious, as the political manifestos of the BJP make clear.[23] Moreover, much of Hindutva ideology can be traced back to neo-Hinduism, which as C. V. Mathew argues is a missionary religion in its ethos. Neo-Hinduism is "the reinterpreted, modernized and revitalized nationalistic Hinduism"[24] Mathew's thesis, coincidently, was validated in a major survey conducted by the Pew Research Center in 2020 on religion in India. Among other things, the survey revealed that a significant majority of voters for the BJP believed that to be Indian one must be Hindu, speak Hindi, and vote for the BJP.[25] It shouldn't come as a surprise then that there are close ties between the rise of Hindutva and the marginalization of the religious minorities in India.

With the rise of Hindutva and the *Hinduization* of India, the rise of anti-minority violence is inevitable. Moreover, with the implementation of anti-conversion laws in several states, and the drive to "reconvert" (*ghar wapsi*) minorities back to Hinduism, raises serious questions both about the wellbeing of Christians, and the task of Christian apologetics in India.

---

legacy of the land and collectively called "Dharma." RSS Website, accessed November 16, 2021, https://www.rss.org/Encyc/2012/10/22/rss-vision-and-mission.html.

22. As of 2022, the BJP had over 170 million members, by contrast the Communist Party of China is the second largest party with 96 million members. (See: BJP v. CCP: The rise of the world's biggest political party, accessed December 10, 2022, https://www.smh.com.au/world/asia/bjp-v-ccp-the-rise-of-the-world-s-biggest-political-party-20220916-p5bise.html

23. In its political manifestos (1984) before the BJP became the ruling party, it argued that the need of the hour was for national integrity, unity, and cohesion. The reestablishment of national consensus around the secular identity of the country, preserving its democracy and constitution, especially in the light the diverse and inclusive nature of India was stated as a non-negotiable to pursuing the wellbeing of all. However, in 2019 when the BJP came to power, the manifesto speaks about its "nation first" policy, the overall economic development of the country, and the preservation and development of Indian (read Hindu) cultural heritage. Conspicuous by its absence was any reference to preserving the secular or diverse nature of India. The manifestos of the BJP are available for the public to access online. "Party Booklets & Manifestos: Bharatiya Jana Sangh & Bharatiya Janata Party." accessed November 18, 2021, http://library.bjp.org

24. C. V. Mathew. *Neo-Hinduism: A Missionary Religion* (Madras: Church Growth Research Centre, 1987) 15.

25. Based on the Pew Research Center survey of religion conducted across India, based on nearly 30 thousand face-to-face interviews of adults conducted in seventeen languages between late 2019 and early 2020. See: The dimensions of Hindu nationalism in India in "Religion in India: Tolerance and Segregation,"—accessed on November 27, 2022. https://www.pewresearch.org/religion/2021/06/29/religion-in-india-tolerance-and-segregation/ Published on June 29, 2021.

Apologetics in the New Testament
Review and Reflections

From the time of the apostles, the main task of apologetics has been presenting faith in Jesus Christ as reasonable, despite the suffering it brought. Our English word "apologetics" is derived from the Greek word *apologia* (noun), which literally means offering a reasonable defense. Apologetics, in that sense has always been an integral part of the practice of bearing witness to Jesus, that is of evangelism, and is always contextually conditioned.

The New Testament (qualitatively and quantitatively) uses at least three distinct apologetic devices: miracles, fulfilled prophecy, and personal testimony of eyewitness. In what follows I will focus primarily on select sections from Luke's apologetic work: Luke-Acts, and consider the apologetic thrust of the New Testament in its light.

The evangelist Luke offers one of the best examples of the work of an apologist in his two-volume magnum opus: Luke-Acts. F. F. Bruce, refers to Luke as the pioneer among Christian apologists and his work in Acts gives us "contextualized" models for apologetics in various settings such as to civil authorities, to Jews, to pagans, to philosophers and sceptics, and even to rulers.[26]

Luke's work is unique in that unlike any other gospel, Luke is the only work written with a sequel (Acts). Moreover, Acts is the only canonical account of the early church and much of Paul's writings would be devoid of a context if we did not have Acts. While it is very important to recognize these aspects, it is also important to note that, Luke is the only Gospel writer to state the purpose of his narrative (Luke 1:1,4; Acts 1:1–3).[27]

The introduction of Jesus also follows a similar pattern. Luke uses context specific motifs to expose the identity of Jesus. To Mary, a devote Jew, from the house of David, he introduces Jesus as "Son of the Most High" who will sit on David's throne and rule over the house of Jacob forever, his kingdom will never end (Luke 1:32–33, c.f. 2 Sam. 7:6–16). Jesus is introduced as "Christ the Lord" to the shepherds by a host of angels (Luke 2:11b). Simeon a righteous and devout man, through the Holy Spirit, recognizes Jesus as "the Lord's salvation . . . a light for revelation to the

---

26. See, F. F Bruce, *The Book of the Acts,* New International Commentary on the New Testament (Grand Rapids, MI: Erdmann, 1988), 13. Likewise Joel Green argues, that "the genre of Acts suggests Luke's concern with legitimation and apologetic" that is primarily eschatological, centered on the invitation to participate in God's project. J. B. Green, "Acts of the Apostles," in *Dictionary of the Later New Testament and Its Development*, ed. Ralph P. Martin and Peter H. Davids (Downers Grove, Leicester: InterVarsity Press, 1997), 17.

27. A close read of Luke's "undertaking" (ἐπεχείρησαν) will reveal that Luke was especially concerned to offer a contextual apology for the completed work of Christ and the continuing work of the Holy Spirit.

gentiles and for the glory of his people Israel" (2:30–32 c.f. Isa 60:1–3). Anna the prophetess proclaims him as the one the Jews were looking forward to for the redemption of Jerusalem. And both of these assertions were brought together in John the Baptist's declaration that in Jesus "all mankind will see God's salvation" (Luke 3:4–6, c.f. Isa 40:3–55, 52:10; Ps 98:2, 3). While both John and Matthew quote from Isaiah 40, Luke alone includes, *and all mankind will see God's salvation.*

It is important to recognize the contextual emphasis in Luke's account. Luke's focus is to announce God's salvation to Jews and gentiles alike through the person and work of Jesus and the continuing work of the Holy Spirit, through the disciples (and by extension, the church today). These themes can also be found in Mark and Matthew but presented somewhat differently.[28]

While not as well defined or elaborate as Luke, the apologetic use of the rest of the New Testament is beyond doubt. Jesus did not appeal to faith devoid of knowledge, rather he persuaded people to believe in Him because of the evidence that corroborated his claims.[29] In Mark 2, Jesus demonstrates that he has the power to forgive sin (which the Jews recognize is something only God can do) by healing the paralytic of his physical disability, begging the question of who Jesus really is.[30] In Matthew's account of the healing of a demon-oppressed man (Matt 12:23–30), in the discussion that ensued, Jesus reasons with the unbelieving sceptics to help them see the truth about his identity.[31] Likewise, John affirms that what he writes about is what he had seen (John 1:14); which in 1 John 1 he

---

28. If Jesus is a prophet in Luke, he is more of a teacher in Matthew with Mathew emphasizing fulfilled prophecy as an apologetic for the claims of Christ (See, for example, Matt 1:2–23; 2:6, 15, 17–18.). Matthew and Mark present Jesus's message more in terms of the kingdom of God or heaven, whereas Luke has a more salvific thrust. In Luke we see Jesus making it known that everything that happened (his life, death, and resurrection) was in fulfilment of what was written about him in the Old Testament (Luke 24:44, c.f. Pss 2,16, 22, 69, 72, 110, and 118). Specifically, that his suffering, and rising from the dead on the third day was a fulfilment of Old Testament prophecy (Luke 24:46b, c.f. Isa 2:3). Witnessing, preaching repentance, and forgiveness of sins from Jerusalem to all nations in his name was also foretold in the Old Testament (Luke 24:47). The disciples will be his witnesses to all these things through the enabling power of the Holy Spirit (Luke. 24:48, 49). Isaiah prophesied through the Holy Spirit that some Jews would not accept the gospel of Christ (Acts 28:25, c.f. Isa 6:9]. God's salvation was sent to the gentiles, and they will listen (Acts 28:28). The gospel was being preached in Rome without hindrance (Acts 28:31).

29. For more appeals to objective evidence is the New Testament, see: John 19:31–36; 20:24, 30–31; Acts 1:1–3; 2:32; 3:6–16; 4:8–14, 20; 9:3–8; 14:8–14, 20; 17; 22:6–9, 14; 26:12–18, 26; 1 Cor 15:1–8; 2 Pet 1:16.

30. The authority Jesus exercised over nature, disease, demons and even death gave rise to the same question—*Who is this man?* A similar line of argumentation suffuses the Gospel of John (see John 2:18–21; 10: 30–31, 32–33, 37–38; 15:24–25; 20:24–29).

31. In Matthew 12 we see Jesus argue from analogy thrice (vv. 25–26, 27, 29), appeal to the law of logical inference twice (vv. 26, 28–29); expose the absurdity of their erroneous reason (vv. 25–26); apply the law of non-contradiction and uphold the law of excluded middle (v. 30).

argues is what "we have heard, which we have seen with our eyes, which we looked upon and have touched with our hands," and he continues, "that which we have seen and heard we proclaim also to you, so that you too may have fellowship with us; and indeed, our fellowship is with the Father and with his Son Jesus Christ. And we are writing these things so that our joy may be complete" (1 John 1:1–4).

Like the apostles, the early followers of Jesus commended Jesus to others. In Acts 18:25–28 we read that Apollos was "instructed in the way of the Lord, and fervent in Spirit" (v. 25) and he "powerfully refuted the Jews in public, showing by the Scriptures that the Christ was Jesus" (v. 28). The Greek word for "powerfully refuted" (διακατηλέγχετο) literally means to argue, dispute, or reason. The same word is used in Paul's apologetics and instructions in Acts 17:2–3, 11, 17, 22–31; 18:4, 19; 19:8–9; 26:25; and 1 Timothy 6:20.

Apologetics in the New Testament perform the twofold task of commending the truth and contesting errors about Jesus Christ and confirming the continuing work of the Spirit in the world through the church.[32] The New Testament also makes it plain that God is sovereign in making himself know. Apologetics, therefore, is not about "arguing" or "reasoning" people into the kingdom of God. The apologist does not shoulder the burden of conviction, but clear communication. Conviction and conversion are the work of the Holy Spirit.[33] Moreover, the very ability to "hear," "consider," and "respond" to the gospel is the gift of God.[34] This does not preclude the use of reason and evidence; on the contrary, it provides the proper place for the use of it. The use of evidence and the appeal to rationality in the New Testament was not to undermine the authority of the Scriptures, or to undervalue the work of the Spirit, on the contrary, it is because of the authority of the Word, that the Christian can "argue" for the truth (without being argumentative), empowered by the Spirit. The goal of Christian apologetics, then, is the glory of the risen Lord Jesus Christ, its resources are the Word and the Spirit, and its reward is the salvation of souls.

Truth *Enfleshed*
An Apologia *for Embodied Presence*

Dialogue is also foundational to engagement in a religious pluralistic environment, especially when the sociocultural-religious context is in flux, as it is with India today. With the BJP consolidating its position and political influence over

---

32. To dispel error, one has to defang or dismantle arguments against Christianity (2 Cor 10:3–5; Titus 1:9–11) and to preserve truth we must embody truth truthfully (1 Pet 3:15; Acts 1:3; Luke 24:39; Rom 1:19–20).

33. Only the Holy Spirit can enable a person to believe in Jesus Christ as Lord and Savior (see John 1:13; 6:44, 65; 16:8–11; Rom 9:16; Eph 2:8–10; 1 Cor 2:14). This is necessary due to human sin (see 1 Cor 2:13–14; 2 Cor 4:4; Eph 4:18).

34. See Rom 1:17; 3:10–13; Eph 2:8–10, and Acts 17:22–31, 34; 1 Pet 3:15.

the past decade, Hindutva is on the ascent and Hinduization of the Indian identity is in full swing. Apologetics in this context, appropriating what Pachuau
insists contextualization does, must attempt "to relate the gospel to both traditional culture and the changing sociopolitical [context of India]."[35] Moreover,
developing an apologetic that genuinely engages, adapts to, and appropriates the
religio-cultural aspects of India (Tanchanpongs 'context-to-text approach"),[36]
which calls for a posture in which elements in the receiver/interpreter's context is
held as "dynamic and modifiable," and is in constructive dialogue with Scripture
is invaluable. This is especially true in urban India given the increasing popularity of the discipline of apologetics. "We stand at the dawn of the grand age of
human apologetics," observed Os Guinness, "and never before in human history"
have we had the means to engage in the "business of relentless self-promotion."[37]
Yet, it is hard to miss the signs warning us that apologetics is deemed by many
as unnecessary, disadvantageous, even detrimental to the Christian faith. The
grand age of apologetics is not without its troubles.[38] The greater the persuasion
to follow Jesus, the louder are the dissenting, disillusioned, and disappointed
voices that disapprove of apologetics.

As earlier noted, a careful read of the Luke-Acts account of the early Church
shows how the first followers of Jesus were almost always engaged in persuading
others to follow Jesus.[39] It should come as no surprise that the history of missions
is the story of the lives of "ordinary" Christians, living lives faithful to Jesus, in
tangible ways—as "integrated members of their communities."[40] Nor should it
surprise us that persuading others to follow Jesus, even if it costs them their lives,

---

35. Pachuau, *World Christianity*, 141–142.

36. Green, Pardue, and Yeo, *Majority World Theology*, 69.

37. Os Guinness, *Fool's Talk: Recovering the Art of Christian Persuasion* (Downers Grove, IL:
IVP Books, 2015), 15.

38. The contemporary challenges to apologetics can be attributed in part to what Lyotard in *The
Postmodern Condition* calls "incredulity towards metanarratives," but mostly because of why
(and how) it is practiced, which in my view is a greater problem. Sean McDowell highlights four
reasons why apologetics has a bad name: (1) apologists often overstate their case, (2) apologists
often do not speak with gentleness, love, and respect, (3) apologists are often not emotionally
healthy, and (4) apologetics is often done in a cold, mechanical, and rationalistic manner. See,
"Why Apologetics Has a Bad Name." https://seanmcdowell.org/blog/why-apologetics-has-a-
bad-name, accessed on December 7, 2022.

39. F. F. Bruce points out that Luke's work in Acts gives us "contextualized" models for apologetics in various settings such as to civil authorities, to Jews, to pagans, to philosophers and
sceptics, and even to rulers. (Bruce, *The Book of the Acts*, 13).

40. Edward L. Smither, *Mission in the Early Church*, electronic edition (James Clark & Co,
2014), 43.

was the "normal" Christian life in the early Church. That was how they were encouraged and empowered to live.

Apologetic discourses in India, then, will have to be dialogical—both with the contemporary context and the ancient text, and among believers and those who are yet to believe in Jesus—if they are to be meaningful and fruitful. This calls for the Christian community in India to embrace a posture of servitude, even in the face of suffering, modelling our defense of Jesus with Jesus's way.

Earlier I had proposed four aspects (context, canon, community, and Christ) form the building blocks of doing apologetics in India today. I had also noted that the work of apologetics in India calls for an unflinching commitment to the Lordship of Jesus Christ, and to engage those who are yet to believe in Jesus as a community that believes in Jesus, in love. In other words, the church's genuine participation in society—drawing principles from the canonical text based on the patterns of divine-human interactions in it—is foundational to its apologetic. It sets the stage for the gospel to be meaningfully communicated and communities to be genuinely transformed as well.

Three implications for apologetics follow: first, the need for a community that is unafraid to love unreservedly, even the undeserving. Second, an unflinching resolve and willingness to engage with gentleness and respect, and third, a visible demonstration of Jesus's tangible lordship.

The foundation of the gospel is love, and so the fountainhead of the gospel must also be love. This is especially so because the Scriptures reveal a God whose love compelled him, through the pain of his participation in human affairs, through his incarnation, to redeem humanity. The Scriptures also call us to follow his example (1 Pet 2:21; Matt 11:28–30; John 20:21, 1 Cor 11:1). Reflecting on the life of Jesus in the Scriptures as a community of believers gives us three of the four building blocks with which to construct an apologetic for India—Christ, canon, and community.

The eight key findings about Christians in India from a 2021 Pew Research Center study on "Religion in India" listed below provide us with the fourth building block: context.[41] For the purposes of this chapter I will focus my attention on points 1, 4, 5, 6, and 8.

1. Among Indians, 0.4% of adults are Hindu converts to Christianity.
2. There is no clear majority denomination among Indian Christians

---

41. While the eight findings in the list are not always true for everyone, everywhere in India, it is a good representation of the Indian context, and offers us a helpful reference point for our discussion on developing an apologetic that is contextually framed. See Ariana Monique Salazar, "Religion in India: Tolerance and Segregation," (July 29, 2021), accessed on November 27, 2022. https://www.pewresearch.org/fact-tank/2021/07/12/8-key-findings-about-christians-in-india/.

3. Three-quarters of Indian Christians (76%) say religion is very important in their lives, and Indian Christians engage in a variety of traditional beliefs and practices.

4. Substantial shares of Indian Christians follow religious practices and beliefs not traditionally associated with Christianity.

5. Indian Christians disproportionally identify with lower castes (74%), including 57% with Scheduled Castes (SC) or Scheduled Tribes (ST).

6. Lower-caste Indian Christians are much more likely than upper-caste (also called General Category) Christians to hold both Christian and non-Christian beliefs.

7. Overall, Indian Christians are less prone toward religious segregation than some other groups.

8. Politically, Christians favor the opposing Indian National Congress (INC) over the ruling Bharatiya Janata Party (BJP).

The first finding (only 0.4 percent of adults are Hindu converts) alerts us to the challenges associated with witnessing to the vast majority of Indians in India. Points 8 and 5 should help us appreciate that the objectives and goals of Hindu Nationalism will make it increasingly difficult for Christians in India to be proud Indians and unashamedly Christian at the same time. This is clearly seen in both the growing sentiment that Indian and Hindu are synonyms, and the growing discrimination (especially among the SC, ST) meted out against Christians. Points 4 and 6 reveal that the vast majority of Christians in India still hold on to beliefs that are at odds with Christian beliefs and practices that might serve are bridges.

With the rise of Hindu nationalism, the growing number of states enforcing the anti-conversion law, and the steady shift of the Indian identity from "secular" toward "*Hinduness*," persecution of religious minorities is to be expected.[42] This makes witnessing for Christ in India more challenging today. However, this should not deter Christians from engaging in apologetics; instead, it should help reframe Christian engagement to reflect the biblical response to suffering, which is not "to escape" (suffering), but to learn to "suffer well" and "love well" (Jas 1:2–4; Rom 5:3; Heb 10:36; 2 Pet 1:6).

---

42. While it is true that Jawaharlal Nehru, India's first Prime Minister, explicitly stated that Christianity is very much a part of the Indian fabric, with the decline of his "secular vision" of India and the rise of Hindutva, the populist propagandists will continue to paint a picture of Christianity as a Western faith, or worse a corrupting, exploitative, and destabilizing influence, detrimental to national interest.

Apologetics in India, then, will do well, to first, persuade Christians to follow Christ's example and love unreservedly, even those who harm them unjustly, just as God demonstrated his love for us, while we were still sinners, in that Christ died for us (Rom 5:8). The Gospel accounts of Jesus are replete with reports of him taking the initiative to reach out and participate in the lives of others, in love.[43] For any predicament to be dealt with appropriately and adequately one must be present, and in Jesus, human predicament was met by divine presence, and learning from him, we too must persuade one another to love each other, and the world, as Jesus did.

Second, apologetics in India should not only present a persuasive case for the historical veracity of the resurrection to the unbeliever, but also encourage and empower the believes to offer a cogent demonstration "being born again into a living hope" because of the resurrection of Jesus Christ (1 Pet 1:3) by being unafraid of those who persecute them and relentless in doing good to them.

Third, India needs an apologetic that nurtures an unflinching resolve and willingness to engage with gentleness and respect. Any apologetics of the gospel must be done in love, gentleness, and respect; failing which we will only sow seeds of discord and reap dissentions. Moreover, through our engagement (in love), we learn to demonstrate the lordship of Jesus without compromise (teaching, rebuking, correcting, and training) or coercion, as we seek to be an invitational community that embodies the love of God for the other. It is in this context that we maintain a posture of servitude to Jesus that shows the lordship of Jesus as good, as set before the world the as the reason for the hope that is in us, for their good.

Communities that embody the loving, self-giving presence of Christ, engaged dialogically making every effort to relate the gospel to Indians who are yet to be Christians, with gentleness and respect, will offer a compelling apologetic for the gospel of Jesus Christ in an Indian context. Such an apologetic will not only rescue apologetics from reducing the person of Jesus Christ to a mere proposition, but it will also present Christ to Indians as with them and for them—truth *enfleshed*.

Conclusion

Despite two thousand years of Christianity in India, Christians in India are a struggling minority, with a growing sentiment that they don't belong. While it

---

43. The good Jesus went about doing always came at a cost. Sometimes at the expense of a meal (John 4) or risking defilement and ostracizing, which is a big deal for the Jew (Matt 8). He even risked incurring the wrath of the religious and political leaders of his day so that he could do for humanity what only he could—save us from our sin, and so embraced death—even death on the cross (1 Tim 1:15; Phil 2:8).

is true that the Indian constitution grants, guarantees, and guards every citizen's fundamental right to religious freedom, persecution of religious minorities has become commonplace, especially in the light of the rise of Hindu Nationalism. The present condition is bleak, yet therein lies the opportunity for Christian apologetics.

Cradled by the cross, the Christian church is no stranger to persecution. History attests that persecution has been an integral part of the growth and spread of Christianity. Persecution, however, does not mean that the church does nothing about its plight, nor does it imply that persecution guarantees growth. Persecution is not only an opportunity to experience the sovereignty of God but also an invitation to participate in God's work in the world.

In this chapter I offer an *apologia* for embodied presence—truth in the flesh—as an approach to apologetics that is biblical in its content and viable in the Indian context. As a community that embodies and represents Christ faithfully, the task of apologetics is to commend Christ with gentleness and respect, inviting and nurturing participation. The apologetic of embodied presence guards the gospel from being reduced to a proposition, apologetics from being reduced to persuasion, and evangelism from being polarized between proclamation and social action. On the contrary, it nurtures a vision of mission that is holistic, a message that is invitational, and a posture that is participatory, even in the face of persecution and suffering.

CHAPTER NINE

Indian Christian Hymnody

A Missiological Interaction

Arpan Christian

Introduction

ALONG WITH BIBLE translation, one of the significant contributions of the Protestant mission to world Christianity is the printing, publication, and integration of hymnbooks. Hymnody plays a crucial role in the spiritual and ecclesial formation of people. Translating, composing, and singing hymns served as important moments of collaboration between Western missionaries, native poets, and "local" congregations that shaped the church in India during modern missions. Hymnody occupies an important place not only in the spiritual and devotional lives of people but in the collective Christian identity of worshipping congregation in the pluralistic context of India. However, in postcolonial mission studies, the emphasis on Western-indigenous distinction has a tendency to undervalue the interactive and collaborative nature of the relationship between missionaries, native poets, and the "local" congregation that constitutes hymnody. This emphasis sometimes overlooks the spiritual significance of the deeper missiological engagement undergone in the formation of hymnody and inevitably favors *indigenous* tunes and compositions over the *translated* hymns. On the contrary, it is also important to acknowledge that the usage of classical Indian musical traditions (*Hindustani* and *Carnatic*) in compositing indigenous hymns also exhibits hierarchical and dominating tendencies.[1] This chapter attempts to introduce a theoretical principle of "missiological interaction" as a lens to study Indian hymnody that can inform several layers of engagement between missionaries, native poets, and the "local" congregation, which are difficult to categorize into a Western-indigenous binary.

---

1. For instance, Hephzibah Israel, in her studies of Tamil hymnody identifies that the sectional division between *hymns* and *lyrics* (or *Keerthanigal*) represents a point of conflict to establish Protestant identity based on caste-hierarchy than the issues of Western influence. Cf. Hephzibah Israel, "Authority, Patronage and Customary Practice: Protestant Devotion and the Development of Tamil Hymn in Colonial South India," in *Constructing Indian Christianities: Culture, Conversion, and Caste*, ed. Chad M. Bauman and Richard Fox Young (New Delhi: Routledge, 2014), 86–109. See also, Zoe C. Sherinian, *Tamil Folk Music as Dalit Liberation Theology* (Bloomington, IN: Indiana University Press, 2014).

Defining Missiological Interaction

My understanding of *missiological interaction* partly relies on historian Jeffrey Cox's analysis of the *Punjabi Psalter* and the emerging ethnomusicological scholarship.[2] Cox observes that the Punjabi village converts who were largely among the poor and often "illiterate" Christians were distinct in embracing a hymnody that was based exclusively on singing the Psalms. This appears to be a direct theological influence of the United Presbyterian missionaries who emphasized metrical Psalms adhering to the teachings of the sixteenth century reformers. However, missionary accounts of the popularity of the Psalms are attributed to the triumph of the indigenous contribution, particularly, to an Urdu poet, catechist, and mission pastor, I. D. Shahbaz (1846–1921). Even further, it was the Punjabi vernacular language and Punjabi tunes that gave the instant popularity of the metrical Psalms, especially during the "mass conversion" movements in Punjab. According to Cox, *Punjabi Psalter* is a distinct hymnody that represents a "dialect process of hybridity and synthesis" and which might not fit into the conceptual notion of binary opposition.[3]

Language of "hybridity" and "interaction" emerges in the recent missiological studies under the influence of postcolonial linguistic studies.[4] Cox defines *interactions* as a dynamic engagement between the missionaries and the non-Westerners and even the non-Christians in collaborations and in "living often in relationships of hierarchy and conflict and sometimes outright domination, but also of spiritual intimacy, friendship, love for their adopted land, and sometimes inter-marriage."[5] The primary emphasis is that the interaction between European and non-European cultures during modern missions creates

---

2. Cf. Jeffrey Cox, "Sing unto the Lord a New Song: Transcending the Western/Indigenous Binary in Punjabi Christian Hymnody," in *Europe as the Other: External Perspective on European Christianity*, ed. J. Becker and B. Stanley (Göttingen: Vandenhoeck & Ruprecht, 2013), 149–163. The article is based on his previous research in India, which is published as a monograph. Cf. Jeffrey Cox, *Imperial Fault Lines: Christianity and Colonial Power in India, 1818–1940* (Stanford, CA: Stanford University Press, 2002).

3. Jeffrey Cox, "Sing unto the Lord a New Song," 149.

4. The postcolonial linguistic studies responding to Edward Said's *Orientalism* (1978) are represented by Homi K. Bhabha, *The Location of Culture* (London: Routledge, 1994); and Mary Louise Pratt, *Imperial Eyes: Studies in Travel Writing and Transculturation* (London: Routledge, 1992). Cited in Judith Becker, Brian Stanley, and Institut für Europäische Geschichte (Mainz, Rhineland-Palatinate, Germany), eds., *Europe as the Other: External Perspectives on European Christianity*, Veröffentlichungen Des Instituts Für Europäische Geschichte Mainz. Supplement 103 (Göttingen: Vandenhoeck & Ruprecht, 2014), 16. (1–28)

5. Jeffrey Cox, "Global Christianity in the Contact Zone," in *European Missions in Contact Zones: Transformation through Interactions in a (Post-) Colonial World*, ed. J. Becker (Göttingen: Vandenhoeck & Ruprecht, 2015), 27–43, cited at, 32.

a "contact zone" that has the potential to create new "contact cultures" transcending both traditional cultural boundaries.

Along with Cox, I also rely on the emerging ethnomusicological scholarship that pays attention to the central role played by the "local" worshipping congregations in the process of transformation or "hybridity." The editors of *Making Congregational Music Local in Christian Communities Worldwide* include eleven such ethnographic studies from around the world. These scholars are focusing on the critical frontline role taken by "local" communities in adopting and innovating traditions that may not fit into the local-global binary. While they are well aware of the nuances of the missiological principles of *inculturation, contextualization*, and *indigenization*, to emphasize the performative dimension of hymnody, they preferred to call the process of indigenous hymnody a "musical localization."[6] This implies the primary role of the singing congregations or the practicing Christians in "localizing" the musical tradition as per the ecclesial needs in a particular context, may it be Western or indigenous, local or global. Zoe C. Sherinian who also studies Tamil folk hymnody is one of the editors,[7] who along with others defines "musical localization" as "a variety of musical practices—some considered 'indigenous,' some 'foreign,' some shared across spatial and cultural divides; some linked to past practice, some innovative— and make them locally meaningful and useful in the construction of Christian beliefs, theology, practice, or identity."[8]

The insights from Cox and the ethnomusicological scholarship can complement each other to define missiological interaction. While Cox pays attention to the transformative process beyond the binary, ethnomusicological studies help to see the decisive role of the "local" congregation. Missiological interaction represents a process of deeper collaborative engagement and mutual transformation. While missionaries and poets were directly engaged with the "text" of the hymnody, the worshipping congregations collectively participated through their concrete engagements in the "context." The principle of missiological interaction can help us to explore the diverse layers of complexity involved in Indian Christian hymnody beyond the binary opposition. The three primary layers of

---

6. While the Catholic Church prefers the term *inculturation* to show the concern for the institutional authority; the Protestant church prefers *contextualization* to show the concern for the Scriptural authority and its sociocultural implications; the anthropological studies prefer *indigenous* describing the process of "foreign" beliefs become adopted into "local." Cited by Monique M. Ingalls, Muriel S. Reigersberg, and Zoe C. Sherinian, eds., "Introduction," in *Making Congregational Music Local in Christian Communities Worldwide* (London and New York: Routledge, 2018), 1–32.

7. Cf. Zoe C. Sherinian, *Tamil Folk Music as Dalit Liberation Theology* (Bloomington, IN: Indiana University Press, 2014).

8. Cited by Ingalls, Reigersberg, and Sherinian, "Introduction," 13.

engagement include the publication of vernacular hymnals, the process of translation and musical settings, and the influence of the *Bhakti* movement. However, along with the written text, the distinctive layers of evangelistic singing bands and the stories of the lives of the poets and laypeople as illustrated in the case of the North Indian regions, particularly, Gujarat add the dynamics of oral traditions. More than a mixing of Western and indigenous traditions, the Indian Christian hymnody represents a lyrical affirmation of witnessing people and their wider influence even in times of persecution and challenges.

Missiological Interaction in the Publication of Vernacular Hymnals

A cursory glance at the "Foreign Mission" section of John Julian's (1839–1913) ambitious dictionary of hymnology, first published in 1892,[9]provides some interesting details of collaborative engagement as well as some disagreements between missionaries and the native poets in publishing vernacular hymnbooks in India.[10] The section provides a survey of fourteen regions and regional language hymnbook publications in India which become one of the crucial intersections between mission agencies and the worshipping congregation.[11] The section recognizes the presence and distinguished leadership of some of the first-generation native poets. I could identify at least thirty-one names of poets along with several others whose names are not mentioned but who were deeply engaged with missionaries and their respective "local" congregation.[12] Some of them are recognized for their distinctive characteristics. For instance, in the case of "Uriya" (present Odisha state) hymnody, the first hymnbook was published in 1844 through the efforts of missionary Rev. Amos Sutton (1802–1854) and the area's first native convert, Gangu Dhor. However, this hymnbook did not survive

---

9. John Julian, *A Dictionary of Hymnology: Setting Forth the Origin and History of Christian Hymns of all Ages and Nations.* 2nd rev. ed. (New York: Dover, 1907), 746–759. Cited at https://ccel.org/ccel/julian_j/hymn1/hymn1.i.v.html accessed on December 12, 2022.

10. The section of *Dictionary of Hymnology* called "Missions, Foreign" is written by W. R. Stevenson, and includes Asian and Indian hymnodies, see pp. 746–759.

11. Regional languages include Bengali, Uriya (i.e., Orissa), Hindi, Urdu, Marathi, Gujarati, Punjabi, Sindhi, Tamil, Telugu, Malayalam, Canarese (i.e. Kannada), Tulu and Assamese; Tribal languages in which hymnbooks emerged include Kolh, Santalia, and Khasi.

12. The poets include: Krishna Pal, Rev. Jacob K. Biswas, Babu Bipra Charan Chakrabutty, Amrito Lal Nath, Gogou Chunder Dutt, Madhu Sodon Sircar, Gunga Dhor, Makund Das, Shem Shau, Kartick Samal, Bamadeb, Daniel Mahanty, Mansell Gill, Janvier, Shujat Ali, Walji Bechar, Krishnaraw Ramaji Sangle, Pastor J. Paul, Rev. Abliah Samuel, Rev. Justus Joseph, Philippos, Vethanayagam, Purshattam Chowdry, Rev. P. Jagganandham, Nathannel Tuagu, Manidah Tassu.

long. Later, it was Makunda Das who is identified as "Dr. Watts of Orissa," and who widely popularized the hymns among the congregation through his gifts of native compositions.

The following case illustrates some of the distinctive developments which appear to be spontaneous and beyond the control of missionaries. In the case of Marathi hymnody, the origin of *Kirttans* is attributed to native poet and catechist, Krishnaraw Ramji Sangale. The missionaries were surprised by the "enthusiastic reception" even from the neighboring villages when the first Marathi *Kirttans* performed under his leadership in Ahmednagar in 1862. Stevenson records in detail the entire setting of the event. He also mentions the diverse local instruments like *sarangi*, *symbols*, and *dholak*, and tries to explain their Western equivalents. He further describes the entire worship order which is significantly different from the liturgical order. "The words of the chorus became the text for a brief exhortation, delivered in a musical tone, and leading the way to another chorus, the whole performance occupying around two hours." He further connects the new pattern of *Kirttans* with other such developments of the use of *Bhajans* or *Lyrics* in Christian worship which brought initial dissonance. "The use of *Lyrics* in public worship was at first opposed by many missionaries, principally because the associations with the tunes were objectionable; but they are so much preferred by the people and suit so well the genius of the language, that the opposition has almost ceased, and in many village congregations they are used exclusively."[13] The popularity of this new pattern of worship made a profound impact on missionaries beyond their imagination.

The section also records some of the disagreements among the missionaries about the native hymnals. For instance, Stevenson mentions an important remark of Baptist missionary Rev. G. H. Rouse regarding the native Bengali Baptist hymnal. He critiques that though the hymnody is rich in native tunes, "joyous Christian experience is very deficient in the native church . . ." Stevenson does not fully endorse this remark and adds that probably the understanding of music in this region was "melancholy." Contrary to that, he identifies the popularity of the native meter hymns for "Bazar preaching" and for the church and the surpassing contribution of native poets in the Bengali hymnody. For instance, Bengali poet and leader Rev. Jacob K. Biswas who was a tutor at the Divinity School of CMS, composed more than a thousand hymns in both Bengali and English meter and whose hymns have a wider impact in the Indian church even transcending denominational and regional boundaries.

The dissonance over the usage of poetry in composing hymns was also witnessed in the case of Joseph van Someran Taylor (1820–1881). His story is interesting because he was non-native and yet became known as the "father of Gujarati

---

13. Cited in Julian, *A Dictionary of Hymnology*, 753.

grammar" and made significant efforts in learning and loving the "local" language and composing hymns that touched the hearts and minds of the people.[14] He was born to an London Missionary Society missionary in Bellary, Karnataka, and grew up speaking Kannada, Marathi, and Tamil. He chose to stay back in Gujarat due to his love for the language and became the first to publish Gujarati hymnbooks using indigenous tunes. His story witnesses some dissonance with fellow missionaries over the use of Gujarati poetic tunes. The Irish missionaries were strongly influenced by certain home traditions which did not allow musical accompaniment or hymns apart from metrical Psalms. However, he along with five native poets, together composed around four hundred hymns out of which the majority are still regularly sung during church worship.

This brief survey based on Stevenson's article informs the collaborative engagement as well as some dissonance in the publication of vernacular hymnals. However, the work of publishing hymnals became instrumental in integrating the gift and experiences of the native poets and the oral traditions that emerged as a surprise. The deeper engagement between missionaries and native poets not only generated written liturgy for the church for years to come but also created a movement by which diverse forms of worship could spread across India.

Translation and Musical Settings

The second kind of missiological interaction that appears in hymnody is translation and musical settings—both of which are inseparable in hymnody. The process of translation of hymns is founded on the pioneering Protestant missionary work of the vernacular Bible translation. Lamin Sanneh helps to see critically what is involved in the translation process beyond the popular notion of colonial imperialism. "The translation role of missionaries cast them as unwitting allies of mother-tongue speakers and as reluctant opponents of colonial domination."[15] It was through "translation," that collaboration, the back-and-forth discussions, and relational intimacy developed and made the missionaries "unwitting allies" with the natives. Music in hymnody adds to the dynamic an element of a collective appeal to emotion. Hymnody invites one to partake in collective worship along with the totality of Christian tradition

14. Some of his contributions and details are studied by Indian historian and missionary R. H. S. Boyd. See Robin H. S. Boyd, "An Outline History of Gujarati Theological Literature-I," *The Indian Journal of Theology* 12, no. 2 (April–June 1963): 43; Robin H. S. Boyd, "An Outline History of Gujarati Theological Literature-II," *The Indian Journal of Theology* 12, no. 3 (September 1963): 83–100.

15. Lamin O. Sanneh, *Translating the Message: The Missionary Impact on Culture*, 2nd ed., American Society of Missiology Series 42 (Maryknoll, NY: Orbis Books, 2009), 95.

transcending the "local" particularities. Hymns bring the theological language of the Bible into everyday metaphors and colloquial conversations. Hymnody also asks to bring in diverse musical gifts and experiences that can create a shared experience a concrete visible space amid their fellow citizens witnessing their new identity in Christ.

Tamil hymnologist and theologian M. Thomas Thangaraj helps to identify some of these constitutive dynamics in the historical formation of Indian hymnody influenced by language and musical settings. He classifies them as *Western, classical, folk/tribal,* and *light music.*[16] During the Western influence, the focus was on the translated hymns from English or German as introduced by the missionaries. Subsequently, the first-generation poets and the local people utilized the musical resources and skills from the *Classic Hindustani* in North India and *Carnatic* in South India. Several of the skillful poets and musicians who took leadership in Tamil Christian hymnody, such as Vedanayagam Sastriyar and H. A. Krishna Pillai, were from the upper caste. However, due to a lack of a kind of improvisation and ornamentation peculiar to Indian classical music, as observed by Thangaraj, the early converts had become used to singing Western hymns and even the indigenous hymns sounded like Western congregational songs. However, the emergence of *folk* and *Dalit* Christian resources challenged this development. It appealed to the issues of justice and liberation through hymns in which folk dance, non-literal day-to-day colloquial language, and ordinary matters became the focus of hymn composition. Similarly, the interaction between the missionaries and the tribal people in the northeastern mountain regions added a distinctive dimension of indigenous music, drumming, and dancing that was different from classical music or the Hindu religious traditions. Finally, *light music* is a hybrid music that creatively integrates both, the Western and Indian musical traditions. It became popular among the Protestant churches under the influence of Pentecostal and Charismatic movements and televangelists, and through popular digital media like cassettes (in tge 1970s), and CDs.

"What is Indigenous Hymnody?"—Thangaraj raises this question and believes that it is almost impossible to define indigenous hymnody in India. First, because of several historical shifts, the interaction between languages and musical traditions evolved in the formation of the Indian Christian hymnody. Second, he finds that the forces of globalization in the form of Western music and praise songs through digital media are common in church worship and create a

---

16. M. Thomas Thangaraj. "Indian Christian hymnody," in *The Canterbury Dictionary of Hymnology,* http://www.hymnology.co.uk/i/indian-christian-hymnody, accessed on March 20, 2023.

culture of English as a new *lingua franca*.[17] The triangulation of the missionaries, the native poets, and the languages and musical traditions of both made Indian hymnody a missiological contact zone. While on the one hand, we see a tension between the missionaries and the native poets over the use of Western tunes and indigenous tunes, on the other hand, there is a form of hybridity in which both merge to create a distinctive Indian hymnody.

The hybridity and interaction in Indian hymnody also generated inter-state or regional language exchange. Not only among the North Indian languages but also in a crisscrossing of "Dravidian" languages with the North Indian languages through hymnody. For instance, Stevenson finds that the Bengali Methodist hymnal's (2nd ed., 1886) 322 hymns also contained fifty-one *lyrics* of a kind very popular in all parts of India like *Tamil* and *Marathi*. Here, by *lyrics,* he is referring to *Bhajans* of northern and central India which he qualifies as "usually sung in processions at festivals, to the accompaniment of a drum and cymbals"[18] and later defines as originating from "Dravidian" languages, especially referring to the *Tamil Lyrics* of Vedanayagam Sastriyar (1774–1864) which was widely circulated and translated in other regional languages. Several of the hymns migrated from one region to another transcending cultural boundaries and thus creating a shared space of a Christian common experience that invokes dialogue and interaction beyond the written text. The preference for vernacular language over the *Sanskrit* script, as we see in the next section, is one of the important social contributions of hymnody.

Missiological Interaction and *Bhakti* Movements

Another layer of missiological interaction that appears in the hymnody is theological in nature and also integrates different "local" movements as well. Historian and missiologist, Arun Jones provides an analysis of the missiological interaction between American Evangelicalism and "local" religion, that is, constituted at the interface of Hindu *Bhakti* and the poetic traditions such as *Kabir Pant* and *Sufi* in *Islam* during the period 1836–1870. He observes that even before the arrival of the missionaries, a grassroots movement led by medieval *Bhakti-poets*[19] cultivated a religious "third space" into which evangelicalism "was drawn" and

---

17. Thangaraj, "Indian Christian hymnody."

18. Cited in Julian, *A Dictionary of Hymnology*, 752.

19. Such as, Kabir (fifteenth to sixteenth century) Surdas Ravidas (sixteenth century) Mirabai (sixteenth century) in Hindi; Nammalvar and Antal (nineth century) in Tamil; Namdev (fourteenth century) and Tukaram (seventeenth century) in Marathi; Baba Nanak (fifteenth to sixteenth century) in Punjabi; Narsi Mehta (fifteenth to sixteenth century).

"was able to establish itself and grow there because of certain crucial similarities with the otherwise dissimilar *bhakti* movements."[20]

During the medieval period religious reformed movements known as *Bhakti* employed the medium of poetry and songs to channel religious enthusiasm to intense devotion, worship, and community participation. This also contributed to national integration by knitting together different regions, classical periods and modernity, and tension between *Dalits* and *Brahmins*.[21] The preference for the vernacular languages and poetry over the scriptural language of *Sanskrit* is one of the ways the medieval *Bhakti* movements (ca. 500–1700 CE) cultivated a "complex network of grassroots communities" into which the newly arrived missionaries were drawn.

Jones identifies five shared characteristics between *Bhakti poets* and evangelicalism in the northwest region: theology, religious expression, reformation, social formation, and social location.[22] Theologically, both evangelicalism and *bhaktas* look to and worship a divine savior. The relational intimacy with the savior empowers the worshipper in the highs and lows of life. Second, both traditions reflect "heart religion" and the affective dimension at the center. The transformation of the heart and the love of God are recurring themes in the hymns. Third, both, the *Bhakti* movement and evangelicalism in their own distinct ways have catalyzed theological reformation by which approaching the divine became accessible to all castes and social reform in which appropriate religious devotion could be practiced, cultivated, and developed over time. Finally, both these movements found a majority of their adherents from the lower ranks of society.[23]

The confluence and divergence of the "local" movement in the Indian Christian hymnody are well illustrated by historian Alan M. Guenther in his analyses of the Methodist hymnody in North India (first published, in 1890, followed by several revised editions).[24] He identifies distinctive interreligious aspects in the process based on the structure and usage of the hymnal.[25] The

---

20. Arun W. Jones, *Missionary Christianity and Local Religion: American Evangelicalism in North India, 1836–1870*, Studies in World Christianity (Waco, TX: Baylor University Press, 2017), 6.

21. John Stratton Hawley, *A Storm of Songs: India and the Idea of the Bhakti Movement* (Cambridge, MA, Harvard University Press, 2015), 3.

22. Jones, *Missionary Christianity and Local Religion*, 6.

23. Jones, *Missionary Christianity and Local Religion*, 12.

24. Alan Guenther, "Ghazals, Bhajans and Hymns: Hindustani Christian Music in Nineteenth-Century North India," *Studies in World Christianity* 25, no. 2 (2019): 145–165.

25. Cf. J. W. Waugh ed., *Hindustani Kalisiyaki GitKi Kitab, Jismen Git, Bhajan, O Gazalen aur Sande Iskul Ke Git Mundraj Hai* (Lucknow: Methodist Publishing House, 1890) [Title

three sections in the hymnal, that is, *ghazals*, *bhajans*, and *hymns* for the church worship and for Sunday schools, represent respectively, the influence and mixing of Muslim, Hindu, and Christian cultures. The composition process includes interaction with people who were not yet baptized and still played an important role. It also confirms the historical experience of Christianity that emerged in relation to and continues to exist in, the tension between the other two religions. In the following section, the story of poet Wahlji Bechar, a follower of *Kabir Pant*, will further illustrate the role native poets played in interreligious engagement through their life and work.

The Role of a Local Poet
The Case of Wahlji Bechar

Jones mentions the example of Gujarati Irish Presbyterian pastor and poet Pandit Wahlji Bechar who as early as 1881 published studies on *Kabir Pant* (the sect consisting of the followers of *Kabir*). He was indeed a scholar and probably the first native poet (born, ca. 1830) who laid the foundation for Gujarati hymnody along with the missionaries. Considering his case will provide important insights into the missiological interaction between the *Bhakti* poetic movements, the missionaries, and his wider influence during the *mass* movement in the northwest region of India. Robin H. S. Boyd (1924–2018), an Irish theologian, missionary, and Gujarati church historian explains Becher's method as an approach to "fulfillment to Hinduism which is yet to be found and published in J. N. Farquhar's *The Crown of Hinduism* (1913)." He illustrates an apologetic approach of Becher in which he compares Kabir with the Word (*Sabda*), who is also the Creator (*purusa*) who becomes incarnate *avatara* as the son of the Word (*vachan vansa*). He then demonstrates how these conceptions are fulfilled in Christ, the Son of God. Becher also wrote a similar book on the Sikh religion, entitled *Hari Charitra or Comparison between the Adi Granth and the Bible* (Lodiana Mission Press, 1894).[26]

Even prior to these publications, Becher was among the first five native poets who contributed original hymns to the Gujarati hymnbook, in close association with Joseph van Someran Taylor (1820–1881). Bechar also translated metrical Psalms in Indian meter in 1876, but as per the preface, he was not convinced of his skillfulness to translate them, his love for the Scripture and the biblical account of David had encouraged him to give a try on insistence

---

translated by Guenther as *A Book of Songs of the Hindustani Church, in which Hymns, Bhajans, Ghazals, and Sunday School Songs are included*]

26. Boyd cites this reference from J. C. B. Webster, *The Christian Community and Change in Nineteenth Century in North India* (Delhi: Macmillan, 1976), 104, 280.

of the missionaries. Even prior to this, in 1864, Becher published a book of Christian doctrine in verse entitled *Atam Bodh* ("The Way of Wisdom") and had already written hymns in Indian meter.[27] Being pastor, leader, and evangelist of a small Presbyterian congregation in times of resettlement during the crisis due to the withdrawal of the Society for the Propagation of the Gospel in Foreign Parts in 1851 and the London Missionary Society in 1860, Bechar also had to take leadership of a small Christian community in the absence of the missionaries. As Boyd records, Bechar worked compassionately with this newly established small mixed (caste) Christian community in Borsad to bring them "at equal footing as brethren and members of one body of Christ," who were from different castes, *Brahmin, Patidar,* and *Dhed*. Bechar's compositions which are still popular in Gujarati hymnody compassionately bridge the issues faced by "local" Christians without neglecting a constant theological engagement with the issues that emerge from the wider socioreligious context. The poets were not passive recipients even though not always recognized. However, their critical presence embodies the very words of their compositions making a deeper qualitative impact in the community. Bechar's case informs about the dynamics by which a native poet exceptionally engages to integrate the message of the gospel in light of his own reading and in conversation which missionaries.

Evangelistic Singing Bands and Mass Movements

The following story of Karshan Ranchhod, a converted leader of *Kabir Pant*, illustrates yet another dimension of lay people's engagement in the formation of hymnody and their wider social influence. Ranchhod was a contractor supplying sweepers (scavengers) for municipal needs in Mumbai and was a sweeper by caste. He and a few of his friends became Christian through Methodist missionaries around the 1880s and returned to Gujarat becoming the first evangelists to their native village of Kasar, near Bhalej. They could not but tell their relatives and friends of their newfound joy and Savior. Missionary Frederick Woods comments about this incident in the following way: ". . . a work of grace commenced among the Gujarati-speaking people. Karsan Ranchhod who was filled with an overflowing love for the Savior who had found him, returned to his native village in Gujarat and witnessed for Christ with such power and conviction that scores began to seek the Lord, and this inaugurated the Gujarat Mass Movement, and led our church to open work in Gujarat."[28]

---

27. Robin H. S. Boyd, *A Church History of Gujarat* (Christian Literature Society, 1981), 101.

28. Ithiel Virjibhai Master, "A History of Methodist Church in Gujarat, India," 17 [BD Dissertation, Asbury Theological Seminary, Wilmore, 1954]

The Methodist missionaries became one of the key catalysts during the "mass movements" in Gujarat. "Mass movements" are generally perceived as a social phenomenon or a colonial influence rather than a spiritual transformation.[29] However, unlike the popular perception of huge gatherings and instant baptism, the early twentieth century journals record meticulous efforts made by lay people like Ranchhod, in organizing evangelistic singing bands to help spread the message. The annual journals also describe this critical grassroots development of the evangelistic singing bands, *melas* (festival gatherings), and a month of evangelism. These practices provide a lens to see the leadership role taken by the grassroots in shaping each other and in spreading the message of Christianity over the course of several years of intensive engagements. Wesleyan emphasis on "the redemption as an invitation to all" created an openness to the marginal communities and the emphasis on the experience catalyzed revival and freedom of worship through the inclusion of diverse indigenous music instruments and traditions. In the missiological analysis, more attention is given to the statistic than to the consistent grassroots practices of the "local" worshippers.

The evangelistic singing bands were distinct in form and practice. While the congregational songs are primarily sung during worship on Sunday mornings, the evangelistic singing bands are primarily performed outside the church premise and in the evenings. These songs are more basic in the written script but expand in the oral vernacular due to a tendency to improvisation. These songs are narrative and descriptive. They also include the scriptural stories but also remain open to questions raised by the listeners. They also invite them to join not only in singing but also in the story by performing or dancing. The musical instruments were also different from those primarily used in the Sunday worship services. The singing bands were also arranged in a circle leaving a space for the dance and performance at the center. For instance, one of the most famous songs is *Samaritan Woman*. While singing the song it is usually, a male worshipper who stands up and dances with a pot on his head and acts like a Samaritan woman. The Methodist mission has significantly relied on these forms of worship for a month of evangelism and the special observations during *Melas* (religious festival gatherings).

---

29. The issue of mass conversions is one of the criticisms of Christianity in Gujarat, especially during the famine of 1900/01 in which the converts were characterized as "rice Christians." On the other hand, Gujarati theologian and author, Manilal C. Parekh in his book *Christian Proselytism in India—a Great and Growing Menace* (1947) replying to J. W. Pickett's *Christian Mass Movement in India* (1933), because he was deeply dismayed by the "shallowness" of the Christianity among the converts. He was convinced that these movements are not producing better fruits. Cited at H L Richard, "Manilal C. Parekh (1885–1967): Moving Beyond the Church, Christianity, and Christo-centrism," *Margnetowrk* (2016), accessed January 25, 2023 https://margnetwork.org/manilal-c-parekh/.

Melas are organized in which small-band evangelistic preaching was adopted as the primary means of preaching the gospel. Almost all the journal records of the first half of the twentieth century witnessed matriculate efforts toward organizing evangelistic bands and *melas*. For Instant, Rev. R. P. Christy, a poet and the district superintendent of Baroda in 1945, was deeply involved in organizing five to seven *melas* every year in different regions of his work. He writes in his annual report regarding the importance of the evangelistic singing bands by which his own spiritual life is shaped and which "inspired him to compose new Christian songs." He further emphasizes the wider impact of such practices. "Through singing bands, thousands of people, old and young, have come to the feet of Christ, hence I have always taken a keen interest in organizing singing bands in the district. Several bands have come into existence during this year. . ."[30]

During *melas,* several international and national missionary leaders visited Gujarat and many were inspired to share these experiences with the rest of the world. In 1895, Bishop Foss and the American Methodist Episcopal church deputation visited Gujarat. Dr. John Goucher was among them and at the Bhalej mass meeting in the native village of Karshan Ranchhod around three hundred people who formerly were being discipled were baptized. Goucher and others made frequent visits to Gujarat. No wonder then, his experiences might have contributed to his popular statement. "I heard more about the Holy Spirit in the time I was in India than in thirty years of preaching here in America" as quoted by Brenton Badley.[31]

The distinctive form of oral hymnody became a crucial point of missiological interaction in which the worshipping congregations take leadership. This process also shaped the church that emerged during modern missions. During the month of evangelism, the entire congregation was divided into small bands, and they all participated in reaching out to the neighboring villages. Today, these practices are transformed into open-air street gatherings and preaching during the Lent season. The congregation members open their houses and arrange open-air meetings while their neighbors would either join or hear them singing and preaching. However, today two sets of worship patterns emerge, mainly in village settings, in which one can distinguish the "singing bands" and the Sunday morning congregational worship. While historically, the singing bands were evangelistic in nature, currently, these practices are formational and invitational. During my more than ten years of pastoral work, I have been part of these dynamics. I also understand how the singing bands take leadership during the evening meetings.

---

30. Official Journal of the Gujarat Annual Conference of the Methodist Church in Southern India (GAC), Seventh Session, Baroda, 1945. 37.

31. Brenton T. Badley, *Warne of India: The Life-story of Bishop Francis Wesley Warnes* (Madras: Madras Publishing House, 1931), 17.

On Sunday mornings, I oversaw liturgy and the selection of hymns, but during the evening fellowships, the singing bands were in charge.

Evangelistic Spirituality and Persecution

There are several other native poets whose stories and hymns witness deeper spiritual and authentic discipleship even to the point of martyrdom. At times, people are touched and transformed by the text and tune of the hymns, even though the stories behind the hymns are difficult to extract. Such hymns inform deeper engagement with the spiritual experiences of the people and a careful presentation of the Lordship of Jesus Christ. Such is the case of the following popular hymn that emerged in the region of Assam, which made a global evangelistic impact during the twentieth century evangelical revival, especially, as an "altar-call" or "commitment hymn."

> *I have decided to follow Jesus;*
> *I have decided to follow Jesus;*
> *I have decided to follow Jesus;*
> *No turning back, no turning back.*[32]

The hymn is translated into almost all the regional languages of India, but its English version has traveled all around the world since the 1950s. The earliest publication is found in *Choice Life and Life Songs* (Winona Lake, IN, 1950). C. Michael Hawn's article evaluates three historical accounts associated with the hymn and considers Simon Kara Marak's story as the most plausible one. Marak was pastor and A.chik Baptist evangelist from Jorhat, Assam.[33] The hymn represents Marak's tragedies and the tears in his life as he traveled as an evangelist during the 1930s and '40s. His children grew up listing to the hymn and after they got married, they spread the hymn in the places they lived. In conversation with one of the surviving daughters, it is indicated that Marak meant "the song should be sung wherever the good news of the gospel was being preached." According to Hawn, "The ultimate efficacy of 'I Have Decided to Follow Jesus'

---

32. Lyrics found on the website of the Hymn Society in the United States and Canada, accessed on October 2, 2022 at https://hymnary.org/text/i_have_decided_to_follow_jesus#instances. The hymn is published in more than sixty-two hymn books as per the data found on the website and widely circulated during the 1950s.

33. For a historical discussion on the hymn, see historian C. Michael Hawn's "History of Hymns: 'I Have Decided to Follow Jesus,'" published by the Discipleship Ministry, the United Methodist Church, June 2020. Cited at https://www.umcdiscipleship.org/articles/history-of-hymns-i-have-decided-to-follow-jesus accessed on October 2, 2022.

lies in its intrinsic message and compositional coherence that come together in a way that expresses the experience and faith of those who sing it."

Even though the specific details of the origin and composition is difficult to extract, the hymn represents a missionary narrative of faith and martyrdom, a lyrical autobiographical response to a life full of struggle and pain, and a collective witness, evangelism and deeper interaction between missionaries and native Christians on Indian soil. During the 1970s and '80s, or even today, Indian Christians would warm-heartedly relate with and testify how the words of the hymns have played a decisive role to express their faith and enable them to be resilient in the face of adversity. This hymn and hundreds of other such hymns witness deeper spiritual thrust and cross-generational theological formation embedded in the Indian Christian hymnody. There are several other Indian hymns that transcend the regional and national boundaries and travel across the globe during modern missions and witness a spirituality originated in Indian soil. We can call this process as a kind of "reverse-translation," in which Indian original hymns, tunes, and stories of poets were translated into English and became part of the global nexus of relationship. For instance, Krishna Pal's (1764–1822) Bengali hymn "O Thou My Soul Forget No More" (1801) was translated into English and became popular in nearly a hundred different denominational hymnals.

Conclusion

It is almost impossible to either extract or present a comprehensive image of the complex process of the Indian Christian hymnody which emerged within the wider frame of the modern Protestant mission. The findings of this essay are but an attempt to develop a perspective that can help see beyond the binary of Western-indigenous in shaping hymnody and to explore some of the underlying constitutive currents. The formation of hymnody is also an important intersection in which the multidimensional missionary interaction occurs between missionaries, poets, and the congregation. Hymnody becomes instrumental in creating a distinctive ecclesial identity in the diverse religious and cultural context of India. Reading from the perspective of "missiological interaction," the Indian Christian hymnody proves to be a distinct theological and missiological contribution though difficult to define or to fit into the binary categories. The proximity and collaboration between missionaries and natives were more determinative and constituent in shaping the Indian church than their perceived distinction. The publication of the vernacular hymnals, the usage of language and musical tradition, and the confluence and divergence of the *Bhakti* movements became some of the primary grounds of interaction. However, without the active and central role played by the "local" congregation the spiritual and theological significance of the hymnody remains ineffective. The distinctive stories of poets and laypeople, the intentional endeavors by the entire congregation, and the consistent witness of individuals during the times of persecution were deeply interwoven in the lyrical affirmation of Christian hymns. The lens of missiological interaction can also guard against the binary tendencies that devalue *translated* hymns and overestimate the *indigenous* hymns, which consequentially, disconnects Indian ecclesiology from the historical legacy of spiritual and theological collaborations undergone in the publications and singing of the hymns. It is through the collective and repeated singing, revising, and editing, of the familiar tunes, over time, that the credibility of the Christian faith is established in India.

Part III

Social and Cultural Dimensions

CHAPTER TEN

Indian Christians in the Political and Civic Life of India

Manohar James

Introduction

GOD'S MISSION, AS gleaned from the Bible, not only involves the propagation of faith but also includes political emancipation, military victories, the development of sociopolitical and religious structures, and the provision of assistance to the impoverished and disadvantaged. Christians who actively engage in mission exhibit their faith by participating in a range of sociopolitical and community efforts to fulfill their divine calling.

Christianity's mission in India has been comprehensive and transformative. As an agent of transformation, using parochial services as well as political assistance, Christianity demonstrates its dedication to the holistic mission in the nation by addressing the physical needs of the people alongside spiritual activities. Indian Christians, in turn, play their part in nation-building by engaging themselves in the planned social system in the areas of liberation, education, social change, literacy, health, promotion of justice and peace, economic progress, and community development to help, heal, and uplift people as their faith calls them to.

This chapter provides a concise examination of the involvement of Indian Christians in the political and civic spheres of India since the last quarter of the nineteenth century. This study aims to illustrate the efforts made by Indian Christians in their commitment to serving the nation through the promotion of human values, advocacy for political independence, preservation of the dignity of life, and support for democratic socialism through a wide array of initiatives.

Nationalism and Indian Christians

Canon Subir Biswas, Vicar of St. Paul's Cathedral, Kolkata (Calcutta), and President of the National Christian Council of India (NCCI), once said, "Our main job is to put our fingers in the pulse of God at work in our nation and not be continuously on the defensive if our rights are in danger. Rather, we should be concerned about the rights of all the people."[1] Going a step further, Mathai

---

1. Mathai Zachariah, *The Christian Presence in India: Editorials in the N.C.C. Review* (Madras: Christian Literature Society, 1981), 73.

Zachariah, the ecumenical leader and the former general secretary of the NCCI, wrote in an editorial that "the church should no longer be just a 'gathered community,' 'a chosen people,' or not even a 'scattered community;' it should be a people's movement, helping community by being its pathfinder."[2]

In India, Christians appear to have withdrawn from politics in the face of oppressive forces, but they are not absent. They display their patriotism as a Christian virtue. In a country like India, where politics can be divisive, Indian Christians, who were expected to show "patriotism" like every other Indian, are proud of their country and continue to work for the advancement of the country. During the pre-independence era, while some Christians demonstrated their support for political independence through a variety of channels, others participated directly in the freedom movement without seeking authoritarianism. But the Christian contribution to the freedom movement has received marginal attention in the history of independent India, if not undermined or dismissed by many as irrelevant.

The first war of India's independence, which began with the Sepoy Mutiny in 1857, eventually led to the formation of an organized movement known as the Indian National Congress (INC) in 1885, marking a rapid growth of national consciousness among the people of India for political independence from the British. As a Christian precursor to Indian nationalism, in 1867, Womesh Chunder Bonnerjee, a Bengali barrister, demanded Indian representation in the British government of India. He was the INC's cofounder. In 1874, Krishtodas Pal, Justice of the Peace and Municipal Commissioner of Calcutta, also proposed similar thoughts through his article "Home Rule for India" in the *Hindoo Patriot Beginning*, an English weekly, which he edited and published from Calcutta, Bengal, in the latter half of the nineteenth century. In the following years, political thinkers across India mobilized the public with ideas of Indian nationalism by organizing themselves into associations such as the Indian League (1875), the Indian Association (1876), the Bombay Presidency Association (1870), the Poona Sarvajanik Sabha (1867), the "Mahajan Sabha" of Madras (1884), and the Indian Association of Calcutta (1883) until the INC was formed under the leadership of Allan Octavian Hume, a retired member of the Indian civil service, with an ideology to promote national unity in the areas of development, diversity, and nationalism. At the beginning, the INC transcended religious differences.[3] By around 1900, with the emergence of Hindu fundamentalists like Bal Gangadhar Tilak, Bipin Chandra Pal, Lala Lajpat Rai,

---

2. Mathai Zachariah, ed., *The Church: A Peoples' Movement* (Mysore: NCCI & Wesley Press, 1975), 9.

3. George Thomas, *Christian Indians, and Indian Nationalism 1885–1950: An Interpretation in Historical and Theological Perspectives* (Frankfurt: Verlag Peter D. Lang, 1979), 87.

and others, the main aim of the INC had shifted to Indian nationalism and political independence, along with some religious communal ideas.

With the coming of Mohandas Karamchand Gandhi, the freedom movement gained new impetus within the INC. He brought international attention to Indian national identity and consciousness. His strategic "non-violence" efforts through movements such as Swadeshi, Satyagraha, non-cooperation, civil disobedience, and Quit India undoubtedly yielded fruit and rewarded the country with political liberty in 1947, making him the Father of the Nation.

To achieve this monumental independence, tens of thousands of people from various religious, social, linguistic, economic, and political spectrums have come together for the Congress's united action. Some have suffered beatings, imprisonment, and even death. Away from the so-called leaders that history keeps record of, there is a vast majority of common people from the main and marginal socioreligious communities that have patriotically participated in the freedom movement and whose names or contributions are not captured by history due to linguistic, social, political, or religious limitations or barriers. Those unsung heroes from various minority communities fought for the nation without any recognition or national attention.

Indian Christians in the Freedom Movement

In the overwhelming history of the freedom movement in India, the account of the participation of Indian Christians often goes unnoticed, especially when India is being Hinduized politically. Undoubtedly, the national movement drew a sizable number of Christian leaders and laymen from various Christian groups across the country, some from close quarters and others from afar, in support of Indian nationalism. Some raised their voices publicly by joining the INC, while others participated through activism or written speeches. Indian Christian associations also organized camps and conferences to discuss and debate social issues, including political problems, and sent letters to the concerned authorities, thereby making Indian Christians' voices heard.[4]

Early Christian Movements for Nationalism

As early as the 1850s, Indian Christians began to sense the need for nationalism. It was Lal Behari Day, an ordained minister in the Free Church of Scotland, who was the earliest among Indian Christians to question the status of Indian clergymen in relation to European clergy.[5] His questioning of the imperial ethos and the racial superiority of the Western missionaries gave rise to self-consciousness

---

4. Atula Imsong, "Christians and the Indian National Movement: A Historical Perspective," *Indian Journal of Theology*, 46 no. 1 and 2 (2004): 101.

5. Thomas, *Christian Indians, and Indian Nationalism 1885–1950*, 66.

in the Indian Christian leadership and a desire for national independence. Gopi Nath Nandi in the 1840s, Krishna Mohan Banerjee in the 1850s, and Samuel Sathianandhan in the 1890s felt the same way about European missionaries' views and treatment of Indian clergy,[6] which led to the formation of Indian Christian associations and journals across India that began to express the need for Indianizing Christianity and a theological justification for nationalism.[7]

The Bengal Christian Association, which was the first Indian group founded in Calcutta in 1878, also played a role in the national movement by awakening the national consciousness in the minds of Indian Christians, creating public awareness. Krishna Mohan Banerjee served as its first president, and Kali Charan Banerjee was one of its active members. Similarly, in 1886, S. Parani (Pulney) Andy, an Indian medical doctor, along with his colleagues, founded the "National Church of India" in Madras. Parallel to the Brahmo Samaj, K. C. Banerjee and Joy Govinda Shome formed the "Calcutta Christo Samaj" in 1887.[8] Similarly, the Poona Christian Association and the Lucknow Christian Association were formed in 1892. In 1908, the Christo Samaj of Madras was formed. Its prominent leaders were P. Chenchiah, V. Chakkarai, S. K. George, P. A. Thangasami, and others who met every year to discuss socioeconomic, religious, and political matters.

The All-India Conference of Indian Christians (AICIC) was the first national political organization of Protestant Indian Christians, founded in Calcutta in 1914. Its leaders met annually in December in various cities across India to discuss the political burdens of the Indian Christian community and express their political ideas and views. Presenting itself to the government as the mouthpiece of Indian Christians, the AICIC advocated for communal harmony, the rights of Indian Christians, and self-rule in a united independent country. Allying itself with the Indian National Congress in 1920, the AICIC said, "Indian Christians should take part in all healthy political movements of the country and oppose all that is harmful to the country and the government of the land."[9] Exhibiting their unwavering support for the freedom movement, several Indian Christian associations declared their support for the civil disobedience movement by giving open statements through weekly magazines, newspapers, and periodicals. For instance, in 1930, the *Guardian* published, "We feel sure that the Christians, in common with the Sikhs and

---

6. Geoffrey A. Oddie, "Indian Christians and National Identity, 1870 1947," *The Journal of Religious History*, 58, no. 3 (2001): 350.

7. Imsong, "Christians and the Indian National Movement," 104.

8. Thomas, *Christian Indians, and Indian Nationalism 1885–1950*, 75.

9. Lalchhuanliana, "A Study of Indian Christians Involvement in the Political Developments in India from 1885 to 1947" (Unpublished MTh thesis, Bangalore: UTC, 1973), p. 73. quoted in Imsong, *Christians, and the Indian National Movement*," 102.

other important minorities, are as earnest in their desire for self-government as the Hindu Community."[10]

The Student Christian Association of India, which was formed in 1912, also contributed to the spread of national consciousness, especially among the student community.[11] Although the Young Men's Christian Association (YMCA) of India did not directly involve itself in political affairs due to its foreign ties, it allowed its members to express their political opinions in its magazine, *The Young Men of India*, promoting national consciousness among Indian Christians during the national movement.[12] But the NCCI, which was formed in 1914, has shown its active participation in the national movement since 1940, when its leadership was transferred to Indian Christian leaders. The NCCI, led by Bishop V. S. Azariah, passed a political resolution in January 1944, saying, "Educated Indian Christians fully share the national aspirations of their countrymen. Consequently, they also share the sorrow and disappointment aroused by the present political deadlock."[13] Similarly, a group of Christians from Tirunelveli and Palayamkottai released a statement, showing their intense national spirit, that said, "The Indian Christians were not behind any other community in their desire for freedom and in their readiness to work and suffer for it."[14]

Christians in the Indian National Congress (INC)

The membership of the INC included some prominent Indian Christians like Rajkumari Amrit Kaur of Punjabi royal lineage from Uttar Pradesh, George Joseph from Kerala, S. K. George from Nagpur, J. C. Kumarappa from Tamil Nadu, and H. C. Mookerjee from Bengal, who were closely associated with Gandhi. They actively propagated the idea of political independence and participated in the INC's strategic meetings. In the INC session held in Madras in 1887, there were thirty-five Christian participants among the 607 registered delegates.[15] Given the percentage of the Indian Christian population, the proportion of Indian Christian delegates to the Congress session was much higher

---

10. "Indian Christians and Present Politics," *Guardian*, June 5, 1930, 267.

11. Imsong, "*Christians and the Indian National Movement*, 102.

12. By 1891, there were thirty-five YMCAs in the country with 1,896 members.

13. Imsong, "Christians and the Indian National Movement," 102.

14. Editorial, *Guardian*, May 14, 1931, 218.

15. D. Arthur Jeyakumar, "Christians and the National Movement in India: 1885–1947," in *Nationalism and Hindutva: A Christian Response: Papers from the 10th CMS Consultation*, ed. Mark T. B. Laing (New Delhi: ISPCK, 2005), 92.

than the proportion of other delegates compared to their populations. In the Sixth Congress session held in Calcutta in 1890, there were sixteen Christian clergymen.[16] Christian leaders like K. C. Banerjee from Bengal, C. G. Nath from Lahore, and Peter Paul Pillai from Madras, along with R. S. N. Subramanian, a prominent barrister from Madras, and Madhusudan Das, a lawyer from Orissa, also represented Christians from across India and played major roles in the Congress sessions. Pillai was one of the founding members of the Congress.[17]

On the other hand, there were some Western attempts to prevent Indian Christian leaders who were under the direct employment of Western mission agencies from participating in the national movement.[18] Educational institutions that were financially connected to the West were threatened with the withdrawal of student grants if they became involved in the freedom struggle.[19] While some Western missionaries despised national politics and advised Indian Christians not to participate in the Congress, several notable Western missionaries, including C. F. Andrews, T. E. Slater, E. Greaves, J. Waskom Picket, Stanley E. Jones, Jack C. Winslow, R. R. Keithahn, E. Forrester-Patton, and Verrier Elwin, not only encouraged Indian Christians to participate in the national movement but also attended Congress sessions in support of the movement. C. F. Andrews, a British missionary who loved India so dearly, stood by Indian Christians and strongly persuaded them to partake in the movement, saying, "It is my own conviction, which grows stronger every day, that Indian Christians will lose a great and noble opportunity if they hold aloof at the present time from the National Movement in India."[20] Offering unwavering support, American missionary Stanley Jones expressed, "I am also interested in India's freedom. I believe it to be the birthright of every nation to express itself in self-government. I believe it will be good for India and for Britain when the right is conceded and implemented."[21]

While Indian Christians were showing their unwavering support to the national movement with or without the support of Western missionaries, in

---

16. B. N. Pande, ed., *A Centenary History of the Indian National Congress, 1885–1919*, vol. 1 (New Delhi: Vikash Publishing House Private Limited, 1985), 581.

17. Thomas, *Christian Indians, and Indian Nationalism 1885–1950*, 89.

18. D. Arthur Jeyakumar, *Christians and the National Movement: The Memoranda of 1919 and the National Movement with Special Reference to Protestant Christians in Tamil Nadu: 1919–1939* (Bangalore: Centre for Contemporary Christianity, 2009), 120.

19. Thomas, *Christian Indians, and Indian Nationalism 1885–1950*, 190.

20. C. F. Andrews, "Indian Christians and the National Movement," *The Young Men of India* 19, no. 19 (1908): 147.

21. E. Stanley Jones, "My Position Restated," *Indian Witness* (April 11, 1940): 233.

the first decade of the twentieth century, Hindu fundamentalists brought militant, religious, and communal ideas into the INC. This, along with prejudices against Christians in general, made it harder for Indian Christians to be seen in the INC in the following years.[22] Despite the fact that Christians continued to support the freedom movement through various publications, special newspaper statements, and public addresses, their nationalism had to be demonstrated and endorsed by Hindus.[23] Some Christian representatives felt unwelcome in the INC as a result of Hindu religious agendas, and they saw the proposed protests as unchristian, contributing to the decline of Christian participation in the INC.[24] However, Indian Christians' patriotism and their participation in nationalist movements in the subsequent years are not to be discounted. In a meeting held by Indian Christian leaders in Bombay in 1930, they passed several resolutions over the prevailing situation, expressing their desire and willingness to be one with Indian communities in their desire to win "complete swaraj" for India. In 1931, they submitted the following memorandum to Gandhi, expressing Indian Christians' attitude toward the idea of *Swaraj*:

> We wholeheartedly support the national demand that real political power and responsibility must be transferred without delay and without reservation from the people of England to the people of India. We stand for full freedom, for the unrestrictive authority to direct, in whichever way, we desire the management of our economic and political affairs. We would, however, welcome Indo-British cooperation based on terms of perfect equality, without the surrender of our sovereign rights.[25]

---

22. Some militant Hindus made accusations against Indian Christians that they are denationalized people and to become Christian means to be a non-Indian! See T. R. Vedantham, *Christianity—A Political Problem* (Madras: The Author, 1984), 11–12; Oddie, "Indian Christians and National Identity," 352, 358. Also see M. S. S. Pandian, "Nation as Nostalgia: Ambiguous Spiritual Journeys of Vengal Chakkarai," *Economic and Political Weekly* 38, no. 51/52 (2003): 5357–5365. http://www.jstor.org/stable/4414434.

23. Pandian, "Nation as Nostalgia: Ambiguous Spiritual Journeys of Vengal Chakkarai," 62.

24. When Gandhi gave a clarion call for the non-cooperation and civil disobedience movements, many Indian Christians participated while some hesitated to partake because they felt those methods were unconstitutional or they appeared un-Christian to them. M. M. Thomas suggests some Christian groups have disregarded the idea of political participation due to their doctrinal convictions. See, M. M. Thomas, compiler. *Christian Participation in Nation-Building: The Summing Up of a Corporate Study on Rapid Social Change* (Bangalore: NCCI & CISRS, 1960), 48.

25. "Indian Christians and the National Demand," editorial, *Guardian* 9, no. 36, (September 10, 1931), p. 423.

In 1942, when Gandhi and other Congress leaders were arrested and imprisoned at the launching of the Quit India movement with mass protests, Christian institutions, church leaders, and councils across India publicly condemned the arrest of the Congress leaders and demanded immediate independence. In 1944, the NCCI released a statement saying, "Imperialism is condemned by Christian conscience, and it is agreed that in India it should be brought immediately to an end . . . ."[26]

Indian Christian Men in the Freedom Struggle

There are records that provide evidence of a collective sense of national identity among Christians throughout India. In 1921, the editorial of the *Harvest Field*, the official voice of the National Missionary Council of India, mentions that "there are some Christians in their patriotism carried away by this movement (meaning the non-cooperation movement) . . ."[27] indicating the presence and self-interest of Indian Christians in the national movement. In a confidential note to the SPG mission, the principal of the Bishop's College, N. H. Tubbs, mentions the deep interest of Christian students in the freedom struggle. He wrote, "They are out and out nationalists as a rule."[28] In 1930, an editorial in the *Guardian*, read, "A number of Christian young men have joined in the civil disobedience movement."[29] S. K. Datta, speaking at the All-India Conference of Indian Christians held in Lucknow between December 27 and 30, 1922, mentioned the imprisonment of some Indian Christians due to their involvement in the national movement.[30] A statement by E. C. Dewick, a British missionary, is noteworthy:

> The old tradition of loyalty to the British Raj, and of imitation of the West in dress and social customs have steadily been giving place to a much more nationalistic outlook, and to expressions of this national customs and national habits. A growing number of the younger Indian Christians have been gathering courage to raise their voices in criticism

---

26. Kaj Baago, A History of the National Christian Council of India 1914–1964, (Nagpur: NCC, Christian Council Lodge, 1965), 64, quoted in Imsong, "Christians and the Indian National Movement," 105.

27. Jeyakumar, *Christians and the National Movement*, 122.

28. Jeyakumar, *Christians and the National Movement*, 123.

29. Jeyakumar, *Christians and the National Movement*, 123.

30. Jeyakumar, *Christians and the National Movement*, 122.

of the British Government and have joined with their Hindu friends in the non-Cooperation and Civil Disobedience movement.[31]

In the wake of Hinduized political groups that question or doubt the patriotism of Indian Christians, it is important to acknowledge some of the names of notable Indian Christian leaders in history who took part in the liberation movement through their leadership, social action, formation of associations, and publications. These Christian leaders represented Christian communities across India, from the north to the south and from the east to the west.

K. C. Banerjee, a lawyer and eminent Christian scholar from Bengal, was an active participant in the INC's early years of formation. He was one of the early Indian Christian nationalists, who not only saw God's saving act in Christ but also in the Aryan cultural traditions of North India.[32] In 1902, there was a proposal that he should lead the annual session of the National Congress that year. As an Indian Christian, he expressed his patriotic stand in the *Bengal Christian Herald* in 1870, stating, "In having become Christians, we have not ceased to be Hindus. We are Hindu Christian ... We have embraced Christianity, but we have not rejected our nationality. We are as intensely national as any of our brethren."[33] He educated his nephew Bhabani [Bhawani] Charan Banerjee, who is known as Brahmabandhab Upadhyay, and went on to become an influential Indian theologian, journalist, and freedom fighter. Since his high school days, Upadhyay leaned toward the Indian nationalist movement for freedom. He edited the Bengali journal *Sandhya* through which he carried out his "God-appointed mission of Swaraj" and gave a clarion call to people toward nationalism. He was arrested on August 13, 1907.[34] His Christian faith did not lessen his national interest; rather, it strengthened it. He made a significant contribution to the shaping of the new India, whose identity began to emerge in the first half of the nineteenth century. According to Thomas George, "Upadhyay was among the mightiest of Indian nationalists who flourished in the first decade of [the twentieth] century."[35]

Narayan Vaman Tilak, a Christian poet from Maharashtra, exhibited his burning patriotism in his writings and actions. He joined the Home Rule

---

31. Jeyakumar, *Christians and the National Movement*, 123–124.

32. Oddie, "Indian Christians and National Identity, 1870 1947," 350.

33. Kaj Baago, "The First Independence Movement Among Indian Christians," 67; Imsong, "Christians and the Indian National Movement," 105.

34. Pande, ed., *A Centenary History of the Indian National Congress, 1885–1919*, vol.1, 239.

35. Thomas, *Christian Indians, and Indian Nationalism 1885–1950*, 104.

League in 1916. Ram Chandra Bose, another Christian from Uttar Pradesh, made contributions to the Congress debates on various issues related to industrial problems, reform of the legislature, and organizational matters of the Congress. During the period of civil disobedience and non-cooperation, Madhusudan Das, an Indian attorney and social reformer who hails from Odisha, backed Mahatma Gandhi's appeal for unity and liberation while serving in a government position.[36] Another prominent Christian, Pandipeddi Chenchiah, an alumnus of the Madras Christian College and a Telugu Brahmin from Andhra Pradesh and a Chief Justice of the Pudukottai High Court, said in support of national freedom, "We want first of all an Indian nation as against Hindu, Muslim, Christian communities, [to] develop an Indian culture and religious background that will weld the communities into a living whole."[37]

Theologian K. T. Paul was another prominent Christian leader whose active participation in the Indian national movement was evidenced by his frequent correspondence with William Paton, the first secretary of the National Christian Council of India, urging him to quickly settle the issues with India's freedom struggle.[38] In paying homage to K. T. Paul, Gandhi called him a thorough nationalist and said his death was a great loss to India.[39] Another Christian leader, Nirad Biswas, who later became the Bishop of Assam of the Church of India, Burma, and Ceylon (CIBC), joined the national campaign of civil disobedience in the 1930s and began making salt outside Calcutta in 1932 in support of Gandhi's call to Salt Satyagraha.[40] Likewise, Vengal Chakkarai (Chakravarty), who served as a mayor of Madras from 1941 to 1942 and the president of the All India Trade Union Congress from 1954 to 1957, attended the annual session of the Indian National Congress at Surat in 1907 and became a follower of Bal Gangadhar Tilak.[41] Later, influenced by Gandhi, he proudly participated in the freedom struggle, joining the Home Rule Movement in 1917 and the non-cooperation movement in 1920. He edited the nationalist Christian journal

---

36. Gordon Hewitt, The Problems of Success: A History of the Church Missionary Society, 1910–1942, vol. 2, 42.

37. Thomas, *Christian Indians, and Indian Nationalism 1885–1950*, 122.

38. Jeyakumar, *Christians and the National Movement*, 134–135.

39. Sherwood Eddy, *Pathfinders of the World Missionary Crusade* (New York: Abingdon-Cokesbury, 1945), 175.

40. Gordon Hewitt, *The Problems of Success: A History of the Church Missionary Society, 1910–1942*, vol. 2 (London: Church Missionary Society, 1977), 43.

41. Pandian, "Nation as Nostalgia: Ambiguous Spiritual Journeys of Vengal Chakkarai," 57–58.

Christian Patriot from 1911 onward. Unfortunately, nationalist literature hardly mentions his name or his participation in the freedom movement.

Augustine Ralla Ram, a pastor from Allahabad, is another prominent leader in the United Church of North India who did not shy away from being a voice in the freedom movement. He risked his job and reputation by issuing a manifesto during his visit to Wales in 1932, in which he questioned the intentions of the British over India and praised the Congress Party and its ideology.[42] Another Christian from Kerala, George Gheverghese Joseph, gave up his law practice to join the non-cooperation movement in 1917 and was imprisoned in 1922 along with Jawaharlal Nehru, Mahadev Desai, Purushottam Das Tandon, and Devdas Gandhi. In the history of India's war for independence, he secures a place as the first Christian to get involved in the nationalist movement from the southern states of India and as one of the pioneers who tried to bridge the north-south divide.[43] Some Christians were not afraid to go to jail for the cause of national independence. For instance, J. C. Kumarappa of Tamil Nadu, a friend of Gandhi and a staunch advocate of Satyagraha and the Quit India movement, went to jail in 1931 and 1945. Paul Ramasamy from Tamil Nadu joined the liberation movement in 1930, at the height of the Salt Satyagraha campaign, and protested outside of Thiruchirappalli's Bishop Heber College. He was taken into custody, given a six-month prison term, and sent to jails in Thiruchirapalli and Alipuram on various occasions.[44] Thevarthundiyil Titus (1905–1980), originally a Marthomite from Kerala, participated in the national movement in Allahabad. Gandhi fondly called him Titusji. Titus had joined Gandhi in the Sabarmati Ashram. When Gandhi made the decision to violate the salt ban in 1930, he picked Titus as one of the seventy-eight people he trusted to be part of the group that marched from Sabarmathi to the Dandi seashore to create salt symbolically. British soldiers thrashed them and then took them into custody.[45] Titus, the only Christian in that group, was proud to suffer for the nation's freedom.

Along the lines of the INC's ideology, V. S. Azariah (1874–1954) wished that India be free from the bondage of the West. His patriotism was found in his slogan, "Indian Christians are Indians first." His famous 1910 Edinburgh speech that ended with "give us friends" was an indicator of his feelings and

42. Jeyakumar, *Christians and the National Movement*, 125.

43. https://indianculture.gov.in/node/2800911, accessed January 20, 2023.

44. Jeyakumar, *Christians and the National Movement*, 131.

45. Thomas John Philip Nalloor, "TITUSJI—An Unknown Hero of the Mar Thoma Church—The Christian Dandi Marcher—Freedom Fighter, 1905–1980," accessed January 20, 2023, https://www.marthomaparishsharjah.com/library/titusji.pdf

appeal for nationalism and indigenous Christian faith in India. In 1930, joining other Anglican bishops, he issued a letter to the *London Times*, in which he questioned India's place in the commonwealth of the nations and insisted that India should have a full voice in determining its own destiny.[46] He pointed out that Indian Christians are no different from other non-Christian brothers and demanded that they be treated equally like other communities in the areas of civil rights, including voting in the general elections. Although Azariah did not agree with Gandhi's interpretation of the intentions of Christian missions in India, he remained a true nationalist Christian. S. K. George, originally from Kerala and a follower of Gandhi, supported the nation's cause by contributing numerous articles on the nationalist movement in various periodicals and journals, including *Gandhi Marg*.[47]

There are many Christian freedom fighters who supported and participated in the liberation cause whose details cannot be captured in this chapter. However, a few more names worth mentioning are: Bombay-based Mangalorean Catholic John Francis Pinto; Jerome Saldanha from the Madras Legislative Council who met Gandhi in Mangalore in 1927; and Maurice Sreshta, a former government employee who served during the British Raj,[48] Felix Albuquerque Pai, the owner of the Albuquerque tile factory in Mangalore; Joseph Baptista (1864–1930), a barrister from Bombay; and the three Canara couples: Thomas and Helen Alvares, Cyprian and Alice Alvares, and Joachim and Violet Alvares. The Tamil Nadu government's "Who is Who of Freedom Fighters" survey lists 15,264 people who took part in the national movement toward independence. Among them are 103 identified as Christians based on their and their family members' names.[49] There may be more Christians on the list whose names are difficult to identify. The fact that Christians in general have favored the Congress Party over other parties since independence is one of the proofs that the majority of Christians supported the Indian nationalist movement.

Indian Christian Women in the Movement

It is worth noting the contribution of Indian Christian women to the cause of the freedom movement and the political independence of India. It is praiseworthy

46. Jeyakumar, *Christians and the National Movement*, 127.

47. M. M. Thomas, *The Acknowledged Christ of the Indian Renaissance* (London: SCM Press, 1969), 323.

48. Ambrose Pinto, "Christian Contribution to the Freedom Struggle," *Mainstream Weekly*, August 20, 2017, accessed January 20, 2023, http://www.mainstreamweekly.net/article7406.html

49. Jeyakumar, *Christians and the National Movement*, 167.

that some of them came forward not only to take part in the movement but also to lead protests at a time when women were treated as inferior to men and largely confined to their homes.

In 1888, when women first attended an INC session in Bombay, there were also Indian Christian women present. Three out of the ten women delegates were Christians: Pandita Ramabai Saraswati, Mesdames Triumbuck, and Shevantibai M. Nikambe, who upheld the right of women to participate in national politics.[50] Ramabai and Nikambe, two Indian Christian women, have actively supported nationalism. Ramabai also led the National Social Conference in 1889. She eloquently articulated the need for the liberation of women from immoral social customs, traditional bonds, and myths. Nikambe assisted Ramabai at Sharda Sadan High School and worked for the education of married women alongside Ramabai.[51]

Another Protestant Christian woman, Rajkumari Amrit Kaur, a close associate of Gandhi, joined the independence movement with dedication and courage. She founded the All-India Women's Conference in 1927. She was jailed in 1942 for her participation in the Quit India movement. *Time* magazine named her "Woman of the Year" in 1947.[52] In independent India, she served as health minister for ten years. The other three Christian women who joined the movement in the south along with their husbands are Violet Alva (1908–1969), wife of Joachim Alva; Helen, wife of Thomas Alvares; and Alice, Cyprian's wife. At Gandhi's call, Helen participated in the movement. She took up the name Alva Devi for herself. She was a fervent supporter of Satyagraha and emphasized it in her speeches in front of crowds. In the 1930s, Alice joined the Quit India movement along with her husband and went underground. In November 1942, she was imprisoned in Bombay. In independent India, Violet became a member of Parliament and served as deputy minister of state for home affairs; she later became the Deputy Chairperson of the Rajya Sabha.

Christian women from Kerala also actively and bravely took part in the freedom movement. Freedom warrior Accamma Cherian (1909–1982) is notable among them. She was hailed for her boldness. She participated in the freedom struggle and has been at its forefront since 1938. At the age of nineteen, she gave

---

50. Thomas, *Christian Indians, and Indian Nationalism 1885–1950*, 90.

51. Manohar Dugaje, "The 'Leaving' Impact of Christianity in Shevantibai Nikambe's Ratanbai: A High-Caste Child Wife," *Journal of Interdisciplinary Cycle Research* 11, no. 12 (December 2019): 8–13, accessed January 15, 2023, https://www.researchgate.net/publication/343057946_ The_'Leaving'_Impact_of_Christianity_in_Shevantibai_Nikambe's_Ratanbai_A_High-Caste_Child_Wife.

52. https://indianexpress.com/article/lifestyle/life-style/indira-gandhi-amrit-kaur-time-magazine-100-women-of-the-year-6302092/

up her job to involve herself in the freedom movement. She organized and led mass protests against the British, fearing no police. She was detained for a year after being arrested on December 24, 1939, and throughout that time, the jail staff ridiculed and tortured her.[53] Her sister, Rosamma Punnoose, as well as their brother, Varkey, joined the movement because of her influence. Between 1946 and 1947, Accamma was detained twice for protesting. Because of her bravery, Gandhi called her "the Jhansi Rani of Travancore," while others saw the goddess Durga in her.[54] Another Christian woman, Annie Mascarene (1902–1963), a lawyer, had also boldly stepped up to support the freedom movement. She traveled to the Sabarmati Ashram to join the movement with Gandhi. In 1946, she became one of the 299 members of the Constituent Assembly that prepared the Constitution of India. After India gained its independence, she helped bring the princely states into the Indian Union.[55] She was the first elected female member of Parliament from Kerala and served as minister of Kerala for health and power.[56] Among other Christian women who actively participated in the freedom struggle are Mary Thomas, Margaret Pavamani, Susannah Joseph, Gracy Aaron, and Constance Premnath Dass.

Christians in the Politics of Independent India

The participation of Indian Christians in politics continued Indian independence. In 1947, the Constituent Assembly appointed six Christians to the Minority Advisory Committee, which included Raj Kumari Amrit Kaur from Uttar Pradesh, H. C. Mukherjee from Bengal, and J. J. M. Nichols Roy from Meghalaya.[57] In that committee, which Sardar Vallabhbhai Patel led, the

---

53. Swetha Ganjoo, "Why Mahatma Gandhi called Accamma Cherian the 'Jhansi Rani of Travancore," *Inuth*, August 11, 2017, accessed January 25, 2023 https://www.inuth.com/india/women-freedom-fighters-of-india/why-mahatma-gandhi-called-accamma-cherian-the-jhansi-rani-of-travancore/

54. Goddess Durga is a female deity in Hinduism. She is depicted as a powerful worrier riding on a tiger or a lion, fighting evil.

55. Jaqueline Kelly, "Remembering the Contributions of Christian Women to the Freedom Movement," *Indian Catholic Matters: A New Home for the Community*, August 13, 2022, accessed January 16, 2023, https://www.indiancatholicmatters.org/remembering-the-contributions-of-christian-women-to-the-freedom-movement/

56. "Annie Mascarene: A freedom fighter erased from history," *New Indian Express*, Thirucananthapuram, August 15, 2019, accessed January 18, 2023, https://www.newindianexpress.com/cities/thiruvananthapuram/2019/aug/15/annie-mascarene-a-freedom-fighter-erased-from-history-2019113.html

57. Graham Houghton, "The Foundation Laid Towards Nation Building by Christian Missionaries," in *Christian Contribution to Nation Building*, ed. Ezra Sargunam (Ayanavaram, Chennai: Mission Educational Books, 2006), 11.

Christian members expressed their dedication to the Christian ideal of oneness and their readiness to join in nation-building, rejecting the necessity for political safeguards to defend their parochial interests.[58] Some of these were instrumental in securing rights for minorities under the Indian Constitution. For instance, Frank Anthony, because of his legal expertise, was appointed a member of several important subcommittees of the Drafting Committee and became a member of Parliament in 1950.[59] After independence, many Christians served as politicians, including Joachim and Violet Alva (Karnataka),[60] who served the country with absolute patriotism. John Mathai (Kerala), an economist, served as India's first railway minister in 1947 and as finance minister in 1948. For his commitment to service, the government of India awarded him the "Padma Shree" in 1954 and the "Padma Vibhushan" in 1959. During the Emergency (1975–1977), while some Christians supported Prime Minister Indira Gandhi's stand on the imposition of a state of emergency in view of protecting Congress' ideals, other prominent leaders like M. M. Thomas and M. A. Thomas did not shy away from condemning it from a humanitarian standpoint.

It is not possible to list all Christian leaders who served the country in independent India, but it is worth noting a few. Beginning in 1969, Margaret Alva was active in politics and served as member of Parliament (Rajya Sabha) from 1974 to 1998; member of Parliament (Lok Sabha) from 1999 to 2004; and governor of various states from 2009 to 2014. M. M. Thomas was a theological and social activist who served as governor of Nagaland from 1990 to 1992. Ajit Promod Kumar Jogi of Chhattisgarh is one of the most well-known Christians who has worked in politics in recent years. Since 1978, he has been a district magistrate, collector, MP, and the first Chief Minister of Chhattisgarh from 2000 to 2003. Christian leadership in dominantly Christian states like Mizoram, Nagaland, and Meghalaya has made contributions to the country's development by improving living standards and extending education to all.[61] George Mathew Fernandes, a statesman and journalist, served as defense minister from 1998 to 2004 and A. K. Antony was the country's twenty-third defense minister. Y. S. Rajasekhar Reddy served as chief minister of Andhra

---

58. Houghton, "The Foundation Laid Towards Nation Building by Christian Missionaries," 11.

59. Louis D'Silva, "Indian Thought, Culture, and National Life," *Christian Contribution to Nation Building*, 60.

60. In November 2008, the Government of India released a commemorative postal stamp in honor of the couple.

61. A few prominent political leaders are Lal Thanhawla, a five-time, and the longest-serving chief minister of Mizoram (1984–1986, 1989–1998, 2008–2018). P. A. Sangma served as the chief minister of Meghalaya from 1988 to 1990, minister of information and broadcasting from 1995 to 1996, and speaker of Lok Sabha from 1996 to 1998.

Pradesh from 2004 to 2009 and Oommen Chandy as chief minister of Kerala from 2004 to 2006 and 2011 to 2016. Y. Jagan Mohan Reddy is currently serving as the Chief Minister of Andhra Pradesh and Conrad Sangma as the Chief Minister of Meghalaya. Apart from these major personalities, there are dozens of other Christian MPs, MLAs, and high government officials in the country.

Although Christian involvement in politics has been minimized by the rise of Hindu nationalist politics in India, Christians are not fully absent from national politics and administration. They serve India with the utmost dedication and great patriotism.

Indian Christianity's Role in the Civic Life of India

On December 7, 2014, while paying a tribute to the Christian community in India, Mr. Ch. Vidyasagar Rao, Governor of Maharashtra, said, "We are proud of you for the work of enriching India's social, cultural, economic, and political life. The idea of India is difficult to imagine without you."[62] Government officials and non-Christian politicians occasionally make such statements that bear witness to the truth, fulfilling the holistic gospel that Christian faith requires. Western missionaries laid the foundation for good works in India in the fields of systematic education, social reformation, adult literacy, women's empowerment, publication of knowledge, health, and rehabilitation, contributing to the welfare of the nation. Indian Christians, who followed the trail, have carried on and even multiplied the legacy handed down to them, uniquely impacting India's civic life in the periods before and after independence. They have served their country with utmost dedication in various capacities, including civil services, military, Indian police, education, science, sports, medicine, social services, and the establishment of movements and organizations that care for neglected communities. It is impossible to enumerate all the contributions Indian Christians have made to nation-building over the past 150 years, but it is worth mentioning a few.

Education, Social Reformation, and Development

From a transformational standpoint, it was Christians who first noticed the untouchability and immoral traditions of the caste system in Indian civilization. William Carey and others have been instrumental in campaigning against

---

62. "Maharashtra Governor Ch Vidyasagar Rao lauds contribution of Christians to India's progress" *Economic Times*, December 8, 2014, accessed January 25, 2014, https://economic-times.indiatimes.com/news/politics-and-nation/maharashtra-governor-ch-vidyasagar-rao-lauds-contribution-of-christians-to-indias-progress/articleshow/45411852.cms?from=mdr

India's social practices of untouchability, sati, child marriage, religious offering of infants, killing of lepers, and human sacrifice.[63] European settlers and Western Christian missionaries contributed to the sociocultural and political reformation of the nineteenth century through educational endeavors and social reformation. Those attempts changed the nation's destiny and provided direction toward progress. Western educational establishments in India gave its people a systematic education (alphabetical characters, textbooks, grammar, and dictionaries) and made a significant contribution to the nation in the fields of language, literature, and journalism.[64]

Indian Christians also played a crucial role in the national education movement. It was Upadhyay who initially envisioned national colleges with a Western outlook, which Gandhi emphasized when he launched the first non-violent revolution in 1921.[65] For Upadhyay, "national education" means colleges operated under Indian control and culture. Later, Tagore and Upadhyay founded a school in the Santiniketan Ashram. In independent India, Christian communities have established numerous educational institutions, including schools and colleges.[66] Those institutions have been instrumental in providing education to a substantial number of individuals from diverse backgrounds and socioeconomic strata. Certain institutions offer scholarships and tuition-free education to individuals from disadvantaged socioeconomic backgrounds. In July 2021, *India Today* published the top ten best art colleges in India, out of which five were Christian. Christian colleges are also ranked among the top ten best colleges in science, commerce, information technology, and medicine.

The involvement of Christians in rural development is huge. As early as 1921, the Indian national movement recognized that "the great poverty and misery" of India was due to the economic stagnation inherent in rural Indian agriculture

---

63. In 1802, infanticide was banned by Wellesley. After hearing reports of 438 widow burnings Carey and his colleagues petitioned the government to outlaw the practice of sati. In 1829, Lord William Bentinck issued an order banning it.

64. In the sixteenth century, the Jesuits first established Christian institutions of learning in India. The German missionaries arrived after them and established schools. Later, Christian schools in both English and local languages were started by the eminent Friedrick Schwartz. In North India, modern education was pioneered by William Carey and the British Baptists who settled in Calcutta in the late eighteenth century. As far afield from Calcutta as Shimla and Delhi in the north and Rajputna in the south, there were 111 schools by 1818.

65. Thomas, *Christian Indians, and Indian Nationalism 1885–1950*, 101.

66. It is estimated that there are over 25 thousand Christian schools, colleges, and universities in India, imparting quality education to people irrespective of differences, contributing to the progress and development of the nation in most altruistic manner.

and land ownership.[67] K. T. Paul, one of the prominent theologians and South Indian nationalists and a friend of C. Rajagopalachari, had concerns about the development of rural India. He envisioned and developed a concept he referred to as "rural reconstruction" as early as 1913. He implemented micro-loan initiatives that effectively liberated the economically disadvantaged rural population from the clutches of usurious moneylenders, consequently garnering significant support from the lower socioeconomic strata of Indian society.

There have been other Christian enterprises that have addressed the broader needs of the entire community at Gurgoan, Martandom, Sevagram, Sriniketan, Bangalore, Tamil Nadu, Andhra Pradesh, and Allahabad and contributed to village development plans.[68] Two examples of agricultural organizations are the Bethel Agricultural Fellowship (BAF) and the ACTS Group. BAF was established in Tamil Nadu in 1963 by Sam Kamalesan and P. Samuel, while the ACTS Group was created in Bangalore in 1979 by Ken Gnanakan. With a motto of "for change we serve," Bethel Agricultural Fellowship has taken initiatives in the areas of agriculture, education, health, and rural development. Their aim was to assist and improve the productivity of farmers. Their dedication to developing a better society has impacted thousands of people. Similarly, ACTS has been focusing on skills training, education, art, and environmental and social entrepreneurship. Gnanakan, who was a "global pioneer of creation care,"[69] initiated the Program for Environmental Awareness in Schools (PEAS), a nationwide association targeted at inspiring students into action. His book *Trees*, an anthology of poems on environmental issues, has been used in various schools.

Another Christian, Varghese Kurien from Kerala, who was popularly known as "the milkman of India," contributed to the nation in the field of dairy development in India. After completing a master's program at Michigan State University, he returned to India to work for the government in a rural setting. He worked at Amul Dairy in Anand, Gujarat, as the general manager and became its chairman in 1949. He received over seventy-five awards, including four prestigious national awards from presidents of India and several international awards, for his outstanding contribution to rural development in the field

---

67. Thomas, *Christian Participation in Nation-Building*, 76.

68. Thomas, *Christian Participation in Nation-Building*, 76.

69. "WEA Remembers Ken Gnanakan, Global Christian Education and Environmental Leader," *World Evangelical Alliance*, June 21, 2021, accessed January 25, 2023, https://worldea.org/news/14655/wea-remembers-ken-gnanakan-global-christian-education-and-environmental-leader/

of dairy.[70] His vision, energy, and action toward dairy development in India made him the so-called Father of Dairy Development and fetched him many accolades.

In literature, art, and culture, people like Narayan Vaman Tilak, Vedanayagam Pillai, Gurram Joshua, H. A. Krishna Pillai, and others stand out. Tilak was a poet who revered the spiritual and intellectual heritage of India by writing Bhajans and poems in Marathi, promoting Christian Bhakti. He saw Indian church as "God's Darbar." There are several Christians who have expressed their faith through Indian religious thought and culture. For example, Brahmabandhab Updhayay expounded the doctrine of trinity as *sat-chit-ananda* while Sadhu Sunder Singh expressed his faith through the lifestyle of a "roaming sadhu." Other Indian expressions include Chenchiah's *yoga* of the spirit, Appasamy's idea of *Moksha*, Chakkari's *Atman* and *Paramatman*, Dvanandan's concept of *maya*, S. K. George's *sarva dharma samabhava* and Tilak's idea of Christ as the *Lord of yoga*. Christian writers, Vedanayagam Pillai (1824–1889) and H. A. Krishna Pillai (1827–1900) produced some of the first Tamil novels in India. To adopt and preserve Indian culture in Christian spirituality, some Christian leaders established and promoted Ashrams. For instance, Pandita Ramabai founded several schools and ashrams for orphan girls and widows, including the Mukti Mission and Sharada Sadan in Mumbai in 1889. In one year, she had about two thousand inhabitants in one of her centers. Ramabai had an impact on thousands of women. On October 26, 1989, the Indian government paid tribute to her for her profound impact on the advancement of Indian women by issuing a commemorative postage stamp. Similarly, Jesudason and Ajit Kumar established ashrams in South India. In consultation with Gandhi and Rajaji, Ernest Paton and Savirirayan Jesudason (Periannan) established the Christukula Ashram in Tirupattur, Tamil Nadu in 1921, and the Christu Seva Sangh and Christa Prema Sangh near Pune in 1921 and 1934, respectively. Their aim was to uplift and empower the downtrodden communities in an Indian way with Indian resources. With a similar thought, D. J. Ajit Kumar established the Kristukripa Ashram in Kerala in 1993 with the aim of giving "the living water in the Indian cup." The orthodox and Marthoma churches have also started similar ashrams in South India, preserving Indian Bhakti tradition.

To bring about reformation, many Indian Christians have also been independently and collectively involved in social action. Madhusudan Das, George Joseph, Sundarabai Pawar, and Francina Sorabji are among many others who participated in pre-independent India by protesting, advocating, and initiating social programs to benefit communities and bring about change. In independent

---

70. Awards. "Dr. V. Kurien." Accessed March 20, 2023, https://drkurien.com/awards/

India also, numerous smaller indigenous Christian organizations mushroomed across the nation to help the country through education for the poor and social services for the needy. Most of them are unsung heroes. In recent years, Auto Raja (Thomas Raja), a criminal-turned-savior, has become a redeemer for the homeless and destitute crowds in the city of Bangalore. He has rescued over ten thousand street beggars in the past twenty years. He took on the burden of cremating about four thousand dead bodies that were lying on the streets. His New Ark Mission of India, located near Bangalore, currently houses 750 people rescued from the streets.[71] He received several awards from secular institutions and was praised by prominent celebrities and news channels.

In the field of journalism, Francis R. Moraes of Goa and K. M. Cherian, B. G. Varghese, and Pothen Philip of Kerala are eminent. Moraes was an outstanding journalist. When Moraes died in 1974, Inder K. Gujral, Minister of Information and Broadcasting, said his death marked "the end of an epoch in Indian journalism."[72] Cherian, Varghese, and Philip received prestigious government awards in journalism, literature, and communication arts. Victor Paranjyoti, who was a towering musical personality, played a leadership role in information and media organizations in India. From 1938 to 1947, he served as a director of All India Radio in Madras, Calcutta, Bombay, and New Delhi. He excelled as an accomplished organizer, painter, singer, lecturer, and critic of music and ballet. He composed classical music in Konkani, Tamil, and Hindi.

Indian Christians have pioneered and contributed to the health care system of India, serving the rural masses through hospitals, clinics, health awareness programs, and the distribution of preventative medicines. In independent India, the Comprehensive Rural Health Project initiated by Raj and Mabelle Arole in Jamkhed, Maharashtra, in 1970, the GEMS Multispecialty Hospital by Augustine Jebakumar in Bihar in 2002, and thousands of rural clinics in various parts of India help hundreds of thousands of financially poor patients with low to no-cost treatment. Christians have also excelled in medical research. In the late twentieth century, the majority of doctors and nurses in all areas of health care or medicine were Indian Christians. The father of modern neurosurgery in India is Jacob Chandi, who contributed to the development of neurosurgery in India. The government of India honored him with the Padma Bhushan award in 1964. He also received recognition from various organizations.

---

71. A. Shrikumar, "The Healing Touch: Meet Auto Raja, the Saviour of Bengaluru's destitute," *The Hindu*, March 16, 2017, accessed January 30, 2023, https://www.thehindu.com/society/meet-auto-raja-the-saviour-of-bengalurus-destitute/article17474857.ece

72. Louis D'Silva, "Indian Thought, Culture, and National Life," *Christian Contribution to Nation Building*, 63.

Conclusion

Undoubtedly, many Indian Christians have been at the forefront of the freedom struggle with unwavering dedication. Some served jail terms for the sake of the nation, while others worked for the benefit of society. Whether the country recognizes the contribution of Christians to the nation or not, they still impact the nation through social services, educational endeavors, entrepreneurship, art, media, and culture. As M. M. Thomas encouraged, Christian participation in the life of the state is a moral duty, a national obligation, and the demand of enlightened self-interest among Christians.[73] Therefore, Christians can be found working in both the public and private sectors of Indian society today. They make up an integral part of Indian culture in all walks of life, from the highest levels of government to the lowest, from doctors and engineers to business executives, and from sports, the arts, and literature to drivers, cooks, and servants.

With the rise of Hindu nationalist politics in India, active Christian political participation has declined in recent times as its involvement has been discouraged, if not hindered, by the dominant political parties. The Niyogi Commission, which was headed by Hindu nationalist leaders in the mid-1950s, interpreted Christian political activities as imperial and subservient to Western missions in its report.[74] Some Hindu nationalist writers deny Christian contribution to the Freedom movement and disapprove of Christian humanitarian activities. For instance, T. R. Vedantham remarked in his work *Christianity—A Political Problem*, "When Mahatma Gandhi launched his campaign of non-co-operation movement the entire Indian Christian Community stood behind the British Government and refused to join the movement."[75] Not recognizing the Christian contribution to nation-building, people like Vedantham still label Indian Christians as non-patriotic. The anti-Christian propaganda and hatred may create religious tensions, but such actions will not discourage Christians from being patriotic and from doing good works in India.

---

73. Thomas, *Christian Participation in Nation-Building*, 49.

74. See Manohar James, *Religious Conversion in India: The Niyogi Committee Report of Madhya Pradesh in 1956 and its Continuing Impact on National Unity* (Oregon: Pickwick Publications, 2022).

75. T. R. Vedantham, *Christianity—A Political Problem* (Madras: The Author, 1984), 15.

CHAPTER ELEVEN

Identity Negotiations and the Hindu Devotees of Christ in India

Vinod John

Introduction

"So, what are you?" I frequently asked this seemingly innocuous question during unstructured conversations throughout my fieldwork in Varanasi, India. This inquiry arose from observing the individuals' fervent and open affirmations of Jesus Christ as God. More than two hundred respondents, belonging to different caste Hindu villages, answered the question exclaiming: "*Hum Hindu hain!*" ("We are Hindus!"). Their unwavering confessions prompted me to delve deeper into their self-identification and understand how they perceived themselves within their social context. Through further observation of these devotees' lived experiences within their birth community, in a predominantly Hindu sacred city, I verified their self-identification as Hindus. This social duality—the phenomenon of simultaneous belonging to both religio-cultural traditions or possessing a hyphenated identity—proved intriguing and raises significant missiological questions about the meaning of being a Christian in a multiethnic, multireligious, and multicultural society like India.

Since ancient times, the Indian subcontinent has been a convergent point for a myriad of cultural and religious traditions that contribute to its multicultural identity. In contrast, spaces once considered monocultural and homogenous "Christian" territories in Western nations have now transformed into landscapes characterized by fervent religious diversity. Contributing to this transformation are factors such as globalization, mass communication, and migrations. Within this diverse milieu exists an inherent ambiguity because, "a culture itself comprises an ambiguous text that is constantly in need of interpretation by those who participate in it ... Meaning is in the act of arguing and negotiating."[1] Consequently, individuals continuously seek understanding while redefining their socioreligious identities through numerous means. These dynamics become particularly relevant in Christian missions when people inexorably bring much of

---

1. Jerome Bruner, *Actual Minds, Possible Worlds* (Cambridge, MA: Harvard University Press, 1986), 122.

their religio-cultural traditions with them when encountering and responding to the gospel message. No wonder issues pertaining to race, ethnicity, and identity have emerged as some of today's most pressing concerns. Given this backdrop, it is crucial to consider how caste Hindus who decide to follow Jesus Christ grapple with these challenges in India and beyond? Many of them engage in a process of negotiating, seeking to redefine their traditional Hindu identity within the framework of their newfound (*bhakti*) devotion to Christ. Thus, it becomes an essential subject for further exploration.

Given the recent trends of national identity politics worldwide, which are intertwined with the construction of self and other identities (ethnic, racial, religious, etc.), it is imperative for missiologists to recognize this as an opportunity to reassess our theories and practices in missions. This necessitates a deconstruction of existing notions that portray Christian identity as monolithic and homogenous. Instead, we must embrace a broader understanding of identity and belonging within increasingly multireligious settings while acknowledging that religious identities serve as dynamic texts of our cultures. This chapter aims to offer guidance in that direction by drawing upon the example of a movement among caste Hindus toward Jesus Christ.[2] Initially, there will be a clarification regarding the concept of identity in general terms followed by an exploration specifically focused on religious identity within the Indian context. Subsequently, I will delve into an examination of the implications when Christ followers choose to retain their Hindu identity without adopting a Christian label.

Identity Construction and Negotiation

The pursuit of one's identity presents a formidable challenge. Despite our best efforts, identity defies conclusive definition due to its constructed and multivalent characteristics. Scholars agree that an individual's constructed self-definition, or how they attribute meaning to themselves, serves as a conduit for conveying their sense of identity. Therefore, identity is about *self*-perception, *self*-consciousness, and *self*-definition. Given the enduring quest to understand one's identity by both individuals and collectives alike, there exists a plethora of perspectives on the formation of identities from sociological, anthropological, and psychological standpoints.[3] Notably, all forms of identity formation follow a binary model whereby "us" is necessarily defined in relation to an "other." Belonging to specific groups not only situates individuals vis-à-vis others but also shapes their perceptions

---

2. For details, see Vinod John, *Believing Without Belonging? Religious Beliefs and Social Belonging of Hindu Devotees of Christ* (Eugene, OR: Pickwick Publications, 2020).

3. As a primer for details, see Mark R. Leary and June Price Tangney, eds., *Handbook of Self and Identity*, 2nd ed. (New York: Guilford, 2012).

and behaviors toward those outside their group boundaries. Consequently, constructing delineations through erecting boundaries and applying labels plays an integral role in shaping individual identities while simultaneously marginalizing outsiders. However, within the framework of any given group or community setting, individual identities assume paramount importance as they engender a sense of harmony and belonging among members. Furthermore, "identity conveys a sense of congruity, a feeling of sameness in the squabble of 'us' versus 'them,' and a common past, along with a longing for continuity with one's sociocultural heritage."[4] Hence, preserving this *continuity* becomes crucial for identity negotiations. Nonetheless, ensuring this continuity demands formulation of *differentness* from others which can inadvertently lead to vilifying those who fall beyond our perceived boundaries.

In any culture, the process of constructing, negotiating, and reconstructing identity involves negotiating through various social, cultural, and religious layers. These layers are constantly in a state of flux, continually shifting with one taking precedence over the others depending on socioreligious and political changes. This fluidity inherent in identities underscores their innate malleability rather than being fixed entities. Moreover, it highlights the contestable nature of identities when it comes to shared myths and historical narratives that shape individual's sense of self. People may even reject an identity ascribed to them by others (etic). As the caste-ridden society of India demonstrates, people resist imposed labels that seek to define their identity. Even amid changing circumstances, a *sine qua non* of identity formation lies in the inherited self-definitions of individuals. These deeply rooted meanings serve as a foundation upon which individuals rebuild their sense of identity and adapt their lives accordingly within the present context. Therefore, due to its multifaceted nature and significance within contemporary socioreligious and missiological discourse, the intricate pursuit for personal identity occupies a prominent position. This is particularly evident in multireligious contexts like India wherein belonging to an ethnic or socioreligious group becomes one of the most pressing concerns for many individuals grappling with questions related to their own sense of belonging and identification.

Religious Identities in India

Religious affiliation assumes a pivotal role in the process of identity formation, often exerting a significant influence that surpasses other cultural constituents. This is because religiosity fosters a sense of belonging and inspires loyalty to a group. This is particularly evident in the context of India, which has long been characterized by its multireligious landscape. Despite the coexistence of diverse

---

4. John, *Believing Without Belonging?*, 167.

religious traditions throughout its extensive history, India's narrative is rife with instances where "the other" has been vehemently treated as an adversary to be eradicated. The arrival of both Moghul (Muslim) and European (Christian) colonizers further exacerbated these conflicts.[5] In more recent times, there has been a resurgence of Hindu ethnonationalism under the BJP administration, intensifying dynamics surrounding identity politics. Consequently, interreligious tensions have escalated significantly resulting in widespread acts of communal violence. These clashes are manifested through arbitrary destruction and defacement of religious sites associated with minority communities.[6]

Despite the presence of a multitude of individuals practicing a variety of native and non-native faiths and offering reverence to countless deities, Hinduism predominates India's multireligious landscape, accounting for approximately 80 percent of the population. However, the accuracy of the official statistics regarding the self-identification of individuals classified as "Hindus" in the census data is questionable. Nevertheless, India's religious identity is primarily shaped by Hinduism, notwithstanding the country's secular constitutional framework. Although Vinayak Savarkar, an ideologue of Hindutva ideology, contended that "the conceptualization of Indian national identity must, at its foundation, be based within the political philosophy of Hindutva,"[7] India chose to establish itself as a secular republic upon gaining independence. Thus, recognition of diverse religious identities has always been a feature of the distinctive Indian version of secularism. Rather than adopting a stance detached from religions altogether, the state is expected to maintain an equal distance from various religions and treat them impartially—at least in theory. Nevertheless, as is the case with all liberal democracies, acknowledging religious identities without essentializing them poses a challenge for India.

The negotiation of identity, particularly in relation to caste, presents an intriguing and distinctive phenomenon observed among Indian Christians. Even after embracing Christianity, members of caste-ridden societies continue to uphold their caste identities. In Indian society, being a follower of Christ entails not only matters of spirituality but also navigating complex dynamics related to either maintaining one's caste membership or acquiring an outcaste

---

5. European colonialism began with the arrival of the Portuguese on the western coast as a trade mission, which soon turned into the Goa Inquisition (1560–1812).

6. See, for example, Sudhir Kakar, *The Colors of Violence: Cultural Identities, Religion, and Conflict* (Chicago: University of Chicago Press, 2022).

7. Vinayak Chaturvedi, "Vinayak & Me: 'Hindutva' and the Politics of Naming," *Social History* 28, no. 2 (May 1, 2003): 169. Hindutva, representing the concept of Hinduness, has emerged as the ideological articulation of Hindu nationalism. Its prominence gained momentum following the electoral triumph of its political wing, the Bhartiya Janta Party (BJP), in 2014.

status within their specific caste/subcaste/*biradari,* along with the associated repercussions. Following their outcasting, many groups have formed new endogamous Christian "castes" that feature all aspects entailed by the traditional caste system. Consequently, missionaries across denominations have grappled with this intricate issue. This observation underscores the significance of a careful consideration by both social scientists and missiologists when addressing the multifaceted questions surrounding religious identity.

Missionaries operating in predominantly monocultural or culturally Christian settings commonly presumed that individuals could identify with a singular religion and profess a single religious identity or no religious identity, which they often conflated with their cultural identity. However, "this Eurocentricity of Christian identity is rejected today by many non-Western and Western Christians alike."[8] It is becoming more apparent that individuals hold multifaceted identities that extend beyond a singular religious affiliation. Globalization and intercultural interactions play significant roles in shaping contemporary identities, resulting in people integrating multiple religious beliefs and embracing diverse cultural customs. Consequently, individuals are not constrained to adhere strictly to one clear-cut religious affiliation or a solitary faith tradition.

For example, among certain Western Christians, there is a noticeable trend toward embracing Hindu or Buddhist religious practices like yoga and meditation. It is not uncommon to find churches hosting these classes within their premises. Moreover, some individuals assert their dual religious belonging to both Christianity and another religious traditions. These practices have raised critical questions regarding the anthropological and theological assumptions that restrict individuals to exclusive religious affiliations at any given time. As Voss Roberts argues, our current definition of religion is "partly responsible for perceptions of multiple commitments as problematic, and . . . the metaphor of belonging obscures important dynamics of religious identity."[9]

---

8. Werner G. Jeanrond, "Belonging or Identity? Christian Faith in a Multi-Religious World," in *Many Mansions? Multiple Religious Belonging and Christian Identity*, ed. Catherine Cornille (Maryknoll, NY: Orbis, 2002), 108.

9. Michelle Voss Roberts, "Religious Belonging and the Multiple," *Journal of Feminist Studies in Religion* 26, no. 1 (2010): 43, https://doi.org/10.2979/fsr.2010.26.1.43. Teresa Morgan highlights that even among the early Christians, it should not be regarded as unusual to encounter "individual Christians identifying with multiple labels, accreting identities, code-switching, or even celebrating their hybridity . . . We should be more surprised not to find evidence of any of these practices—which does not mean that we should take finding it for granted. The more nuanced our understanding of the operation of ethnicity in the world into which Christianity was born, however, the better our chance of recognizing what really is, and is not, distinctive about Christian identity." Teresa Morgan, "Society, Identity, and Ethnicity in the Hellenic World," in *Ethnicity, Race, Religion: Identities and Ideologies in Early Jewish and Christian Texts,*

This notion of multiple belonging is not a recent development, particularly in regions like India where religion is deeply interwoven into the social fabric and intertwined with other cultural categories. However, the term and concept of "religion" as employed in contemporary Western literature falls short in capturing the true essence of religion as practiced in India. Wilfred C. Smith's influential work on religion puts forth a radical argument for comprehending non-Western faiths by suggesting that the term "religion" should be "dropped . . . because of its distracting ambiguity . . . [and] because most of its traditional meanings, are, on scrutiny, illegitimate." While Smith expressed hope that these terms would disappear "from serious writing and careful speech within twenty-five years,"[10] this aspiration did not come to fruition. Nonetheless, he articulated well that assuming other people's usage of terms such as faith, piety, affectionate devotion, or adoration, equates to our concept of "religion" is misguided since this archaic concept of religion fails to fully encompass their rich and multifaceted meanings. Therefore, one must exercise caution when retrojecting the current Christian-based religious ideas onto others' religiosity because, "what we might identify as religion (religio), it is often pointed out, had more to do with cultic practice and dutiful obligation than allegiance to a set of beliefs and doctrines, as the modern notion might be taken to imply."[11] For example, what Paula Fredriksen depicts about religion and ethnicity in the ancient Mediterranean context aptly applies to the Hindu religiosity in India:

> In antiquity, gods were local . . . and attached to particular places, . . . to particular peoples; "religion" ran in the blood. In this sense, one's genos was as much a cult-designation as what we, from a sociological or anthropological perspective, see as an "ethnic" one: ethnicity expressed

---

and in Modern Biblical Interpretation, ed. Katherine M. Hockey and David G. Horrell (London: T&T Clark, 2018), 41–42, http://dx.doi.org/10.5040/9780567677334.

10. Wilfred Cantwell Smith, The Meaning and End of Religion: A New Approach to the Religious Traditions of Mankind (New York: Macmillan, 1963), 17, 194–195. Jonathan Smith, too, contends that "religion is not a native term; it is a term created by scholars for their intellectual purposes and therefore is theirs to define." "Religion, Religions, Religious," in Critical Terms for Religious Studies, ed. Mark C. Taylor (Chicago: University of Chicago Press, 1998), 281. Building upon this perspective, Frits Staal goes further in suggesting that "the concept of religion . . . should either be abandoned or confined to Western traditions." Rules Without Meaning: Ritual, Mantras, and the Human Sciences (New York: Peter Lang, 1989), 415. For an extensive exploration of the historical trajectory of the concept of religion and recent developments surrounding it, see Brent Nongbri, Before Religion: A History of a Modern Concept (New Haven, CT: Yale University Press, 2013).

11. Katherine M. Hockey and David G. Horrell, eds., Ethnicity, Race, Religion: Identities and Ideologies in Early Jewish and Christian Texts, and in Modern Biblical Interpretation (London: T & T Clark, 2018), 6–7, https://doi.org/10.5040/9780567677334.

"religion" (acknowledging the anachronism of both terms for our period), and religion expressed "ethnicity."[12]

Similar to religion itself, the composition and shaping of religious identities have exhibited a dynamic nature rather than being monolithic.[13] All religions appear to have engaged in mutual influence, borrowing and assimilating beliefs from one another and subsequently transforming each other. In fact, "in the wider history of religion, multiple religious belonging may have been the rule rather than the exception, at least on a popular level."[14] Insights from the social sciences further enrich our understanding by highlighting not only the coexistence of diverse religiosities but also individuals' capacity to simultaneously hold elements from different religions when encountering a new faith alongside their existing religious framework.

Hence, when Christianity engages with India's multifaceted religio-cultural milieu, akin to it historical interactions with Greek, Jewish, or Western cultures, it inevitably involves individuals who embrace the Christian faith's hermeneutical framework without severing ties with their traditional religious framework. However, in such gospel encounters, the process of people appropriating the gospel rarely unfolds facilely. Instead, it often engenders friction and strains between the gospel and the cultures implicated in such interactions. While popular religiosity may accommodate concurrent affiliations, most religions typically seek undivided devotion from their adherents. Therefore, this poses a significant theological and missionary challenge when attempting to navigate

---

12. Paula Fredriksen, "What 'Parting of the Ways'? Jews, Gentiles, and the Ancient Mediterranean City," in *The Ways That Never Parted: Jews and Christians in Late Antiquity and the Early Middle Ages*, ed. Adam H. Becker and Annette Yoshiko Reed (Tübingen: Mohr Siebeck, 2003), 39.

13. For insights into the dynamic and historical development of various religiosities, deities, identities, and their intricate interplay among indigenous and foreign religions in India, see Krishna Mohan Shrimali, "The Formation of Religious Identities in India," *Social Scientist* 45, no. 5/6 (2017): 3–27, https://www.jstor.org/stable/26380477. Shrimali, cites an example that sheds light on the complex interactions between different religious communities during the thirteenth century CE. In Gujarat, a local feudal king not only allocated land but also financially supported the construction of a mosque for the Muslim migrants from Iran. Notably, the mosque was "designated as dharmasthana ('a site for religion'). The religious performances at the mosque consisted of daily worship and had provisions of offerings, light, oil, and drinks . . . Like the sacred site, the divinity too is represented as a locally comprehensible concept. . . . Islamic divinity being rendered in the imagery of 'Hindu' deities." Shrimali, "The Formation of Religious Identities in India," 11.

14. Catherine Cornille, "Introduction: The Dynamics of Multiple Belonging," in *Many Mansions? Multiple Religious Belonging and Christian Identity*, ed. Catherine Cornille (Maryknoll, NY: Orbis, 2002), 1.

such complex dynamics. Nonetheless, this perpetual tension is indispensable and can yield fruitful outcomes in fostering genuine and novel expressions of the faith—a phenomenon that has been observed among Hindu followers of Christ.

The ethnographic study conducted in Varanasi, effortlessly dovetails with the testimonies of numerous caste Hindus who profess their adherence to Jesus Christ. Visits, dialogues, and participant observation of their lived experiences within their birth community were utilized to validate their verbal claims. The study "reveals that a vast majority [of followers] identify themselves as Hindus either to their own community members or to outsiders, even though their belief in Christ is not clandestine."[15] The inquiry delves into how participants navigate the discursive conflicts arising from simultaneously following Christ while self-presenting as Hindus. By doing so, it bridges the gap left by mostly theoretical reflections that have only tangentially addressed the issue. It is noteworthy that most of these devotees still inhabit their ancestral (Hindu) villages and abodes. Work-related relocation does not impede their commitment to family and community, as they frequently return home. Such Christward movements and the consequent spiritual transformation among caste Hindus present challenges in the fields of missiology and ecclesiology. The emerging unstructured church and the postponement or avoidance of baptismal rituals observed among these believers cannot be simplistically dismissed as just another instance of syncretism.[16] Instead, such movements toward Christ should be recognized as encounters that engender distinct expressions of Christianity. Historically, in this endeavor, as Jayakiran Sebastian aptly stated, "there were several ways—some known to the missionaries and others quite unknown—in which the missionary versions of Christianity were appropriated, subverted, utilized, adapted, and transformed. This reality has raised a host of questions regarding religion, culture, mission, and conversion."[17]

Religion and the Identity of Hindu Followers of Christ

The self-identification of Christ devotees as Hindus encompasses a complex interplay between ethnicity and religion. It is more of a nuanced ethnoreligious identity than a solely religious one. This should be reckoned as a unified

---

15. John, *Believing Without Belonging?*, 168.

16. See, for example, John, 168; Dasan Jeyaraj, *Followers of Christ Outside the Church in Chennai, India: A Socio-Historical Study of a Non-Church Movement* (Zoetermeer: Boekencentrum, 2010), 411.

17. J. Jayakiran Sebastian, "Interrogating Christian Practices: Popular Religiosity across the Ocean," in *Baptism Today: Understanding, Practice, Ecumenical Implications*, ed. Thomas F. Best (Collegeville, MN: Liturgical, 2008), 256.

Indian identity because, in many contexts, identity often overlaps ethnicity. This self-identification represents a nuanced ethnoreligious identity, which deserves to be deemed as a unified Indian identity since identity and ethnicity tend to overlap in some contexts.

Despite India's pluralistic society, characterized by diverse ethnicities, religions, and languages, the overarching macro identity remains that of being Indian. Within this macro identity, various micro identities thrive as separate groups, subgroups, and faiths while retaining their distinctiveness. This is germane to the discussion of why Christ devotees identify themselves as Hindus.

The term *Hindu* can be traced back to Persia, where it derived from the Sanskrit word "*Sindhu*," as suggested by early references. Several ancient Persian inscriptions contribute to "establishing the primacy of the territorial meaning" of the term which was used to describe the dwellers beyond the river *Sindhu* or the *Sindhu* Valley on India's northwest frontier.[18] In the Greco-Roman usage, *Sindhu* and *Hindu* became "*Indus*." In keeping with this Greco-Roman usage, British colonizers referred to the region as "the Indies" territory in official records dating back to the early eighteenth century when they formalized it as "India."[19] Eventually, when the term "*Hindu*" was employed in relation to the outsiders— the Muslims and Christians—"it lost part of its inclusive character. Still the word Hindu remained inclusive and referred to a host of gods and spirits, faiths, and beliefs representing different castes and communities."[20]

W. C. Smith's point of view holds true in questioning the applicability of the traditional Western conception of "religion" when seeking to comprehend Hinduism as a religion.[21] The notion of Hinduism as a unified religion, demarcated by a fixed set of sacred texts or belief systems, is a relatively recent construct that evolved during the nineteenth century, bolstered by European imperialism in India. To illustrate, unlike the Western linear "mode of thinking that accepts only a single, hierarchically defined system of ideas. [The] Indigenous thought is

---

18. Arvind Sharma, "On Hindu, Hindustān, Hinduism, and Hindutva," *Numen* 49, no. 1 (2002): 2, https://doi.org/10.1163/15685270252772759.

19. For details, including the etymology and application of Hindustan/Hindoostan/Indostan, see Ian J. Barrow, "From Hindustan to India: Naming Change in Changing Names," *South Asia: Journal of South Asian Studies* 26, no. 1 (April 1, 2003): 37–49, https://doi.org/10.1080/085640032000063977. Cf. Manan Ahmed Asif, *The Loss of Hindustan: The Invention of India* (Cambridge, MA: Harvard University Press, 2020), 1–27.

20. D. P. Pattanayak, "Linguistic and Religious Identity in India," *India International Centre Quarterly* 18, no. 4 (1991): 104, https://www.jstor.org/stable/23002249.

21. Smith, *The Meaning and End of Religion*. See note 10 above.

capable of entertaining coexistent and apparently contradictory world views."[22] Consequently, the overarching term "Hindu" covers individuals who encompass a broad spectrum ranging from atheism to polytheism, with adherents embracing monism, dualism, animism, or various combinations thereof situated along this continuum. Despite these diverse beliefs and practices within Hinduism, each individual seeks to maintain their distinct identity while aspiring to coexist under the broader umbrella term of Hindu.

Therefore, the expression *Hum Hindu hain* (We are Hindus) made by Christ's devotees carries implications that extend beyond religion. Instead, it references their ethnocultural and traditional way of life, which forms an integral part of their identity. The definition of who or what a Hindu is is not solely determined by one's beliefs and doctrines but also by the manner in which they live their lives and observe the cultural symbols specific to their community. As Raimon Pannikar succinctly put it, "A hindu [sic] is not constituted by her views or beliefs ("orthodoxy"), but rather by that person's more or less explicit or implicit 'confession', by her practice of being a hindu and her acceptance by a hindu community. It is well known that a theist, a deist, a polytheist, an atheist, etc., all can be hindus without finding any conflict or contradiction therein."[23]

The Legal Conundrum of a Separate Identity in a Multireligious Context

In light of this understanding of Hindu and Hinduism, the insights from Julian Saldhana further aid in understanding the issue from an important legal perspective. This phenomenon is perhaps specific to India's multireligious society as "it is more difficult to be accepted as a Hindu if one was not born such, than to cease to be considered a Hindu if one was born such, even though one may disregard most of the Hindu tenets and practices."[24] In contrast to Hindus and Muslims, Christians in India lack a specific personal law (civil law) that applies to everyone. Consequently, the legal conundrum of determining which civil code or personal law should govern individuals who opt to follow the Christian faith, has only exacerbated their sense of alienation since the colonial era. The British Raj decided against applying the extant civil laws of other communities for the new

---

22. June C. Nash, *We Eat the Mines and the Mines Eat Us: Dependency and Exploitation in Bolivian Tin Mines* (New York: Columbia University Press, 1993), 122.

23. Raimon Pannikar, "On Christian Identity: Who Is a Christian?" in *Many Mansions? Multiple Religious Belonging and Christian Identity*, ed. Catherine Cornille (Maryknoll, NY: Orbis, 2002), 125.

24. Julian Saldanha, *Conversion and Indian Civil Law* (Bangalore: Theological Publications in India, 1981), 56.

followers of Christ and instead placed them under the jurisdiction of the English (Christian) legal regulations. As a result, these individuals began to be identified through negation—defined by what they were not: non-Hindu or non-Muslim. Despite the fact that some Imperial judges addressed this quandary by issuing "rulings that confirmed Christian converts as Hindus (or Muslims, as the case might be) for purposes of law." They largely remained "indifferent to the conditions of liminal existence that converts were forced to cope with . . . left floating in a nebulous space, neither Hindus nor Christians in their social existence."[25] This predicament partly explains why many Hindus or Muslims tend to stick to their birth communities despite following Jesus Christ. This is a judicious move as individuals would not want to encounter legal complications regarding their inheritance rights, property ownership, marriage regulations, and civil liberties solely based on their altered spiritual convictions. Julian Saldanha scrutinizes the legal implications of Hindu identity in postindependence India, and posits:

> Our inquiry discloses that being a Hindu is not a matter of creed, but of social and legal status. There is no particular article of faith which one must profess in order to be a Hindu . . . A Hindu is one who: 1) considers himself a Hindu, i.e., a member of his caste and Hindu community; 2) keeps at least some of the customs and social usages of his community, being content to be governed by Hindu personal law; 3) is accepted as a member by the Hindu community. Thus, being a Hindu is primarily a question of social belonging.[26]

Nonetheless, it is imperative to acknowledge that despite the conceptual understanding of Hinduism as a recent construct and Western religious classifications being inadequate, it remains the dominant religion of the vast majority of Indians and a core aspect of their cultural identity. Hindus continue to embrace this identity, as they always have, while navigating the intricate dynamic of living in a multireligious society. Therefore, Hinduism as a religion offers heuristic advantages when discussing identity today. Resisting the transition from a Hindu to Christian identity can be seen as an act of resistance against colonial Christianity and its ramifications. During the British Raj in northern India, which witnessed the introduction of Christianity, strategic abuse of nomenclature was employed as a tool for promoting imperialism. The government

---

25. Gauri Viswanathan, *Outside the Fold: Conversion, Modernity, and Belief* (Princeton: Princeton University Press, 1998), 81. For details of several court cases in South India, see Chandra Mallampalli, *Christians and Public Life in Colonial South India, 1863–1937: Contending with Marginality* (London: Routledge Curzon, 2004).

26. Saldanha, *Conversion and Indian Civil Law*, 56, 90.

implemented renaming practices for places and people, symbolizing their power and reinforcing imperial control over these territories.

Thus, an individual who identifies as Hindu and has immersed themselves in embracing Hindu practices and beliefs throughout their life can still chose to follow Jesus Christ without severing their ethnocultural identity or renouncing their Hindu community for a different one, provided that Jesus Christ remains the central point of reference. However, this does not imply that nothing from one's traditional religious practices undergoes transformation. Conversely, encountering Christ and being guided by the Holy Spirit inherently leads to a transformative process where nothing remains unchanged. Inevitably fresh symbols and forms of faith will naturally emerge, and it is crucial to embrace these new expressions as they affirm the dynamic essence of World Christianity, as evidenced by studies conducted worldwide.

Viability of Christ's Devotees in a Multifaith Community

Though judicious, is it realistic for adherents of Christ to dwell within their Hindu communities while maintaining their faith in Christ? This has been the subject of inquiry among scholars and mission practitioners. They seek to explore the feasibility of reconciling the inherent incongruity between belief in Christ and living as Hindus within India's diverse cultural milieu. In response to this valid concern, an affirmative stance can be taken based on India's historical legacy of tolerance.

An illustrative example that underscores this culture of tolerance can be found in the experiences of Jewish communities. Persecuted and expelled from other regions, some Jews landed along the western Ghats regions in areas such a Cranganore (Kerala) or Konkan (Maharashtra). It is noteworthy that the Hindu kings not only provided sanctuary to these Jewish settlers but also facilitated in establishing their synagogues where different factions identified themselves as Cochin/Malabar/Black Jews, Pardesi/White Jews, or Bene Israelis while retaining distinctive ethnoreligious identities.[27] This accommodation within the Hindu community can be attributed to cultural norms taking precedence over individual beliefs or creeds. The narrative surrounding Syrian Christians in Kerala (South India) also serves as an apt illustration supporting this observation.

---

27. Nathan Katz, *Who Are the Jews of India?* (Berkeley: University of California Press, 2000), 13–14; Haeem Samuel Kehimkar, *The History of the Bene Israel of India* (Tel-Aviv: Dayag Press, 1937), 4. Katz, responding about their identity, states, "The identity of the Jews of Cochin is seamless: they are simultaneously fully Indian and fully Jewish. . . . the Cochin Jews exemplify a successfully acculturated identity. [They] established and maintained their identity . . . through the skillful adaptation of Hindu symbols and ritual elements within the framework of the Judaic law, and through the emulation of Indian social structure. They were actors in the finely balanced drama of Indian Jewish identity." Katz, *Who Are the Jews of India?*, 9, 91.

Syrian Christians in South India

Syrian Christians, also known as Thomas Christians, hold a significant historical position as one of the oldest Christian communities in India. Their origins can be traced back to migration from Syria in the fourth century CE, although there is a strong tradition attributing their establishment to the first century. According to this tradition, it is believed that the apostle Thomas arrived on the Malabar coast (in Kerala) during this period and engaged in evangelistic activities among caste Hindus. While proudly identifying themselves as Syrian Christians,[28] this community has adeptly integrated their cultural traditions with Hindu practices over generations. They have followed caste norms and adapted certain aspects of the Hindu lifestyle while maintaining their distinct identity. This process of acculturation has resulted in a unique blend of Syrian Christian and Hindu traditions within their religious practices. As a result, the boundaries between these two groups appear blurred, creating a complex interplay of religious identities for the Syrian Christian community.

The observance of customs and regulations regarding ritual pollution is particularly stringent among Kerala's caste Hindus, perhaps more so than in any other part than part of India. Interestingly, however, "within this system the large Syrian Christian community was accorded a position of considerable esteem, on the second or third rung from the top of the hierarchy, as it were, either equal to, or immediately below the Nairs."[29] Since they lived as Hindus practicing the caste system without ever developing a theological justification for it, they were "encapsulated in Hindu society . . . regarded as a caste and had a recognized place in the caste hierarchy . . . accorded a high status within the system . . . [which] seems to have made it possible for Christianity to survive in Kerala, but on condition that it observed the norms of the system."[30] The Syrian

---

28. This moniker is not solely due to their connections with Syria but primarily stems from their adherence to Syriac worship and liturgy until the late 1900s, when they transitioned to using Malayalam, while retaining the Syriac tunes. However, in recent times, a grassroots initiative has emerged with the aim of resuscitating the use of Syriac liturgy in worship. See Martin Antony, "Revival of the Syriac Language in Worship from the Grass Root Level: A New Model of Liturgical Reformation in the Syro Malabar Church," *Nasranis* (blog), October 21, 2022, https://www.nasrani.net/revival-syriac-language-worship-grass-root-level-new-model-liturgical-reformation-syro-malabar-church/.

29. Duncan B. Forrester, *Caste and Christianity: Attitudes and Policies on Caste of Anglo-Saxon Protestant Missions in India* (London: Curzon, 1980), 98.

30. Forrester, *Caste and Christianity*, 99. Besides Forrester, Ninan Koshy, too, in his study of caste among Christians of Kerala, states that "the Syrian Christians" lived as "a distinct caste." Koshy, *Caste in the Kerala Churches* (Bangalore: CISRS, 1968), 51. If they desired to remain in this status, "they had necessarily to conform to the pattern and practices governing a caste society . . . by assimilating themselves in the society in which they lived and by adopting the

Christians recognized and valued their high status because they had "negotiated their position through alliance with the local rulers and maintained their status by adherence to the purity-pollution norms of regional Hindu society."[31] As a consequence of these dynamics, there was little emphasis on evangelization among Syrian Christians since bringing outsiders into one's own caste is considered offensive according to classical Hindu caste hierarchy.[32] This resulted in many Dalit Christians establishing independent churches—leading to a proliferation of indigenous Christian denominations predominantly aligned with Pentecostal traditions.

In present multifaith settings, Hindus who embrace Christ are not obligated to replicate the practices of Syrian Christians, particularly in terms of adopting caste-based discrimination and neglecting evangelization efforts. The multifaceted nature of Indian society is resilient enough to endure if followers of Christ refrain from accentuating the boundary markers and instead confirm to the customs of their birth community while avoiding the mimicry of Western Christians or their values. As far back as 1893, H. Haigh, an English missionary, had implored "That the books which we publish should be carefully related to Hindu thought, expressed in its terms, done in its style, adopting where it can its positions, and leading on, still in Hindu fashion and in its terminology, from points of agreement to essential points of difference. In this way we may, perhaps, be able to furnish an effectual exhibition of legitimately 'Hinduised Christianity.'"[33] Notwithstanding such appeals and the resistance of various Indian Christian leaders regarding colonial missions' insistence on complete separation from the natal community for Christ's followers, mission compounds were established in numerous cities.[34] Consequently, a distinct

---

language, dress, and habits of their Hindu brethren." S. G. Pothan, *The Syrian Christians of Kerala* (New York: Asia Publishing, 1963), 55.

31. Rowena Robinson, "Negotiating Boundaries and Identities: Christian 'Communities' in India," in *Community and Identities: Contemporary Discourses on Culture and Politics in India*, ed. Surinder S. Jodhka (New Delhi: Sage, 2001), 225.

32. It is not just Syrians; other Christians too have not been exempted from the pervasive influence of the caste system. Consequently, they have carried "'dual identities' or have become manifested as possessing 'hybridized' cultural features." Robert Eric Frykenberg, *Christianity in India: From Beginnings to the Present* (Oxford: Oxford University Press, 2008), viii.

33. H. Haigh, "Vernacular Literature," in *Report of the Third Decennial Missionary Conference Held at Bombay, 1892–1893*, vol. 2 (Third Decennial Missionary Conference, Bombay: Education Society's Steam Press, 1893), 667.

34. Prominent among these leaders were individuals such as Krishna Mohan Banerjee, K. T. Paul, R. C. Das, Kali Charan Banerjee, Narayan Vaman Tilak. For a brief discussion of the relevant issue, see John, *Believing Without Belonging?*, 180–192.

communal Christianity surfaced, perceiving itself as a uniform Christian society or *quam*. It emerged through a "process of radical separation from traditional Indian society," where the "individual converts were driven from their homes and communities" thereby disrupting their sociocultural ties with their natal *qaum*.[35] According to Chandra Mallampalli's research on South India's Christian community, perception among Protestant elites was one wherein they deemed this an undesirable development. He states that mostly the South Indian "Protestant elites portrayed the Christian community as something that should never have come into being. They saw themselves as a community in exile from Hindu society and attributed this state of exile equally to the intolerance of foreign missionaries and Hindu families."[36] However, this sentiment was not confined solely to one region; testimonies from North India also merit thoughtful consideration. While initially joining a distinct religious community, some Christ followers eventually grew to rue their decision. The following illustrative statement articulated by Yisu Das Tiwari (1911–1997) is worth noting. Tiwari, hailing from a Brahmin family in Uttar Pradesh (North India), was a baptized adherent of Christ. In his final moments, he conveyed to his son, Ravi Tiwari: "Christ is my *'ishta'* [God], he has never left me, I will never leave him, but I would not have joined the Christian community. I would have lived with my people and my community and been a witness to them."[37]

During my research in Varanasi, I encountered compelling support for Tiwari's perspective within the Hindu community of Christ followers. These individuals have been residing in their birth communities for several years, adhering to local customs while maintaining regular worship of Jesus Christ and expressing unwavering devotion (bhakti) toward him. They firmly assert that their commitment to following Christ has been made possible through his transformative power. In understanding this dynamic, it is essential to consider the insight provided by Judith Lieu, who emphasizes that "social separation is not a Christian characteristic,"[38] during the formative years of the Christ movements. Therefore, the new disciples do not perceive their identification with Christ as a means of socially isolating themselves from others. Historical examples serve to further elucidate this notion.

---

35. Victor Hayward, ed., *The Church as Christian Community: Three Studies of North Indian Churches* (London: Lutterworth, 1966), 130, cf. 79. See John, *Believing Without Belonging*, 180–192.

36. Chandra Mallampalli, *Christians and Public Life*, 14–15.

37. Ravi Tiwari, *Yisu Das: Witness of a Convert* (Delhi: ISPCK, 2000), 24.

38. Judith Lieu, *Neither Jew Nor Greek? Constructing Early Christianity*, 2nd ed. (London: Bloomsbury T&T Clark, 2016), 197.

Early Church Jesus Followers and Their Significance for Hindu Christ Disciples Today

This chapter commenced with the question posed to Hindu devotees of Christ: "What are you?" As already noted, this query elicits crucial missiological questions regarding whether professing Jesus Christ as Lord necessitates a Hindu ceasing to identify as such? Is it incumbent upon a Christ follower to relinquish their association with their caste, community, ethnicity, and nation—elements that shape their very being? Exploring how early Jewish and other disciples of Christ approached the question of their essence can provide insights into this matter. Recent research,[39] suggests that understanding the process by which Hindu followers of Christ define themselves could contribute to our comprehension as it is like the experience of early disciples. Based on my findings, these followers of Christ have engaged in a negotiation process where they seek to integrate Christ's teaching within their existing Hindu framework. However, during this process, there is no inclination among them to sever ties with their ancestral and conventional Hindu religio-ethnic identity. This ongoing social construction and negotiation of identity stems from an inherent desire to establish self-definition and potentially assert it. Consequently, today's Hindu devotees of Christ can be characterized as pilgrims who embark on a similar journey as early-century devotees of Christ.

As W. C. Smith's analysis of the modern notion of "religion" in relation to Hinduism suggests, a similar observation can be made about early Hindu Christ followers and the progression of the Jesus movements.[40] Applying the term "Christianity" to their devotion is anachronistic since Jesus Christ did not establish a new religion that introduced novel worship practices, rituals, temples, or clergy. Instead, his earliest disciples embraced a path referred to as "the Way," as Jesus himself proclaimed to be "the way and the truth and the life."[41] Moreover, they continued to participate in Jewish religious life by worshiping in synagogues and temples, circumcising their offspring, and adhering to kosher dietary laws. Studies indicate that the so-called parting of the ways between Jews and Christians did not occur until the fourth century CE,[42] when the

---

39. For example, see, inter alia, Judith Lieu, *Christian Identity in the Jewish and Graeco-Roman World* (Oxford: Oxford University Press, 2004); Lieu, *Neither Jew nor Greek?*; Philip A. Harland, *Dynamics of Identity in the World of the Early Christians: Associations, Judeans, and Cultural Minorities* (New York: T & T Clark, 2009).

40. Lieu, *Neither Jew nor Greek?*, 2016, 205.

41. Acts 9:2 and John 14:6 NRSVUE; cf. John 1:23, Acts 16:17; 18:25–26; 19:9, 23; 22:4; 24:14, 22.

42. Adam H. Becker and Annette Yoshiko Reed, eds., *The Ways That Never Parted: Jews and Christians in Late Antiquity and the Early Middle Ages* (Minneapolis: Fortress Press, 2007); Lieu, *Neither Jew nor Greek?*; Lieu, *Christian Identity in the Jewish and Graeco-Roman World.*

Roman Empire formally recognized the Church and institutionalized the Christ movement. To exemplify, Paula Fredriksen's copious sources "speak regularly of Christians frequenting synagogues, keeping Sabbath, or feast days with Jewish friends, soliciting Jewish blessings, betrothing their children to Jews or, indeed, marrying Jews themselves."[43] The indistinct boundaries between Jewish ethnicity and Christian faith presented challenges for both followers and apostles of Christ who grappled with reconciling these two aspects. Nonetheless, they exhibited remarkable theological and missiological courage by retaining their Jewish identity while following Christ. Even prominent figures like apostle Paul, despite embarking on missionary vocation to the nations, retained their Jewishness. As Lucian Legrand's aptly stated: "going to the nations, Paul did not turn away from Israel and forswear his Jewish identity."[44]

However, the Christ followers did establish "associations" or "cultural minorities" within their socioreligious or ethnic communities rather than isolate themselves. Such groups in the Greco-Roman era were comparable to "the local devotees of Zeus or Dionysos or the guild of purple-dyers, groups that assembled regularly to socialize, share communal meals, and honor both their earthly and divine benefactors."[45] They were indeed dubbed "Christians" in a derogatory manner, a term that had "its uses but it does not appear to be a primary form of self-definition" until the third century CE. Despite this label, it is important to recognize that "it did not, of course, determine the content of that label nor decide who could claim it."[46] This situation resonates with my own participation in numerous such minority fellowships of Christ followers in Varanasi.[47] Similar to the case of being a Jew and following Christ, it is now conceivable for individuals to be Indian, Asian, Hindu, or Buddhist and follow Jesus Christ. As boundaries become increasingly permeable and hybridity or dual belonging becomes normalized, the fervent devotion displayed by Hindu followers of Christ indicates their ability to identify themselves ethnically as "Hindus" while affirming Jesus, through apostle Thomas's proclamation: "My Lord and my God!"

---

43. Fredriksen, "What 'Parting of the Ways'?," 60.

44. Lucien Legrand, *The Bible on Culture: Belonging or Dissenting?* (Maryknoll, NY: Orbis, 2000), 121.

45. Harland, *Dynamics of Identity*, 45–46. Drawing on archaeological and epigraphic evidence, Harland asserts that among the Christ devotees, one of the self-designations employed was simply "the friends." This term not only expressed filial connections within the group but it was also "sometimes used as the main title for the group itself." Harland, *Dynamics of Identity*, 45. Cf. 3 John 15.

46. Lieu, *Christian Identity*, 259, 267.

47. John, *Believing Without Belonging?*, 107–112.

Is it possible that Hindu devotees adopt this strategy to evade persecution, as some maintain? That notion is not entirely accurate. These individuals are still subjected to persecution, akin to the experiences of early followers. Can we infer from this that Christ would call into question the significance of their Hindu or Indian identity and everything that it entails? The answer is unequivocal. Challenging established norms is intrinsic to the gospel and exemplified by Christ himself, and it will persist as an enduring aspect of faith. The gospel calls upon individuals, communities, castes, and socioreligious structures to acquiesce and transcend their ethnoreligious belongings in order to wholeheartedly follow Christ. This path aligns with the teaching of Christ aimed at liberating humanity from all forms of constraint and enabling them to become a "new creation,"— a new humanity in Christ. As devotees embrace this transformative journey, they progressively experience "being transformed into the [Lord's] image from one degree of glory to another."[48]

Conclusion

When Christ followers assert their identity as Hindus, they are referencing an ethnocultural tradition that places greater emphasis on performative aspects rather than belief systems. This raises relevant questions: Can individuals maintain their cultural and ethnic Hindu identity while professing Jesus Christ as their Lord? Is it practical to follow Jesus Christ and lead a life consistent with his teachings within India's diverse and multireligious society?

The possibility of answering these questions affirmatively exists for those who believe in trans-contextual missions because, "to become Christian after belonging to a non-Christian tradition does not necessarily mean alienation from either the previous cultural and ethnic identity or from one's previous religious identity."[49] Identity being a fluid concept and identity quest always being influenced by context means it remains an evolving construct that is engaged in a dialectic relationship with the challenges it encounters. From this perspective, the quest for identity among Hindu devotees of Christ may not have universal applicability across diverse cultures. However, it holds relevance to the emergence of novel forms of indigenous Christianities. If its corollary were to manifest as a Hindu-Christianity, it would serve as a valuable complement to the diverse spectrum of Christianities—a vibrant flower adorning a beautiful garland.

---

48. 2 Corinthians 5:17; 3:18.

49. Claude Geffre, "Double Belonging and the Originality of Christianity as a Religion," in *Many Mansions? Multiple Religious Belonging and Christian Identity*, ed. Catherine Cornille (Maryknoll, NY: Orbis, 2002), 99.

CHAPTER TWELVE

The Dalit Christian Woman

Caste, Gender, and Constructed Identity in India

Priya Santhakumar Leela

Introduction

THIS CHAPTER AIMS to delineate how the Indian caste system constructs identities for Dalit women and how these identities are reinforced within the Indian church. To expose how caste facilitates the construction of identities for Dalit Christian women, important terms will be defined and the origin and role of the caste system will be briefly elucidated. After an initial exploration of the relationship between caste, gender, and the construction of identities of Dalit women in the larger context of India and its impact on conversions to Christianity, the chapter will investigate these interactions within the Indian church to explain their role in constructing identities for Dalit Christian women and expound on the missional role of the church in this context. This study focuses on the internalization of inferiority forced upon Dalit women by a caste system and patriarchal culture that shapes their self-understanding as the lowest strata of the social and religious hierarchy. This anticipates defining significant terms to render consistent and dependable meaning for them in the study.

Dalits

The word Dalit in Sanskrit is *Dal*, meaning "to fracture, to tear open, or to rupture."[1] Dalits are often dubbed the fifth caste, but in reality are below the lowest of the castes. However, according to Manu, there was no such caste as the fifth caste, though, when such a group emerged due to intermarriages between castes, they were named the fifth caste, or outsiders.[2] Walter Fernandes points out some synonyms for Dalits as *Chandalas* (one who deals with the disposal of corpses), untouchable, depressed classes, and *Harijans* (people of a god named

---

1. Bhagavan Das and James Massey, *Dalit Solidarity* (ISPCK: New Delhi, 1995), 16.

2. S. V. Desika Char, *Caste, Religion, and Country: A View of Ancient Medieval India* (New Delhi: Orient Longman Limited, 1993), 15.

Hari).[3] Krishna Iyer adds more terms which are used to identify Dalits in Indian history such as "outcastes, *Panchamas* [fifth caste], *Antyajas* [an inferior tribe], *Avarnas* [colorless people], exterior castes, depressed classes, untouchables and *Harijans*."[4] As *avarnas*, they are placed under the lowest caste and are considered as "non-caste."[5] Therefore, as discussed they are considered the non-caste, *avarnas* in the Indian caste system.

Caste and the Caste System

Though caste is generally believed to be a part of Hinduism, the Hindu categories of caste saturate almost the whole of Indian society and influence most cultures, with the exceptions of the northeastern tribes who are ethnically different and biologically related to East Asians.

The term caste most likely originated from the Portuguese word "'*casta*' meaning race, lineage, breed or class."[6] Scholars argue that the nuances of the caste system make it a difficult one to define. No one definition can give the full picture of this system. Sebastian Velassery defines it as a hierarchical ordering of subdivisions of ethnic groups who practice intra-marriages.[7] He continues to state that "society is characterized by such a system if it is divided into a large number of hereditarily specialized groups, which are hierarchically superposed and mutually opposed. It does not tolerate the principle of rising in the status of groups' mixture and of changing occupation."[8] This divide in the hierarchy and its impact is stressed by Gerald Berreman who describes the caste system as "institutionalized inequality," which "guaranteed differential access to the valued things of life."[9] Uma Chakravarti further explains this by referring to Bhimrao Ramji Ambedkar's perception of caste as a system of "graded inequality in which castes are arranged according to ascending scale

---

3. Walter Fernandes, *The Emerging Dalit Identity: The Re-assertion of the Subalterns* (New Delhi: Indian Social Institute, 1996), 1.

4. Krishna L. A. Iyer, *Kerala, and her People* (Palghat: Educational Supplies Department, 1961), 38.

5. Gale Ellen Kamen, "The Status, Survival, and Current Dilemma of a Female Dalit Cobbler of India." PhD diss (Virginia: Virginia Polytechnic Institute and State University, 2004), 13.

6. Selvin Raj Gnana, "Caste System, Dalitization and Its Implications in Contemporary India," *International Journal of Sociology and Anthropology* 10, no. 7 (October 2018), 65.

7. Sebastian Velassery, *Casteism and Human Rights: Toward an Ontology of the Social Order.* (Singapore: Marshall Cavendish Academic, 2005), 2

8. Velassery, *Casteism and Human Rights*, 2.

9. Uma Chakravarti, *Gendering Caste Through a Feminist Lens* (Los Angeles: Sage, 2018) 11.

of reverence and a descending scale of contempt."[10] Consequently, Velessamy, Chakravarti, Berreman, and Ambedkar view the caste system as a human-made and institutionalized hierarchy that strengthens disparity. This leads us to the question of the caste system's origin.

Origin of the Caste System

To understand the interconnectedness of caste, gender, and constructed identities one needs to comprehend the origin of the caste system. Anthropologists have determined that some castes have existed as castes for a long time whereas others are identified as immigrant groups.[11] However, many scholars on caste derive its theory of origin from the ancient text of *Manu Smriti* in which Manu explains the order in which four castes are created from various parts of Brahman's body, indicating inferior positioning to "lower castes." However, for Manu, the *avarnas* did not originate from Brahman's body, so are outcastes. Nripendra Dutt argues that in this text Manu was originally referring not to caste but the existence of human diversity.[12] However, George Buhler negates such a view of Manu when he postulated that, the inferior identity is prescribed in this mythical text where Manu suggests that even in the name of a fourth caste there should be elements of disgust.[13] In-depth research of the system's historical origin is a temptation that this chapter will resist as this is a history that has gone into extensive interpretations and such an attempt would be repetitive. However, a significant point to be noted here is that although there are ancient texts that speak against any such inferior positioning or categorization of people, there seem to be intentional efforts in the choice of ancient texts by the creators and advocates of the caste system, consequently demonstrating the desire to establish a certain role for this system in which the Dalits are outcastes.

Main Functions of the Caste System in India

A contextual understanding of the caste system is necessary to understand the interplay between caste, gender, and constructed identities. As the foundations for constructing this system on certain "selected" texts exhibits the aspiration to institute deliberated purposes for this system, the configuration

---

10. Chakravarti, *Gendering Caste Through a Feminist Lens* (Calcutta: Stree, 2003), 7.

11. Irawati Karve, *Hindu Society: An Interpretation* (Poona: Deccan College Postgraduate and Institute, 1961), 12.

12. Nripendra Kumar Dutt, *Origin and Growth of Caste in India*, vol. 1 (London: Kegan Paul, Trench, Trubner & Co., 1931), 4–6.

13. George Buhler, *The Laws of Manu* (Delhi: Motilal Banarsidass, 1964), 31.

of this system delineates its role in achieving these purposes. The two fundamental roles caste plays are constructing an internalized hierarchal identity
and establishing the dynamics of subjectivity and power between each layer
of this hierarchy.

Construction of an Internalized Hierarchy

While sketching the functions of the system, Louis Dumont uses the struc-
turalism approach and underscores the hierarchical order of castes situated
in the "minds" of people and later locates this in the ideology of purity and
impurity.[14] Michael Moffat, while agreeing with the existence of such a ladder
rightly argues that it is enormously internalized and the presupposed hierarchical
order is willingly accepted by most of the Dalits.[15] However, in his anthropological discussion on the features of caste, Dipankar Gupta stresses the *Homo
Hierarchicus* theory of Dumont to understand the caste system and opposes
a view of caste hierarchy as one internalized by those in the lower castes and
Dalits.[16] Nonetheless, Moffat's argument on internalizing seems reasonable as it
is evident that many Dalits in India especially in the past and even in the present
characterize this internalization. Therefore, as opposed to Émile Durkheim's
proposal that social systems must be understood without any contemplation of
the psychology of people,[17] the caste system needs to be understood by contem-
plating the minds of those affected by it. Poignantly, since the "higher" caste in
the order has the decisive power to resolve the standards determining this order,
Dalits are often deprived of the ability to evaluate or question these categories,
and this closes the door to any interaction.[18] The usage of Hindu scriptures by
the advocates of the system to contend that the only way of mobility is through
rebirths consequently closes the possibility of any mobility between these segments in this life.

Chakravarti rightly points out that caste and gender must be studied
together to understand how it dispenses hierarchy in the minds of Dalit women

14. Louis Dumont, *Homo Hierarchicus: The Caste System and Its Implications.* (London.
Weidenfeld and Nicholson, 1970), 82, 71.

15. Michael Moffat, *Untouchable Community in South India: Structure and Consensus* (New
Jersey: Princeton University Press, 1979), 63.

16. Dipankar Gupta, *Interrogating Caste: Understanding Hierarchy and Difference in Indian
Society* (New Delhi: Penguin Books, 2000), 2, 6.

17. L. L. Langness, *The Research of Culture* (Los Angeles: Chandler & Sharp, 2005), 176.

18. Uma Chakravarti, *Gendering Caste: Through a Feminist Lens,* (Calcutta: Street, 2013), 7.

in India.[19] R. K. Kshirsagar points to the usage of texts of Manu to aid the positioning of patriarchal hierarchy in Indian women's minds.[20] Sharmila Rege asserts that this is later reinforced by imposing constraints upon each category.[21] Consequently, many Dalit women internalize that this is an unquestionable system. Hence, it establishes that the caste system functions to institute such a categorization and restricts Dalits from challenging it. Patriarchy adds another layer to the hierarchy for Dalit women. Once the existence of a chain of orders is affirmed and forced to be internalized, it is predictable that there is more to the functioning of such an order. This is where the system establishes the dynamics within this classification.

Construction of the Dynamics of Subjectivity and Power

From the above discussion, we can see that these created orders through cultural categories permeate society and create permanent statuses without the possibility to change orders in the present life. Yet another function of this system is to superimpose a dynamic of interaction between each layer of this hierarchy. Isabel Wilkerson speaks of eight pillars of the caste system understood by Indians as originating from the will and character of God: heredity, intra-marriage, intrinsic with pollution ideologies, labor divisions, demeaning, violence for power, inbuilt superior, and inferior view of human.[22] These features exhibit a dialectical interaction. This is further clarified when Chakravarti posits that in contrast to the opposition between the pure and the impure outlined by Dumont, Berreman provides another set of juxtapositions.[23] Chakravarti asserts that for Berreman the meaning of caste "is power and vulnerability, privilege and oppression, honor and degradation, plenty and want, reward and deprivation, security and anxiety."[24] These dialectics reveal the dynamics between the hierarchies as one between subjectivity and power as will be discussed below. Berreman further illuminates this as he views the caste system as a stratification system, grading people and

---

19. Chakravarti, *Gendering Caste*, 1.

20. R. K. Kshirsagar, *Untouchability in India—Implementation of the Law and Abolition* (New Delhi: Deep & Deep, 1989) 49.

21. Sharmila Rege, "Caste and Gender: The Violence against Women in India," in *Dalit Women in India: Issues and Perspectives*, ed. P. G. Jogdand (New Delhi: Gyan, 1995), 33.

22. Isabel Wilkerson, *Caste: The Origin of Our Discontents* (New York: Random House, 2020) 101–159.

23. Chakravarti, *Gendering Caste*, 10. 12

24. Chakravarti, *Gendering Caste*, 11.

consequently allocating power and privilege to maintain a certain beneficial status for its creators.[25] He further explains that there are widespread influences of these stratifications on the minds of the people within it.[26] This indicates how caste is employed to create and maintain the dual identity of power and subjectivity within the created hierarchies.

Jacques Lacan's theory of subjectivity formation is useful in understanding the way various discourses of this system are created to construct a dynamic of subjectivity for Dalit women. According to Lacan as explained by James DiCenso, "subjectivity" and "identity" are culturally constructed.[27] The culture of the caste system and its patriarchal undertones operate in these women as psychic agencies which are being reinforced through various manifestations of caste. This creates a state of subjectivity for these women and that of power for the "high caste" men. Berreman illustrates this by comparing it with Oscar Lewis's "Culture of Poverty" arguing just as poverty continues to exist as the poor internalize the condition and behave in a certain way and such behaviors are passed down along with the attached identity, stopping the future generations from escaping poverty itself,[28] the caste system attaches itself to behaviors, symbols, and beliefs so that it creates psychological constructs of subjectivity that speak to the minds of Dalit women. The role of caste in creating and establishing internalized hierarchy and the dynamics of subjectivity and power lead to the need to examine the specific identities this system attributes to Dalit women.

Dalit Women and Caste-Constructed Identities

While the system establishes the existence of a hierarchy of subjectivity and power, the ideologies put down by the interplay of patriarchy and the caste system create cultural identities for Dalit women. These identities communicate certain fundamental characteristics to individuals and those around them.[29] Each of these identities is based on the established hierarchy of subjectivity. Subsequently, such constructions facilitate effortless implementations of rules that assimilate power in the hands of the "upper caste" man.

---

25. Gerald D. Berreman, "Caste as Social Process," *Southwestern Journal of Anthropology* 23, no. 4 (Winter 1967): 354, 356.

26. Berreman, "Caste as Social Process," 351.

27. James J. DiCenso, "Symbolism and Subjectivity: A Lacanian Approach to Religion." *Journal of Religion* 74, no. 1 (January 1994), 48.

28. Berreman, "Caste as Social Process," 351.

29. Erik Erikson, *Identity and Lifecycle* (New York: Norton, 1980), 109.

The "Impure Untouchable" Dalit Womanhood

The "upper caste" man's body is considered pure and interactions with those from "lower" ranks are believed to make him impure.[30] Commenting on the role of the purity-pollution dialectic, which reveals the subjectivity of Dalit women in India, A. M. Shah states,

> Ideas of purity/impurity were present all-over Hindu society for centuries: in domestic as well as public life, in exchange of food and water, in practicing occupations, in kinship and marriage, in religious action and belief, in temples and monasteries, and myriad different contexts and situations . . . The Hindu civilization is sometimes called a civilization of purity and pollution, and the Hindu psyche is believed to be pathologically obsessed with it.[31]

To reinforce this impurity on Dalit women, the "high castes" have created rituals to exclude them religiously and culturally, consequently giving them a lived experience to the ground and consistently reminding them of this distinctiveness of being polluted.[32] This is affirmed by Selvin Raj Gnana, "caste discrimination is so strong due to purity-pollution concept in the mind of people which was found in Hindu religion promoted by the Brahmins."[33] This emphasis on its origin in the texts strengthens the dialectic and as Gopal Guru states, a relationship of hierarchy in which impurity is stressed facilitates the internalizing of ritual pollution for these women.[34] This identity creation is further elucidated by Chakravarti through Meillasoux's understanding of purity as one which creates alienation that would superimpose the idea of impurity into the minds of the Dalits.[35] Through this created identity of "impure-untouchable Dalit women," their continuous victimization is justified. Adding to this is another layer of subjective identity bequeathed by the patriarchy that is intrinsic to this system.

---

30. Dean Spears, and Amit Thorat, "The Puzzle of Open Defecation in Rural India: Evidence from a Novel Measure of Caste Attitudes in a Nationally Representative Survey" *Economic Development and Cultural Change* 67, no. 4 (September 2015): 5.

31. A. M. Shah, "Purity, Impurity, Untouchability: Then and Now," *Sociological Bulletin* 56, no. 3 (September–December 2007), 356.

32. Chakravarti, *Gendering Caste*, 14.

33. Gnana, "Caste System, Dalitization and Its Implications in Contemporary India," 67.

34. Gopal Guru, *"Afterward" The Prisons We Broke* (Delhi: Orient BlackSwan, 2008), 64.

35. Chakravarti, *Gendering Caste*, 14.

The "Twice Inferiorized" Dalit Womanhood

Through the interplay of caste and gender stereotyping of patriarchy, another layer of low-grade identity is created for these women. There are differences among scholars on the type of patriarchy Dalit women are exposed to. Guru speaks of a "Dalit patriarchy" that delineates the caste group's patriarchal approach to women.[36] In this reflection, he completely detaches it from Brahminical patriarchy. However, Chakravarti looks at the patriarchy experienced by Dalit women as part of the Brahminical patriarchy but sees uniqueness due to their identity as Dalit.[37] Chakravarti's description seems more reasonable as even though these women are exposed to subjugations from their same caste men, these are rooted in the larger caste system itself. This clarifies that caste and patriarchy are knitted together. This is further affirmed by Sunaina Arya in her reflection on patriarchy as she suggests that caste acts as a "catalyst" in patriarchy that permeates all its layers.[38]

Morton Klass rightly proposes that caste and patriarchy are "created" for a function.[39] However, the function most likely is to generate identities of subjugation as "twice inferior" for Dalit women and "grand power" to the creators of caste. This is reinstated by Uthara Soman, as she explains that patriarchy restricts women's judgment, acts, and options, consequently normalizing their identity within the social structure while denying their independence and ability to protect themselves.[40] This is further explained by Anthony Giddens when he speaks of "patriarchal cultural institutions" as a group of institutions including religious that represent women in a patriarchal picture and this image influences "women's identities" and stipulates suitable values of her manners and acts.[41] Although millions of Dalit women in India have absorbed these identities prescribed by caste and patriarchy and strengthened by rituals, symbols, and practices, these layers of consciousness have also influenced India's religious demographics. This is evidenced in the preponderance of Dalits among converts from Hinduism to other religions such as Christianity, and among them women are the majority. These are women

---

36. Gopal Guru, "Dalit Women Talk Differently," *Economic and Political Weekly* 30, no. 41/42 (1995): 2549.

37. Chakravarti, *Gendering Caste,* 87–88.

38. Sunaina Arya, "Dalit or Brahmanical Patriarchy? Rethinking Indian Feminism." *A Global Journal on Social Exclusion* 1, no. 1 (February 2020): 223–224.

39. Morton Klass, *Caste—The Emergence of the South Asian Social System* (Philadelphia: Institute for the Research of Human Issues, 1980) 175–180.

40. Uthara Soman, "Patriarchy: Theoretical Postulates and Empirical Findings," *Sociological Bulletin* 58, no. 2 (May–August 2009), 262.

41. Anthony Giddens, *Sociology* (Cambridge: Polity Press, 2006), 473.

who through conversion sought to acquire a new identity that would provide safety from the constant abuses of caste and patriarchy bestowed upon them.

Dalit Women and Conversion to Christianity

The subhuman status ascribed to Dalit women in Indian society points to the fact that, when these women converted to Christianity en masse, the need for salvation was not limited to its eternal prospects. Although Gandhi called such conversions as unintelligible "conversions of convenience,"[42] these were women who sought an alternate identity in the church by stripping the heavy burdens laid by the interplay of caste and patriarchy. Scholars like Dumont and Moffat while asserting that caste creates hierarchical consciousness that is internalized also presents the caste system as a system of "consensual values."[43] However, such a generalization of consensual attitude is negated by these women who have strived to create a counter identity away from the one erected by the "upper caste." This is asserted by Fernandes as he clarifies that the Dalit mass movements to Christianity in nineteenth- and twentieth-century India were an attempt to escape the inferior identity and to achieve an equal identity.[44] In these conversions, they have endeavored to find a world that gives them identities of dignity, value, and equal power. In contrast to a superorganic view of culture, the identities created by the culture have impacted these countercultural movements in the churches of India.

Identity of Dalit Christian Women in the Church

As stated earlier, these conversions were accompanied by the hope for a new identity. However, these hopes were not fulfilled always. Lancy Lobo states that the Dalit converts in the church have four layers of discrimination: as a minority due to their religion, as Dalits in the church by caste-centric structures of some churches, as a Dalit in society by the caste system in the Indian culture, and from their caste by detachment through the change of faith.[45] Kshirsagar underscores this when he states that women who converted to Christianity were considered polluted and impure.[46] Two other layers of discrimination can be added to this

---

42. M. K. Gandhi, *Christian Missions: Their Place in India*, ed. Bharatan Kumarappa, (Ahmedabad: Navajivan Publishing House, 1941) 60.

43. Chakravarti, *Gendering Caste*, 6.

44. Fernandes, *The Emerging Dalit Identity*, 5.

45. Lancy Lobo, "Visions, Illusions and Dilemmas of Dalit Christians in India," in *Cultural Subordination and the Dalit Challenge*, ed. Simon R. Charsley and G. K. Karanth (New Delhi: Sage Publications, 2001), 246.

46. Kshirsagar, *Untouchability in India*, 50.

list: being a woman in the larger patriarchal Indian culture and being a woman in the patriarchal theology of most churches.

Ironically, by knocking at the doors of Indian churches the two levels of constructed discrimination they confronted and from which they tried to escape, augmented for most of these Dalit women. The additional discriminations that the churches are accountable for persuaded many of these women to associate themselves with dehumanizing identities within the church based on gender and caste.

"Impure Untouchable" Dalit Christian Womanhood

Caste creation has always been an ongoing process in the history of India.[47] This is analogous to what is happening within numerous Indian churches. The caste system has clothed itself with different features while maintaining its fundamental essence in these churches. Prakash Louis rightly posits that the caste system and its ideologies have permeated the walls of Indian churches.[48] Tanika Sarkar confirms this by stating that in becoming Christians, many Dalit women accumulate newer demeaning identities to the already existing belittling cultural identities.[49] This is confirmed by Louis who states that the identity of impurity and untouchability seeped into churches and was reinforced by practices (i.e., in many churches in South India Dalits are seated at the side or the back and could take communion only after the "high caste" Christians).[50] Buhler agrees with Louis as he elucidates that partaking in church activities is a chief feature that confirmed caste discrimination in Indian churches when Dalits are given less prominent roles in many of these churches.[51] He goes on to say that these identities are reinforced in practices such as denied access to services, not allowing them inside "high caste" member's houses, 'high caste' members covering their mouths while speaking to them, not allowing inter-caste marriages, and so forth.[52] Dejectedly, these discriminations aid in reinforcing an identity of "impure untouchable" womanhood for these women. Ajay Sekher agrees as he postulates "while the caste

---

47. Karve, *Hindu Society: An Interpretation*, 58.

48. Prakash Louis, "Dalit Christians: Betrayed by State and Church," *Economic and Political Weekly* 42, no. 16 (April 2007), 1411.

49. Tanika Sarkar, "Missionaries, Converts and the State in Colonial India," *Studies in History* 18, no. 1 (February 2002), 123.

50. Louis, "Dalit Christians," 1411.

51. Buhler, *The Laws of Manu*, 10.

52. Buhler, *The Laws of Manu*, 10.

conscious Christians thus stitched and re-stitched their touchable identity, the outcasts, the untouchables were pushed to the periphery for a subhuman marginal existence."[53] Many Indian churches reinforce these subjugating identities on Dalit women, from which they sought refuge in these churches in the first place. In addition to these, the interaction of caste and patriarchy also percolated into these churches.

"Twice Inferior" Dalit Christian Womanhood

As discussed, while being Dalit ascribed an inferior identity to these women in many Indian churches, the patriarchal nature of Indian culture added another layer of discrimination. This is underlined through various symbols. One powerful illustration is the usage of gendered language within many Indian churches which is normalized and uncritically absorbed by many churches. This according to Rosemary Reuther, eventually removes the lived experiences of women from culture, making man's voice and experiences more powerful.[54] On the significance of language, Edward Sapir postulates that "it is quite an illusion to imagine that one adjusts to reality essentially without the use of language. . . . The fact of the matter is that the 'real world' is to a large extent unconsciously built up on the language habits of the group."[55] According to Sapir, the usage of vocabulary reflects the thought behind the word.[56] Reuther and Saphir assert the fact that the usage of gender-exclusive language could reinforce the subhuman identity that the patriarchal Indian culture has superimposed on Dalit women. Paradoxically, the movement to Christianity for liberation adds another layer of subjugating consciousness to many Dalit women through gendered practices and language. However, this discrimination bleeds into another level of constructed identity which is specific to the theologizing of certain churches.

"Thrice Inferior" Dalit Christian Womanhood

Many Christian denominations generate a patriarchal theology based on selected biblical texts. The order of creation, the usage of the word "helper," the use of man's rib in the creation narrative, and several texts from the Pauline writings

---

53. Ajay Sekher, "Older than the Church: Christianity and Caste in The God of Small Things," *Economic and Political Weekly* 38, no. 33 (August 2003), 3447.

54. Rosemary Radford Ruether, "Feminist Interpretation: A Method of Correlation," in *Feminist Interpretation of the Bible*, ed. Letty M. Russell (Philadelphia: Westminster Press, 1985): 113, 117.

55. Edward Sapir, "The Status of Linguistics as a Science," *Language* 5 (1929): 209.

56. Richard H. Robbins, *Cultural Anthropology* (California: Wadsworth, Cengage Learning: 2013), 135.

are interpreted as proof of the patriarchy of the churches.[57] Parallel to Hinduism's selective usage of specific texts to imply an inferior identity to women, a subordinate view of women is superimposed by many churches through their theological interpretation of Scripture. This attaches yet another identity of inferiority to these women.

This not only superimposes a subhuman identity but this patriarchal theologizing of the church creates a dilemma in the minds of women, even though there are biblical texts that assert an equal image for all human beings. This is parallel to the dilemma of Hindu women as Christina Manohar postulates, when in some Hindu scriptures women are referred to as goddesses and in other texts they are portrayed as lesser human beings, consequently creating a "contradictory consciousness" in these women.[58] The churches' interpretations of many texts which are not originally intended to be patriarchal, create such an incongruous consciousness in Dalit Christian women that Dalit Christian womanhood is given a third demeaning identity through these uncritical patriarchal hermeneutics.

After the bold step of embracing Christianity, the generational experiences of contradictions, and disappointments that these women experience in these Indian churches that reinforce the man-made substandard identities is beyond the expressiveness of any given language. Yet, we see many examples of moving forward when many Dalit Christian women challenge such identities ascribed to them. A relevant question here would be: What is the church's role in their struggle to retrieve dignity and justice as human beings?

The Dalit Woman in the Body of Christ

The church, as one body of Christ, must identify with these women's struggles. New Testament scholar Craig Keener, while speaking on the New Testament perspective on women, affirms how these writers were beyond their cultures and poses a question for the church to ponder on how they would write for today.[59] This requires an "interpretative drift" as explained by Luhrmann that changes the beliefs of those churches that dehumanize women.[60] One can see this in the story of the Syro-Phoenician woman, a story of a woman challenging

---

57. Frank B. Holbrook, "Symposium on the Role of Women in the Church." Research presented at the General Council of Seventh-Day Adventists, Plainfield, New Jersey (1984) 2, 17.

58. Christina Manohar, "Introduction," in *Women's Issues and Reflections*, ed. Christina Manohar (New Delhi: ISPCL, 2012) 6.

59. Craig S. Keener, "The Role of Women in the New Testament," in *Women's Issues and Reflections*, ed. Christina Manohar (New Delhi: ISPCL, 2012), 53.

60. Robbins, *Cultural Anthropology*, 150.

patriarchal power, according to Aruna Gnanadason.[61] She can be perceived as a representative of Dalit women in India who become followers of Christ. In her conversation, she challenges both the patriarchy and her "outsider" status as impure and thus goes beyond the assigned identity. Jesus's response though initially appears hierarchical, provides her with the chance to express her perception of the identity the culture has assigned to her. This unquestionably was a calculated effort from Jesus so that she could voice her identity and that Jesus could consequently affirm her real identity in Him.

This calls for such an effort from the church to provoke the consciences of those Dalit women who have absorbed the culturally and theologically superimposed identities and affirm the image of God in them. The church must stand with many of these women who challenge the existing symbols that enforce subhuman identity on them. The church of India requires leaders like Martin Luther King Jr to fight against its version of diabolic dehumanizing.

Conclusion

The caste system in India was created to assign a hierarchy of subjectivity and power. For Dalit women, it constructs identities of impurity and inferiority and enforces these on them through different symbols in the larger context and within many churches. Therefore, this chapter calls for deeper research of these interactions in the context of specific cultures within the subcontinent. Dalit women's brave step of embracing Christianity to escape the identities prescribed by the caste system was welcomed by a deeper subjugation by many churches in India. Within the walls of these churches, they still struggle to shed these identities. Before a countercultural movement causes millions of these members to leave the Indian church, it is in the hands of the churches to cleanse themselves of these demonic categories and identify themselves with these women who reflect the face of world Christianity today.

---

61. Aruna Gnanadason, "Jesus and the Asian Woman: A Post-colonial Look at the Syro-Phoenician Woman/Canaanite Woman from an Indian Perspective," *Studies in World Christianity* 7 (2001): 163–164.

CHAPTER THIRTEEN

Multidimensional Poverty, Constitutional Responses, and Holistic Mission in India

Allan Varghese Meloottu and John Amalraj Karunakaran

Introduction

TRADITIONALLY, POVERTY HAS been understood as the lack of money. However, it is much more broadly experienced with multiple simultaneous disadvantages, leading to the situation of lack of money. Therefore, according to the Human Development Index (introduced by the United Nations in 1990), the phrase "multidimensional poverty" is now aptly used to capture a comprehensive picture of poverty, considering systemic factors such as class, caste, and rural divisions (to name the few) that contribute to the persistence of a poverty cycle that manifests in three dimensions: health, education, and standard of living.[1] According to the recent Multidimensional Poverty Index, "16.4 percent of the population in India (228,907 thousand people in 2020) is multidimensionally poor while an additional 18.7 percent is classified as vulnerable to multidimensional poverty (260,941 thousand people in 2020)."[2]

India has seen a long history of poverty alleviation plans by government and economic policy makers. Simultaneously, Indian Christians have also been playing their part in engaging in holistic mission to alleviate poverty. However, the consistent prevalence of poverty presents a missional challenge for the Indian church within the context of governmental, non-governmental organizations, and corporate sector interventions. Therefore, in this chapter, we provide a brief historical analysis of Indian governmental poverty alleviation plans (pre-independence and contemporary) as we highlight various historical holistic missiological responses and conclude by providing few suggestions for

---

1. According to the Multidimensional Poverty Index, these three dimensions are further delineated for the purpose of measuring poverty: accessibility to nutrition and child mortality rate (health); years of schooling and school attendance rate (education); and access to cooking fuel, sanitation, drinking water, electricity, housing and assets (standard of living). Multidimensional Poverty Index 2022, "India" *UNDP*. Accessed October 2, 2023, https://hdr.undp.org/sites/default/files/Country-Profiles/MPI/IND.pdf

2. Multidimensional Poverty Index 2022, "India," 2.

Indian Christians to work alongside with the governmental plans in poverty reduction efforts. First, we begin with a brief clarification on what we mean by "multidimensional poverty" and "holistic mission."

Defining Multidimensional Poverty and Holistic Mission

Although there is a consensus among scholars that poverty should not be narrowly defined as only relating to material poverty, there has not been uniformity in how to define poverty. Christian development theologian Bryant Myers defines poverty as relationships that breakdown, isolate, abandon, and devalue the personhood.[3] In *Walking with the Poor*, Myers proposes the relational definition of poverty while engaging with various other development studies scholars.[4] Unlike non-Christian development scholars, Myers emphasizes the spiritual dimension of poverty and refers to it as stemming from humanity's relational breakdown, with God and other people. At the same time, Myers acknowledges that the diverse scholarly engagements in the field demonstrate various angles of poverty that touch the multifaceted nature of human life. Consequently, any poverty alleviation intervention should require a holistic approach.

Although Myers's emphasis on the spiritual facet is often ignored by other non-Christians in developmental studies, Amartya Sen's theory of "development as freedom" set the development conversation in a multi-dimensional direction specifically shifting it away from quantitative to qualitative economic measures.[5] More importantly, Sen stated that poverty should be understood as a result of deprivation of human freedom. Consequently, recent scholarship has taken the cue and focused more on development issues holistically relating to human well-being and flourishing which are aligned with biblical images. Sen's unapologetic focus on ethical values and human capabilities paved the way not only for governments and international development agencies but also for Christian development organizations and missions to focus on holistic human development as a response to multidimensional poverty.

From a Christian perspective, it also brought forth the pathways to imagining freedom in mission work. Proclaiming freedom as part of the development

---

3. Bryant L. Myers, *Walking with the Poor: Principles and Practices of Transformational Development*, rev. ed. (Maryknoll, NY: Orbis, 2011), 75.

4. Notably, Myers engages with Robert Chambers, who describes poverty as entanglement; John Friedmann, who proposes poverty as a lack of access to social power; Isaac Prilletensky's understanding that poverty is due to diminished personal and relational well-being; Jayakumar Christian, who sees poverty as a disempowering system that results in an individual's marred identity that internalizes the impact of poverty; and Ravi Jayakaran, who notes poverty as the lack of freedom to grow physically, mentally, socially, and spiritually.

5. Amartya Sen, *Development as Freedom*, (New York: Anchor, 2000), 3–11.

work is the mission of God as it challenges that which is seen as not affirming and denying life in all its fullness.[6] In other words, the mission of God, as Esther Mombo describes, is "life in abundance, and in cases where life is threatened in all its totality, the affirmation of life is one of the goals of mission".[7]

In Indian context of multidimensional poverty, Christianity attempts to embody a theology of holism affirming and communicating the "transformative power of the gospel over every aspect of life."[8] Although the practice of such a holistic and integral gospel appears differently from one local congregation to another, there is a general consensus across denominational boundaries to maintain their missiological outlook in terms of holistic mission (evangelism and social action combined).[9] Furthermore, in doing so Christians challenge the inequalities, exploitation, and power structures that bind people in poverty and deprivation.

Pre-independence Christian Mission responses to Multidimensional Poverty
Pandita Ramabai and Bishop Azariah

Even a casual reading of the Indian church and mission history will illustrate that holistic mission was a key characteristic in Indian Christianity before and after independence. Among other issues, poverty was at the heart of any mission work that Western missionaries and Indian Christians could not ignore. Long before the debates on the holistic nature of mission dominated Western evangelical circles, missionaries who came to India initiated projects and founded educational and medical institutions in an attempt to tackle poverty. Furthermore, it was the Indian Christians who served in these institutions while a few also ventured on to found new initiatives. Pandita Ramabai's mission in Pune and Bishop Azariah's mission in Dornakal were two such initiatives that stands out from among the pioneering efforts of Indian mission leaders in the early twentieth century.

---

6. Esther Mombo, "From Fourfold Mission to Holistic Mission: Toward Edinburgh 2010," in *Holistic Mission: God's Plan for God's People*, ed. Brian E. Woolnough and Wonsuk Ma (Eugene, OR: Wipf & Stock, 2010), 40, 43.

7. Mombo, "From Fourfold Mission to Holistic Mission," 43.

8. Aminta Arrington, "American Evangelicalism, Social Action, and Christianity in India," in *Christianity in India: Conversion, Community Development, and Religious Freedom*, ed. Rebecca Shah and Joel A. Carpenter (Minneapolis: Fortress Press, 2018) 119.

9. Jayakumar Christian provides an apt discussion on how various denominational models differ in their approach towards their work of poverty alleviation. For details, see, Jayakumar Christian, *God of the Empty-handed: Poverty, Power and the Kingdom of God* (Monrovia, CA: MARC, 1999), 92–111.

Pandita Ramabai had a remarkable spiritual journey from her traditional Hindu faith to being a follower of Christ. She was a well-known social reformer advocating for Indian women,[10] especially during the great Indian famine of the late nineteenth and early twentieth century, and addressing issues of poverty. Ramabai, using her personal charisma and network of supporters developed during her international travels, mobilized financial resources to respond to domestic crises.[11] However, Ramabai's holistic mission had vehement opposition from the Hindu social reformers who accused her of wrong motives in her personal conversion as well as proselytization of the widows and orphans who lived in the shelter homes she founded.[12] In 1889, Ramabai first founded a destitute home for high caste widows called *Sharda Sadan* (home of learning) in Mumbai and then later shifted to Pune as she faced opposition from Hindu nationalists who objected to the women in her home becoming followers of Christ.[13] She eventually moved away from the city of Pune to Kedagaon, and in 1890 established *Mukti Mission* (liberty), a community on a hundred acres of land to shelter widows and orphans.[14] Her work included vocational training, nursing, tailoring, embroidery, weaving of cloth and carpets, operating a printing press, gardening, dairy farming, agriculture, and so forth, involving all the residents creating a community transformed holistically to serve others around them.

While Ramabai was impacting vulnerable communities in West India, Bishop Azariah played a pivotal role in the South. Azariah, was born into a family where his father was a first-generation Christian from a Hindu background (who also became a village pastor).[15] Serving as the traveling secretary for the Young Men's Christian Association (YMCA), Azariah used his leadership platform to

---

10. Robert Eric Frykenberg, "Pandita Ramabai Saraswati: A Biographical Introduction," in *Pandita Ramabai's America—Conditions of Life in the United States*, trans. Kshitija Gomes, trans. ed. Philip C. Engblom (Grand Rapids, MI: Eerdmans, 2003), 8.

11. Heather D. Curtis, *Holy Humanitarians: American Evangelicals and Global Aid* (Cambridge, MA: Harvard University Press, 2018), 163–170.

12. Meera Kosambi, "Women, Emancipation and Equality: Pandita Ramabai's Contribution to Women's Cause." *Economic and Political Weekly* 23, no. 44 (1988): 41–42.

13. Meera Kosambi, *Pandita Ramabai Through Her Own Words—Selected Works* (New Delhi: Oxford University Press, 2000), 4–8.

14. Meera Kosambi, "Women, Emancipation and Equality," 38–49.

15. A. R. Chelliah, *Bishop Vedanayagam Samuel Azariah—A Life in Indigenization* (Delhi: ISPCK, 2016), 2.

build networks across India and other countries.[16] His exposure to the worldwide mission movement inspired him to give leadership to the founding of two missionary sending societies—Indian Missionary Society (1903) and National Missionary Society (1905).[17] However, it was only when he answered the call to serve cross culturally in Dornakal, a remote village (in Andhra Pradesh) that Azariah's vision of holistic mission came to the fore.[18] The people were social outcastes, illiterate, and living in economic poverty. Azariah and his wife along with their children lived among them.[19]

His incarnational living extended from encouraging his congregation to be indigenous in worship, using culturally relevant songs, music, and symbols,[20] to empowering village development, lay involvement in caring for the poor, establishing literacy programs, and schools for the children.[21] Although Azariah's mission work received backlashes, especially from prominent figures like Gandhi who accused him of possible inducement of economic development for the mass movements,[22] Azariah's focus was on embodying the holistic nature of the gospel to the poor. Furthermore, Azariah's understanding of poverty among the vulnerable resulted in a focus on value-based education to stimulate their sense of individuality, leading them to regain their dignity to actualize spiritual and economic progress.[23] Azariah's holistic mission resulted in one of the major mass movements among the lower castes in Dornakal and surrounding regions.[24]

---

16. S. Sam Victor, "Azariah, Vedanayagam Samuel" in *A Dictionary of Asian Christianity*, ed. Scott Sunquist, John Hiang Chea Chew, and David Chusing Wu (Grand Rapids, MI: Eerdmans, 2001), 49.

17. Carol Graham, "The Legacy of V S Azariah" *International Bulletin of Missionary Research* 9 no. 1 (1985): 16–19.

18. Chelliah, *Bishop Vedanayagam Samuel Azariah*, 7–8. Azariah belonged to the Anglican church and was ordained into priesthood and later consecrated as the Bishop of Dornakal Diocese.

19. Graham, "The Legacy of V S Azariah," 17.

20. Chelliah, *Bishop Vedanayagam Samuel Azariah*, 61.

21. Samuel Jayakumar, "The Work of God as Holistic Mission: An Asian Perspective" in Woolnough and Ma, *Holistic Mission*, 90–93.

22. Lalsangkima Pachuau, "A Clash of 'Mass Movements'? Christian Missions and the Gandhian Nationalist Movement in India," *Transformation* 31, no. 3 (2014): 166–167.

23. Jayakumar, "The Work of God as Holistic Mission," 93.

24. Graham, "The Legacy of V S Azariah," 17.

Leading into the postindependence era, the works of Ramabai and Azariah provided a foundational purview for the Indian church and mission as Western missionary involvement was drastically reduced amid the changing political scenario. Even before the Western evangelical landscape embraced holistic and integral mission at the Lausanne consultation of 1974 to reconcile and integrate evangelism and social concern,[25] Indian evangelicals were active in such endeavors as ground realities compelled them to respond holistically.

One of the main issues that churches, mission organizations, and Christian development organizations in India are grappling with concerns how to work alongside the government on poverty alleviation rather than being a competitor. Before considering how the churches may collaborate with the government, it is essential to examine, briefly, the constitutional policies that paved way for the contemporary state of India's poverty alleviation approach. Hence, we turn our attention to the postindependence era of Indian poverty alleviation plans while we briefly note how Indian Christians engaged in some historical points.

Postindependence Indian Poverty-Alleviation Plans (1940s–2020)

From Top-down Governmental Intervention to Decentralized Grassroots Approach

The Indian poverty-alleviation journey has been a slow progression in the last seventy years as the nation has been through various government transitions and policymaking.

1947–1950
Establishing Political & Economic Structures toward Poverty Alleviation

When the architects of an independent India set to lay out a plan for the nation, the plight of the poor and the marginalized low caste people was in the cards. At one of the early Constituent Assembly debates, Jawaharlal Nehru emphasized the constitution's role in poverty alleviation. He said, "The first task of this Assembly is to free India through a new constitution, to feed the starving people, and to clothe the naked masses, and to give every Indian the fullest opportunity to

---

25. Timothy C. Tennent, *Invitation to World Missions: A Trinitarian Missiology for the Twenty-First Century* (Grand Rapids, MI: Kregel, 2010), 388–393.

develop himself according to his capacity."[26] The constitution became modern India's foundation to safeguard the liberty and equality of all Indians within its motto "to be a sovereign, socialist, secure and democratic republic" (Preamble to the Constitution of India).

Subsequently, with the insertion of the Directive Principle of State Policy in the Indian Constitution (Article 36-51), the lawmakers aimed to provide the constitutional principles that would direct the government to make socioeconomic and political policies and programs to promote economic growth and alleviate poverty. These constitutional directives became foundational toward "state planning, welfarism and mass democracy."[27]Additionally, following the drafting of the constitution, through the Constitution Order 1950, the term "scheduled castes" (initially proposed in 1935 by the British)[28] was also incorporated into the constitution (listing 821 groups as scheduled castes) for the "purposes of targeting in development programs, compensatory policies to amend for prior discrimination, and policies to prevent violence against untouchables."[29]

Along with these constitutional directives, the Planning Commission was also established in 1950 as a government agency to provide directions to the government of India in the form of five-year plans to oversee the country's economic and social development. Therefore, the first two Five Year Plans (1951–1956 and 1956–1961) provided an assessment and recommendations on the "programmes of Development," in anticipation of creating economic growth. The first plan's developmental drive was based on the notion of understanding development structurally with the wider objectives such as full employment and the removal of economic inequalities along with legislation for abolition of the traditional Zamindar system that controlled the agricultural sector and was a root cause of the poverty among India's weaker sections. It hoped to spur economic growth that would foster poverty alleviation efforts. The second five-year

---

26. Quoted in Stuart Corbridge, Glyn Williams, Manoj Srivastava, René Véron. *Seeing the State: Governance and Governmentality in India* (Cambridge: Cambridge University Press, 2005), 54.

27. Nandini Gooptu, "The Construction of Poverty and the Poor in Colonial and Post-Colonial India: An Overview," in *Persistence of Poverty in India*, ed. Nandini Gooptu and Jonathan Parry (London: Routledge, 2017), 48.

28. In 1935 "the British listed the lowest-ranking Hindu castes in a Schedule appended to the Government of India Acts for purposes of statutory safeguards and other benefits." (Lelah Dushkin, "Scheduled Caste Policy in India: History, Problems, Prospects," *Asian Survey* 7, no. 9 [1967]: 630).

29. Maitreyi Bordia Das and Soumya Kapoor Mehta, *Poverty and Social Exclusion in India: Overview* (World Bank, Washington, DC, 2012), 1. https://openknowledge.worldbank.org/handle/10986/26337

plan continued along with the agenda of economic growth as development in rural India; however, the focus began to move toward industrializing agricultural sectors.[30] Subsequent five-year plans held on to the industrialization principle in generating economic capital. In doing so, the Commission and the government believed the assumption that such "economic growth would automatically foster poverty alleviation efforts."[31]

Along the same time, a significant move toward poverty alleviation was made (July 1962) when a working group of economists set up by the Planning Commission advocated for a standard determining the national poverty line. The group "advocated a national minimum expenditure for every household of five persons (or four adult consumption units) at Rs 100 [approximately USD 1.25] per month or Rs 20 [approximately USD 0.25] per capita per month in terms of 1960–61 prices so as to provide a minimum nutritional diet in terms of calorie intake as well as to allow for a modest expenditure on items other than food."[32] Hence, Rs 20 [approximately USD 0.25] per person became the norm for the Indian Poverty line, meaning, "individuals falling below this line were said to be 'poor,' or suffering from 'absolute poverty'."[33]

1960s
Agricultural Production, Green Revolution, and Poverty Alleviation

In the early 1960s, as well as establishing the poverty line, attention was also given to the production of food as part of economic growth and poverty alleviation plans. The government launched programs such as the Intensive Agricultural

---

30. For an analysis of agricultural growth and industrialization, see C. Rangarajan, "Agricultural Growth and Industrial Performance in India," (1982) accessed on September 15, 2023, https://ageconsearch.umn.edu/record/42186/?ln=en

31. Caroline Bertram, "Counting the Poor in India: A Conceptual Analysis of Theory and Praxis of the Government Approach," *South Asia Chronicle* 2 (2012), 166.

32. EPW Research Foundation, "Special Statistics-2: Poverty Levels in India: Norms, Estimates and Trends." *Economic and Political Weekly* 28, no. 34 (1993): 1748.

33. Corbridge et al., *Seeing the State*, 63. Determining the poverty line based on sufficient income necessary to meet basic calory levels became a standard methodology until the 1990s. Various study groups since the 1990s—Lakdawala Expert Group (1993), the Tendular Expert Group (2009) and the Rangajan Committee (2014), have proposed to reform the basis of the poverty line (Seema Gaur and N. Srinivasa Rao, "Poverty Measurement in India: A Status Update," Ministry of Rural Development [Working Paper], 2020, 6).

District Programme (IADP) and Intensive Agricultural Areas Programme (IAAP) to improve agricultural production (in line with their objective to increase industrialization). The IADP was undertaken as a pilot project in corporation with the Ford Foundation.[34]

However, food production was strained, and a national food shortage was also exacerbated due to the Bihar drought and famine in 1966/67. On January 23, 1966, the popular Indian newspaper *Hindu* published an alarming article stating, "Thirty million people in India are facing 'dire distress' at present in getting food. This estimate has been made by the Union Food Ministry on the basis of information received from different states."

Following the Bihar famine in 1966/67, Prime Minister Indira Gandhi opted for the slogan *Garibi Hatao* ("down with poverty") for her political campaign in the 1970s attempting to revamp India into the path of Nehruvian development. *Garibi Hatao* became an important component in the fourth (1966–1974) and fifth five-year plans (1974–1979). During this period, one of the significant steps in using agricultural production as a poverty alleviation plan was adopting the High Yielding Varieties Programme (HYVP). As Dayabati Roy notes, the high yield varieties program, "known as Green Revolution Technology (GRT), had actually been the most trumpeted state programme of the central government, and has still been continuing in most parts of the country as an exclusive mode of cultivation."[35] However, the total eradication of poverty, as Indira Gandhi envisioned, was a distant dream.

During the 1960s, Christians also went to work in pursuit of alleviating poverty, especially in the context of the Bihar famine. The Evangelical Fellowship of India, an alliance of evangelical churches and organizations responded by forming a committee on emergency relief in 1967.[36] This committee evolved into a department and later an independent identity known as Evangelical Fellowship of India Commission on Relief (EFICOR), emerging as the leading Christian relief and development agency. One of the features of EFICOR was not just to be a channel for humanitarian aid but also a partner on the ground enabling

---

34. The Ford Foundation representative team arrived in January1959 and "completed what came to be known as the 'food crisis report' by mid-April. Their recommendation . . . generated the Intensive Agricultural Development Program" (Carl C. Malone and Sherman E. Johnson, "The Intensive Agricultural Development Program in India." *Agricultural Economics Research* 23, no. 2 [1971], 25).

35. Dayabati Roy, *Employment, Poverty and Rights in India* (London: Routledge, Taylor and Francis Group, 2018), 24.

36. Evangelical Fellowship of India Commission on Relief, *Parivarthan, The First Forty Years of EFICOR* (New Delhi: Mountain Peak), 2007, 6.

church planting missions to be more holistic.[37] EFICOR's various programs were not only to provide relief and development, but also to train missionaries, new believers, community leaders and government officials with a holistic model of development providing the theological framework.[38] Furthermore, EFICOR also empowers ground-level workers to be autonomous in planning and implementing projects. Such mobilization to address multidimensional poverty in community development brought credibility to EFICOR with the government.

During the 1970s, as volunteer mission societies became the flag bearers of evangelicals involved in mission, we also had several Christians from South India obeying God's call to go to North India independent of existing ecclesiastical and mission structures and pioneering new church planting ministry along with holistic mission. In 1972, Augustine Jebakumar from Tamil Nadu responded to such a divine call to go to Bihar in North India which was known as the graveyard of missionaries.[39] In spite of severe resistance to gospel preaching, the extreme poverty contributing to cerebral malaria and other infectious diseases led Jebakumar to establish Gospel Echoing Missionary Society (GEMS).[40] At first, Jebakumar and his wife were burdened to open an orphanage but were reluctant as they felt it may shift their focus away from preaching the gospel until a well-wisher volunteered to assist financially.[41] Coming from a Pentecostal background, Jebakumar's goals were to preach the gospel, evangelize, and plant churches. However, the social need prompted them to expand their approach to incorporate educational, medical, and humanitarian assistance—even rescuing children from bonded labor and starting a polio rehabilitation home for children. Jebakumar's and GEMS's understanding of poverty in a multidimensional perspective resulted in a holistic mission. They integrated evangelism and social engagement together in their organization by creating two categories of staffing—missionaries who focused on evangelism and tentmakers who served as teachers and administrators.

In 1960s and '70s, when India as a nation, under the banner *Garibi Hatao* was engaged in various efforts to lift herself from poverty, the works of EFICOR and GEMS stand as testaments of Christian efforts to alleviate poverty.

---

37. Evangelical Fellowship of India Commission on Relief, *Parivarthan*, 7.

38. Evangelical Fellowship of India Commission on Relief, *Parivarthan*, 24.

39. Augustine D. Jebakumar, *No One Else*, Rev. 2nd ed. (Chennai: Gospel Echoing Missionary Society, 2017), 42–43.

40. Gospel Echoing Missionary Society, "About Us," accessed on March 30, 2020. https://www.gemsbihar.org.

41. Jebakumar, *No One Else*, 127–129.

1980s
Establishing the Other Backward Classes (OBCs) and Decentralization Toward Poverty Alleviation

The post–Indira Gandhi governments continued to heed the suggestions of the Planning Commission, initiating a top-down approach toward economic growth and poverty alleviation. In the sixth five-year plan period (1980–1985), more anti-poverty programs were approved for "wage employment, self-employment and nutritional support."[42] At the same time, another vital step toward poverty alleviation was made in the form of identifying the other backward classes (OBC) to extend the reservation quotas which were allocated to only those belonging to the scheduled castes (SC) and scheduled tribes (ST).[43] The Mandal Commission under the chairmanship of B. P. Mandal produced its report in 1980 recommending 27 percent reservation for the OBC,[44] as the Supreme Court had limited the total quantum of reservation to 50 percent.[45]

During the 1980s, the seventh planning commission (1985–1990) proposed greater decentralization following their assessment of the Integrated Rural Development Programme (IRDP). In doing so, the Commission recognized the lack of effectiveness of the central government, an "outsider," in implementing the programs on the ground and deemed the IRDP a failure.[46] As a response, the government proposed to decentralize poverty alleviation plans from the central government to the grassroots level. It became the village body's responsibility to identify the programme beneficiaries. Subsequently, the Jawahar Rozgar Yojana (JRY) was formed in 1989 as a merger of the National Rural Employment Programme (NREP) and Rural Landless Employment Guarantee Programme

---

42. Anjini Kochar, "The Effectiveness of India's Anti-Poverty Programmes." *Journal of Development Studies* 44, no. 9 (2008), 1291.

43. Reservation quota is an affirmative action policy for socioeconomically marginalized people to help in their proportional representation in educational opportunities and government jobs. The quota system in India traces its history to the Hunter Commission of British India in 1882. The Indian constitution provided reservation quotas based on caste and tribal identities that included seats in the parliament and state legislatures limited to the first ten years but subsequently extended by the parliament up to the year 2060.

44. The Mandal Commission concluded that the "population of OBCs which includes both Hindus and non-Hindus is around 52 percent of the total population." A. Ramaiah, "Identifying Other Backward Classes," *Economic and Political Weekly* 27, no. 23 (1992): 1204.

45. Due to political dynamics and a change in the government, the Mandal Commission recommendations were shelved until 1989, but in 1990, Prime Minister V. P. Singh implemented them.

46. Kochar, "The Effectiveness of India's Anti-Poverty Programmes," 1292.

(RLEGP).[47] "The JRY aims to alleviate poverty through creating supplementary employment opportunities for the rural poor during agricultural slack periods" by entrusting 80 percent of the central government-sponsored funds to local government bodies such as "the District Rural Development Agency (DRDA) and/or the Zilla (District) Parishad at the district level, and the gram (village) panchayat at the village level."[48] Such decentralization was further strengthened by the 73rd Constitutional Amendment in 1993, which provided constitutional authority for the Gram Panchayats to be self-governing bodies.[49] Through this decentralization process, there was further emphasis on helping people from the schedule caste and schedule tribes to receive the benefits of the government poverty alleviation programs.

1990s
The Era of Liberalization, Privatization, and Globalization (LPG)

During the 1990s, the government of India implemented vital economic reforms that brought globalization to the shores of India. The then finance minister Manmohan Singh's proposal toward liberalization, privatization, and globalization (LPG) was a pivotal move that Jairam Ramesh called "the day that changed India forever."[50] Although Singh's concern was to lift India from financial turmoil, he was also seriously considering the economic upliftment of the poor in the nation. As Singh envisioned, "globalization creates opportunities . . . freer trade, if it is genuinely free, and India's labor-intensive products can find markets abroad that will help to get new jobs in our country. That will help to relieve poverty."[51]

---

47. The RLEGP initiative was during the prime ministership of Rajiv Gandhi.

48. Raghav Gaiha, P. D. Kaushik, and Vani Kulkarni. "Jawahar Rozgar Yojana, Panchayats, and the Rural Poor in India," *Asian Survey* 38, no. 10 (1998): 928, 929.

49. The Jawahar Rozgar Yojana (JRY) was further redesigned into the Sampoorna Grameen Rozgar Yojana (SGRY) in 2001. The SGRY also consolidated all the government's employment programs. As Kochar notes, "SGRY guidelines . . . state that all work relating to the co-ordination, review, supervision and monitoring of the programme at the village level is the responsibility of the Village Panchayat" (Kochar, "The Effectiveness of India's Anti-Poverty Programmes," 1291).

50. Jairam Ramesh, "Twenty-five years ago this day," *The Hindu* (2016), accessed January 25, 2023, https://www.thehindu.com/opinion/lead/Twenty-five-years-ago-this-day/article14504910.ece

51. Manmohan Singh made this statement in an interview conducted by PBS in 2001. For the full transcript of the interview, see https://www.pbs.org/wgbh/commandingheights/shared/minitext/int_manmohansingh.html#5

Consequently, India's service sector, which covers a wide variety of businesses from hotels and restaurants to real estate and IT companies, reshaped the role of Indian cities in its development as it integrated globalization. Collaterally, such a global urban space has accelerated the pace of rural-urban migration[52] of the poor with the hope of an upward economic movement.[52] As globalization in India struggles to provide a substantial change in the Indian agriculture sector, which is predominantly centered in rural India, the poor embark on migration with the hopes of finding jobs. Furthermore, frequent droughts, ineffective rural agriculture economic policies, lack of modern technology, and the like, have resulted in farmer's woes and suicides driving the rural to urban migration. Fast tracking to the contemporary migration trends, the recent economic growth since 1990s has shown significant movement of people specially from underdeveloped regions to developing metropolises like Mumbai, Delhi, Chennai, and other urban centers. The number of migrants by place of last residence in India was 453.6 million in 2011 with a decadal growth rate of 44 percent.[53] The census report further states that among these migrants nearly 70 percent are women.

At the same time, in the urban spaces, as Sanjay Ruparelia writes, "The desires, habits and patterns of consumption of the country's urban middle classes, increasingly under the 'moral political sway of the corporate capitalist class,' spurred the drive to build 'entrepreneurial cities' as zones of technological innovation, commerce and finance, and modernist residential enclaves."[54] Such "zones" indeed helped revive the Indian economy. However, for the poor, due to the lack of education and skill set to compete within the globalized service sector, most of them ended up finding jobs in the manufacturing sector (such as brick making and textiles). Subsequently, the low-income jobs combined with high city costs prompted the poor to find refuge in slums. Hence, the relationship between poverty and rural-urban migration remains complex without any hope for the poor to break away from the vicious cycle of poverty.

---

52. According to the Economic Survey (2017) conducted by the government of India, "an average of 5–6 million Indians migrated annually between 2001 and 2011, leading to an inter-state migrant population of 'about 60 million and an inter-district migrant population 'as high as 80 million" (quoted in Irudaya S. Rajan and R. B. Bhagat, "Internal Migration in India: Integrating Migration with Development and Urbanization Policies," *KNOMAD Policy Brief* 12 (2021), accessed on January 20, 2023, https://www.knomad.org/publication/internal-migration-india-integrating-migration-development-and-urbanization-policies).

53. Samrath Bansal, "45.36 Crore Indians are Internal Migrants" *The Hindu*, (blog) December 3, 2016, https://www.thehindu.com/data/45.36-crore-Indians-are-internal-migrants/article16748716.ece.

54. Sanjay Ruparelia, "India's New Rights Agenda: Genesis, Promises, Risks," *Pacific Affairs* 86, no. 3 (2013): 578.

Such is the context of urban poverty in which the urban churches engage. For example, in the last fifteen years, the capital city of Aizawl began to see a change as migrants from different parts of India arrived. Initially there was a lot of resistance and cultural conflicts but soon, the Mizoram Presbyterian Church recognized the realities and found opportunities to serve the migrated manual laborers from the Hindi speaking states of India in practical ways. In response, many of the migrants have chosen to worship Jesus in their own mother tongue and follow Him.

2000s
Era of 'New Rights Agenda' Toward Poverty Alleviation

As the trend of internal migration continued into the 2000s, India saw the introduction of the "New Rights Agenda" with numerous rights-based acts by the then government of India to help alleviate inequality and institute development.[55] Some of the well-known acts are the Right to Information Act (2005), the Scheduled Tribes and Other Traditional Forest Dwellers (Recognition of Forest Rights) Act in 2006, the Right to Education Act (2009), and most notably for poverty alleviation, the National Rural Employment Guarantee Act (NREGA) in 2005, re-named in 2010 as the Mahatma Gandhi National Rural Employment Guarantee Act (MGNREGA). The MGHREGA became "a national anti-poverty program," which aimed to offer "up to 100 days of unskilled manual labor per year on public works projects."[56]

Compared to previous governmental anti-alleviation policies, what was new about the MGNREGA is that through this enactment, "the government would encourage that the people should take initiatives for their own benefit instead of sitting 'idly' in expectation of the government's doles or other kinds of actions."[57] In other words, the program provided institutional structures or the "formal institutional mechanisms," as Ruparelia puts it, "obliging poor citizens to demand their rights, . . . [and] encourage the development of basic political capabilities."[58] This "new rights agenda" built upon the capitalist structures of growth from the 1990s, along with a decentralized implementation method (where the opportunities are made available and monitored by the village

---

55. Ruparelia, "India's New Rights Agenda," 569–590.

56. "Brief: An Evaluation of India's National Rural Employment Guarantee Act," *World Bank*, https://www.worldbank.org/en/programs/sief-trust-fund/brief/an-evaluation-of-indias-national-rural-employment-guarantee-act

57. Roy, *Employment, Poverty and Rights in India*, 43.

58. Ruparelia, "India's New Rights Agenda," 588.

panchayats), enabled India's poor to make some headway in securing employment and generating income. For example: between 2004/05 and 2009/10, poverty declined with the national headcount of people in poverty falling from 37 percent to 30 percent. And "between 1990–1991, 2000–2001 and 2007–2008, gross domestic savings as a percentage of gross domestic product (GDP) increased from 22.8 percent to 23.7 percent to 37.7 percent."[59] Therefore, since its inception in 2005, the Employment Guarantee Act (MGNREGA) has been making progress in generating income for the poor as well as increasing the national GDP.

However, scholars have also noted that the slow pace of poverty alleviation and the drawback of the MGNREGA make any substantial changes in eradicating structural inequalities difficult (which perpetuates poverty). To succinctly put it, the Indian political governance has not responded effectively to the social demands "for greater material equality."[60] In other words, although these programs have attempted to provide some respite in the form of providing means of income, they have not been successful in materializing equality for all Indian citizens, let alone alleviating poverty. People's lack of awareness on the grassroots level and the lack of accountability among the lower bureaucrats at the village level are a couple of the key areas that need reforming in order for policies and acts to be successful in reducing poverty and creating systems (based on equality) for sustainable development.

It is also important to note that the workfare programs that the various government administrations have put forth since India's independence have not contributed substantially to overall human development. Some of the long-held systemic inequalities in Indian society persist, impeding the complete alleviation of poverty and human flourishing despite government interventions. Although recently, in 2021, the government of India officially adopted a national multidimensional poverty index (MPI) and published a detailed base reports on the national multidimensional poverty index,[61] there is a very long way to go for the poor to break free from poverty.

Contextual Christian Response to Poverty and Contemporary Poverty Alleviation Programs

The Covid-19 pandemic only exacerbated the stark economic realities of the people who are oppressed. In India, the images of migrant poor people along

---

59. Ruparelia, "India's New Rights Agenda," 577.

60. Ruparelia, "India's New Rights Agenda," 571.

61. For the complete National Multidimension Poverty Index Baseline Report, see the document; https://www.niti.gov.in/sites/default/files/2021-11/National_MPI_India-11242021.pdf

with their families walking home from the bustling Indian cities to their villages will remain with us for a long time. Having migrated from their villages to the cities, to provide for their families, the pandemic forced them to return to their villages with no job, no source of income, and an uncertain future. After all these years of Indian governmental economic development and poverty alleviation plans, it appears that we are back to square one. The poor migrants have been deprived of their freedom to make choices to fulfill their human capabilities. It is in this context that the Indian Christian missiological landscape to embody "development as freedom" as a holistic development goal and witness to the freedom Gospel brings in constructive ways.

The church in India is an agent of development even though it may have its own strengths and weaknesses. Using the Mar Thoma Church as a case study, Salmon Kalarikkal affirms the role of the church as a catalyst for development by promoting economic equality, human dignity, justice, freedom and equity through its theology and biblical teaching.[62] Kalarikkal goes on to suggest that the church should evaluate its understanding of development and calles for the church to expand its initiatives to work on human trafficking, human rights violation, corruption, caste discrimination, and the like.[63] The local churches may not be as professional as mission organizations and Christian developmental organizations (CDOs) but they can still be actively involved in the community as an agent and catalyst for poverty alleviation and development.

At the same time, in some instances the local churches can work with the mission organizations and CDOs as "co-agents of missional transformation."[64] From the South Indian context, Duerksen equates the work of CDOs and churches as an "uneasy but divine marriage" where the close collaboration between the two creates some adaptive challenges.[65] Yet when churches partner with CDOs, they "allow the development ideas and concerns brought by a CDO to permeate, mix and help shape their sense of mission; when the CDO values and honors the church's primacy as mission agent in that place . . . it is probable that the calling of the Christian development organization will contribute to God's mission in ways not otherwise possible."[66] Although Duerksen's vision of co-partnering is admirable, for an Indian grassroots Christian, such a co-partnering work with a CDO often results in the local church following the CDO's vision of social

---

62. *Salomon Kalarikkal, The Trigger, Church as Catalyst of Development: Mar Thoma Church: A Case Study* (Delhi: Christian World Imprints, 2021), 118–121.

63. Kalarikkal, *The Trigger, Church as Catalyst of Development*, 121–122.

64. Duerksen, "What God Has Joined Together Let No One Separate," 146.

65. Duerksen, "What God Has Joined Together Let No One Separate," 146.

66. Duerksen, "What God Has Joined Together Let No One Separate," 147.

transformation. Most notably, the churches and Christians contend by making compassionate contributions to provide immediate relief but failing to form a robust theology or practices to tackle the systemic evils of inequalities that perpetuates and sustains poverty in India.

However, in light of the above-discussed context of already existing governmental poverty alleviation programs, we contend that the church should not limit itself to only partnering with mission organizations and CDOs to provide compassionate acts. Instead, the churches, as grassroots civil society organizations, should advocate for the poor in their neighborhoods by ensuring the implementation of the government poverty alleviation policies and programs.

The church's prophetic nature to be representative of God's kingdom calls for the church to be discerning of the earthly powers that wage war against what a flourishing God intends for the poor. Such a prophetic discernment enables the church to hold the corrupt bureaucrats accountable to ensure the reservation quotas and poverty alleviation programs are equally distributed to all the deserved members of the low castes. Being an assembly of local citizens of India, the local church is constitutionally endowed with the Right to Information Act (RTI). Sujay Ghosh refers to the RTI as a "seed right, where accountability is the gateway to other rights/entitlements via empowerment."[67] Furthermore, the RTI contributes to democratization when it captures ordinary people's discontent over asymmetrical power relations and transforms it into articulation of their awareness that corruption affects inalienable aspects of life such as food security, livelihood, and overall well-being. The massive involvement of surrogates such as political parties, non-governmental organizations (NGOs), and civil society organizations (CSOs) carries the process forward.[68]

The local church, as a CSO, in Ghosh's terms, can serve as a "surrogate" for the poor and demand accountability and information from the local bureaucrats to perform their democratic role in dispersing the affirmative action plans to the rightful beneficiaries. In their capacity as CSOs, churches can also provide awareness to the poor about their rights and provisions available through the poverty reduction programs. In such a capacity, the local churches are called to advocate for the poor beyond their church members and other religious adherents with the perspective that people are created in the image of God. However, in situations where the local churches are becoming voiceless due to religious persecutions, the responsibilities should be recognized as individual Christians who are also citizens to be aware of their rights to help the poor through the RTI or being engaged with the existing governmental poverty

---

67. Sujay Ghosh, "Accountability, Democratisation and the Right to Information in India," *Asian Studies Review* 42, no. 4 (2018): 627.

68. Ghosh, "Accountability, Democratisation and the Right to Information in India," 627.

alleviation schemes. Individuals or a group of concerned individuals can act as citizens without using the organizational structures. Even when individuals (who are Christians) cannot engage through their local church organizations, they should not lose sight of their belonging to the "church" of believers beyond their organization. They are called to be part of the universal church of Jesus Christ to stand as witness of the love and care of Christ to the oppressed and the marginalized.

More importantly, the church has the theological message of the kingdom of God that Jesus Christ entrusted the church to live out. Hence, being endowed by the "kingdom power," as Jayakumar Christian puts it, the local church has the mandate to be inclusive toward the poor who have been excluded by the world's powerful on account of caste and class.[69] Additionally, the church is also entrusted by God (as Jesus's followers) to make the poor aware of the truth concerning their dignity and worth (being made in the image of God) against the historical "web of lies" that was cultivated around caste consciousness.

Conclusion

The chapter's objective was to provide a brief look into the history of Indian governmental intervention toward poverty alleviation and map the role of Christians in such a pursuit. Even after seventy-five years of Indian independent governance, the nation faces the challenge that more than 365 million people (around 28 percent of the population) live in poverty. The Covid-19 pandemic added another six to ten million. The policymakers—in Indian and outside, are hard at work developing strategies that will initiate change. Recently, the Nobel laureate and economist Abhijit Banerjee and colleagues, based on a multi-national empirical study, demonstrated that a multifaceted program that provides productive asset grants, training and support, life skills coaching, temporary cash consumption support, access to savings accounts, and health information and services seems to increase income and well-being for the ultra-poor sustainably and cost-effectively.[70] This indicates that there is no one specific strategy or action plan to combat multidimensional poverty; we need multiple interventions to serve the poor.

In this process of poverty alleviation, the role of the Indian church is pivotal. In a nation of multiple religions, the Indian Christian population is around 30 million, and about 80 percent of them come from the lower economic strata of the society. Poverty is undoubtedly a missional challenge of the Indian church.

---

69. Christian, *God of the Empty-handed*, 182–206.

70. Abhijit Banerjee et al., "A Multifaceted Program Causes Lasting Progress for the Very Poor: Evidence from Six Countries," *Science* 348, no. 6238 (2015). https://www.science.org/doi/10.1126/science.1260799

At this stage, perhaps a more realistic approach would be to speak of poverty reduction instead of poverty alleviation, as John Toye notes.[71] Nonetheless, there is hope. As Christians, we have a social and political duty to speak in the name of God for justice and compassion and, as a prophetic church, speak the words of truth to the local government and bureaucrats.[72] Vinod Ramachandra emphasizes that the church is called to be present before the public gaze the "forgotten" people in our societies—the poor, the disabled, the elderly, and the outcasts as a demonstration of our understanding of them being created in God's image.[73]

The global church has partnered with the Indian church in its holistic mission task. However, the theological biases, old mission paradigms, and the continuing anti-colonial suspicion of the Indian political leadership are issues that have not adequately addressed in the challenge of poverty. The missing link for the Indian church is its failure to advocate effectively on behalf of the poor and oppressed in partnership with local authorities, the government, and development organizations, rather than focusing on building our own relief and welfare institutions and programs that are seen as competition. However, our prayer is that the prospects listed in this chapter would provide a vision for Christian leaders to see churches as communities of God's people and communities of national citizens with the responsibility to act on behalf of the poor in India, advocate for their rightful constitutional provisions, and hold local bureaucrats accountable for their caste biases against the low caste people, while continuing to provide relief from their own resources.

71. John Toye, "Poverty Reduction," in *Deconstructing Development Discourse*, ed. Andrea Cornwall and Deborah Eade (Oxfam: Great Britain, 2010), 47.

72. Howard Marshall, "Biblical Patterns for Public Theology," *European Journal of Theology* 14, no. 1 (2005), 73–86

73. Vinod Ramachandra, "Learning from Modern European Secularism: A View from the Third World," *Evangelical Review of Theology* 27, no. 3 (2003), 213–233

Part IV

Missional Challenges

CHAPTER FOURTEEN

Gender Inequality and Domestic Violence
A Missional Challenge in India
Hepziba Arputharaj

Introduction

GENDER INEQUALITY IS a common phenomenon in most societies around the world. Though gender equality is a basic human right, inequality is deliberately practiced in certain societies, including in India. Amartya Sen, the Indian Nobel Laureate, quips, "gender inequality is not one homogenous phenomenon, but a collection of disparate and inter-linked problems."[1] Among many problems caused by gender inequality, domestic violence (hereafter DV) stands out and needs critical attention. Regardless of religious, educational, economic, ethnic, or cultural status, DV is a common phenomenon in most societies. Recent data (2021) collected on DV in Indian Christian homes reveal that while 55.6 percent of women encounter physical violence, 88.9 percent of women reported that they go through nonphysical (verbal, emotional and psychological) violence in their homes.[2] This affirms that the sociocultural practice of abuse and violence does not spare the Christian community. This is also a threat to the witnessing Christian lifestyle and the growth of missions in India. Hence, in this chapter, I argue that India's practice of gender inequality often results in DV against women, becoming a hindrance toward the growth of missions. Therefore, the Indian church must use its voice to speak against gender inequality, eradicating abuse and DV among her members and members of other faith communities. This requires the churches to orient themselves on gender equality and to raise their voices against DV toward eradicating domestic abuse first among the Christian homes, and then in society at large. While the first part of this chapter highlights gender inequality in India, the second part focuses on the causes and effects of DV, demanding local churches to interfere, act, advocate, and educate society

1. Amartya Sen, "Many Faces of Gender Inequality," accessed November 22, 2022, https://www.sas.upenn.edu/~dludden/MANY%20FACES%20OF%20GENDER%20INEQUALITY.htm.

2. A. Lozaanba Khumbah and Bonnie Miriam Jacob, *Violence against Women in Indian Christian Families* (New Delhi: Theological Research and Communication Institute (TRACI), 2023, 19.

to create a culture of dignity, respect, equality, and harmonious relationships. Finally, I conclude by demonstrating the Indian churches' responsibility to redemptively engage the victims and abusers by advocating for, educating, and empowering families with healthy relationships resulting in a greater witness and impact in God's mission.

Gender Inequality in Indian Society

While gender discrimination is a global issue, women in India are doubly discriminated against (socially and religiously). As Martha C. Nussbaum rightly says, in Indian culture, people worship female deities and talk highly of gender equality only in literature, but it is a totally different reality on the ground.[3] According to statistics, the literacy rate of females in 2011 was 65.46 percent compared to 82.14 percent for males (fortunately, this literacy aspect is changing for good in recent years).[4] When it comes to health, boys are given priority. On many occasions, girls are denied education and health care, and are sent to work as daily wage laborers or housemaids. Statistics prove that "among children in the age group of 10–14 years reported as neither working nor attending an educational institution, girls (4.6 million) outnumber boys (3.9 million),"[5] which confirms that such a huge number of girls come under unaccounted child laborers. Religiously, it is hard to find women in leadership roles, and in certain religious practices, women are restricted from entering the temple or partaking in the rituals.[6] Gender discrimination is also practiced in Christianity. Women are expected to serve, but are not encouraged or accepted as leaders.[7] Gender-based violence in the form of rape, sexual assault,[8] physical abuse/intimate partner violence, kidnapping, deserting

---

3. Martha C. Nussbaum, *Women and Human Development: The Capabilities Approach*, John Robert Seeley Lectures (Cambridge: Cambridge University Press, 2000), 24.

4. https://indiafacts.in/literacy-rate-india-2011/, accessed on October 20, 2022.

5. "5 Facts about Child Labour in India," International Year for the Elimination of Child Labour, June 24, 2021, accessed October 20, 2022, https://endchildlabour2021.org/5-facts-about-child-labour-in-india/

6. "Sabarimala Temple: India's Top Court Revokes Ban on Women," *BBC News*, September 28, 2018, sec. India, accessed on November 15, 2022, https://www.bbc.com/news/world-asia-india-45652182

7. NA. "Indian Church Council against Move to Ordain Women Bishops," *The Indian Express* (blog), February 18, 2009, https://indianexpress.com/article/india/india-others/indian-church-council-against-move-to-ordain-women-bishops/. Accessed on October 30, 2022.

8. Rhea Mogul, Swati Gupta, and Manveena Suri, "Alleged Rapist and His Mother Set Teenage Girl on Fire after Learning She Was Pregnant, Indian Police Say," CNN, October 12, 2022,

girl children at birth,[9] selling or giving in marriage against their will, the dowry system, and the many more evil practices against women and girls prove the inexhaustible presence of gender inequality in Indian society.[10]

Gender Inequality and Domestic Violence

Domestic Violence is an outcome of many fundamental issues such as dowry, economic oppression, honor/shame societal pressure, and male dominance. Nonetheless, they all boil down to the one root cause that is gender discrimination. DV not only destroys the physical, emotional, and social well-being of the victims, but society as a whole suffers, since family is the basic unit of society.[11] Raaj Mondol's research records that "violence in India kills and disables as many women between the ages of 15 and 44 as cancer,"[12] which attests to Joni Seager's statistics that say, 60 to 80 percent of women in India encounter abuse in some form and that 42 percent are beaten physically.[13] Considering the insecurity and other challenges that come with it, roughly 77 percent of women who experience DV do not mention it to anyone and less than 1 percent of the women actually seek help from the police.[14]

Having been absorbed in a culture that prioritizes honor/shame, most women silently go through DV in order to protect the honor of their family and

---

https://www.cnn.com/2022/10/12/india/india-girl-rape-pregnancy-attempted-murder-intl-hnk/index.html. Accessed on November 25, 2022.

9. M. Sabari, "Parents Abandon New born Female Triplets in Tamil Nadu's Salem Citing Poverty," *The Hindu*, November 5, 2022, sec. Tamil Nadu, https://www.thehindu.com/news/national/tamil-nadu/parents-abandon-newborn-female-triplets-in-tamil-nadus-salem-citing-poverty/article66100971.ece. Accessed on November 19, 2022.

10. Priti Jha and Niti Nagar, "A Study of Gender Inequality in India," *International Journal of Indian Psychology* 2, no. 3 (June 25, 2015): 6–7, https://doi.org/10.25215/0203.045. Accessed on October 20, 2022.

11. Emmanuel Clapsis, ed., *Violence and Christian Spirituality: An Ecumenical Conversation* (Brookline, Mass: Holy Cross Orthodox Press, 2007), 9.

12. Raaj Mondol, "Gender-Based Violence: Recovering the Tradition of Lament to Break the Culture of Silence." (306–323), In Bonnie Miriam Jacob. *Public Theology : Exploring Expressions of the Christian Faith /*, First edition. (Bengaluru: TRACI & Primalogue, 2020), 308.

13. Joni Seager, *The Penguin Atlas of Women in the World*, 4th ed. (New York: Penguin Books, 2009), 29.

14. Shrey Banka, "DV In India: Has Anything Changed?" *Countercurrents*, December 25, 2020, accessed November 10, 2022, https://countercurrents.org/2020/12/domestic-violence-in-india-has-anything-changed/

avoid being shamed by society. Sarah England writes, "The honor/shame complex is also one of the main cultural concepts that shapes gender violence in India."[15] As part of protecting the honor, a woman's life is restricted to reproduction and tending to family needs. Considering it as a shame, families do not complain about the DV and abuse that women encounter.

Factors that contribute to DV include economic standing, addiction, and past experiences of DV either as victim or perpetrator, or lived in such a cultural context. In most Indian families, women are not allowed to work and earn regardless of their educational qualifications and skills so as to keep them dependent on the male members of the family and limit their lives to childbearing and household work. On the other hand, there are families in which men are unemployed and addicted to alcohol while women work tirelessly as housemaids or in small-scale industries. Amutha (pseudonym) is a mother of two children, living in Chennai. Her day begins at 5 a.m. as a sweeper on a school premises, followed by working at another school as a facilities staff from 8:30 a.m. to 5:30 p.m. After this, she works as a housemaid before she comes home by 8 p.m. to provide for her family. Her husband stays home, saying that he does not get enough orders in his tailoring unit and so spends the day with friends and alcohol, comes home late only to pick a fight, and abuses his wife and children. When asked, "Why do you cling to this abusive marriage?" she replied that she is worried about society's criticism and also feels unsafe to live as a single mother in Indian society.[16]

Though illegal, the practice of the dowry system continues to abuse and kill women in India today. According to National Crime Records Bureau data, in 2020, a total of 6,966 cases of dowry deaths were recorded.[17] Unreported events of dowry-related cases outnumber the reported ones. As I write this chapter, my friend informed me that a few days ago, a young graduate woman in her neighborhood was allegedly killed by her husband and in-laws due to a dowry issue within a year of marriage. Of the hundred sovereign gold and four hundred thousand rupees in cash as the dowry commitment, the woman's family gave seventy sovereign gold and four hundred thousand rupees in cash during the marriage. While the woman's parents worked on arranging the remaining dowry, the girl was verbally and physically abused by her in-laws and restricted from talking with or visiting her parents despite, living in the same town. At this

---

15. Sarah England, "Gender Violence: Honor, Shame, and the Violation of Bodies in Guatemala and India," in *The Pacific Basin: An Introduction* (Routledge, 2017), 191.

16. Amutha, personal conversation. WhatsApp call, October 24, 2023.

17. "19 Women Were Killed for Dowry Every Day in 2020: NCRB," cnbctv18.com, September 16, 2021, accessed March 20, 2023, https://www.cnbctv18.com/india/19-women-were-killed-for-dowry-every-day-in-2020-ncrb-10758421.htm

time, her husband returned from the Middle East to sort out the issue but ended up aggravating violence and taking the newly married woman's life early.[18] This is one example of many cases of DV against women in Indian society.

No particular religion seems to protect women from being unequally treated and abused, despite most of them demonstrating a high regard for women in their scriptures. Though the Bible teaches that *both* male and female are created in God's image, Scripture is often misinterpreted according to the convenience of the cultures and contexts. For example, the teaching on family in Ephesians 5 is interpreted as women are to submit totally to their husbands as subjects who act according to their rule and desire and that women do not even have a voice in the family decisions and can be beaten when disobeyed.[19] Women around the world, particularly in India, stay in abusive relationships due to the society's traditional views about home and family.

Creating an egalitarian and abuse free society is important for healthy growth and development. Michael Kimmel speaks that practicing gender equality leads to a peaceful life with equal opportunities, improves the nation's economy, and creates healthier communities. Especially, gender equality empowers women to thrive economically and professionally with confidence and higher self-esteem, and it eradicates DV.[20] So it is important and worth striving for a healthy egalitarian and abuse free community. To this extent the churches are invited to engage in a challenging responsibility of eradicating DV, as seen further.

The Role of Churches in India

Local churches are God's powerful and primary tools to influence communities with love, gender equality, and godly values. God calls every local church to engage actively in transforming the culture of violence,[21] replacing it with healthy practices of mutual love and respect. Unlike any other religion, the Bible teaches equality of every person, and no one is under anyone. Diane Langberg writes, "women and children are not possessions to be owned, but

---

18. "Woman Killed for Dowry in Tuticorin? Police Investigation," *India Posts English*, January 14, 2023, accessed May 22, 2023, https://india.postsen.com/trends/247249.html

19. A. Tali Ao, ed., *Voices against DV: Biblical, Theological & Sociocultural Appraisal of the Experiences of the Oppressed Tribal, Children, Men & Women*, CCPRA Publication Series, no. 8 (Mokokchung: Clark Centre for Peace Research and Action, Clark Theological College & Christian World Imprints, 2016), 43.

20. Michael Kimmel, *Why Gender Equality Is Good for Everyone—Men Included* (Ted Talk), accessed December 12, 2022, https://www.ted.com/talks/michael_kimmel_why_gender_equality_is_good_for_everyone_men_included?language=zh

21. Stephen Offutt et al, *Advocating for Justice: An Evangelical Vision for Transforming Systems and Structures* (Baker Academic, 2016), 129.

persons created in God's image to be loved, nurtured, and treated as crea-
tures that are responsible before him."[22] To this extent, the Indian church is
called to practice and teach values of equality, respect, and dignity. Thus, local
churches cannot be silent on devastating public issues like abuse and turn a
deaf ear toward it.[23] Hence, I believe that the churches ought to play a key
role in recognizing and teaching against DV, while creating protection and
empowerment measures that serve the victims, and advocate for the same.
Accordingly, the following initial steps are mandatory: (1) acknowledge and
recognize, (2) teaching, training, and counselling (3) protection and empowerment, and (4) advocacy and awareness through which the churches can engage
in eradication of DV.

Acknowledging the Presence of DV and Abuse

Thomas Varghese's research reveals that despite the reality of abuse and violence
in Christian homes, the church leaders are of the opinion that DV is not present
or if it is, it is trivial and can be ignored. To serve the communities that are
afflicted with abuse, the churches need to acknowledge the presence of abusive
situations within Christian families.[24] When a local church deliberately denies
any abuse, it cannot and will not treat the victims fairly or offer any support.
Affirming the same, Swagman writes that acknowledging the pain and misery
of the victims should be the first and foremost response of any local church and
its leaders. By acknowledging the verbally or physically abused victims who seek
help, the church leaders reinstate that living in abuse is not the plan of God for
humanity. People are to be treated with dignity, respect, and love. Unless the
reality of abuse is recognized and treated, DV will grip families, settling for a
negative presentation of Christian witness. Rather than suggesting immediate
remedies such as leaving the relationship or reconciliation, active listening to
the cry of the victims would be the best response that the leaders can offer.[25]
Following the example of the Scriptures (2 Sam 13:1–22; Psalm 55), Mondol calls
for the churches to "lament" instead of "being silent." He warns the churches not

---

22. Diane Langberg, *Suffering and the Heart of God: How Trauma Destroys and Christ Restores*
(Greensboro, NC: New Growth Press, 2015), 253.

23. K. W. Clements, *Learning to Speak: The Church's Voice in Public Affairs* (Edinburgh: T&T
Clark, 1995), 11.

24. Thomas Varghese, *Abuse of Women in Indian Christian Families: Roles of Clergymen, Church
and Theological Institutions* (Delhi: Indian Society for Promoting Christian Knowledge, 2013), 5.

25. Beth Swagman, *Responding to DV: A Resource for Church Leaders* (Faith Alive Christian
Resources, 2002), 163.

to ignore the oppression and cry of the abused, but to acknowledge their pain and express solidarity with the afflicted ones.[26]

Paul Hegstrom acknowledges that many churches turn a blind eye to believers who are being abused in their homes. He writes, "It is a sad state of affairs in the church that when a woman has been abused, it seems that the congregation, her friends, and her clergy shy away from dealing with the situation."[27] The church is called to impact and influence society by its proclamation and demonstration of support for the abused.[28] Affirming the same, C. S. Tiwary argues that, regrettably, most churches in India are still drenched in the patriarchal and hierarchical practices which restrain women from contributing significantly to the growth of the church. He continues, "The emerging theological articulations of women in every region of the world calls for a church that will be truly the church of Jesus Christ, ready to shed itself of some of its institutional power and privilege which has in itself been a stumbling block for change."[29] It is the need of the hour that the churches recognize the presence of the abuse, voicing against and emphasizing on the importance of practicing respect and care for the other gender at home and so leaving an example for others to follow.[30]

Teaching, Training, and Counselling

Emphasizing the role of churches in dealing with this insidious abuse, Varghese emphasizes the need for church leaders to be aware, trained to counsel, and prudent to assist victims in need.[31] Practicing Christian spirituality has to be extended beyond Sunday services as everyday practice. Pastors and Christian leaders should not limit themselves to preach on faith, prayer, evangelism, heaven and the like, but also teach about responsibility, accountability, transparent communication, and gratitude toward others. Challenges of marital relationships ought to be addressed among believers toward healthy interpersonal

---

26. Mondol, "Gender-Based Violence," 309.

27. Paul Hegstrom, *Angry Men and the Women Who Love Them: Breaking the Cycle of Physical and Emotional Abuse* (Beacon Hill Press of Kansas City, 1999), 124.

28. Clapsis, *Violence and Christian Spirituality*, 21.

29. C. S. Tiwary, *Gender Equality and Religious Identity in World Religions* (Medhashri Publications, 2010), 23–24.

30. Aruna Gnanadason, *No Longer a Secret: The Church and Violence against Women*, Risk Book Series (WCC Publications, 1993), 40.

31. Varghese, *Abuse of Women in Indian Christian Families*, 89.

and spousal relationships. Church leaders are to hold themselves responsible to interpret the word of God rightly and teach. They should also hold the abusers accountable to their local church and society for their deliberate action. Family seminars, workshops, and counselling classes should be conducted on a regular basis. They should also boldly rebuke the abusive deeds of church members and families. Amid all of these, the teachers are to practice their teaching and in doing so, they may influence and disciple others. Remembering the call of God on their lives, they are to consider themselves responsible for the smooth functioning of every church family.[32] Varghese emphasizes that the churches should focus on the importance of practicing equality in marriage that can save families from abusive practices. Recognizing their limitations and the need for professional assistance, church leaders can also direct the victims and the perpetrators to the right counselors so that they find help and support. Counselling can go a long way in dealing with abuse in Christian families, as counselors try to find the root cause of the issue and help deal with that by suggesting immediate solutions.[33]

Protection and Empowerment

It is important to provide protection and support, particularly to the victims when needed. The perpetrators also should be monitored in their treatment along with offering moral support and helping them be responsible for their abusive behaviors.[34] It is very clear that the God of the Bible hates abuse (Isa 1:17; Jer 22:3). So, churches should take a stand to protect the victims which includes encouraging, supporting and separating the victim from the abuser since timely separation could protect the victim and children from lasting damages.[35] Another significant factor in dealing with this issue is to empower women to access control over the challenges in their lives. They need to be empowered socially, financially, intellectually, and spiritually. Being empowered will obviously improve their self-confidence, self-respect, and boldness. Gleaning from the government's and nongovernmental organizations' initiatives on empowering women, the churches, in partnering with them can develop projects that could be beneficial to the church women to be socially and economically empowered. On the spiritual side, the churches must practice equality by letting more women participate and take up leadership roles in the church and ministries.

---

32. Varghese, *Abuse of Women in Indian Christian Families*, 82–85.

33. Varghese, *Abuse of Women in Indian Christian Families*, 91–93.

34. Swagman, *Responding to DV*, 165.

35. Varghese, *Abuse of Women in Indian Christian Families*, 94–95.

Advocacy and Awareness

Finally, I suggest that churches also be willing to spread awareness of the relevant laws and opportunities available to victims and be advocates of the abused in establishing justice. The Christian mission does not end with spreading the message of salvation and hope. As David J. Bosch rightly says, "Those who know that God will one day wipe away all the tears will not accept with resignation the tears of those who suffer and are oppressed now."[36] So, it is very clear that according to our beliefs and proclamations, the church is to actively participate in advocating for the pain of the oppressed and the marginalized. Stephen Offutt et. al suggest three ways, through which the churches as a social reality, can practice transformational advocacy: advocacy *for,* advocacy *with,* and advocacy *by.* In the *advocacy for* approach, even if a particular church does not encounter abused individuals or families, it still can speak up for the victims of domestic abuse in their community. Proverbs 31:8 reminds us, "Speak up for those who cannot speak for themselves, for the rights of all those who are destitute." In the *advocacy with* method, the churches ought to stand with the victims in support as they fight for their rights and dignity. By this, the victims are motivated to speak up. In the *advocacy by* approach, the affected ones, despite threats and backlash, choose to confront the injustice.[37] The church needs to be a part of this great venture. Along with this, local churches in partnering with other churches and NGOs can also organize awareness programs in the community, educating not only Christians but all Indians on persisting issues and challenges in our society.

Conclusion

In this chapter, I argued that gender inequality results in the presence and acceptance of DV in society. Despite the enormous amount of growth and development in many areas of social life, gender discrimination continues to exist both in Christian families and in society at large. Unless gender inequality is addressed among the local churches, DV will ruin the Christian witness. The local churches ought to respond creatively and constructively to the issue of gender inequality and work to eradicate DV through teaching, training, protecting, empowering, and standing with the abused and the marginalized. While being reminded that we can never become a prescription pill for all social problems, we ought to be doing our part in healing the broken world as God's image bearers, as equal human beings who are unique and respectful.

---

36. David Jacobus Bosch, *Transforming Mission: Paradigm Shifts in Theology of Mission*, American Society of Missiology Series (Orbis Books, 1991), 400.

37. Offutt, *Advocating for Justice*, 124–126.

CHAPTER FIFTEEN

The Deadly Virus of Human Trafficking in India

A Prophetic Call to Action

Uma John

Introduction

HUMAN TRAFFICKING IS one of the fastest-growing organized criminal industries in the world. The United Nations defines human trafficking as "the recruitment, transportation, transfer, harboring or receipt of people through force, fraud or deception, with the aim of exploiting them for profit."[1] In other words, it is modern-day slavery. Its victims include women, children, and even men and it presents an ongoing and escalating problem throughout the world. It is imperative that society—both local and global—fight against trafficking and work for the welfare of the victims. This is especially true for Christians and Christian organizations since the Bible consistently and unequivocally calls for social action to be united with faith. Specifically, the prophetic books of the Bible urgently exhort its readers to participate in social justice. This chapter seeks to engage with this prophetic voice and puts forth three particular actions for addressing human trafficking: to prosecute the perpetrators, to protect the victims, and to prevent further acts of trafficking. This study focuses specifically on the issue of trafficking in India and solicits a call for action from, but is not limited to, Indian Christians and churches.

Statistics of Human Trafficking in India

According to a 2018 Polaris report,[2] it is estimated that globally there are 20.9 million victims of human trafficking.[3] Of those, 68 percent of the victims are in

---

1. United Nations, "United Nations: Office on Drugs and Crime," https://www.unodc.org/unodc/en/human-trafficking/human-trafficking.html.

2. Polaris is a nonprofit organization that works to fight and prevent trafficking in North America.

3. Kim Maryniak, "An Overview on Human Trafficking" *AMN Healthcare Education Services*, 2019, https://www.rn.com/headlines-in-health/overview-human-trafficking/.

forced labor of which 55 percent are adult females and 26 percent are children.[4] According to a *Reuters* study,[5] on average there are 16 million women and girls who are victims of sex trafficking in India.[6] Legal services in India has recorded that, four girls enter prostitution in India every hour, and three of them are forced to enter without their consent,[7] making human trafficking, tragically, one of the biggest industries in India.

There is a demand for teenage girls because of the misconception that a man has a reduced risk of contracting HIV/AIDS by having sex with a young girl, on the presumption that young girls are less likely to have HIV/AIDS than women who have been prostitutes longer. Furthermore, the demand for young girls who are virgins is especially high because of the myth that one may cure impotence or HIV/AIDS through intimacy with a virgin. Humans are trafficked for various reasons, including, predominantly, sex trafficking, but also for child labor, the organ trade, marriage, and pornography. Recently there also has been trafficking for fertility egg reproduction. In these cases, young girls are trafficked and forcefully injected with clomiphene to such an extent that it causes the girl to produce multiple eggs at a time so that these eggs can be sold to hospitals which then sell them to infertile couples.[8] Thus, sex trafficking represents only one of the many reasons why women and children are trafficked.

Major Causes of Human Trafficking in India

There are multiple reasons why trafficking is so high in India and a few of the more prominent reasons will be examined here. These reasons emanate from

---

4. Maryniak, "An Overview on Human Trafficking."

5. Reuters is one of the largest news agencies in the world and its headquarters is in London.

6. There are another four million additional women who choose to be in commercial prostitution but are not "victims" in the technical sense. See Hamaad Habibullah, "Explained: Why Human Trafficking Remains One of the Top Organized Crimes In India," *IndiaTimes*, October 2021, https://www.indiatimes.com/explainers/news/human-trafficking-in-india-552763.html.

7. Habibullah, "Explained." According to the data from the 2019's National Crime Records Bureau (NCRB), it is estimated that every eight minutes a child goes missing. Sushmita Panda, "'A Child Goes Missing in India Every Eight Minutes,'" *The Sunday Guardian Live*, 2020, https://www.sundayguardianlive.com /news/child-goes-missing-india-every-eight-minutes. Also see, Shreya Shah, "India's Missing Children, By the Numbers," *Wall Street Journal*, 2012, https://www.wsj.com/articles/BL-IRTB-16945. Shubhashish Singh Rehal, *Human Trafficking in India: Detailed Analysis for UPSC CSE*, IASPrimers, 2021, https://www.youtube.com/watch?v=RyfQvRCUSeA&ab_channel=IASPrimers.

8. Jennifer Lahl, "Is Egg 'Donation' and Surrogacy the Newest Form of Human Trafficking?" *Center for Bioethics & Culture Network*, 2019, https://cbc-network.org/2019/09/newest-form-human-trafficking/

two essential factors, which may be termed "push" and "pull" factors.[9] The "push" factors include poverty, natural disasters which project the vulnerable into destitution, lack of education, and lack of job opportunities. The "pull" factors, alternatively, include lucrative job opportunities in big cities, the promise of good pay, the need for young girls for marriage in other territories, and the demand for low-paid shop labor. A victim of trafficking, therefore, is simultaneously being "pushed" by poverty and destitution while also being "pulled" by the false promise of a better life. I will detail a few of these problems below.

Lack of Job Opportunities or Income

As of 2024, India is the most populous country in the world and the poverty in India is extreme. As Vimal Vidushy notes, "It appears from the case studies that extreme poverty and other causes of deprivation not only push people to fall into the [trap of] the traffickers, they also create for some an incentive for trafficking."[10] As the National Institution for Transforming India (NITI) Aayog policy notes, 25 percent of the Indian population is poor; so, every fourth person in India lives in poverty.[11] In 2021, the global multidimensional poverty index (MPI) ranked India as the sixty-sixth poorest out of the 109 nations that were surveyed for multidimensional poverty.[12] In the same year, the total male population living in poverty in India was about 45 million;[13] whereas total number of women living in poverty was around 53 million.[14] One of the reasons for high poverty rates is the unemployment rate, as well as the low pay for those who are employed. The 2022 World Inequality Report describes India as a "poor country and very unequal, with an affluent elite,"[15] where 57 percent of national income

---

9. Vimal Vidushy, "Human Trafficking in India: An Analysis," *International Journal of Applied Research* 2 (2016): 168–171, here 169.

10. Vidushy, "Human Trafficking in India," 169.

11. The Global Statistics, "Poverty Rate in India Statistics 2022 | Poorest State in India," *The Global Statistics*, 2022, https://www.theglobalstatistics.com/poverty-in-india-statistics-2021/.

12. Elisha Vermani, "Multidimensional Poverty Index: Everything You Need to Know," *India Development Review*, 2021, https://idronline.org/article/inequality/multidimensional-poverty-index-everything-you-need-to-know/.

13. Poverty here refers to those who struggle to provide for their daily food, clothing, and shelter.

14. Sanyukta Kanwal, "India: Total Population Living in Poverty by Gender 2021," *Statista*, 2022, https://www.statista.com/statistics/1270990/india-total-population-living-in-poverty/

15. Shivaji Sarkar, "India's Low HDI Rank Reflects Poverty, Inequality," *The Pioneer*, September 2022, https://www.dailypioneer.com/2022/columnists/india---s-low-hdi-rank-reflects-poverty--inequality.html.

is from 10 percent of the nation's population, and the bottom 50 percent of people live in a challenging life due to poverty, poor paying jobs, and so forth.[16]

Unlike in cities, rural India does not have many job opportunities. According to the World Bank, 65 percent of India's total population in 2021 was considered rural.[17] Usually, people in rural areas depend on farming. And once the farming season is over or if there are droughts and floods, then the families and villages struggle to earn their living. IT companies and other industries which provide job opportunities are rarely seen in rural villages. Due to such conditions, many people from such locations try to migrate to cities to find a job and feed their families. In those circumstances, unfortunately, some fall into the hands of procurers who offer them alluring jobs in cities. However, once they arrive at their destination, they are forced into prostitution. When I was working for a government aftercare home,[18] one of the girls, Ramya (a pseudonym), said she was trafficked when she was only eleven years old when she was looking for a job because of severe poverty at her home. During her job search, she was lured to Mumbai, tortured, and forced to serve as a prostitute. In my time with an anti–human trafficking organization (2013–2018), it became evident that most slums in Goa had migrants from North Karnataka. Upon further research, we found that the migrants came due to a lack of employment and droughts in North Karnataka.[19] During this process, and because Goa is a tourist state in India, many children get trafficked to entertain the tourists. Such is the status of some of the rural states in India.[20] Thus, unemployment, or employment that does not provide sufficient income, is one of the reasons for trafficking.

Lack of Awareness

Rural villages have little to no awareness of many of the illegal and immoral activities that happen in the cities. As mentioned, women and men migrate to different states for jobs and survival. In this journey, due to their naivete, they

16. Sarkar, "India's Low HDI Rank Reflects Poverty."

17. World Bank, "Rural Population (% of Total Population)—India," *World Bank*, 2022, https://data.worldbank.org/indicator/SP.RUR.TOTL.ZS?locations=IN.

18. The state government in India is required by the Juvenile Justice (Care & Protection of Children) Act, 2000, to run an aftercare program for the care of juveniles or children to facilitate their transition from an institution-based life to independent life.

19. "Goa's Slums Are Full of Karnataka Migrants: Study," *Times of India*, May 15, 2017, https://timesofindia.indiatimes.com/city/bengaluru/goas-slums-are-full-of-karnataka-migrants-study/articleshow/58676868.cms.

20. Gauree Malkarnekar, "After Karnataka & Maha, UP Gives Goa the Most Migrants," *Times of India*, August 14, 2019, https://timesofindia.indiatimes.com/city/goa/after-ktaka-maha-up-gives-goa-the-most-migrants/articleshow/70666598.cms.

get lured and trafficked. Illiteracy is one of the reasons for their lack of awareness. According to UNESCO,[21] as of 2014, India had 287 million illiterate adults which represents 37 percent of the total world population.[22] Although the literate population keeps increasing, due to the high population in India, the percentage of illiteracy rate remains around the same.[23] As of 2021, 65 percent of females in India were literate,[24] and, correspondingly, 35 percent of women in India were illiterate. Thus, lack of education and awareness especially of the women and children makes them easy targets for trafficking. As Kiril Sharapov and others have rightly pointed out, "awareness-raising and information provision is the most common tool in the arsenal of *prevention* activities."[25] The National Agency for the Prohibition of Trafficking in Persons (NAPTIP) says that "ignorance was still driving human trafficking to thrive in the country."[26]

Lack of a Properly Functioning Government

One of the other reasons why trafficking is so prominent in India is because of the irresponsibility of the government. There are various programs (which will be mentioned later) that are set to abolish trafficking and to help the victims, yet most of the programs are not rightly implemented by the government employees. It is reported that "cases involving corruption in trafficking in persons where public officials involved in the identification, investigation, prosecution, or referral of human trafficking in their country had also been involved in related corruption."[27] Corruption is extremely high in India. Corrupted police officials play a significant role in fostering and facilitating the crime of trafficking by recruiting, transporting, and exploiting the victims.[28] Regularly, police officers

21. United Nations Educational, Scientific and Cultural Organization

22. Nilanjana Bhowmick, "37% of All the Illiterate Adults in the World Are Indian," *Time*, January 29, 2014, https://world.time.com/2014/01/29/indian-adult-illiteracy/.

23. Bhowmick, "37% of All the Illiterate Adults."

24. Census 2021, "Literacy Rate of India 2021 || State Wise Literacy Rate," *Census 2021*, 2022, https://censusofindia2021.com/literacy-rate-of-india-2021/.

25. Kiril Sharapov, Suzanne Hoff, and Borislav Gerasimov, "Editorial: Knowledge Is Power, Ignorance Is Bliss: Public Perceptions and Responses to Human Trafficking," *Anti-Trafficking Review* 13 (2019): 1–11, here 4.

26. David O. Royal, "Ignorance Still Driving Human Trafficking to Thrive in Society—NAPTIP," *Vanguard News*, 2022, https://www.vanguardngr.com/2022/03/ignorance-still-driving-human-trafficking-to-thrive-in-society-naptip/.

27. United Nations Office on Drugs and Crime, "The Role of Corruption in Trafficking in Persons," *UNODC* (2011): 3–32, here 4.

28. UNODC, "The Role of Corruption," 9.

release traffickers in exchange for bribes.[29] Likewise, many government officials take bribes and turn a blind eye to traffickers and do numerous favors for them.[30] When I was interning for a nonprofit in India, the NGO employees informed the local police, as required by law, about a brothel raid that the NGO would be undertaking. On the day of the raid when all the NGO staff along with others accompanying them went to raid, the whole brothel was vacant; neither the victims nor the madams were present. Later when we inquired about this, we learned that the police had been bribed by the owners of the brothel and in return informed them about the upcoming raid, giving them time to vacate the premises. Such situations are common in India.[31] Although the laws exist, their enforcement is awfully weak.

Other Reasons

Added to all these human factors are natural disasters. Floods, drought, and tsunamis all lead many to lose their families and employment and thus fall into the risk of trafficking. For example, Covid-19 brought drastic changes to India: poverty and unemployment increased which led to an increase in trafficking. A significant group of people who were already vulnerable to such illegal businesses became even more vulnerable. Due to the lack of workers during the lockdown, children were forced into hard labor to ensure that manufacturing units continued to operate.[32] According to the survey of the Centre for Monitoring Indian Economy, within two months of the start of the lockdown in India, 122 million people lost their employment; and 75 percent of them were daily wage laborers and small business traders.[33] It is surveyed that during the Covid lockdown,

---

29. India News, "Noida Cops Take Bribe to Let Off Drug Trafficking Suspect; Suspended," *NDTV.Com*, 2022, https://www.ndtv.com/india-news/3-noida-cops-suspended-for-taking-bribe-to-let-off-drug-trafficking-suspect-3353487. TV9 Marathi, "Maharashtra Shocker: Police Inspector Among Three Held for Demanding Bribe From Drug Trafficking Suspect in Malegaon," *LatestLY*, 2022, https://www.latestly.com/india/news/maharashtra-shocker-police-inspector-among-three-held-for-demanding-bribe-from-drug-trafficking-suspect-in-malegaon-4274375.html.

30. Ravikanth B. Lamani and G. S. Venumadhava, "Police Corruption in India," *International Journal of Criminology and Sociological Theory* 6 no. 4 (2013): 228–234, here 231.

31. UNODC, "The Role of Corruption," 9.

32. United Nations, "Impact of the Covid-19 Pandemic on Trafficking in Persons," *Covid-19 Response*, 2021, https://www.unodc.org/documents/Advocacy-Section/HTMSS_Thematic_Brief_on_COVID-19.pdf.

33. Leeza, "Human Trafficking and Exploitation in India during the Covid-19 Pandemic," *Caritas*, 2020, https://www.caritas.org/aa.

within eleven days, 92 thousand cases of child abuse within the family and in the communities were filed with the government helpline.[34] Selling children to earn some money and performing child marriages to avoid having to feed another person in the house became extremely common.[35]

Thus, due to these various reasons and needs, humans get trafficked. Victims who fall into such traps face serious issues physically, mentally, emotionally, and spiritually. The need to advocate for these victims and fight against this evil is urgent and imperative.

The Need for Christian Social Action

Social work and advocating for justice are not just responsibilities of governments and non-profit organizations, rather it is the task of every human being to take care of other humans. Mollie Marti, the founding CEO of the National Resilience Institute says, "helping others in need is not only a responsibility of life; it is what gives meaning to life."[36] For Christians in particular, this becomes a mandatory obligation. Jesus preached several times about helping the sick, poor, and naked. He starts his ministry using a quote from Isaiah 61 which describes his mission to the poor, broken, captives, and prisoners (Luke 4:16–18). In Jesus's parable on separating sheep and goats in Matthew 25:31–46, he separates them based on their deed to the poor, sick, naked, and imprisoned rather than who prophesied and performed miracles. The whole Bible intensely encourages and warns about serving others as an important aspect of Christian life. Thus, it can be attested that the social aspect is part and parcel of the Christian faith. As John Stott correctly observes, "social action not as a means to evangelism but as a manifestation of evangelism."[37] And he also says it is even better to say social action is a partner of evangelism as "both are expressions of unfeigned love."[38]

Although the entire Bible speaks of social engagement, I will exclusively focus on prophetic literature to present the need and the course of action required for social activism from the prophetic corpus alone. Prophetic literature widely speaks about social justice and actions. It requires its audience to stop ritualistic religion and focus on true religion which includes social activism. Therefore,

---

34. Leeza, "Human Trafficking."

35. Divya Arya, "India's Covid Crisis Sees Rise in Child Marriage and Trafficking," *BBC News*, 2020, https://www.bbc.com/news/world-asia-india-54186709.

36. Mollie Marti, *Walking with Justice: Uncommon Lessons from One of Life's Greatest Mentors* (Austin, TX: Greenleaf, 2012).

37. John Stott, *Christian Mission in the Modern World* (Westmont, IL: InterVarsity Press, 1975), 27.

38. Stott, *Christian Mission in the Modern World*.

following the examples of the prophets who lamented and warned the Israelites,[39] it is the task of every church and true Christian to take up the task of social activism along with evangelism. As this chapter focuses on trafficking, I will propose three ways a church or a Christian can work on anti-trafficking programs.

Three Approaches from the Prophetic Literature

The United States Congress has taken various actions to address crime. One such action directed at anti-trafficking in 2000 is called the "3Ps" approach which stands for protection, prosecution, and prevention.[40] Various countries including India take a similar three-step approach to seriously work for the victims and prevent trafficking.[41] Even NGOs take a similar approach in their work. We can find these three aspects in the prophetic literature as well. God commands his people to *protect* the vulnerable, *prosecute* the unjust, and *prevent* someone from stumbling and falling. The rest of this chapter will present how the prophets encouraged Israelites to focus on these three areas to help the needy and downtrodden which the churches can also use for the cause of anti-trafficking. Not all churches in India may take up the following steps due to various limitations related to manpower, adequate training, financial restraints, and so forth, however, if the church is able, it is highly recommended that they take up these steps to help the victims.

Protection

Protection of the victims of trafficking, slavery, violence, or any other evil is an important task. After these victims are officially rescued, many families nevertheless reject and refuse to accept them in their families because of shame. Even though society rejects them, the church must accept these women and children as proposed by the prophets. Isaiah 16:3–4 says, "Give counsel, grant justice; make your shade like night at the height of noon; hide the outcasts, do not betray the fugitive; let the outcasts of Moab settle among you; be a refuge to them from the destroyer." The Hebrew word for "refuge" is סֵתֶר, and the literal meaning of

---

39. Isa 1:17, 21; 5:7; 16; 9:7; 10:2; 11:4; 16:3; 25:4; 32:1; 33:15, 41:17; 42:1, 3, 4; 51:4, 14; 54:14; 56:1, 58:3, 6, 7; 59:8, 11; 59:14, 15; 60:14; 61:1, 8; Jer 2:34; 5:28; 7:6; 9:24; 21:12; 22:3, 15, 16, 17; 23:5; 30:20; 33:15; 50:33; Ezek 16:49; 18:7, 12; 22:29; 45:8; 9; Dan 4:27; Hos 12:6; Amos 2:7; 4:1; 5:1, 7, 15, 24; 8:4, 6; Mic 2:2; 3:9; 6:8; 7:3; Hab 1:4; Zec 7:10; Mal 3:5.

40. Tammy Toney-Butler, Megan Ladd, and Olivia Mittel, "Human Trafficking," *StatPearls* (2022), https://www.statpearls.com/ArticleLibrary/viewarticle/36310.

41. United States Department of State, "2021 Trafficking in Persons Report: India," *United States Department of State*, 2022, https://www.state.gov/reports/2021-trafficking-in-persons-report/india/.

the word is "hiding place, covering or protection."[42] In some instances like in Isaiah 28:17, "refuge" "is to be a hiding place in threatening legal circumstances, [and] here in 16:4 it is meant as protection from ruin."[43] The nifal form of נִדָּחִים "outcast" here means those who "(allow oneself to) be drawn away, led astray[44] or to be seduced."[45] Moabites here are displaced and desperate people who are petitioning for justice, counsel, and mainly protection from their enemies.[46] George Buchanan Gray says that either the Moabites are seeking the Judeans to decide the case between Moab and their enemies or asking Judeans to protect them from the hot anger of the enemies and that they will also hide them so that the enemies will not discover them.[47] The metaphor of shelter and shade from the sun refers to protection.[48] John Oswalt notes that "a shelter from the noonday sun is a figurative way of asking them (Judeans) to take steps to become a refuge from the terrible blows which had so demoralized the Moabites."[49] God is making a petition to the Judeans to receive and protect the refugees from Moab, a non-Israelite community, who were seduced or led astray.

Isaiah 61:1 is the verse Jesus used when he started his ministry (Luke 4:16–17): ". . . to bring good news to the poor. He has sent me to proclaim release to the captives and recovery of sight to the blind, to let the oppressed go free." Many LXX manuscripts have πτωχοῖς, meaning "poor." There is a debate among scholars whether the poor referred here is economic, or spiritual.[50] But John Goldingay says that the word "poor" itself refers to "people's relationship to power and to power structures" who are unable to withstand the oppressive

---

42. BDB, s.v. סֵתֶר.

43. *HALOT*, s.v. סֵתֶר.

44. *DCH*, s.v. נִדָּחִים.

45. *HALOT*, s.v. נִדָּחִים.

46. Walter Brueggemann, *Isaiah 1–39*, Westminster Bible Companion (Louisville: Westminster John Knox, 1998), 141.

47. George Buchanan Gray, *A Critical and Exegetical Commentary on the Book of Isaiah, I–XXXIX*, ICC (New York: C. Scribner's Sons, 1912), 288–289.

48. Patricia K. Tull, *Isaiah 1–39*, SHBC (Macon, GA: Smyth & Helwys, 2010), 296.

49. John N. Oswalt, *The Book of Isaiah, Chapters 1–39*, NICOT (Grand Rapids, MI: Eerdmans, 1986), Isaiah 16:3–4 (electronic version).

50. See Brevard S. Childs, *Isaiah: A Commentary*, OTL (Louisville: Westminster John Knox, 2001), 504–506. John D. W. Watts, *Isaiah 34–66*, WBC 25, rev. ed. (Nashville: Thomas Nelson, 2005), 873–874. Claus Westermann, *Isaiah 40–66: A Commentary*, OTL (Philadelphia: Westminster, 1969), 366–367. Goldingay, *A Critical and Exegetical Commentary on Isaiah 56–66*, 293–294.

and powerful people over them.[51] Walter Brueggemann says that in general all the verbs mentioned in Isaiah 61 refer to the rehabilitation of the impoverished and powerless: "The proclamation is something of a test case for the way in which the Old Testament holds together *theological vision* and *concrete economic practice*."[52] In Ezekiel 34, we see that God is speaking against false shepherds and one of the complaints God has against them is that they do not strengthen the weak or bound up the wounds or bring back those lost– "You have not strengthened the weak, you have not healed the sick, you have not bound up the injured, you have not brought back the strayed, you have not sought the lost, but with force and harshness you have ruled them" (34:4). The shepherds in the current era are pastors, church leaders, or others who are in charge over the flock on the church and missional places. They have a similar task as shepherds in the Ezekiel era. Daniel Isaac Block says these pastors are "the antithesis of the responsible shepherd (as) they have shown no concern for the physical health of the flock."[53] It is the duty of the shepherds and Christians who are in charge, and every Christian, to bring back the oppressed and assist the weak and poor, to make sure the flock is heading in the right direction and that their necessities are being taken care of. As Leslie C. Allen puts it: "Behind the shepherd language lies the typical royal duty of welfare of society's weaklings."[54]

The Ministry of Women and Child Development (MWCD) funds NGO- and government-run rehabilitation centers like the *Ujjawala* scheme for female trafficked victims and the Swadhar Greh scheme that helps women in any difficult situations that need institutional support by providing shelter, food, clothing, security, and so forth.[55] The church as an organization should make use of such schemes to help protect the women and children who are abused and misused. Also, the church should become a refuge by providing shelter, basic needs and teaching them some helpful life skills.

Prosecution

In the matter of trafficking, there is so much need for prosecution. Usually, prosecution involves judicial involvement. Often churches spiritualize their role

51. Goldingay, *A Critical and Exegetical Commentary on Isaiah 56–66*, 298–299.

52. Walter Brueggemann, *Isaiah 40–66*, Westminster Bible Companion (Louisville: Westminster John Knox, 1998), 213–214.

53. Daniel Isaac Block, *The Book of Ezekiel, Chapters 25–48*, NICOT (Grand Rapids: Eerdmans, 1997), 283–284.

54. Leslie C. Allen, *Ezekiel 20–48*, WBC 29 (Dallas: Word, 1990), 161.

55. National Informatics Centre (NIC), "Parliament of India Lok Sabha House of the People," *Lok Sabha*, 2018, https://loksabha.nic.in/Members/QResult16.aspx?qref=61198.

in the world, and they tend to not get into judicial matters much, but prosecution is necessary. The prophets do propose taking legal action for the needy and oppressed. Isaiah strongly commands: "Learn to do good; seek justice, rescue the oppressed, defend the orphan, plead for the widow" (Isa 1:17). The Hebrew for "rescue the oppressed" is אַשְּׁרוּ חָמוֹץ, the literal meaning of אשר is "to stride, to lead."[56] J. J. M. Roberts says that אשר which means "lead on," can be understood as leading things in the right direction, that is, "set the mistreated back on the road to justice."[57] "Defend the orphan" in Hebrew is שִׁפְטוּ יָתוֹם. The word שפט comes from the other Semitic language root words. In Ugaritic, it means "on the one hand to control, rule, and on the other hand to make correct, help to obtain justice."[58] שפט has the meaning of administering justice and leading a person or community that has lost justice to get back their justice.[59] "Plead the widow": In Hebrew, the root word for "plead" is ריב meaning "to strive." According to *HALOT*, the word is typically used in legal circumstances or when there is a need to plead for someone's legal need or cause.[60] Thus, we see that all these verbs have the meaning of administering justice or helping someone get their justice done in the court. Brueggemann says that these vulnerable people mentioned in Isaiah 1:17 are without an advocate and thus under political and economic exploitation.[61] Roberts says that even in the ancient Israelites' era, it was enormously tough for an orphan or a widow to get legal justice in court unless they had an influential person beside them.[62] And thus "right neighbor practice (*justice*)"[63] by being an advocate for the vulnerable is required from the Judeans. Patricia K. Tull says that the verbs mentioned in this verse have specific judicial understandings. She says, "What is sought here is not charity. Rather, 'the leaders, in particular, and the people, in general, are instructed to use the courts for their fundamental purpose, to protect those least able to protect themselves.'"[64] Thus, as Tull and other scholars clearly point out, apart from charitable services to the

---

56. *HALOT*, s.v. אשר.

57. J. J. M. Roberts, *First Isaiah: A Commentary*, Hermeneia (Minneapolis: Fortress Press, 2015), 24.

58. *HALOT*, s.v. שפט.

59. *HALOT*, s.v. שפט.

60. *HALOT*, s.v. ריב.

61. Walter Brueggemann, *Isaiah 1–39*, Westminster Bible Companion (Louisville, KY: Westminster John Knox, 1998), 19.

62. Roberts, *First Isaiah*, 24.

63. Brueggemann, *Isaiah 1–39*, 19.

64. Tull, *Isaiah 1–39*, 63.

poor, going to court to seek justice for the weak and vulnerable is required by the believer of God.

In another instance in Isaiah, the writer asserts that God hates the ritualistic religion of sacrifices and offerings. Instead, he prefers a different religion: "Is not this the fast that I choose: to loose the bonds of injustice, to undo the thongs of the yoke, to let the oppressed go free, and to break every yoke?" (Isa 58:6–7). The figure of speech used here is "yoke." A yoke is an instrument of wood that holds two (or more) animals to be coupled in order to work together. Metaphorically, the Bible used the term for bondage.[65] Here the slaves are similar to animals bound by the yoke, and freeing them is like cutting the ropes of the yoke.[66] In Targam *muṭṭeh* (yoke) implies "injustice" that is "in the sense of illicit legal decisions."[67] It is interesting to note that the Hebrew "thongs of yoke" (אֲגֻדּוֹת מוֹטָה) is translated as στραγγαλιὰς βιαίων in LXX meaning "knot of violent transactions."[68] And the Hebrew "break every yoke" (וְכָל־מוֹטָה תְּנַתֵּקוּ) is translated as συγγραφὴν ἄδικον διάσπα meaning "tear unjust contract asunder." Joseph Blenkinsopp says that the primary task mentioned is releasing people from bondage, especially a judicial one.[69] So thus it is clear that these verses refer to unfair contracts that a human is bound up with which is so similar to trafficking. The women and children are bound up with illegal contracts and bondage, and breaking such knots of violent transactions and unjust contracts is a duty of every Christian and church in the capacity that they are capable of.

As in the ancient era, there is a similar struggle in India today. Some of the judicial authorities do not fully stand with the victims of lower status. Unless a person is wealthy or influential, a person's case is not easily considered in court. Bribery and corruption always delay justice or even deny justice. When it comes to orphans and trafficked victims, they are mostly women and children who either do not have families or are usually from poor backgrounds, and do not have anybody to fight for their justice. Hence there is a need for the church and Christians to take up this responsibility. Churches should take the step of defending legal cases on behalf of the needy and oppressed. First AG Church in Bangalore is a good example of this. They run an anti-trafficking network and pull together different NGOs and churches to stand for justice and fight

---

65. *BEB* "Yoke," 2173.

66. John Goldingay, *A Critical and Exegetical Commentary on Isaiah 56–66*, ICC (London: Bloomsbury, 2014), 174.

67. Goldingay, *A Critical and Exegetical Commentary on Isaiah 56–66*, 174.

68. The LXX translations are from Lexham English Septuagint

69. Joseph Blenkinsopp, *Isaiah 56–66: A New Translation with Introduction and Commentary*, AYB 19 (New Haven: Yale University, 2008), 179.

legally. Various laws and codes are present in India to help trafficked women and children. Section 370 of the Indian Penal Code (IPC) proscribes trafficking offenses that involve any kind of physical sexual or slavery exploitation. Punishments include seven to ten years of imprisonment and fines depending on the age of the victim. Sections 372 and 373 of the IPC criminalize the exploitation of children through prostitution and have a similar punishment. Other laws like the Protection of Children from Sexual Offenses Act (POCSO) and the Immoral Traffic Prevention Act (ITPA), also criminalized crimes concerning commercial sexual exploitation. The Juvenile Justice Act prohibits the recruitment of children under the age of 18 for labor or illegal activities. In the constitution of India, 1949, article 23 (1) prohibits the traffic of human beings and declares it as a punishable offense. Churches should be aware of the acts that exist for these downtrodden groups and should fight for them using these law codes. Sometimes, getting justice is not easy as corruption is common, yet churches should not give up trying for justice for the weak and vulnerable.

Prevention

The third step, prevention, is the most significant of all. Trafficking causes a lifetime of struggles for the victims; many will have health issues such as sexually transmitted diseases, HIV, AIDS, and the like. All victims are usually mentally traumatized. Usually, there is a loss of family as traffickers transport victims away from their hometowns. Feelings of shame and disrespect abound in the victims. Hatred toward God and other human beings is also common. Hence, it is exceptionally important to work on prevention.

Prevention is also a key aspect we find in the prophetic literature. It is asked of the biblical audience to seek out the needy and help them in their struggles. Isaiah contends on religious fasting: "Is it not to share your bread with the hungry, and bring the homeless poor into your house; when you see the naked, to cover them, and not to hide yourself from your own kin?" (58:7). The term "your kin/flesh" means here, "fellow human beings."[70] During this context of the early Persian era, there were droughts, irregular harvests, unemployment, and social unrest.[71] All of this led people into poverty who had to seek help from the upper classes and fall in their injustice. Hence Isaiah was commanding his audience to seek out their fellow human beings who need basic things, and this was considered as true fasting. In Isaiah 35:3 we see imperative commands to "strengthen the weak hands and make firm the feeble knees." The redeemed of

---

70. Blenkinsopp, *Isaiah 56–66*, 175.

71. Cf. Hag 1:5–6, 10–11; 2:16–17; Zec 8:10. See Blenkinsopp, *Isaiah 56–66*, 178.

the Lord are tasked to strengthen and make strong the vulnerable and the weak so that they do not fall victim to the powerful and corrupt and become weak and despair. Ezekiel 16:49 says: "This was the guilt of your sister Sodom: she and her daughters had pride, excess of food, and prosperous ease, but did not aid the poor and needy." As Daniel Isaac Block says, "Ezekiel portrays Sodom's crimes as social and moral rather than cultic."[72] It is a sin to not care for the people who are struggling and so it is required for people to care for the poor and provide for the needy.

Churches need to work on helping the poor materially. However, churches should not be satisfied by giving money to the poor, instead churches or Christians, as they are able, should make efforts to find ways to serve by educating people or helping them find a job or skills training so that they would not fall into the trap of corruption. As one of the greatest proverbs says "Give a man a fish, and you feed him for a day. Teach a man to fish, and you feed him for a lifetime." Notably, churches should work on trafficking prevention programs in their churches, and outreach activities. January is human trafficking awareness month. They can get involved in movements like "Walk for Freedom," where the organization conducts awareness events about human trafficking.[73] Churches can make use of the month to do outreach programs to bring awareness on trafficking. Thus, helping a person with education, whether formal or informal, skills training, job placements, and creating awareness programs would be some of the few steps churches and capable Christians can take to prevent the trafficking of victims. Churches can also colaborate with other anti-trafficking non-profit organizations to help them with their programs. Thus, churches should step forward to help the poor and desperate before a pimp misuses and enslaves them.

Conclusion

In this chapter, many current statistics, and proposals to help the anti-trafficking cause are described. However, if the chapter remains just information and reporting, its purpose will be unfulfilled. James says, "You see that a person is justified by works and not by faith alone. For just as the body without the spirit is dead, so faith without works is also dead" (Jas 2:24, 26). As adherents of God, we are required to get our hands dirty by working for such a great social justice

---

72. Daniel Isaac Block, *The Book of Ezekiel, Chapters 1–24*, NICOT (Grand Rapids, MI: Eerdmans, 1997), 509.

73. Walk for Freedom 2023, *The Movement India*, https://www.themovementindia.com/content/walk-for-freedom/gjjvnd.

need in society. Although the above proposal is from the prophetic literature, the whole corpus of the Old and New Testament intensively encourages social intervention. To be specific, God desires a religion that has a social dimension. Let me conclude with James's words: "Religion that God our Father accepts as pure and faultless is this: to look after orphans and widows in their distress and to keep oneself from being polluted by the world" (Jas 1:27).

CHAPTER SIXTEEN

Missiological Reflections on Disability Discourse in India

How the Church Can Respond

T. S. John

Introduction

PEOPLE WITH DISABILITIES in India form a significant part of the population. According to the 2011 Census, 2.1 percent of India's population has some form of impairment, but the World Health Organization (WHO) believes the actual rate is 16 percent or higher, totaling over 22.4 crore individuals.[1] Unfortunately, the majority of Indians with disabilities face stigma, marginalization, poverty, and lack access to the gospel. Disability will likely touch the lives of nearly all Indians, either through personal experience or caring for a loved one with an impairment. While the church in India has established institutions that have served people with disabilities for almost two centuries, there has been limited theological or missiological reflection on the subject from an Indian perspective. This chapter aims to contribute to the conversation by discussing current, secular discourse on disability and examining it through a missiological lens. Its thesis is that such an analysis is generative for developing a response to disability in India that is well informed by current scholarship. I proceed by analyzing definitions of disability, briefly describe the challenges faced by Indians with disabilities, survey four "models" of disability, reflect on them missiologically, and conclude with a missiological response that offers the church suggestions on how to proceed into the twenty-first century.

Disability Definitions and Complexities

According to India's Rights of Persons with Disabilities (RPWD) Act, 2016, disability is defined as "a long-term physical, mental, intellectual, or sensory impairment that, in interaction with barriers, hinders full and effective participation in society equally with others."[2] WHO further expands on this definition,

1. "Disability," WHO (World Health Organization), accessed April 10, 2020, http://www.who.int/topics/disabilities/en/.

2. "The Rights of Persons with Disabilities Act, 2016," Pub. L. No. ACT NO. 49 (2016), https://legislative.gov.in/sites/default/files/A2016-49_1.pdf.

stating that disability is "an umbrella term encompassing impairments, activity limitations, and participation restrictions."[3] WHO goes on to admit, "disability is a complex phenomenon that arises from the interaction between an individual's bodily features and the societal context in which they live."[4]

Three important insights can be drawn from the above definitions. First, the distinction between "impairment" and "barriers" indicates disability is not simply about bodily impairment but includes society's negative response to that impairment. When combined, these create "disability." Second, disability is "complex" because it involves varying social responses that are not consistent across the whole spectrum of disability. Consequently, disability is an "umbrella term" which indicates there is a broad range of impairments and social responses that vary greatly.

Despite disability's complexities, scholars have identified a handful of disabling experiences shared by most Indians with disabilities. Social exclusion is cited both globally and in India as the most common disabling experience across the disability spectrum. In India, exclusion manifests within the family and in the wider society. It is compounded when combined with other marginalizing experiences like castes, gender, religion, and so forth. Poverty is another experience of disablement widely recognized as a common phenomenon among Indians with disabilities despite recent increases in government expenditure on disability issues. Forty-one percent of Indians with disabilities are multi-dimensionally poor and their poverty is exacerbated by a context of poverty:[5] India's low human development index of .633 which ranks 132nd globally and fifth among the eight SAARC nations.[6] Disability scholar Anita Ghai obverses a vicious cycle that exists between disability and poverty. "If you are poor, you are more likely to be disabled, and if you are disabled, you are more likely to be poor."[7] Finally, a lack of access to churches for Indians with disabilities is also an issue that holds particular relevance to the topic at hand. The limited geographic dispersal of churches in India coupled with attitudinal and physical barriers that are assumed to exist (as will be more fully interrogated below) prevents Indians with disabilities from experiencing the love and fellowship of Christ's people.

---

3. "Persons with Disabilities (Divyangjan) in India-A Statistical Profile: 2021" (Ministry of Statistics and Programme Implementation, Government of India, n.d.), 2, http://www.nhfdc.nic.in/upload/nhfdc/Persons_Disabilities_31mar21.pdf.

4. "Persons with Disabilities (Divyangjan) in India-A Statistical Profile: 2021," 2.

5. Mónica Pinilla-Roncancio et al., "Multidimensional Poverty and Disability: A Case Control Study in India, Cameroon, and Guatemala," *SSM—Population Health* 11 (May 3, 2020): 100591, https://doi.org/10.1016/j.ssmph.2020.100591.

6. United Nations, "Human Development Index," *Human Development Reports* (United Nations), accessed February 14, 2023, https://hdr.undp.org/data-center/human-development-index.

7. Anita Ghai, *Rethinking Disability in India* (New Delhi: Routledge India, 2017), 103.

Social exclusion, poverty, and lack of church access are areas of concern for disability advocates in the Church. In the following section, we will examine scholarly perspectives on the underlying causes for these issues.

Survey of Disability Models and Their Critiques

Scholars who are focused on social issues related to disability analyze the historical, political, and cultural factors behind the various constructs of disability and frame them as "models" of disability. The models most frequently analyzed in the literature are the moral model, the charity model, the medical model, and the social model. Below, I survey each model, briefly describe their secular critique, and offer a missiological response. Since this is a survey, my explanations of positions and responses only scratch the surface. But in scratching the surface, readers can begin to grapple with the issues and consider responses that are informed by some of the most respected voices in the field.

Moral Model of Disability

The moral model of disability is a traditional understanding of disability that has its roots in religious beliefs. The model asserts that disability is caused by the moral failing of the person with an impairment or of their family. Many disability advocates and scholars attribute disabling conditions in India to this model, as disability is widely associated with karmic retribution. Ghai emphasizes this perception, stating, "the common perception is that disability is retribution for past karma (actions) from which there can be no reprieve."[8] The stories and statements from Hinduism's authoritative texts, such as the Mahabharata, the Ramayana, and the Upanishads, further support these beliefs.[9] Consequently, disability is seen as a tragic fate befalling those with bad karma. Ghai observes, "perhaps, this notion was instrumental in the widespread belief that disabled people are seen as better dead than alive."[10]

Belief in karmic retribution also impacts the self-perception of individuals with disabilities. As Shubhangi Vaidya notes,

> Disablement is regarded not only as retribution for misdeeds committed in past lives, but also the consequent discrimination, marginalization, and suffering is to be internalized and borne in a spirit of resignation to atone for previous sins and transgressions.[11]

8. Ghai, *Rethinking Disability in India*, xx.

9. For a thorough overview see, Ghai, *Rethinking Disability in India*, 21–71.

10. Ghai, *Rethinking Disability in India*, xx.

11. Anita Ghai, ed., *Disability in South Asia: Knowledge and Experience* (New Delhi: Sage, 2018), 247.

This sense of retribution extends beyond the individual to the entire family such that the whole family is viewed as "karmically impaired" and experience social barriers as a consequence. Regrettably, the Christian community in India is not immune to this way of thinking about disability. Engage Disability India's *Disability Inclusion Toolkit*, asserts, "Unfortunately, this interpretation linking disability to sin has caused significant harm to people with disabilities and has become a source of exclusion even among Christians."[12]

Secular Critique of the Moral Model

Ghai argues that the moral model exists as an example of "othering." Drawing from Michael Foucault's theory of "The Other," the process of "othering" occurs when groups in power develop social constructs that portray other groups as less than human thereby justifying their marginalization and oppression.[13] According to Ghai, this "othering" is the basis for oppressive and marginalizing constructs of disability in India.[14] For traditional societies, the moral model provides a simplistic yet compelling explanation for disabilities, using spiritual language to justify the marginalization of people with disabilities and support the status quo.

Missiological Critique to the Moral Model

The theological arguments against the moral model are many and explaining them all here is beyond the scope of this chapter. What is more relevant from a missiological perspective is interrogating how the church came to adopt beliefs about people with disabilities that are clearly not biblical. Disability scholar Benjamin Conner argues that these wrong perceptions of disability are the result of the church becoming too indigenized within the surrounding culture (a reference to Andrew Wall's indigenizing principle).[15] Conner also helps us see how the church has a tendency to conflate manifestations of worldly power—prosperity, health, physical and mental prowess, influence, etc.—with God's power, and interpret this power as a sign of moral or spiritual superiority. Conversely, those without power are believed to suffer from some form of moral or spiritual dysfunction. Sadly, people with disabilities get entangled in this interpretation.

---

12. *Disability Inclusion Tool Kit* (India: Engage Disability India, 2016), 43, https://engagedisability.in/wp-content/uploads/engage_disability_toolkit_2019.pdf.

13. Ghai, *Disability in South Asia*, 300.

14. Ghai, *Disability in South Asia*, 300.

15. Benjamin T. Conner, *Disabling Mission, Enabling Witness: Exploring Missiology Through the Lens of Disability Studies*, Missiological Engagements (Downers Grove: IVP Academic, 2018), 42.

Charity Model of Disability

The charity model of disability is a response to disability that also has its roots in religious beliefs. Often inspired by religious teachings, this model encourages providing aid to the needy and fulfilling duties for the disabled, with the belief that such acts bring positive karma to the do-gooder. Likewise, Christians consider charitable acts toward people with disabilities as part of their Christian duty.

India has a long history of charitable initiatives toward people with disabilities. However, according to disability scholar Jagdish Chander, the perception and service toward Indians with disabilities gained greater importance only after the arrival of foreign missionaries in India.[16] Their presence, coupled with their international ties, brought about a new era of disability service in India.

Critique of the Charity Model

Since the charity model is linked to the benefactor's remission of sins, bad karma, fulfillment of religious duty, and the like, it is viewed by scholars as a construct that, like the moral model, exists to ultimately support the status quo rather than change it. The charity model helps maintain the benefactor's privileged position by securing for themselves the moral high ground through acts of charity and benevolence. Conversely, the charity model does little to alleviate the oppression and marginalization of the disabled and it is certainly not intended to empower them such that they have a voice in the social order. Usha Bhatt, one of India's early disability scholars, aptly asserts, "pity, although somewhat positive, makes its object feel inferior and fails to result in constructive efforts to improve the situation."[17]

Missiological Critique of the Charity Model

Disability theologian Amos Yong shares Bhatt's aversion to the charity model, arguing that the Judeo-Christian concern for those in need has often degenerated into treating people with disabilities as mere recipients of charity.[18] According to Yong, this influences a Christian's reading of Scripture and unintentionally reinforces the view that people with disabilities in the Bible are merely objects of charity.[19] From a mission history perspective, the charity model is strikingly similar to

---

16. Jagdish Chander, "Self-Advocacy and Blind Activists: The Origins of the Disability Rights Movement in Twentieth-Century India," in *Disability Histories*, ed. Susan Burch and Michael Rembis (Urbana: University of Illinois Press, 2014), 365.

17. Ghai, *Rethinking Disability in India*, 51.

18. For example, see Amos Yong, *The Bible Disability and the Church: A New Vision of the People of God* (Grand Rapids, MI: Eerdmans, 2011), 10–12.

19. Yong, *The Bible Disability and the Church*, 10–12.

the past belief held by foreign missionaries that indigenous people were incapable of leading themselves and would always require the benevolence and leadership of the foreign "Mother Church" for guidance and care. A similar sense of paternalism, superiority, and dependence pervades the charity model of disability.

Medical Model of Disability

The medical model continues the assumptions of the moral and charity models and views impairment as the cause for an individual's suffering and disablement in society. However, it distinguishes itself from the two previous models by demystifying the cause of impairment, rejecting sin and bad karma as causes, and instead turning to science for answers and solutions.

The medical model emerged in India from the nineteenth century from the medical missions movement which became a willing vehicle of modern advances in the medical sciences. Advances in rehabilitation following World War II fueled a global rehabilitation movement that worked from the premise that people with disabilities could become self-reliant contributors to society through the rigorous application of medical and rehabilitative techniques.

Secular Critique of the Medical Model

The medical model, though seemingly a step in the right direction, led to several developments that proved problematic. First, its use of science to label impairments as "abnormal" had powerful, negative implications for people with disabilities. Put in Ghai's terms of "othering," the medical model mobilized arguably the most powerful ideological force in human history to provide a scientific basis for "othering."[20] Second, the labeling of abnormality led to exclusionary societal responses, some of which were highly objectionable. These included the mass institutionalization of those with cognitive or mental disabilities, eugenics practices like the forced sterilization of the congenitally disabled, and, in some cases, the extermination of those deemed unfit to live.[21] Third, postcolonial critics argue that the global scale of the medical model displaced indigenous constructs that were more inclusive and culturally relevant. Fourth, people with disabilities continued to be portrayed as objects of pity by medical institutions which further reinforced stigma. Finally, the approach continued to deflect attention away from society's responsibility for social barriers. While the medical model is largely rejected by disability scholars, ongoing efforts by the medical

---

20. See Ghai, *Rethinking Disability in India*, 306–307.

21. For a detailed summary of the history of eugenics, see Amos Yong, *Theology and Down Syndrome: Reimagining Disability in Late Modernity* (Waco, TX: Baylor University Press, 2007), 49–54.

establishment to reduce or eliminate impairment are hotly contested by secular scholars as vestiges of the medical model. Their reasoning will become clear in the description of the social model below.

Missiological Critique of the Medical Model

Disability scholars generally have a negative view of the foreign medical missions movement because they contend Christian missionaries introduced the medical model and its corrosive effects to India. Moreover, Christian medical institutions remain involved in aspects of the medical model that disability scholars deem controversial, such as reducing or correcting impairment. Their reasons for holding these views will be introduced below, along with critiques of these views. What is important here is to be open to critics of the medical model and I believe a brief recap of colonial mission history will help us see things from their perspective.

Western missionaries once portrayed indigenous people as abnormal because their ethnicity, culture, superstitions, and traditional beliefs where considered retrograde. Hence, their approach to missions was to "normalize" indigenous people by replacing their culture and traditions with Western culture. This was grounded in the belief that Western culture exemplified the very definition of being made in God's image. What this view failed to realize was that all people are created in God's image and all cultures have God's creative stamp on them. Both manifest the great diversity of God's human creation. Likewise, the medical model fails to recognize the possibility that some impairments may not be impairments at all but examples of the physical and cognitive diversity of human creation. This will be explored more fully below.

Social Model of Disability

The social model of disability pioneered a powerful, new way of thinking about disability that broke from previous models. At the core of this model lies the belief that "impairment" is not a deficit to be eliminated but a facet of human diversity. Disability arises not from impairment itself but from society's failure to accommodate such diversity. Therefore, the social model focuses on promoting the rights of the disabled and removing barriers in all realms of society (physical, social, political, educational, employment, religious, etc.) in order to create a more just and inclusive world.

The social model emerged from the disability rights movements of the 1970s in the United States and spread to India in the 1980s.[22] In India, this move-

---

22. For a more detailed overview of the movement in India see, Jagdish Chander, "Disability Rights Law and Origin of Disability Rights Movement in India," in *Disability in South Asia: Knowledge and Experience*, ed. Anita Ghai (New Delhi: Sage, 2018), 3–20.

ment was supported by legislation first through the Persons with Disabilities Act (1995) and then the Rights of Persons with Disabilities Act (2016). The Indian church followed suit by formulating its own conventions, declarations, and policies centered on disability inclusion and empowerment. Recent examples include the Engage Disability India National Conference (2022)[23] and the National Council of Churches document "India's Disability Inclusion Policy Guidelines" (2019).[24]

Secular Critique of the Social Model

Despite the positive influence of the social model in promoting disability rights and securing greater inclusion in society, the social model is not without its critics. Scholars like Meenu Bhambhani,[25] Miles and Houssain,[26] and Rao and Kalyanpur[27] argue that while the social model prioritizes human rights and equity-related issues, people with disabilities in developing economies like India grapple with challenges related to basic survival. Moreover, rights-based approaches to solving problems of exclusion do not always serve the best interests of the disabled in their communities.[28] Yong adds that the social model may not adequately represent the experiences of those with intellectual disabilities.[29] Critics also challenge the model's tendency to downplay the body and imply that impairment is not a problem.[30] Science may not explain the totality of bodily experiences in terms of normal or impaired but it can explain some things in those terms and is useful in India where correction of impairment is vital to flourishing in a social context that is filled with disabling conditions. Finally, the social model's focus on securing individual rights and agency privileges

23. Shemron S. Vinod and Jessica Richard, "Persons with Disabilities Take Centre Stage at the Third National Conference of Engage Disability 2022" (Hyderabad, TG: Engage Disability India, November 26, 2022), https://engagedisability.in/2022/12/03/persons-with-disabilities-take-centre-stage-at-the-third-national-conference-of-engage-disability-2022/.

24. "Disability Inclusion Policy Guidelines (2019)" (National Council of Churches in India—Indian Disability Ecumenical Accompaniment (IDEA), 2019), https://ncci1914.com/wp-content/uploads/2019/09/8.2-Disability-Policy-Guidelines-Final-presented-in-EC-1-Mar-2019.pdf.

25. Ghai, *Disability in South Asia*, 26.

26. Ghai, *Disability in South Asia*, 39.

27. Shridevi Rao and Maya Kalyanpur, *South Asia and Disability Studies: Redefining Boundaries and Extending Horizons*, vol. 15, Disability Studies in Education (New York: Peter Lang, 2015), 6.

28. Rao and Kalyanpur, *South Asia and Disability Studies*, 15:6.

29. Yong, *Theology and Down Syndrome*, Kindle edition.

30. Rao and Kalyanpur, *South Asia and Disability Studies*, 15:290.

individualist cultures over collectivist ones. Ultimately, the conclusion of many disability scholars in India, and of theologians of disability in general, is that the social model of disability does not fully represent everyone's experience of disability and cannot be fully applied in the Indian context.

Missiological Response to the Social Model

As noted above, the church in India has been positively influenced by the social model. Theological discourse has also benefited from its influence as manifested through a new field of theology known as "disability theology," a disability-informed theological perspective that argues, among other things, that all are made in God's image, all must be included in the body of Christ, and disability is an aspect of human diversity. However, just as postcolonial critiques have identified the tendency of social model advocates to downplay bodily impairments so also disability theologians can downplay bodily impairments; even questioning healing narratives that they interpret as aligning Jesus with a medical model approach.[31] What appears to be behind this tendency is the same tendency that is apparent in the social model; a tendency to universalize and privilege the disability experiences of the West and impose assumptions of Western individualism and individual agency onto other cultures. For this reason, it is vital that Indian theologians of disability and practitioners in the fields of medicine, rehabilitation, and community-based service, and Indians with disabilities themselves, critically analyze the disability constructs propagated by the West, drawing out that which is helpful in the Indian context and discarding that which is unhelpful.

Postcolonial Critique

As alluded to above, Indian scholars influenced by postmodern or postcolonial thought, are questioning the validity of disability models that are projected as universal. Consequently, they argue that neither the medical model nor the social model adequately capture the complexity of the disability experience. They contend that disability constructs vary across cultures and appropriate responses to disability depend on the local context. Tom Shakespeare echoes the sentiments of many postcolonial or postmodernist thinkers in India when he asserts that "disability is the quintessential post-modern concept because it is so complex, variable, contingent, and situated."[32]

---

31. See Yong's analysis of the debate in Yong, *Theology and Down Syndrome*, 227–258.

32. Tom Shakespeare and Nicholas Watson, "The Social Model of Disability: An Outdated Ideology?," *Research in Social Science and Disability* 2 (2002): 19.

Accordingly, Kalyanpur and Rao question the universality of disability constructs propagated by international institutions like the UN and WHO since they rely heavily on Western notions of individualism, agency, justice, and equity. They argue, "the time has come for moving beyond Northern constructions of disability" and believe disability constructs and responses should be based on local epistemologies, languages, and realities.[33] They support a "strength-based perspective" to disability which places the strengths and resources of individuals, communities, and their environments at the core of disability responses, rather than focusing on problems and pathologies. Ghai adds that reversing disabling views within society requires that society adopt an "epistemology of disability," that is, an understanding of the world from the perspective of people with disabilities.[34] She believes academia and specifically the field of disability studies has a pivotal role in disseminating this disability epistemology throughout Indian society.[35]

Missiological Response to Postcolonial Critique

I believe most in the field of missiology will find the postcolonial critique quite compelling. The emphasis on the local context, the value it places on local constructs of disability, and the call to critically evaluate non-local concepts of disability align well with basic tenants of contextualization and cultural sensitivity. However, as with most postmodern, postcolonial theories, there are issues that evoke criticism. The first and most glaring from a Christian perspective is the fact that the postcolonial critique and its foils, the medical and social models of disability, do not engage with religion other than to critique its complicity with disablement. Since so much of Indian society's opinion about disability is shaped by religion one would expect more proactive, positive engagement with religions. Furthermore, spirituality is an important aspect of coping and finding meaning amid experiences of marginalization. Second, Ghai's call for Indian society to embrace a disability epistemology is noteworthy since it seeks cultural transformation as the solution. But her epistemology is not grounded in anything except the experience of people with disabilities. Likewise, Rao and Kalyanpur's proposal for an ongoing North/South discourse is notable but it too lacks grounds for determining what are true and false constructs of disability. This lack of grounding in anything other than one's experiences can lead to moral relativism and lacks any constructive alternative to that which is criticized. When

---

33. Rao and Kalyanpur, *South Asia and Disability Studies: Redefining Boundaries and Extending Horizons*, 15:289.

34. Ghai, *Rethinking Disability in India*, 319–323.

35. Ghai, *Rethinking Disability in India*, 323–325.

alternatives are offered, they inevitably privilege some experiences over others with no legitimate grounds to do so.

In summary, the models of disability and their associated critiques all have weaknesses. The moral model is not only erroneous but exists to deflect societal culpability. The charity model suffers the same problem but also insidiously disguises itself as charitable when it is in fact a manifestation of a benefactor's self-interest. The medical model uses one of the most powerful ideologies in history—science—to construct universal definitions of disability that can create and reinforce stigma and continues the game of deflecting blame away from society to the individual. The social model helpfully identifies the role society plays in disability but can be as guilty as the medical model in imposing an approach that is foreign and negates local constructs in the process. And, finally, the postcolonial critique is right in emphasizing local constructs but lacks a foundation on which to develop and implement alternatives to that which it criticizes.

A Missiological Response to What We Have Learned

Amid these flawed conceptions of disability and the weaknesses of their critiques, what does the church in India have to offer people with disabilities and how should the church proceed? The following attempt at answering these questions is not intended to be exhaustive but touches on some of the most pressing issues identified in the analysis above.

What Can the Church Offer?

First, the church can offer the gospel as the grounds for understanding disability; a grounding that is universally accepted by the global church and provides the church a basis for its disability discourse locally and globally—something the postcolonial critique does not have. Admittedly, certain interpretations of Scripture have led to exclusionary beliefs and practices represented by the moral model. Yet, it has also guided the church to renounce those interpretations and practices. In fact, often, it has inspired exemplary practices of compassion and inclusion that resist the errors within the moral model and the charity model. Moreover, it allows for engagement with spiritual issues that are of central importance to most Indians yet completely missing in the solutions offered by the social model and postcolonial critique. Such engagement has the potential for spreading the disability epistemology Ghai seeks but in a way that is much more profound since it calls people to go beyond "putting on the mind of disability" and instead calls them to "put on the mind of Christ" (Phil 2:5). The mind of Christ, for which disability theologians have provided greater clarity, accepts all people regardless of ability as created in the image of the Triune God. This counters the moral model that views impairment as a sign of corrupted humanness resulting from sin or bad karma and replaces it with the possibility of interpreting impairment as a manifestation of human diversity or an anomaly that can be corrected. Furthermore, disability theologians have pointed out that a Trinitarian perspective paves the way for seeing interdependent relationship as the fundamental characteristic of our image bearing, thus enabling the church to accept even the most dependent of persons as fully reflecting God's image. In other words, dependence is not a sign of disability but a sign of the Triune God.

Second, churches as the representatives of the Triune God, can offer the kind of mutuality, friendship, and acceptance of people with disabilities that is reflective of humanity's Triune image and repeatedly mentioned in the literature as necessary for the flourishing of people with disabilities.[36] In the Indian context, this friendship will include relationships not just with the individual with disability but their family members and possibly even the broader community, keeping in mind the communitarian nature of the disability experience in India. As all stakeholders come together, the dialogue does not begin with changing impairment or social barriers, but prayer as exemplified in the Serenity Prayer: "God, grant us the serenity to accept the things we cannot change, courage to change the things we can, and the wisdom to know the difference."

Third, this friendship needs to entail not just mutual affection and listening but concrete acts of service and advocacy that most Indians affected by disability require to flourish. With almost two centuries of experience ministering to Indians with disabilities through its sister institutions working in the fields of medicine, rehabilitation, educational institutions, job training, and community development, the church in India is well positioned to offer this service and advocacy. But it should do so following a "strength-based approach" recommended by the postcolonialists, yet also guided by the universal truths of Scripture.

Fourth, the local, regional, and global connections of the church in India also position it to offer the disability discourse that postcolonialists believe is vital for learning new insights and practices. In fact, this has been taking place for decades (if not centuries) and received additional impetus through the formation of the Engage Disability India network in 2014.[37] Moreover, the church in India has over two millennia of experience in contextualizing new insights and practices that effectively reach the grassroots in ways that are culturally relevant and transformative. This practical, grassroots impact is something postcolonialists and social model advocates still struggle with.

---

36. For example, see Samuel George, *Church and Disability* (Delhi: Indian Society for Promoting Christian Knowledge, 2021), 38–39.; Yong, *Theology and Down Syndrome*, 173–174; Conners, *Disabling Mission: Enabling Mission*, 113–114

37. See "Engage Disability India," accessed September 29, 2023, https://engagedisability.in/.

Finally, along with the Indian church's vast network comes access to their resources and technical expertise. The church in India already is a conduit for resources and technical expertise from local, regional, and global sources which have reached into some of the most remote communities in India and filled voids that are not being filled by the government or local communities. Granted, this is a passionately contested issue and many of the criticisms are valid. When rightly applied, the sharing of resources and technical expertise can not only have a transformative impact, but also is a reflection of the interdependent nature of our human existence. If the question is right application, then the church in India has access to an epistemological and ethical perspective that ensures resources and technical assistance are rightly applied.

How Should the Church Proceed?

The first priority of the church in India should be to exemplify disability inclusion within the church. This inclusion does not simply mean inclusion as members of congregations but inclusion in leadership roles, as missionaries, service professionals within parachurch organizations, and members of staff, volunteers, and so forth. In other words, Indians with disabilities should be part of the church at every level and within every manifestation of the church. This is necessary for several reasons. As alluded to above, Indians with disabilities and their families need the friendship, spiritual nurturing, and, if necessary, services that the church can provide. Conversely, the church needs Indians with disabilities not only to reveal a new way of thinking about God that exposes the lies of power and privilege, but also to reveal a new way of thinking about humanity. Accordingly, Conner asserts,

> People with disabilities are understood to be an essential part of the diversity of the human experience and necessary contributors to the calling of the church to bear witness to the ongoing redemptive work of God in this world by proclaiming the kingdom of God is at hand.[38]

The best hope the church has in disseminating a disability epistemology that reflects the mind of Christ is to have people with disabilities in their midst, relating as equals within the church at all levels, and sharing their gifts and perspective with the church. In turn, this will witness to India what true, disability inclusion looks like.

Second, the church in India needs to multiply since the vast majority of communities in India lack a congregation. This is not a call to multiply monuments of denominational, caste, or ethnic identity but a call to multiply Christward

---

38. Conner, *Disabling Mission, Enabling Witness*, 59.

movements wherein existing identities are transformed by the mind of Christ in ways that are culturally relevant. Indians with disabilities, their families, and their communities need these Christward mission movements. Granted, the church in India is faced with new challenges that are making mission increasingly difficult. But missiologist Prabhu Singh believes these new challenges call us not to abandon our mission but to employ new approaches that are creative, contextualized, and courageous.[39] One relatively newer paradigm that holds promise is the house church movement that has seen scores of Indian come to Christ over the last two decades.[40] In the book *Undivided Witness*, David Greenlee and colleagues provide a groundbreaking glimpse at how mission is accomplished among the marginalized in contexts resistant to the gospel.[41] Regardless of the mission strategy, the lesson is this: just as the postcolonialists have called for a new construct of disability that reflects Indian realities, so also the church in India must create new constructs of mission that act as catalysts of disability inclusion reflective of the Triune God in whose image all humanity is made.

39. Prabhu Singh, "Surfing the Third Wave of Missions in India," *Lausanne Global Analysis*, March 2017, https://lausanne.org/content/lga/2017-03/surfing-the-third-wave-of-missions-in-india.

40. For examples, see Victor John and Dave Coles, *Bhojpuri Breakthrough: A Movement That Keeps Multiplying* (Monument, CO: WIGTake Resources, 2019).

41. David Greenlee, Mark Galpin, and Paul Bendor-Samuel, *Undivided Witness: Jesus Followers, Community Development, and Least Reached Communities* (Oxford: Regnum Books International, 2020).

CHAPTER SEVENTEEN

Envisioning Mission as "Walking Alongside" amid the Mental Health Crisis in India

Joy Jemima Singh and Allan Varghese Meloottu

Introduction

ACCORDING TO THE World Health Organization (WHO), mental health is defined as "a state of mental well-being that enables people to cope with the stresses of life, realize their abilities . . . and contribute to their community."[1] Mental health as a discipline includes various professions, such as psychology, psychiatry, counseling, psychotherapy, and social work. All of these contribute to understanding and improving the well-being of a person which in turn affects multiple dimensions of their life. This holistic model is also known as the *bio-psycho-social model*.[2] Because the field of mental health is vast in its practice and focus, it is impossible to map all the contemporary developments in each field that pertains to it. Furthermore, it would be daunting to comprehend the full diversity of the mental health field within the vast growing demographics of India which includes multiple ethnoreligious diversities. Therefore, the goal of this chapter is not to provide an exhaustive analysis of the field of mental health in India but to highlight historical and current beliefs and practices. Consequently, this chapter presents an introductory analysis of the mental health crisis in India from a missiological framework as we believe that is pivotal for Christian missiological integration.

While India's rich cultural heritage and community-based culture is an asset in fostering human well-being, India is also facing a huge mental health crisis which has further deteriorated since the Covid-19 pandemic.[3] Not only does India have one of the highest prevalences of mental illness, but there is also a shortage of psychiatrists and psychologists. India is estimated to have only

1. World Health Organization, "Mental Health" (June 2022), accessed April 10, 2023, https://www.who.int/news-room/fact-sheets/detail/mental-health-strengthening-our-response.

2. G. L. Engel, "The need for a new medical model: A challenge for biomedicine," *Science* 196 (1977): 129–136.

3. Amanda Ryan, "India's Mental Health Epidemic: Deteriorating amidst the Pandemic," *Towson University Journal of International Affairs* (May 2021), https://wp.towson.edu/iajournal/2021/05/10/indias-mental-health-epidemic-deteriorating-amidst-the-pandemic/.

"0.75 psychiatrists for every 100,000 patients."[4] Due to the need and the shortage of professionals, any conversation concerning Christian missional engagement in India should not overlook this crisis. To attain that objective, first we shall provide a brief historical discussion on mental health practices in India, cultural perceptions, and the challenges it presents. Second, considering Indian Christian understanding of mental health, we propose a missiological paradigm of "walking alongside" (informed by the experience of disciples on the road to Emmaus) to respond to the mental health crises. In doing so, we hope this analysis will serve as a conversation starter to encourage Christians to engage in mental health pursuits to advocate for a long-term change in Indian society.

Mental Health Engagement in India

In using the phrase "mental health concerns," for the sake of this chapter, we are referring to a broader definition as put forth in India's Mental Health Care Act (2017). The act defines "'mental health disorders' as a substantial disorder of thinking, mood, perception, orientation, or memory that grossly impairs judgment or ability to meet the ordinary demands of life, mental conditions associated with the abuse of alcohol and drugs."[5]

Although mental health professions are gaining ground in India, we find that there is a lack of engagement in society and culture in regard to mental health related concerns. The Covid-19 pandemic only highlighted this gap and brought it to the forefront. However, to engage in the contemporary aspects of mental health, it is vital to have a brief historical understanding of the perspectives, services, and practices surrounding mental health in India.

Historical and Statistical Outlook

During the first half of the twentieth century, the resources available for people struggling with mental health disorders were limited, and the scope was seen as "custodial rather than therapeutic."[6] As seen in the enactment of the 1912 Indian Lunacy Act—which was the first of its kind—the goal was to protect the masses from people with mental health disorders rather than to provide support for the

---

4. Anisha Padukone, "India's Mental Health Conversation is Opening Up: Better Access to Treatment is the Next Frontier," *World Economic Forum* (Feb 2022), https://www.weforum.org/agenda/2022/02/india-mental-health/

5. Quoted in A. Mishra A. Galhotra, "Mental Healthcare Act 2017: Need to Wait and Watch," *International Journal of Applied & Basic Medical Research* 8, no. 2 (2018): 68.

6. N. G. Desai, S. C. Tiwari, S. Nambi, B. Shah, R. A. Singh, D. Kumar, J. K. Trivedi, V. Palaniappan, A. Tripathi, C. Pali, N. Pal, A. Maurya, and M. Mathew, "Urban Mental Health Services in India: How Complete or Incomplete?," *Indian Journal of Psychiatry* 46, no. 3 (2004): 195–212.

patient to be able to function better. Such a "custodial" notion of mental health care was evident in how asylums were placed far from cities, with heightened security presences comparable to prisons.

However, the growth in caring for those struggling with mental health disorders has been progressing, albeit slowly. In the 1970s, qualitative change began with the setting up of General Hospital Psychiatry Units (GHPUs). According to Desai and colleagues, "the next breakthrough came about in the 80s, with the increasing involvement of NGOs and the private sector in providing mental health care to the community."[7] Additionally, the 1982 National Mental Health Program (NMHP) provided a framework for mental health services and decentralized care, making them more approachable to the general population.[8] In 2013, the Mental Health Care Bill was presented in Parliament and was launched in 2014 as the first national mental health policy. It was further revised as the Mental Health Care Act in 2017, "with the objectives of providing equitable, affordable, and universal access to mental health care."[9] Furthermore, a recent India state-level study from the Indian Council of Medical Research, New Delhi[10] and the National Mental Health Survey of India 2015–16 from the National Institute of Mental Health and Neurosciences (NIMHANS) Bengaluru[11] also shed further light on the current state of mental health disorders and the lapse in health institutions meeting the challenges in the nation.

The recent statistical estimation, based on the 2017 study, states that "197.3 million (95% uncertainty intervals; 178.4–216.4) people had mental health disorders in India, including 45.7 million . . . with depressive disorders and 44.9 million . . . with anxiety disorders."[12] This proportion leads to the estimate that "one in seven Indians were affected by mental disorders of varying

---

7. Desai et al., "Urban Mental Health Services in India," 196.

8. As part of this decentralization plan, as Desai et al. notes, "two pilot projects at NIMHANS, Bangalore and PGIMER, Chandigarh, [were launched encouraging] the integration of mental health with Primary Health care . . . at the district level covering a population of two million between 1984 and 1990" (Desai et al., "Urban Mental Health Services in India," 197).

9. India State-Level Disease Burden Initiative Mental Disorders Collaborators. "The Burden of Mental Disorders across the States of India: The Global Burden of Disease Study 1990–2017." *Lancet Psychiatry* 7, no. 2 (February 2020): 149.

10. India State-Level Disease Burden Initiative Mental Disorders Collaborators. "The Burden of Mental Disorders across the States of India."

11. National Institute of Mental Health and Neurosciences. *National Mental Health Survey of India, 2015–16: Summary* (Bengaluru, 2016), 1–62. Available at http://indianmhs.nimhans. ac.in/Docs/Summary.pdf

12. India State-Level Disease Burden Initiative Mental Disorders Collaborators. "The Burden of Mental Disorders across the States of India," 148.

severity in 2017."[13] Furthermore, the National Mental Health Survey of India (NMHSI) indicates that "1 in 20 people in India suffer from depression."[14] We also find a high prevalence of substance use disorders.

In contemporary India, a key factor influencing the trajectory of mental health disorders is the rapid urbanization of India and the rising mental health concerns among the urbanites.[15] According to NMHSI, "the prevalence of schizophrenia and other psychoses (0.64%), mood disorders (5.6%) and neurotic or stress-related disorders (6.93%) was nearly 2–3 times more in urban metros."[16] With continuing urbanization, experts are only expecting a rise in these trends and calls for "an urban specific mental health program."[17]

It is also important to highlight the gender differentials concerning mental health illness. While mental health disorders are prevalent in men, women, and children, there is a higher rate of stress-related disorders among women, "nearly twice as much as males."[18] The NMHSI notes that "specific mental disorders like mood disorders, depression, neurotic disorders, phobic anxiety disorders, agoraphobia, generalized anxiety disorders, and obsessive-compulsive disorders were higher in females."[19] Furthermore, given the cultural backdrop of patriarchal practices fueling gender discrimination—marrying at a young age, husbands' substance misuse habits, and domestic violence—it seem like females are almost "predisposed to mental disorders" as Venkatashiva Reddy and colleagues put it.[20]

---

13. India State-Level Disease Burden Initiative Mental Disorders Collaborators. "The Burden of Mental Disorders across the States of India," 148.

14. National Institute of Mental Health and Neurosciences. *National Mental Health Survey of India,* 16.

15. Jitendra K. Trivedi, Himanshu Sareen, and Mohan Dhyani, "Rapid Urbanization—Its Impact on Mental Health: A South Asian Perspective, *Indian Journal of Psychiatry* 50, no. 3 (2008).

16. National Institute of Mental Health and Neurosciences, *National Mental Health Survey of India,* 15.

17. National Institute of Mental Health and Neurosciences, *National Mental Health Survey of India,* 15.

18. National Institute of Mental Health and Neurosciences, *National Mental Health Survey of India,* 21.

19. National Institute of Mental Health and Neurosciences, *National Mental Health Survey of India,* 19.

20. Venkatashiva Reddy B., Arti Gupta, Ayush Lohiya, and Pradip Kharya, "Mental Health Issues and Challenges in India: A Review," *International Journal of Scientific and Research Publications* 3, no. 2 (2013): 2.

Cultural Beliefs, Stigma and the Existence of "Non-Medical Models" of Engaging with Mental Health

India is a collectivistic culture that places a high emphasis on community and its core values include harmony and collectivism. Indian culture promotes health and healing through close-knit families and religious communities. While this can be a powerful tool to foster communal-based therapeutic approaches toward mental health, it has also become detrimental in some ways. Irrespective of urban or rural India, there is a lack of space for individual retrospection to keep personal emotional well-being in check. Furthermore, there is also less room for critical reflection to challenge age-old beliefs and traditions that impede the flourishing of mental health individually and communally. The general expectation to perform and carry on these traditions adds on to the pressure and certainly has a detrimental effect.

People with mental health disorders feel alienated due to social stigma. Although popular notions are changing positively where people are becoming more concerned about mental health, deep-rooted communal factors are still firmly situated causing social stigma in the Indian context. Stigma surrounds anyone who admits they struggle with their mental health due to the cultural belief that mental health struggles are associated with weakness or inadequacy. In 1982 while discussing the present state of psychotherapy in India, V. K. Verma highlighted seven distinct features of the Indian population that impede the practical impact of psychotherapy in Indian practice.[21] Verma's observation include concerns that the common populace lack the verbal abilities to reflect emotionally, hierarchical notions between the doctor and patient resulting in the patient's unwillingness to express their thoughts, religious belief in rebirth and fatalism, the social notion of shame, lower emphasis on confidentiality as a society, and a lapse in personal responsibility to implement change.[22] Consequently, "the stigmatized individual experiences social distancing, fear, rejection and ill treatment from others in the society."[23] This stigmatization can be attributed to the socioreligious belief about the *source* of an illness and intervention.

The extent of these beliefs is also reflected in how medical professionals address mental health conditions. Within the Indian socioreligious cultural

---

21. V. K. Varma, "Present State of Psychotherapy in India," *Indian Journal of Psychiatry* 24, no. 3 (1982): 211–214.

22. We understand stigma as a negative attitude attached to a person due to a condition they struggle with. "Stigma results from a process whereby certain individuals and groups are unjustifiably rendered shameful, excluded and discriminated against" (quoted in Ramaprasad Dharitri, Suryanarayan N. Rao, S. Kalyanasundaram, "Stigma of Mental Illness: An Interventional Study to Reduce its Impact in the Community, *Indian Journal of Psychiatry* 57, no. 2 (2015): 166.

23. Dharitri et al., "Stigma of Mental Illness," 166.

context, the chief cause of mental disorders or conditions is ascribed to the breach of taboo (misdeed) either by the victim or by their ancestors in their present life or previous incarnation. Other common reasons are personal sin, evil intent, angry deities, soul loss, intrusion by various elements, sorcery, and so forth. For example, as Ramakrishna Biswall and colleagues note, "a prevalent belief among rural villagers is that if a person had killed a cow during his past life, he would suffer from mental illness in the present life."[24] These beliefs are not isolated incidences. Instead, it is a common occurrence to the extent scholars have noted them as "non-medical models of mental health disorders" existing parallel to the "medical model" that "adheres to an objective and scientific analysis of mental health conditions."[25] The etiological explanations of mental health disorders centering around "spirit possession, witchcraft, breaking of religious taboos, divine retribution, capture of the soul by spirit, and many more"[26] makes the non-medical models practiced by traditional healers the first point of consultation for people with mental illness.[27]

Now that we have briefly outlined the general contour of mental health discussion in the Indian context and examined it as an impeding challenge, it is essential to reflect upon how Christians may position their mission to engage those who struggle with mental health.

Mental Health Understandings, Indian Christians, and the Missiological Implications

In the Indian Church context, it is common to find theologies that promote the idea that mental health disorders are a result of a "lack of intimacy with God," or due to "a specific sin," or "demonic influence."[28] This thinking has caused a strong belief, that if one believes in God and has a "good" relationship with God, one will not struggle with mental health disorders. This belief

---

24. Biswal R, Subudhi C, Acharya SK. "Healers and Healing Practices of Mental Illness in India: The Role of Proposed Eclectic Healing Model," *Journal of Health Research and Reviews* 4, no. 3 (2017): 92. https://www.jhrr.org/text.asp?2017/4/3/89/216066

25. Biswal et al., "Healers and Healing Practices of Mental Illness in India," 89.

26. Biswal et al., "Healers and Healing Practices of Mental Illness in India," 89.

27. Through the analysis of other existing studies, Biswal et al. states that "45% of psychiatric patients have sought about 1–15 sessions with folk healers in South India and nearly about 40% of patients consult faith healers in Northern India before resorting to psychiatric care" (Biswal et al., "Healers and Healing Practices of Mental Illness in India," 92).

28. Paul D. Meier, Frank B. Minirth, Frank B. Wichern and Donald E. Ratcliff, *Introduction to Psychology and Counselling: Christian Perspectives and Applications*, 2nd ed. (Grand Rapids, MI: Baker Books, 1991), 257–261.

puts unconscious pressure on people to sustain the image of being perfect or having a good relationship with God thus causing them to suppress and even deny the existence of their mental health struggles. Within the Indian cultural context, where folk beliefs, spirit possessions, witchcraft, and the like are popularly seen as sources of mental health disorders, we find that Christian communities also fall prey to such notions without critically examining them scripturally.

These strong convictions fail to account for the undeniable gravity of the existential reality of sin that influences humanity.[29] At the same time, to blame a specific act of sin as a cause for mental health disorder would be a grave mistake, as we see the sinful reality has marred all aspects of humanity—contributing to the genetic and biological aspects of mental illness. Therefore, as Monica Thomas Chandy and Jamila Koshy note, the question of whether mental disorders are a "sin" or "medical illness" is based on faulty reasoning. They write,

> It is not an either or situation. All the aspects of a problem need to be handled, the biological part by therapies, and indeed, in this case, by warning those with addictions in a family to never even "try" a possibly addictive substance; the psychological, social, and the spiritual part can be helped by therapy and pastoral counseling. Similarly, it is without a doubt now that many mental illnesses have a genetic–a biological–contribution, and cannot be branded as "sin" alone.[30]

In other words, it is important to recognize that there is a holistic theological and physiological rationale toward understanding mental illness, than just attributing the causation solely to a particular sin or spirit possession. Nonetheless, missionally, the church is called to meet people where they are in their mental health journey.

Although, historically, mental health or psychological aspects were not incorporated into missiological inquiries (predominantly evangelical), in 2004, the *Holistic Mission Issue Group of the Lausanne Movement Forum for World Evangelization* explicitly included mental health as part of a holistic mission. The report notes: "Holistic mission is mission oriented toward the satisfaction of basic human needs, including the need of God, but also the need of food, love,

---

29. One could trace the causation of mental health illness to the reality of sin, which has marred the divine image in human beings and led to misplacing our source of security, self-worth, and significance from God to self or others. Selwyn Hughes, *Christ Empowered Living* (Surrey, UK: CWR, 2002), 99–135.

30. Monica Thomas Chandy and Jamila Koshy, "Public Health and Mental Health," in *Public Theology: Exploring Expressions of the Christian Faith*, ed. Bonnie Miriam Jacob (Traci Publications: New Delhi, 2020), 352–353.

housing, clothes, physical and *mental health* and a sense of human dignity."[31] Furthermore, in 2009, the Movement created a new Senior Associate role in Care and Counsel as Mission. In 2016, the focus on mental health was defined as "Global Mental Health and Trauma" (GMHT),[32] reinstating the importance of mental health in missiological discourse.

With such a development in global missiological thinking, it would also be appropriate to imagine a model conducive to meeting the mental health challenges in the Indian context. Therefore, in the final session, we propose a missiological approach as *walking alongside*, specifically considering the mental health challenges. The paradigm is constructed from the scriptural passage that recounts the experiences of two disciples on the road to Emmaus (Luke 24: 13–35).

Mental Health Practices as Mission "Walking Alongside"

In Luke 24: 13–33, Luke narrates the story of two disciples on the way to Emmaus from Jerusalem on the same day the news of Jesus's resurrection started circulating. As they talked to each other about what was happening, a third person, Jesus, came near and walked with them. "But their eyes were kept from recognizing him" (v. 16). Furthermore, as they looked sad, Jesus asked, "What are you discussing with each other while you walk along?" (v. 17, NRSV). Jesus's open-ended question led to a very engaging back and forth conversation, possibly an emotionally animated one, which gave room for the disciples to open up about the issue that caused them a deep mental health distress. In the narration, Luke makes sure to incorporate the emotional presentation of the disciples, who were grieving Jesus's death and trying to make sense of the news of his body being missing (v. 23). Such an exchange led to the disciples' emotional response which Luke phrases as "hearts burning." Although Luke's account on the conversation abruptly ends as Jesus "vanished from their sight" as they arrived at Emmaus (v. 31), when the disciples reflected, they asked each other, "Were not our *hearts burning* within us while he was talking to us on the road, while he was opening the scriptures to us?" (v. 32). The word, *kaieomene*, translated as "burning," used here to communicate an "emotional experience,"[33] perhaps an "intense inner

---

31. C. R. Padilla, "Holistic Mission," *Lausanne Occasional Paper No. 33: Holistic Mission* (2005), 11–23, https://lausanne.org/content/holistic-mission-lop-33. Emphasis added.

32. https://lausanne.org/content/lga/turning-the-churchs-attention-to-mental-health; Consequently, in 2021, Lausanne produced eleven videos under the *Lausanne Global Classroom: Mental Health and Trauma* to serve the global church to think of Mental Health aspects in light of Mission. (https://lausanne.org/lausanne-global-classroom/mental-health-and-trauma-episode)

33. Frederick William Danker. *A Greek-English Lexicon of the New Testament and other Early Christian Literature*, 3rd ed., (Chicago: University of Chicago Press, 2000), 499.

warmth."[34] Although, scholars are not sure of the full extent of the meaning, the emotionality of the phrase is undeniable.

While one can identify various missiological themes from the above Lukean narration, we would like to emphasis the theme of *walking alongside* as Jesus walked alongside the disciples. Furthermore, in light of the mental health conversations, the use of *emotive language* (hearts burning) in the disciples' reflection provides an apt reason for missiological integration. However, more specifically, we take inspiration from Jesus's posture in the conversation to put forth the "walking alongside" missiological model. Jesus entered the disciples' conversation in a *listening posture* while *engaging* with them carefully to demonstrate how God *does not deny* their current emotionally distressing situation. Jesus asked *important questions* that not only enabled the disciples to *make meaning* of the traumatic experience they witnessed, but also *redirected* their imagination to see that God's plan for the Messiah was still intact (vv. 26, 27), even amid this distressing situation.

The Model of Walking Alongside—Creating Space to Engage

As we strive to educate our congregations and help reduce the stigma surrounding struggles with mental disorders, we would like to present a model of "walking alongside" based on the above scriptural reflection that can be practiced as an intervention in the following five stages. We will also highlight the story of the Samaritan woman as an example of this model in action.

1. Creating Safety Our first emphasis while beginning this process should be to create a safe environment for those with mental health disorders within the church. There is evidence to show that a lack of secure connection limits people from exploring their problems and being able to work through their beliefs about self and others. Creating safety means *making space* for people where they can share their fears, process their trauma, engage with emotions and make meaning of their condition without the fear of judgement. The goal is to increase a sense of belonging. Fostering a sense of belonging through hospitality is necessary to ensure that people with mental illness are not marginalized and in doing so, the local church emulates the footsteps of Jesus Christ.[35] Similar to Jesus's encounter

---

34. Temper Longmann III, David E. Gorland, Walter L. Liefeld, David W. Pao, Robert H. Mounce, and Richard Longenecker, *The Expositor's Bible Commentary*, Volume 10, *Luke-Acts*. rev. ed. (Grand Rapids, MI: Zondervan, 2007), 348.

35. Curtis S. Lehmann, William B. Whitney, Jean Un, Jennifer S. Payne, Maria Simanjuntak, Stephen Hamilton, Tsegamlak Worku, Nathaniel A. Fernandez. "Hospitality towards People with Mental Illness in the Church: A Cross-cultural Qualitative Study," *Pastoral Psychology* 71, no. 1 (2022): 1–27.

with the disciples on the way to Emmaus, we also see Jesus creating a safe space for the Samaritan woman at the well (John 4:5–30). Jesus bypassed the sociocultural hindrances, even let his disciples go away for a while, so the women could converse with him. Jesus intentionally crossed the social boundary and created an emotionally safe space for her to foster a sense of belonging. Similarly, our goal as a church is to be an emotionally healthy church that chooses to embrace the marginalized and build a safe space for them to foster a connection with God in their pain.

2. Entering and Engaging Just as Jesus entered the conversation, it is the responsibility of the church to enter the lives of people, in the posture of non-judgmental listening. Engaging can be defined as a two-step process—first is to be present and second, to use open ended questions as a way to continue exploration or conversation. To quote Thich Nhat Hanh, "the most precious gift we can offer others is our presence."[36] Being present outweighs having solutions and suffering is reduced when shared with others. As Jesus walked alongside the two disciples on the way to Emmaus, he was actively present with them and used open ended questions with care and love to engage with them in their pain. Furthermore, the engaging questions enabled the disciples to verbalize and externalize their concerns, struggles, and fears. Similarly, as Christians, we are called to continue the process of engaging with those who are hurting by being present and asking non-threatening open-ended questions with a listening posture.

3. Acknowledging and Validating In cultivating an emotionally healthy space in our congregations, we promote the truth that being vulnerable about the reality of our struggles does not make us less "Christian." Instead, in our vulnerability, we are able to acknowledge and engage in the reality of God's presence amid our sufferings. We can testify that the promised counsellor, the Holy Spirit is with us in our wrestling. To quote Susan M. Johnson, "shared vulnerability builds bonds."[37] At the same time, as we position ourselves with a caring space, we testify that Jesus is Immanuel, "God with us" to the communities surrounding us. Considering the trinitarian perspective, Jesus's incarnation, more specifically his engagement with the disciples on the road to Emmaus, affirms the realities of the human experience and points to God's knowing of these experiences.[38] While

36. Oliver, J. Morgan. *Counseling and Spirituality: Views from the Profession* (Lahaska Press, 2007), 132.

37. Susan M. Johnson, *Attachment Theory in Practice* (Surrey: Guilford Press, 2019), 6.

38. Veronica L. Timbers and Jennifer C. Hollenberger, "Christian Mindfulness and Mental Health: Coping through Sacred Traditions and Embodied Awareness," *Religions* 13, no. 1(2022): 62

validating the existence and weightiness of painful life instances the pastoral goal is to normalize the struggle and foster a sense of safety to reduce the sense of aloneness and shame people may associate with their problems or traumatizing life-events. Returning to our text, we find that in Jesus's interaction with the disciples, Jesus acknowledges the life-event and validates their experience of abandonment, uncertainty, loneliness, and fear. Hence one could infer that God validates humanity's needs, limits, and strengths, using embodied experiences as tools for spiritual growth and social redemption.

4. Recapturing the Role of Emotions The emotional wounds that are embedded in every individual as a result of the sinful reality can be innumerable and inevitable.[39] Those with mental health challenges recognize their emotional wounds more readily than others. As Diane J. Candler notes, "emotional wounds are an inevitable outcome of life, and no one escapes their fury, even those with stable relational foundations and secure attachments."[40] These wounds are from myriads of relational dynamics, "most notably the actual or perceived absence or withdrawal of love, attachment, acceptance, security and well-being."[41] Our emotional reactions are indications that we have more to learn about God's love for us through "our emotional participation."[42] In an emotionally engaged church where there is safe space the goal then is not to deny emotional reactions or to negate them but to engage with them. The early desert fathers emphasized the importance of sitting with one's emotions to connect with God in it.[43] It is vital to exercise emotional intelligence by perceiving, understanding, and managing such emotions so that our deeper emotional wounds are acknowledged and surrendered to God in prayer to be healed. In doing so, we participate with our emotions, "reconciling one's self-image with the way that God views us, as being worthy recipients of God's love."[44]

5. Making Meaning and Redirection Our process does not just end with identifying painful emotions, it continues in finding meaning by redirecting the person to relate with others from a place of healing. "Reframing in order to

---

39. Romans 3:23.

40. Diane J. Chandler, *Christian Spiritual Formation: An Integrated Approach for Personal and Relational Wholeness* (Downers Grove, IL: IVP Academic, 2014), 94.

41. Chandler, *Christian Spiritual Formation*, 94, 95.

42. Charles M. Cameron, "An Introduction to 'Theological Anthropology,'" *Evangel* 23, no. 2 (2005): 8.

43. Timbers and Hollenberger, "Christian Mindfulness and Mental Health."

44. Chandler, *Christian Spiritual Formation*, 93.

shift the meaning . . . to shift a client's perspective from a problem-reinforcing mindset to one that expands awareness and acknowledges underlying attachment vulnerabilities."[45] While Jesus created space, engaged with open-ended questions, acknowledged and validated the traumatizing life event in the disciples' life, Jesus did not stop there. He entered into the conversation with insights that reframed how disciples approached the incident. We also see such a parallel in Jesus's inter-action with the Samaritan woman at the well. While Jesus acknowledged the emotional pain due to rejection in the life of the woman he did not just stop there, he begins to invite the truth of God's ability to fulfill the deepest of human needs. Furthermore, we find the woman reframing her life story. Subsequently, she gathered up the courage to go back to the same people who once rejected her and help them find the peace and healing she just received through her Jesus encounter. Contribution, helping others, and a heightened sense of empathy is the final result of healing and becoming whole. Through serving others who may be on a similar journey as us, we continue the process of healing in our own lives.

The above model should be deeply rooted in *the presence and direction of the Holy Spirit* the divine counselor, who is the one who ultimately begins and ends the formative process of experiencing emotional and mental healing and wholeness. However, emotionally attuned Christians and churches should be able to cul-tivate space for people with mental health challenges to go through the process of healing.

Conclusion

This chapter presented an introductory look into the often-ignored mental health crisis in India and subsequently called upon Christians in India to engage in mental health conversations with a missiological posture of care and compassion. To that extent, we proposed a missiological paradigm of "walking alongside" to respond to mental health challenges. An emotive reading of Luke 21:13–33 noting the experience of disciples on the road to Emmaus, presents a robust scriptural approach to walk alongside folks going through mental health chal-lenges. Finally, we highlighted five steps of interventions to engage in mental health conversations to "walk alongside" with people witnessing the embodied gospel of Jesus Christ: (1) creating safety, (2) entering and engaging, (3) acknowl-edging and validating, (4) recapturing our emotions, and (5) making meaning and redirecting.

Although these factors are not an exhaustive interpretation of Scripture, we believe these will help others perceive the scriptural truths in light of mental

---

45. Johnson, *Attachment Theory in Practice*, 70.

health conversations and provide impetus to create a more effective care pathway in our missiological discourse. We also recognize that not every problem or emotional response has to be dealt with within the church setting. In such cases, it is important to seek professional help. However, church leaders should be informed about mental health challenges and develop a culture where leaders are trained periodically to identify and refer people to seek help. Such an approach could be integrated into the church's missiological engagement. A mental health–competent church may also maintain accessible resources to better help their congregants.

Furthermore, we hope that the analysis in this chapter will serve as a conversation starter in the Indian church to encourage Christians to engage in mental health pursuits to advocate for a long-term change in the societal perception of mental health concerns.

CONTRIBUTORS

Hepziba Arputharaj is currently a PhD candidate at Asbury Theological Seminary. She holds an MA (Eng), a BD, and MPhil (Christian Studies) from Madras University. She served as a Bible school teacher and associate pastor for twelve years, and later as a development practitioner working among underprivileged children for two years in Chennai, India. She is passionate about working with children, women, and their families, researching and advocating on issues such as domestic violence, and gender inequality in Christian families and churches.

Arpan Christian is a PhD candidate at Asbury Theological Seminary, working on developing mission spirituality embedded in modern hymnodies from a cross-cultural perspective. Arpan and his wife Anpa are ordained elders of the Methodist Church in India and served seven years as teachers at the Methodist Bible Seminary, Gujarat.

Matthias Phurba Sonam Gergan has family ties across India's Himalayas among the Indo-Tibetan people. He currently serves as the Digital Content Editor at Asia Theological Association (ATA). He is also a PhD candidate at Asbury Theological Seminary where his research helps the Indian Himalayan Church to discern its identity and mission despite increasing political, social, and ethnic tensions. He encourages the Himalayan Church and Christians in the diaspora to celebrate gospel-centered unity and diversity, particularly in contexts where they live as minorities.

Manohar James served in India as an evangelist, church planter, and seminary professor for twenty years. He received a PhD in intercultural studies (2016) from Asbury Theological Seminary. His most recent book is *Religious Conversion in India* (2022). He currently leads Serving Alongside International, Inc., and serves as pastor of intercultural ministry at High Point Church in Madison, Wisconsin.

T. S. John is founder and director of a mission organization serving people and families affected by disability in South Asia since 1997. He holds an MA in intercultural studies from Wheaton Graduate School, an MBA from Hope International University, and is currently carrying out doctoral research in the field of disability mission at Asbury Theological Seminary.

Uma John is a PhD candidate in biblical studies at Asbury Theological Seminary. Her dissertation focuses on imprecation in the Old Testament and trauma theory. One of her recent publications is "Tracing a Redemptive Movement within Pentateuchal Slavery Laws" (*Wesleyan Theological Journal*, 2023). Prior to her doctoral studies, Uma spent six years working with anti–human trafficking organizations in India. She holds a MA in theology (Mysore University) and MDiv (SAIACS).

Vinod John is a scholar-practitioner who has lived, studied, and worked in both Eastern and Western cultures. His research interests include the cross-cultural and inter-religious interaction of the gospel, the transcontextualization of Christian witness, and the responses of indigenous cultures and religions to the gospel. His most recent publication is *Believing Without Belonging? Religious Beliefs and Social Belonging of Hindu Devotees of Christ* (2020). In addition to pastoring a multicultural and multilingual church in Edmonton, Canada, John teaches missiology in India and North America.

John Amalraj Karunakaran grew up as a pastor's child and was involved in local church ministries. His education spans law, management, political science, theology, and intercultural studies. Cross-cultural living and multi-cultural communities are his learning context. Having served with Indian mission organizations in leadership roles for three decades he is researching Indian cross-cultural missional leadership at Asbury Theological Seminary. Along with his wife and two sons, he has lived in four cities in India and Singapore while traveling widely.

Lalenkawla is an ordained minister of the Presbyterian Church of India, Mizoram Synod. He completed his bachelor of divinity (Aizawl Theological College) and master of theology (United Theological College, Bangalore). He has also been in pastoral ministry as an ordained minister since 2009. He is currently doing his PhD (Biblical Studies) at Asbury Theological Seminary.

Priya Santhakumar Leela is pursuing a PhD in intercultural studies at Asbury Theological Seminary. Previously she worked with the Union of Evangelical Students of India (UESI) in the teaching and training department (Delhi), taught theology at Master's College of Theology, and served as the internship director at the Theological Research and Communication Institute (TRACI), India. Her articles and research interests include public theology, issues of street children, gender, and sex trafficking.

Shivraj K. Mahendra (PhD, Asbury Theological Seminary) is dean of online studies and associate professor of history of Christianity and missiology at

New Theological College, India. He is general secretary of the Church History Association of India (CHAI) and member of the International Association for Mission Studies (IAMS) and American Society of Church History (ASCH). His publications include the award-winning *Lived Missiology: The Legacy of Ernest and Phebe Ward* (2021) and nine other books and Hindi translations of over twenty theological books.

Allan Varghese Meloottu is the registrar at the Asbury Theological Seminary in Wilmore, Kentucky and is also a PhD (IS) candidate at the Seminary, researching the intersection of Indian Pentecostalism and social engagements. Some of his research has been published in journals, including *Nidan: International Journal for Indian Studies* (2019), *Religions* (2023) and the *Asian Journal for Pentecostal Studies* (2023). He holds a masters in social work (Christ University, Bangalore), an MA in integrative psychotherapy (London School of Theology), a certificate in theological studies (University of Oxford), and a master in theological studies (Duke Divinity School, Duke University).

Lalsangkima Pachuau (PhD, Princeton Theological Seminary) is the J. W. Beeson professor of Christian mission and dean of advanced research programs at Asbury Theological Seminary. Among his recent books are *God at Work in the World: Theology and Mission in the Global Church* (Baker, 2022) and *World Christianity: A Historical and Theological Introduction* (Abingdon Press, 2018).

Jose Philip has been active in Christian Ministry for over a decade in Southeast Asia, serving as an apologist and evangelist, pastor, and teacher. With postgraduate degrees in both science and theology, a keen interest in philosophy and culture, and a passion for building gospel-shaped communities. Jose is engaged in research at Asbury Theological Seminary and focuses on cross-cultural communication of the gospel of Jesus Christ and teaching others to do the same.

Sochanngam Shirik is from Manipur, India, and recently graduated with a PhD in intercultural studies (Historical and Theological Studies) from Asbury Theological Seminary, Wilmore, Kentucky. He finished his MDiv and ThM from the Southern Baptist Theological Seminary, Louisville, Kentucky.

Joy Jemima Singh is a licensed clinical mental health therapist. She graduated with her MA in mental health counselling from Asbury Theological Seminary, Kentucky, and currently works for the Isaiah House where she enjoys working with women in addiction and recovery. She is passionate about trauma awareness and education in the church.

INDEX

Praise for *Christians and Christianity in India Today*

This edited volume brings together a set of substantial essays that offer a range of trajectories through the incredibly multifaceted reality of Christianity in India, placing the lived experiences of practicing Christians at the forefront of the investigation. Most of the writers assembled represent a new generation of scholar-practitioners. Their acumen and ability to handle the big-picture questions, without losing sight of the practitioners who have inhabited and continue to dwell in the local religious spaces of multicultural and multifaith India, is laudable.

—J. Jayakiran Sebastian, dean and H. George Anderson
Professor of Mission and Cultures, United
Lutheran Seminary, Philadelphia

Christians and Christianity in India Today highlights many original reflections and offers a credible case for Christianity in India being a microcosm of World Christianity. The authors' sketches of the regionally varied forms of Christianity throughout history, expositions of its theology in context, and reconstructions of the missional challenges in India's dynamic milieu all richly demonstrate Indian Christianity's prophetic presence within World Christianity today.

—David Emmanuel Singh, senior research tutor,
Oxford Centre for Mission Studies

Christians and Christianity in India Today is a scholarly tribute to Asbury Theological Seminary's centenary celebration. Divided into historical, theological, sociocultural, and missional sections, the book illuminates Christianity's journey across India's diverse landscape. It uncovers caste dynamics, interfaith relations, and faith's cultural expressions, addressing pressing issues like gender inequality, mental health, and human trafficking. The book showcases how Christianity has intricately woven itself into India's cultural tapestry, resulting in a fusion of identities. This meticulously argued yet accessible collection invites readers to a journey of faith, history, and identity.

—Finny Philip, principal, Filadelfia Bible College, Udaipur, India;
author of *The Origins of Pauline Pneumatology*

India, the world's most populous nation, has been home to Christians and Christianity for almost as long as Christianity has existed. However, if Christianity doesn't reorient, reinvent, and redefine itself in every age, it loses its vital essence. *Christians and Christianity in India Today* is a unique contribution from the practitioners of Christian faith to the current Indian Christian conversation. I strongly recommend it to all dedicated scholars and students of Christianity in the Global South.

—Samuel George, professor of Christian theology and principal, South India Biblical Seminary, Bangarapet, India; author of *Jesus Beyond Borders: Towards a 'Glocal' Christology*

This book presents the history of Indian Christians, their theological interactions, and their social realities as a minority community. Written from insiders' perspectives by Indian scholars, the chapters provide excellent reflections on the stories of Indian Christians, their responses to contextual challenges, and their contributions to larger Indian society. The multidimensional missional challenges for Indian Christians are also clearly reflected.

—K. Lalrinkima, senior administrative secretary (general secretary), Presbyterian Church of India

This is a fascinating resource on Christians and Christianity in India from a multidimensional perspective. It uniquely allows readers to look at Christianity in India, which is as old as Christianity itself, through various paradigms. I highly recommend this new book to anyone who is interested in knowing about the latest on Christianity in the present-day India.

—V. V. Thomas, chair of the department of the history of Christianity, United Theological College, Bangalore, India

It is not easy to fully grasp the multifaceted, variegated nature of Christianity in India, which is one of the few countries with all seven major streams of historic Christianity present. It is a phenomenon as old as St. Thomas and as fresh as the rapidly growing indigenous church movements that are less than five years old. *Christians and Christianity in India Today* provides an insightful introduction to some of the facets of the grand story of Indian Christianity. These essays all flow from Indian pens and remind us afresh that this is a story which, in the end, can best be told by Indians.

—Timothy C. Tennent, president, Asbury Theological Seminary